Economic Planning & Politics in Britain

Economic
Planning & Politics
in Britain

JACQUES LERUEZ
translated by Martin Harrison

PREFACE BY J. E. S. HAYWARD

BARNES & NOBLE
BOOKS
10 East 53d St. New York 10022
(a division of Harper & Row Publishers, Inc.)

English translation © Martin Harrison 1975

The original French edition was published in 1972 by Librairie Armand Colin et Fondation Nationale des Sciences Politiques.

French edition Preface by André Mathiot. Université de Droit, de Sciences Sociales et d'Economie, and Institut d'Etudes Politques, Paris.

This revised English edition was first published in the U.K. by Martin Robertson & Company. Published in the U.S.A. 1976 by Harper & Row Publishers Inc., Barnes & Noble Import Division.

ISBN 0-06-494190-6

Typeset by Santype (Coldtype) Ltd., Salisbury.
Reproduced, printed by photolithography and bound in Britain
at The Pitman Press, Bath. 76-4467

Contents

Preface

The French planning phenomenon has attracted a good deal of attention, not least from British scholars, publicists and public men, but there has been relatively little French discussion of the misfortunes of national economic planning in its British incarnation. So it is with particular interest that British readers will peruse this work by a native of Normandy who knows Britain well thanks to frequent scholarly invasions. We are still not entirely clear on why we failed to achieve continuous economic growth whereas France succeeded. Following the fiascos of the 1960s, the smugness of the 1950s is in danger of being replaced by the fatalistic defeatism of the 1970s, so a reassessment of the record is desirable and comes best from someone who has both the detachment and insight of a well informed outsider. My impression is that perhaps out of a mixture of politeness and sympathy for a country for which he has a warm affection, Jacques Leruez has sometimes pulled his punches. Nevertheless, at a time when the incessant din of the dirge is in our ears, we may take more kindly to tactful euphemisms than to sadistic overstatements. In that state of mind, it is possible that we may finally face the facts, although to do something about them will probably require harsher medicine.

The author appropriately begins by presenting the heterogeneous inter-war ideological matrix out of which the advocacy of planning developed in Britain. Here, the subject was much more highly charged with ideological polemics than was the case in France. There, planning was successfully depoliticised except for the Communist Party, which in any case was outside the working political system from 1947–65. While the French were the true pragmatists, unobtrusively establishing a permanent national economic planning process that exerted some impact upon policy — making, in Britain pragmatism was interpreted as coping by improvisation with day to day crises, without reorganising the structures and processes of economic policy-making. Leruez shows that while the Labour Party freely used the rhetoric of planning in the 1940s, it had little understanding of its practical implications. Instead, behind the slogans there was little more than the pious hope that the wartime consensus could be extended into the post-war period and that corporatist practices would be continued under new auspices. However, the reliance upon seconded private businessmen and trade association officials to control the business sector proved disastrous when the 'national interest' became identified with the establishment of socialism. The reluctance to rely upon a traditional bureaucracy lacking the necessary expertise and activism and the inability to call on technocratic new men, who were to organise and direct the resurgence of the French economy, placed the Labour Government at the mercy of their political enemies.

The failure to create an instrument for continuous modernisation of the economy in the 1940s meant that a reliance upon Keynesian techniques of economic management was thought to be sufficient for steering the economy. An increasing awareness of their ineffectiveness in the 1950s led to the adoption of the panacea of planning which, it was believed, would spare the government painful choices, whereas if it was to be taken seriously, planning meant abandoning the cosy assumption that one could somehow 'muddle through'. Both the 1963 National Economic Development Council 'plan' under the Conservatives and the 1965 Department of Economic Affairs 'plan' under Labour appeared to confuse planning with exercises in economic forecasting, coupled with indications of the obstacles to growth and attempts to persuade organised business and labour that they should cooperate voluntarily in eliminating such obstacles. In fact, the evidence suggests that without really believing in their planning rhetoric, both Conservative and Labour leaders unsuccessfully used their 'plans' as public relations devices for securing wage restraint and industrial peace from the workers and greater investment and exports from businessmen. Whether or not he deluded himself that there would be a twenty-five per cent increase in the standard of living by 1970, the economic unreality of the 1965 National Plan served Harold Wilson's short term political objective of winning the 1966 general election, just as pre-electoral consumer demand booms gave the Conservatives a resounding ('You never had it so good') victory in 1959 and nearly saved them from defeat in 1964. The credibility of medium term planning was destroyed by its perversion into an electoral expedient. 'Stop–go' was perpetuated under the paradoxical appellation of planning.

Given that references to the abandonment of planning make little sense when once it is conceded that planning never seriously got started, this book is primarily a study of British economic policy in the late 40s and since the early 60s. If Jacques Leruez has no solution to Britain's intractable economic problems, he does remind us in remorseless detail of the extent to which we have repeated the same series of mistakes rather than shown any disposition to learn from them. Instead of acquiring any ability to utilise successive economic crises for the purpose of forcing through the backlog of overdue change in personnel and policies, political leaders have preferred to indulge the national weakness for institutional musical chairs, in which the semblance of spectacular change masks the underlying inertia. Repeated exposure of the pretensions of British politicians has encouraged the mass public to pursue their sectional interests with increasing cynicism.

Under the inflationary pressures exerted by external developments and internal forces over which they have little control, British governments seem condemned partially to retreat to the 1930s in the sense that they will in practice abandon the commitment to full employment and the generous 'welfare state' services that have hitherto been regarded as the sacrosanct achievement of the mid-1940s. Unable to control inflation through an effective curb upon private consumption, even a Labour Government now seems resigned to cuts in public expenditure that will dwarf into insignificance earlier attempts to nibble at public consumption through what the author calls 'squalid little economies' on school meals and milk. Jacques Leruez's book documents with scrupulous fairness how we reached this sorry pass, when governments act as though they are the creatures of circumstances and not in any sense their masters. In such a situation, planning ceases to have any meaning. It will only acquire a meaning when the government recovers both the capacity and the will to steer economic development and not merely improvise piecemeal adjustments to accommodate itself to the decisions of others.

Jack Hayward
Professor of Politics
University of Hull

Translator's Note

This book is substantially different from the original edition, published by Armand Colin in 1972 under the title *Planification et Politique en Grande Bretagne, 1945–1971*. In addition to a new introduction, Part IV has been completely rewritten, and the earlier chapters contain a large number of detailed revisions. This version was prepared in close consultation with the author, who in addition to being a political scientist is also a graduate in English. In almost all cases where quotations originally appeared in English they are quoted here from the original English; in the few instances where the original could not be traced, this has been indicated appropriately in the source footnote.

M. H.

Acknowledgements

I want to thank the officials and colleagues who have helped me at the time of my research, for the French edition or the English edition of this work. I am particularly indebted to Professor André Mathiot of l'Université de Droit, d'Economie et de Sciences Sociales and l'Institut d'Etudes Politiques in Paris, who supervised my research and wrote a preface for the French edition, to Professor Jack Hayward of Hull University who advised me at various stages and wrote the preface to the English edition, and to Professor Martin Harrison of Keele University who not only was brave and friendly enough to undertake the translation but advised me all along. I am also grateful for their material help to le Centre National de la Recherche Scientifique, la Fondation Nationale des Sciences Politiques and especially its Centre d'Etudes et de Recherches Internationales – to which I have belonged since 1968 – whose Director is Monsieur Jean Meyriat.

List of Abbreviations

BEC — British Employers' Confederation
CEPS — Central Economic Planning Staff
CIC — Capital Issues Committee
CPRS — Central Policy Review Staff
DEA — Department of Economic Affairs
DOE — Department of the Environment
DTI — Department of Trade and Industry
EPB — Economic Planning Board
FBI — Federation of British Industry
FCI — Finance Corporation for Industry
ICFC — Industrial and Commercial Finance Corporation
IDE — industrial development executive
IEA — Institute of Economic Affairs
IMF — International Monetary Fund
IRC — Industrial Reorganisation Corporation
Mintech — Ministry of Technology
NEDC — National Economic Development Council
NEDO — National Economic Development Office
NIC — National Incomes Commission
NIB — National Incomes Board
NIESR — National Institute for Economic and Social Research
NIRC — National Industrial Relations Court
NPAC — National Production Advisory Council
PAR — Programme Analysis and Review
PEP — Political and Economic Planning
PES — Public Expenditure Survey
PESC — Public Expenditure Survey Committee
PIB — Prices and Incomes Board
PWLB — Public Works Loan Board
RIDB — regional industrial development board
TUC — Trades Union Congress
UCS — Upper Clyde Shipbuilders

INTRODUCTION

The Emergence of the Idea of Economic Planning in Britain

In considering the birth of the idea of planning in Britain we are essentially considering the decline of a certain conception of liberalism – a decline that began at the very moment when liberalism had apparently triumphed. For although the Treaty of Versailles set the seal on the birth of a series of states, all duly equipped with liberal–democratic constitutions, in place of the old, defeated autocratic empires, this victory was short-lived. For even then a formidable new challenger was looming on the horizon with the advent of the first Marxist state, bearing so many and such varied hopes. Moreover, the First World War had disrupted the old system of world trade dominated by a free-trading Britain, and had impoverished not only the losers but many of the victors (with the notable exception of the United States, which emerged from the war with her power, if not her desire for international co-operation, immeasurably enhanced). Europe was accordingly turned in on herself far more than she would be after 1945.

Such was the context in which the 1929 crisis broke, with the various countries attempting to tackle the situation with outmoded attitudes and inappropriate expedients. The emergency measures by which governments tried to overcome the depression, together with the evidence of foreign experience, were to be the genesis of the idea of planning in Britain.

In the wake of the economic crisis of 1930 and the political crisis of 1931 the National Government took a series of emergency measures. Some were strictly short-term measures that were in no way novel, such as cuts in public expenditure and increases in direct and indirect taxation. They were in any case purely temporary: by 1935 levels of taxation and public expenditure were already back to what they had been in 1930. But this was not the case with the series of Acts increasing import duties and extending their scope.[1] The most important was the Import Duties Act of 1932, which imposed a standing duty of 10 per cent on all imports apart from primary products like wheat, tea, meat, wool, cotton, etc. In addition a duty of 22.5 per cent was levied on steel and steel products. Only the dominions and colonies were exempt as a result of the introduction of 'imperial preference', which was confirmed at the Ottawa conference of 1932. Britain was of course by no means the only country to take such action, but since she had so long been the standard-bearer of the free trade movement the measures had a special significance. Britain had taken a decisive step towards protectionism.

Domestically too liberalism was under attack. The May and Macmillan reports of 1931 recommended widespread rationalisation, particularly in the major exporting industries, as a way of making British prices competitive again in world markets.[2] Rationalisation was to have the greatest impact in coal, engineering, cotton and shipbuilding. The impetus came from the government, particularly in the mining industry which was reorganised under Labour's moderately 'interventionist' Coal Mines Act of 1930. However, *dirigisme** first appeared in a fully worked out and coherent form in agriculture with measures designed to restore some order to markets, which had virtually collapsed in the twenties. In 1931 the government set up marketing boards for the main agricultural products, after consulting the producers. The intention behind the creation of the boards was to help deal with the problem of surpluses. They were given considerable financial and regulatory powers. They were financed by a system of levies or borrowing either from the State or in the money market, and they made loans to their members, to scientific research centres or to agricultural training schemes. They could either regulate the selling prices and fix production quotas, or they could become trading monopolies with producers being required, on pain of heavy fines, to sell their entire output to the board. By 1934 five marketing boards had been established, for hops, potatoes, pork, bacon and milk; others were added later for most major products. Within the terms of this study their significance lay in the way they showed that when there was a crisis the State was bound to intervene, but that intervention need not take an authoritarian form. The boards were established only after the farmers had indicated their full agreement, and the men running them were elected by the producers; consequently they enjoyed a high measure of confidence.

Thus by 1935 it could no longer be said with strict accuracy that Britain had a truly liberal economy. But as yet the new *dirigisme* was very fragmentary, and it was generally looked on as a mere collection of short-term expedients. Indeed the government's new measures did not spring from any well defined political or economic philosophy or view of society; they were simply intended to stave off economic disaster — and in this they were of course successful. So it was not surprising that some people would have preferred the State to act more

---

* A succinct distinction between terms may be useful at this point. *Dirigisme*, for which no really satisfactory English equivalent exists, denotes a situation in which the State intervenes in the economy by controlling economic machinery so as to improve its functioning. But, while obviously at the opposite end of the scale from *laissez-faire*, unlike interventionism it implies systematic action affecting the whole economy; unlike socialism it does not imply a prior transformation of the political system; and unlike planning it is essentially concerned with vigorous short-term action (and is less concerned with the longer term and the future). However, during the thirties planning was often confused with *dirigisme* (and vice-versa), particularly in Britain. It was a long time before the distinction was made clearly, either in learned journals or in the press. In France the distinction has been clearly understood since at least 1945; thus during the 1974 presidential election campaign the candidate of the Left, M. Mitterrand, was able to accuse his right-wing opponent, M. Giscard d'Estaing, who at the time was Minister of Finance, of both being a *dirigiste* and having abandoned planning, without any fear of being accused of having contradicted himself!

systematically and coherently, setting out a series of principles on which intervention should be based, as a number of other countries had done.

Among them was Oswald Mosley, one of the most brilliant members of the second Labour government – though at no time a full member of the cabinet. First as a minister (in the Mosley memorandum), later as a backbencher (in the Mosley short-term programme), Mosley put forward proposals for tackling unemployment which implied a measure of 'socialist planning' – 'going beyond Keynes', as he put it. The programme had four main points: (a) a reform of the Whitehall machine; (b) proposals for 'long-term economic reconstruction'; (c) short-term work plans; (d) a radical reform of 'finance and credit policy' favouring producers rather than the financiers. Apart from his third point, his proposals were almost completely rejected because of opposition from the Treasury and the chancellor, Snowden, and also because they alarmed a government that was devoid of both imagination and initiative and was to collapse shortly after. Mosley himself left the government, for which he had little but contempt, in May 1930, and the Labour Party in 1931 before going on to found the British Union of Fascists. But his economic proposals still continued to be dominated by the ideas in the 'memorandum', which was probably the boldest proposal for tackling the crisis at the time.[3]

The Economic Ideas of British Socialists and the Impact of Foreign Experience

Until the end of the twenties British socialists had rarely succeeded in setting down at all precisely in concrete terms just how a socialised economy would be run. It was of course agreed that the means of production would be nationalised but little was said about what would happen after that. However, by 1930 at least two major questions did seem to have been resolved. The first was the rejection of a violent revolutionary takeover. Most socialists had come to accept the principle of coming to power by legal means at a general election – a view that was encouraged by Labour's rising fortunes at the polls. The logical corollary of this in economic as in other matters was the abandoning of any idea of a radical transformation of society and an acceptance, as the Webbs said, of 'the inevitability of gradualism' (a phrase that made Mosley very angry). Secondly, guild socialism, which had been so influential in the early twenties, had been discarded. Led by Cole and Tawney, the guild socialists had campaigned for a highly decentralised system in which the basic unit, the autonomous workshop, would have very broad freedom to run its own affairs, with a central body of some kind exercising a rather ill defined co-ordinating role. But other socialists favoured a more centralised form of organisation in which the individual production units had little independence, and they put heavy emphasis on strong central co-ordination. This school eventually prevailed. On the whole the Webbs could be numbered among them. They accepted that there should be a measure of political and administrative decentralisation, but they were acutely aware of the futility of isolated efforts in an economy where the automatic co-ordinating effect of the market had been eliminated.

Moreover, their *Constitution for the Socialist Commonwealth of Great Britain*, published in 1920, pointed towards a centrally run economy. The Webbs grasped at a very early stage how unsuited the existing Parliament was to controlling the economy, so they proposed the creation of a 'social parliament' with broad powers in economic and social affairs. This social parliament would serve two main functions: not only to deal with the living conditions of the current generation, but also (and this was their most novel suggestion) to prepare for future generations. But to prepare for the future it was essential to control what was happening in the present. Consequently, the social parliament would need to have supreme control over economic and social matters — and thus of the country's capital resources and the industries employing them, of the whole range of social services, transport and other means of communication, scientific research organisations and bodies promoting the arts. To avoid clashes between the two Houses, they devised an ingenious method of resolving differences, including the possibility of the two Houses meeting in joint session. The Webbs made a commendable effort to formulate a systematically worked out scheme which they thought would be as appropriate for dealing with the economy in the future as in the present. Admittedly the magic words 'plan' and 'planning' were never mentioned, but they were unquestionably moving in that direction.

Around the same period considerable interest was raised by the experience of a number of other countries, notably the short-lived social-democratic experiments in Germany and Austria, the dramatic economic recoveries of Italy and Germany and, of course, the Soviet experiment.

When the German and Austrian socialists came to power in 1919, like their comrades in other countries they had no clearly worked out plan of campaign. But they were able to profit from wartime experience in controlling the economy. As in Britain, a large machine had been set up to organise food and raw material supplies. But whereas in Britain liberal orthodoxy led to the wartime machinery being dismantled immediately the war was ended, in Germany and Austria it was realised that they formed a useful basis for a permanent system of planning. In Germany a socialisation commission was established and socialist economists like Professors Lederer, Heimann and Rathenau drew up plans for extending socialisation. These plans were followed by the first social-democratic governments. In 1919 Herr Wissel, the Weimar minister of economic affairs (and at that time the every existence of such a ministry for the economy was in itself significant) and his deputy, Herr Moellendorf, drew up a plan which could not be implemented because of the unstable political situation, but which nevertheless created something of a stir and directly inspired several proposals that were discussed in Britain during the thirties. The discussion was by no means limited to Britain; the planning movement was gathering strength elsewhere in western Europe in the wake of the publication of Henri de Man's plan in Belgium in 1933—4. In France the CGT (the largest trade union confederation, which at that time was under socialist leadership) also put forward a plan in 1935. The aim of such proposals was to try and find some effective democratic alternative to the authoritarian *dirigisme* on which several other European countries had embarked, which was making a strong impression on many people in the democracies, which still seemed paralysed by the depression.

First there was the Italian example. Taking power in 1922 after a long period of anarchy, for which they were themselves partly responsible, the Fascists had succeeded in bringing about a rapid improvement in the situation, getting people back to work again by means of a massive programme of public works; raising customs duties with a view to making themselves self-sufficient (Italy had had at least as grave a problem of unemployment as Britain, but by 1929 the economy was again working at full capacity); improving the operation of the public services; increasing industrial production (particularly iron and steel — at a price) as well as agriculture (with the draining of the Pontine marshes and the 'battle for wheat'). All this was achieved through determined action by the State in every sector of the economy. After 1930 Italy was, like other countries, affected by the world economic crisis and fascist rule was generally less successful. But from 1933 its place as an 'example' was taken by the new German National Socialist regime, which also secured a striking improvement in the economy in less than four years (production rose sharply and unemployment was virtually eliminated), owing largely to a big public works programme and a huge rearmament programme, but also to very skilful use of monetary and budgetary methods and to a quite unprecedented emphasis on self-sufficiency (symbolised by the word Ersatz). In comparison with these innovations the measures taken by the democracies seemed extremely timid. Even the New Deal, launched in 1933, which tended to prime the pump by means of devaluation of the dollar, public works and a programme of economic reorganisation, seemed really convincing only when American industry began to benefit from rearmament.

But whether they were socialist or not, all these experiments in *dirigisme* were seen by British socialists, notably the Webbs, as less significant for the future than the transformation of the economy arising from the Russian Revolution. The Webbs at first had made no secret of their lack of enthusiasm, even hostility, for the Bolshevik revolution. But when Sidney Webb retired from active politics at the end of 1931, disillusioned by the experience of two Labour governments, he began reflecting on the failures of the British economy. However, it was only when the glowing reports of the success of the first five-year plan began coming in that the Webbs showed any enthusiasm over the Soviet experiment. This enthusiasm was deepened by their trip to the USSR in May—June 1932, which led to the publication of their monumental *Soviet Communism: A New Civilisation?*[4]

Gosplan was founded in 1923, but it was only in 1928 that the first five-year plan (together with a fifteen-year plan for electrification) was put into force. By

1935 Gosplan had a council of 158 members (shortly afterwards reduced to 72) and a staff of around a thousand statisticians and other experts and several thousand clerical and secretarial workers. Together with bodies like the Central Administration for National Accounts, the Institute of Economic Research and the Academy of Planning, a total of over two thousand experts were involved. These experiments in planning — 'this outstanding discovery in economics',[5] as they put it — were the main reason for the Webbs' visit to the Soviet Union. They noted that experience of trying to run the economy before the introduction of planning had shown the impracticality of controlling industry through the Soviets. This of course confirmed their long-standing antipathy towards guild socialist ideas, and with no little satisfaction they reported that: 'It seems clear that this particular idea [i.e. the running of the economy through Soviets] when put into operation, failed to commend itself to . . . even its warmest advocates . . . . What was fatal and irremediable . . . was that each factory . . . necessarily judged and decided its policy exclusively from the standpoint of its own wishes and interests.'[6] Later they commented that: 'The idea of the "self-governing workshop", the dream of the anarchist and the syndicalist, which had misled whole generations of socialists, had to be abandoned. Workers control, though not eliminated for other functions, was definitely deposed from management.'[7] Finally, they pointed out that while a fully collectivist system of the Soviet type was bound to have a plan for the economy as a whole, as a method planning could be made to serve quite different ends. 'In itself, it is merely a statistical process without a purpose. Logically, however, planning implies a purpose outside itself, a purpose to be decided and determined on by human will.'[8] That was why it did not lie with Gosplan to decide either ends or even the means to be used in achieving those ends; that was the job of the political leadership.

The Webbs also emphasised that planning was not only a technical instrument; it also had a psychological role. It set out a clear objective towards which the energies of the people could be directed. The Webbs concluded that a planned system offered several advantages. Firstly it secured better co-ordination of the instruments of production and the highest possible level of productivity. It was not limited by the dictates of profitability and was not required to support two entire social groups in idleness — the capitalists at one end of the scale and the unemployed at the other. (The Webbs assumed that as there was no unemployment in the USSR this meant that planning eliminated it.) It was not hampered by lengthy strikes. It could build huge factories in the certainty that their productive capacity could be used to the full. Finally, it allowed a rational development of natural resources. There was nothing fundamentally wrong in these arguments — but it was by no means clear whether the Soviet Union's rapid advance was really due to planning or to the command-type political system that operated there until well after the Second World War. After all, a wartime capitalist economy had many similar characteristics; it, too, eliminated unemployment and under-used capacity. Nevertheless, in the mid-thirties the rapid pace of Soviet economic development was one of the best advertisements for planning.

The Ideology of Planning

The interest roused by such foreign examples provoked a number of warnings, particularly from the economists, most of whom had remained faithful to the traditional tenets of economic liberalism. The main argument of these liberal economists was that the degree of compulsion inherent in national economic planning was incompatible with liberal democracy. For planning rests on the abolition of the market economy, and this necessarily limits the freedom of the producer and, ultimately, of the consumer — as the Soviet example showed.

Before considering the 'planners'' reply, we should first see just who they were. Since most of the foreign examples mentioned had a socialist inspiration, not surprisingly in Britain initial support for planning came mainly from socialists. But not exclusively so. For during the thirties planning created a new line of political cleavage cutting across traditional party lines. Nevertheless, among the 'planners' one could distinguish two main schools of thought, reflecting their socialist or non-socialist origins. For some, planning was a way of overcoming the most flagrant deficiencies of capitalism, which had been highlighted by the economic crisis; others wanted to replace the capitalist system with a planned socialist system. Yet in the immediate run the aims of these two schools very largely coincided, and particularly where they shared a belief in political democracy — which meant the immense majority of cases — there was very considerable common ground.

Both groups agreed on rejecting the allegation that planning and tyranny went hand in hand. They saw a clear distinction between political and economic organisation, and between political freedom and economic freedom. While national economic planning unquestionably involved some curtailing of economic freedom, it did not necessarily diminish political freedom or jeopardise the parliamentary system. For at that period government and Parliament took few economic decisions; consequently a planned economy meant replacing an economy run by private individuals who escaped any form of democratic control, and which was in no way rationally organised, by one run by a public body appointed by a government elected through the ballot box. Such a system did not spell the demise of democracy; it meant that democracy would exist where previously there had been none — in economic decision-making.

The reason for the total absence of democracy in the USSR was that the principles on which its political system rested were diametrically opposed to those on which the British parliamentary system was based. There was not the slightest evidence that if the form of economic organisation that existed in the USSR was detached from the communist political system the consequences for democracy would be the same. In other words, while planning was the only way of running an economy under a system of the Soviet type, the converse was not necessarily true — that planning required a Soviet-type political system. Thus the 'planners'' first contention was that economic planning did not necessarily mean the rejection of traditional political institutions and liberties.

But some went further. In 1938, when liberal democracy seemed particularly threatened — and not only by the Soviet regime — a number of politicians, such as the young Harold Macmillan, came to see planning as the only way of saving democracy. As they saw it, the internal danger was greater than the external one, not just because a number of democratic countries had powerful right- and left-wing revolutionary parties, but also because in every country there was a sizeable minority of individuals at the bottom of the social scale who derived little or no benefit from political democracy. Planning offered a way of integrating such people more securely into the national community by seeing that all had a job and some share, however small, in the country's wealth. As Macmillan said, 'It is not enough to deplore and condemn the political excesses and economic inadequacies of the totalitarian states. We must *prove* that democracy can do better.'[9] He went on: 'The preservation of freedom is intimately related to economic and social progress.'[10] Clearly in the minds of the 'planners' planning and social and economic progress were inseparable. But it was also inseparable from other concepts that came to the fore around this time, such as 'full employment' and 'growth'. Then and subsequently the way in which many people thought about such questions was profoundly influenced by the work of Hobson and even more by Keynes.

In Hobson's view it was clear that underemployment of capital and labour was a characteristic of industrial economies.[11] Consequently he considered it absurd to lay such emphasis on raising productivity, for even the existing level of productivity had given rise to a quite unacceptable level of underemployment. While his argument would infuriate most contemporary economists, we should not lose sight of the economic context in which he wrote. However, it was the conclusions Hobson drew from this argument which were of particular interest to the 'planners'. He maintained that the problem was not one of overproduction but of underconsumption. Consequently, before trying to raise productivity it would be better to increase the purchasing power of the most deprived sections of the community, because any increase there would be almost wholly directed into consumption, thus stimulating demand and therefore production, and consequently reducing unemployment. The French Popular Front government of 1936 based its economic policy directly on this theory of underconsumption. But unfortunately it committed the error of simultaneously introducing the forty-hour week, thus cutting production and vitiating the experiment, which duly collapsed amid inflation.

Hobson's theories of underemployment had a hostile reception from his contemporaries. It was really only with the publication of Keynes's General Theory that unemployment came to be seen as something that could be avoided and controlled rather than as part of the natural order of things. With the General Theory Keynes developed the theoretical framework to support the views he had been expressing on unemployment (notably against the efficacy of cutting wages) throughout the twenties, in opposition to prevailing orthodox opinion. While, like Hobson, he did not directly advocate planning, his work helped swell the tide of interventionism, firstly by its assumption that the State needed an economic policy, and secondly by the importance he attached to public investment as a way of redressing the inadequacies of private investment, and to the need for a more equitable distribution of income, and the adoption of protectionism if the circumstances required.

But Keynes's work was not solely concerned with securing full employment; it also implied an expanding economy, since this was the only way of ensuring that everyone had work. This was important because at the time the National Government had restored the balance of the economy firstly by throwing more men out of work and secondly by cutting back production where there were surpluses, which in practice meant in almost every industry. Opposing this approach, the 'planners' emphasised that planning was a way of developing the economy rather than of holding it back. For instance G. D. H. Cole, in a Labour Party pamphlet published just before the war, stressed that:

> This book is about the means to plenty — that, and nothing else . . . . What is essential at the outset is that we should have a clear vision of our aim. There has been a great deal of so-called 'planning' during the last few years under the auspices of the National Government, but really all of it has been planning for scarcity and not for plenty . . . . There is no magic virtue about 'planning' as such: it depends on what the planning is for. Our planning must be for plenty.[12]

The same view was also held by a number of non-socialists. As we have already seen, Harold Macmillan thought that social progress was democracy's best line of defence. But social progress implied sustained growth, and consequently he wrote in much the same terms as Cole:

> So far as the present writer is concerned, the object of planning is *not* to restrict production and solve the problem of plenty by creating an artificial scarcity . . . the object of economic effort must be to *increase* the production of wealth and, as a result of rising prosperity, to enable society to increase the leisure and cultural opportunities of all the people.[13]

Planning Methods

For most of those who supported planning, it implied reform of existing institutions and the creation of new ones. It was widely felt that the kind of political institutions that had grown up in democracies like Britain were quite unsuited and incapable of resolving economic problems. Reforms would accordingly be needed to make governments and parliaments more efficient than hitherto. Their view of Parliament was best summarised by Barbara Wootton:

> It is generally agreed that democratically elected parliaments have proved themselves quite incapable of dealing with all the economic technicalities in which they have been entangled in recent years. There is no part of their job which parliaments do worse than their economic work, and no department of affairs in which the theory of democratic control is further removed from actual practice.[14]

In view of their inadequacy, how could parliaments be involved in the planning process? Barbara Wootton suggested a procedure for keeping the House of Commons fully informed of the preparation of plans, and enabling it to make its views known at the appropriate moment. Initially Parliament would adopt a motion giving general guidance on the aims of the plan indicating, for example, what the increase in production should be, how far incomes should be equalised, or which industries should have priority for public investment. The Planning Commission would go to work on the basis of these general instructions. The draft plan would be submitted to Parliament, providing a further opportunity for discussion not only by Parliament but by all sections of the public. The resulting comments, suggestions and criticisms would then be reviewed by the planners, who would incorporate some and reject others. Barbara Wootton thought that the experts should have the final word, but if they stuck to their original proposals in the face of substantial criticism they would have to give reasons for doing so. The reason she thought it 'absolutely necessary' for them to have the last word was that 'otherwise their position will quickly be rendered impossible by the importunity of unexpert persons who want them to include all sorts of things in the plan without any idea of the practical or technical consequences which these notions entail'.[15]

There would be no direct relationship between Parliament and the Planning Commission; it would operate through the government. Responsibility for proposing the general guidelines to Parliament would be with the cabinet. But it was dubious whether the cabinet was really capable of doing this. In practice the chancellor had overall responsibility for economic policy, and most chancellors in the thirties engaged in economic policy-making much like M. Jourdain speaking prose. It was not surprising that these policies were rarely very coherent. Again, chancellors tended to see their job in essentially negative terms: opposing additional expenditure, worrying over the financial consequences of decisions rather than their overall economic consequences and so on. Consequently most of the 'planners' also thought there should be a ministry of economic affairs (Wootton, Macmillan) or a ministry for planning (Cole). Macmillan even favoured reducing the cabinet to six: the prime minister, the chancellor and four 'overlords' for foreign affairs, economic affairs, social affairs and defence. Most of the 'planners' thought three types of new institution were needed: a planning commission with regional and local offices, a national investment fund, and some kind of national employment fund.

But they naturally devoted most attention to the central planning body — sometimes called the Planning Authority, sometimes the Planning Commission and sometimes the National Economic Council. Some thought it should be a very large body; others that it should be small. Socialists tended to see it in terms of Gosplan; non-socialists preferred something like the Royal Commission model. But nobody wanted the sort of social parliament the Webbs had advocated, perhaps mainly because this would have been recruited in much the same way as existing national parliaments, and consequently it was unlikely to be any more capable of dealing with planning. The 'planners' had no wish to set up economic and social councils of the kind established by several continental countries during the thirties. These had turned out to be rather unwieldy because those who set them up tried to reconcile two different principles: expertise and representativity. Most were too big and the members were too much like conventional politicians with a sprinkling of experts. In fact, while the 'planners' were fairly clear about what they did not want, they were not at all precise about what they did want. Most seemed to favour a rather small council of experts under the chairmanship of a minister for economic affairs, and a staff comprising a statistical service and divisions responsible for preparing the plan and implementing it.

Most of the 'planners' envisaged some degree of decentralisation — naturally enough in view of the imbalance between regions, the seriousness of which had become particularly obvious during the economic crisis. While some areas, mostly around a line running through London and Birmingham, remained relatively prosperous even during the depression, others were severely affected. The three areas that suffered most were Lancashire, the North East and South Wales, but Scotland and the West Riding were also hard hit. The problems of these regions were due largely to their undue dependence on ageing and declining industries like coal, cotton, iron and steel and shipbuilding. The aim of regional planning would be to secure a better balance between the regions.

The proposal for a National Investment Fund was an old idea of Keynes who saw it as a sort of bank promoting and financing the introduction of activities that were essential to the national interest but were not financially viable. The 'planners' wanted the Fund to control loans and investments in accordance with the needs of the plan.

The idea of a National Labour Corps was largely Cole's. He had first floated it in 1929. Surplus manpower was all too common an occurrence in Britain, and Cole was attempting to find a permanent remedy for underemployment. The National Labour Corps would provide a pool of manpower at the disposal of those running the economy. The question was not simply one of keeping as many men as possible in employment, but of seeing that they did work that would otherwise not have been done at all. They would have had the 'task of making the country as a whole both a pleasanter place to inhabit and a more efficient productive concern'.[16] A characteristic feature of the Corps would be that its members 'would have to be prepared to turn their hands to many jobs and to take lightheartedly a certain amount of "roughing it" under somewhat primitive conditions'.[17] Its members would all be volunteers who were prepared to accept periods of separation from their families. The value of the Corps would be two-fold: it would provide a number of men with temporary employment, and it would prepare them to resume a normal working career by seeing they were properly trained in some skill.

Though Cole was a socialist, there was little likelihood of his Corps finding favour with the unions. Nevertheless this somewhat utopian proposal foreshadowed two later developments: the establishment of national schemes for vocational training and retraining, and the emergence in the sixties of those armies of immigrant workers that were to serve as mobile reserves of manpower in most Western industrial countries, undertaking work that the country's own workers were no longer prepared to do.

The Ambiguities of the Planning Movement

A plan can be worked out in greater or lesser detail. The less confidence there is that private individuals will do what the plan expects of them, and the greater trust there is in collective action, then the greater the amount of detailed planning there is likely to be. Whatever the ends and the means involved, the ambiguity stems from a long-standing fundamental disagreement between individualists and socialists over how far the economy should be socialised, and who should own or control the means of production. As far as the socialists were concerned, the anarchy of capitalism could not be eliminated without abolishing capitalism itself, that is without socialising the means of production, distribution and exchange. 'As long as capitalism is in the saddle, the horse cannot gallop. It will only be allowed to trot, for fear it may throw the rider if it is urged to a faster pace.'[18] That was how Cole saw the problem; a few pages further on he was more categoric still: 'Capitalism, by reason of its very nature, *cannot plan*, whereas Socialism can and must.'[19]

On the other hand, the proposals of the non-socialists did not spell the end of private ownership of industry; in their view the capitalist firm should remain the basic unit in the economic community. As Macmillan put it, 'I want to argue . . . for the deliberate preservation of private enterprise in a field lying outside the range of minimum human needs. I support it for the purely economic reason that it ensures initiative, the adoption of new methods, the exploration of the market possibilities of new products, and speculative experimentation with new scientific discoveries.'[20]

But Macmillan was too much of a realist not to be aware that ever since World War I in most industrial societies there had been an apparently irresistible trend towards collectivism, and he realised that the same tide was carrying planning forward with it. In assessing how far the British economy had been socialised in *The Middle Way* he showed a keen awareness that as yet capitalism had been unable to solve the problems of working-class poverty and insecurity. As we have seen, Macmillan believed that genuine political freedom required a high level of social welfare. In this area there had to be state intervention, perhaps even a state monopoly. So when Macmillan proclaimed faith in private enterprise he qualified this by saying, 'I shall advocate all the more passionately on grounds of morality, of social responsibility, as well as of economic wisdom, a wide extension of social enterprise and control in the sphere of minimum human needs.'[21]

What Macmillan ideally wanted was a mixed economy with a system of flexible planning, which might enjoy the advantages of both economic systems, and perhaps even reconcile them:

> I realise, of course, that it is contended both by Socialist planners and by the anti-planners that this mixed system . . . is an impossibility. . . . I profoundly disagree with that view. Britain has been moving along the road towards economic planning for many years now in accordance with the traditional English principles of concordance and adjustment. Unless we can continue this peaceful evolution from a free capitalism to a planned capitalism or, it may be, a new system of capitalist and socialist theory, there will be little hope of preserving the civil, democratic and cultural freedom which, limited as it may be at the moment by economic inefficiency, is a valuable heritage.[22]

The war and its attendant trials helped extend the influence of both Macmillan and his ideas in the Conservative Party. So it is not surprising that the economic and social reforms of the postwar Labour government suffered no major challenge from the Conservative opposition. However, in 1939 socialists found little that appealed to them in Macmillan's 'middle way'. One of the questions raised by Labour's period of rule between 1945 and 1951 was whether it succeeded in going beyond the 'middle way'. We shall return to this later. What is clear is that from 1939 there gradually emerged a consensus over how to ensure that all sections of the community shared to some extent the economic and social progress. It was this consensus that made possible the major wartime and postwar reforms.

PART I

Planning Between 1945 and 1951

CHAPTER 1

Theory and Practice in 1945

There may well never have been a moment in the history of Britain when harmony between social classes was greater, at least superficially, than at the close of the Second World War. Everyone, from the humblest worker to the future Prince Consort, had suffered danger and privation, and everyone who had shared in the war effort felt that the entire country was entitled to a better life, and that everything possible must be done to prevent a return to the hardships and crises of the prewar years. This yearning to build a better society seems the main reason why Labour won its unexpected election triumph in 1945 despite the enormous prestige of Churchill. It also found expression in a measure of consensus over the ends the economy should achieve, and the role that the State should play in it. This consensus was most apparent over proposals for social reform — which were in part prepared under the wartime coalition. But it was by no means negligible in economic matters, though here the apparent emergence of areas of agreement was at times deceptive.

One demand took precedence over all others: full employment. All three major parties had bound themselves to maintain it in the 1944 White Paper on unemployment.[1] Together with this recognition of the right to work went the intention of introducing an all-embracing system of social security, of maintaining the high levels of income tax brought in during the war and of democratising the educational system. Inspired by the desire for greater material and intellectual equality for all, these proposals were outlined in a series of White Papers which won widespread approval. The most celebrated was the Beveridge Report of 1942, which declared that: 'The plan for social security is first and foremost a method of redistributing income, so as to put the first and most urgent needs first, so as to make the best possible use of whatever resources are available.'[2] Only ten years previously such a remark would have been inconceivable in an official report! Now such visions of social reform were well on their way to being accepted as basic assumptions for economic policy-making from which politicians would diverge only at their peril. Thus the State found itself permanently playing a central role in the economy. This gave rise to the idea of a moderately interventionist welfare state which was quite different from the old prewar liberal idea of a 'neutral' state. From Right to Left, all across the political spectrum, the principal parties and pressure groups showed no disposition to challenge this development.

Among the first to realise that, at least in the short term, there could be no return to *laissez-faire* were organisations representing trade and industry. In

1942 the Association of British Chambers of Commerce suggested that a Council for Industry should be set up:

> The work of the Council would ensure cooperation between the government and private enterprise in order that trade and industry might be carried on for the benefit of the community as a whole. The guidance thus given by the Council of Industry would enable the government of the day, with the approval of Parliament, to give general directives as to the policy to be followed. The Association recognises that it will be inevitable for certain controls to be continued for some time after the war, but urges that every endeavour should be made to ensure that in no case should the period of control be unnecessarily prolonged.[3]

At about this same time the leading association of employers, the Federation of British Industry, adopted a similar position.[4] The Conservative Party could not be unaffected by these conciliatory views, and in January 1944 it published a report that argued on very similar lines, though it emphasised that the last word must always lie with the government. State control of industry should continue for only as long as was necessary for the transition from war to peace, but the government must retain control over the location of industry. While the Conservatives rejected the idea of nationalisation, they accepted the view that industry had a responsibility to society and should conform to both its written and unwritten laws.[5] The Liberals adopted more or less the same line on nationalisation but laid particular emphasis on consumer and user interests, which they held to be crucially important. They were also long-standing advocates of having some kind of economic general staff to co-ordinate economic decision-making.

While Labour statements had a more radical tone, in essence they were really not all that different. A motion adopted at the party's 1943 conference spelled out its views as follows:

> The adjustment of industry to the needs of peace, the adoption of a policy of economic expansion at home and the organisation of our export trade, will all call for wide measures of central regulation and control. The governing principle should be this: industry to be the instrument of public policy — not public policy the instrument of industry. . . . Industry in many fields will seek the help of the State to finance and organise itself. There must be no such help without supervision and control to the full extent that the public interest requires.[6]

Also in 1943 the TUC expressed very similar views on the immediate postwar period, calling for 'measures of public control over prices, food, distribution and consumption at least equal in effectiveness to those established and maintained during the war itself'.[7] It also insisted that 'public and private investment must be controlled and directed'.[8]

The extent of the similarity between these various statements is quite striking. The only differences relate to the extent and duration of state control, rather than to the basic principle of state intervention. This high level of agreement was inevitable once there had been an acceptance of full employment and greater equality as the main objectives of social policy. But there were also more strictly political reasons for this convergence in the parties' views. Firstly, both industry and the Conservatives remembered the lessons of the period immediately after the First World War, when a hasty return to freedom (including the restoration of the convertibility of the pound in 1925 without an accompanying devaluation and at a quite unrealistically high exchange rate) had led first to financial disorder and then to economic crisis. They were also acutely conscious that the country was determined that there should be no return of prewar social problems. Finally, a new generation of Conservatives, such as Harold Macmillan, who had taken an unorthodox line during the thirties, was to rise to the higher reaches of the party during its years in opposition between 1945 and 1951. These new Conservatives genuinely believed in the political and moral case for 'welfare democracy'.[9]

After the 1931 débâcle Labour had taken refuge in an aggressive radicalism. But since May 1940 they had been sharing office with the two other major parties, and they had hopes of being able to form a majority Labour government. During the war they had shown that they could govern. Having gained confidence, though remaining committed to a number of principles like nationalisation, they were concerned not to frighten moderate voters — particularly since they were aware that support for their views was growing steadily. Attlee, who was then deputy prime minister in the coalition government, and responsible for domestic policy, commented on this change in a letter to Harold Laski in 1944:

> I have witnessed now the acceptance by all the leading politicians in the country and all the economists of any account of the conception of the utilisation of abundance . . . . It colours all our discussions on home economic policy. There follows from this the doctrine of employment . . . . You will appreciate that in discussions with cabinet colleagues not of our party the full acceptance of these conceptions concedes much of our case in advance . . . . Take up the whole conception of state planning and the control of the financial machine by the government and not by the Bank of England and the City. Here again I see the changes since the days of 1931. In my time in our movement, now getting quite long, I have seen a lot of useful legislation, but I count our progress much more by the extent to which what we cried in the wilderness fifty or thirty years ago has now become part of the assumptions of the ordinary man and woman.[10]

This analysis was, in a way, a tribute to the Fabians, who had always argued that time was on the side of the reformers, and that the progressive permeation of people's minds by the ideals of socialism was preferable to hasty or drastic action. It also gives due credit to the coalition government for laying the groundwork for peace despite its immediate preoccupation with war, thus opening the way for the experiment in reformist democracy on which Labour was about to embark.

But these conversions and proposals contained more than a little ambiguity, and some significant shades of meaning. For while there was practically universal agreement on the retention of wartime controls, many of the non-socialists thought that this should be purely temporary. Consequently it was very probable that, once the economy had returned to something like normal peacetime conditions, there would be demands for a return to a greater measure of freedom. Also, some observers feared that Labour might resort to a measure of compulsion that would threaten democracy itself. For although Labour statements invariably emphasised the party's determination to carry its programme through by strictly democratic means, the warnings of F. A. Hayek[11] had alarmed some sections of the public, particularly those who recalled that before the war some of the leading lights of the Labour Party, such as Harold Laski and Stafford Cripps, had expressed doubts about whether the British system of parliamentary democracy was capable of achieving a transition to a socialist society. There were some who felt their views threatened the rights, and perhaps even the existence, of the opposition parties.[12]

Events were to prove these fears unfounded, since Labour was to operate entirely within existing institutions, which was an indication of the strength of both the government's and the opposition's attachment to democracy. But this raises a quite basic question, which will be discussed later: whether the absence of serious constitutional conflict was due to the strength of the opposition's respect for majority decisions, or to the relative moderation of Labour's reforms. For it should not be forgotten that, beyond the introduction of a planned economy, the avowed aim of the Labour leaders, as countless speeches from the time confirm, was to bring into being a democratic socialist society which would stand between the liberal capitalism of the United States and the authoritarian communism of the USSR. There were no illusions about the difficulty of such an undertaking. Michael Young, for instance, warned the electorate on behalf of the party that:

> To achieve socialism, while preserving and enlarging the full freedom of the individual and the structure of political democracy, will be in many ways far more difficult than it would be if there were a sudden and necessarily violent revolution. As a problem in technique, it cannot be easy to provide the framework within which privately owned industry can function while some sections of the economy are being directed by public enterprise. Planning by persuasion is bound to be technically more complex than planning by coercion. But there is no doubt about the significance for the world of what is being attempted in Britain. People everywhere will be watching to see whether in practice planning according to socialist principles can be reconciled with freedom.[13]

So the aim was set out clearly enough. Consideration of Labour planning between 1945 and 1951 cannot be separated from this wider vision of a transformation of the social and economic structure of Britain. That is why any assessment of Labour planning must also try to establish what became of the 'grand design' of 1945.

The Theoretical Debate

The public, the parties and pressure groups were thus for the most part in favour of planning, taken in the broad sense of state intervention with a view to co-ordinating the working of the economy and settling the broad lines of future development. What conclusions should be drawn from this was a matter of more dispute. Among the economists and political commentators who joined in the ensuing debate were some, such as Hayek and Jewkes, who solemnly warned their contemporaries of what they considered to be a dangerous trend, while others, such as Evan Durbin and Barbara Wootton, welcomed the trend and were concerned to explore the meaning and implications of planning more deeply.

One of the precursors of this debate was Schumpeter. In 1941 he had noted what he considered to be an irreversible trend in capitalism towards socialism. He saw Britain as a prime example of this process:

> Moreover, English people on the whole have become state-broken by now. English workmen are well-organised and as a rule responsibly led . . . . [A] policy of socialisation is conceivable that, by carrying out an extensive programme of nationalisation, might on the other hand make it possible to leave untouched and undisturbed for an indefinite time all interests and activities not included in that programme.[14]

In Schumpeter's view the implementation of such a programme implied nationalisation of a list of basic industries: banking, insurance, internal transport, building and iron and steel (the last two being less urgent). This list bears a strong resemblance to the programme actually undertaken by the 1945 Labour government. However, there was one important difference: Labour did not tackle the banking system as a whole. From the standpoint of economic planning this was to prove a serious drawback.

Events were to show that Schumpeter's view of the 'inevitable' transition to socialism was, to say the least, speculative. However, he was by no means alone in the forties in detecting such a trend. While in Schumpeter's view it was not incompatible with democracy, Hayek and Jewkes viewed it with dread, fearing it would pave the way to totalitarianism. The starkness of their titles — *The Road to Serfdom* and *Ordeal By Planning* — shows the intensity of their opposition.

The Opponents of Planning

Hayek
Professor F. A. Hayek was born in Austria in 1899 and moved to London in the thirties, adopting British nationality in 1938. At the London School of Economics he was an unwavering advocate of both political and economic liberalism. Hypersensitive to anything recalling the initial stages of fascism, he

was convinced that socialism had facilitated the emergence of totalitarianism by making it seem normal and acceptable for freedom to be limited in a number of respects, and by fostering an authoritarian spirit. Since German social democracy had led to Hitler, any form of socialism, no matter how moderate it claimed to be, was bound to pave the way for fascist or communist autocracy:

> How even a formal recognition of individual rights, or of the equal rights of minorities, loses all significance in a State which embarks on a complete control of economic life, has been amply demonstrated by the experience of the various Central European countries. It has been shown there that it is possible to pursue a policy of ruthless discrimination against national minorities by the use of recognised instruments of economic policy, without ever infringing the letter of the statutory protection of minority rights,[15] [for it should not be forgotten that] the idea of a political party, which claims to guide the individual from the cradle to the grave, which claims to guide his views on everything, and which delights in making all problems questions of party-*Weltanschauung*, was first put into practice by the socialists.[16]

Many readers were so shocked by these rather simplistic comparisons that they saw only the exasperating side of Hayek's arguments. Yet this Whig or 'liberal—individualist' criticism, as Raymond Aron calls it,[17] was both more moderate and more pertinent when applied to planning in the strict sense of the word. In Hayek's view planning grasps the economy in an iron grip which makes competition impossible — and competition is a *sine qua non* of a market economy. Thus if there had to be a choice between planning and the market, Hayek chose the market. In an economy as complex as that of Britain, regulation — to the extent it could be attained at all — must be achieved by means of a mechanism that was at once automatic, neutral and decentralised. Only the price mechanism could do this:

> This is precisely what the price system does under competition, and which no other system even promises to accomplish. It enables entrepreneurs, by watching the movement of a relatively few prices, as an engineer watches the hands of a few dials, to adjust their activities to those of their fellows. The important point here is that the price system will fulfil this function only if competition prevails.[18]

Like others who espoused economic liberalism, Hayek would allow the State to intervene only in order to control monopolies and restrictive practices and to maintain free competition.

During the thirties arguments of this kind formed the main basis of the case against planning by Hayek and others.[19] But they were complemented by other more directly political arguments which, in Hayek's case at least, linked with his prime political preoccupation. Since socialism was the source of authoritarianism, and planning stemmed from socialism, then the development of planning was bound to be at the expense of democracy. In Hayek's view one unfailing sign of this was the enthusiasm for planning among 'technical experts' (or 'technocrats' as we would now call them). This enthusiasm was suspect because it was surely due to the fact that they hoped that planning would give them a freer hand to do what they wanted, for it was certain to involve the setting up of a whole new range of technical bodies which would not be completely accountable through the normal constitutional processes, and which as a result would exercise disguised autonomous power. This was in fact one of the fundamental dangers of planning — that too much would escape democratic parliamentary control: 'The delegation of particular technical tasks to separate bodies ... is yet only the first step in the process whereby a democracy which embarks on planning progressively relinquishes its powers. ... The belief is becoming more and more widespread that, if things are to get done, the responsible authorities must be freed from the fetters of democratic procedure.'[20] This was a cogent criticism which impressed the supporters of planning.

Another defect of planning in Hayek's view was that it extended the area in which the State intervened in the life of the individual. On the one hand it meant a considerable increase in the number of decisions that had to be taken at a political level, either directly or by delegation. On the other, it required the whole body of individuals constituting a nation to reach agreement on a far greater number of issues. This meant that there would be many more occasions when the will of the majority would prevail over the wishes of the minority than would be the case under a strictly liberal system. Since there would be more such decisions, affecting progressively wider areas of life, planning meant the diminution, perhaps even the death, of personal freedom. To Hayek, freedom was less a matter of freedom *to* than of freedom *from*. Noting this, Raymond Aron comments that 'freedom is identified with the guarantee of a private sphere in which everyone is master of himself'.[21] It was precisely this 'private sphere' which Hayek considered to be threatened by planning: 'The various kinds of collectivism, fascism, etc., differ between themselves in the nature of the goal towards which they want to direct the efforts of society. But they all differ from liberalism and individualism ... in refusing to recognise autonomous spheres in which the ends of individuals are supreme.'[22] This was not to say that liberals reject the rules of society, but that the only constraint they would accept was that of law, in so far as it was universal, neutral and unvarying. According to Hayek a liberal system was characterised by a general framework of laws which fixed formal rules determining the conditions under which available resources may be used, leaving it to individuals to decide for what ends they are to be used. The characteristic of such rules was that 'we do not know their concrete effect ... we do not know what particular ends these rules will further or which particular people they will assist. They do not involve a choice between particular ends or particular people'.[23] For Hayek, selective or discriminatory measures were bound to be in some measure arbitrary and thus, quite simply, they were incompatible with the rule of law. Yet without discriminatory measures there can be no effective planning.[24]

Hayek's critique was therefore reactionary in the strict and non-pejorative sense of the word. He is open to the criticism of failing to take into account the powerful body of opinion that saw no reason why a curtailing of economic freedom should not be compatible with an extension of political freedom. However, his attack had the merit of drawing attention to the risks inherent in an undue extension of state intervention, and of stinging the socialists to replies which resulted in a much clearer understanding of the limits beyond which freedom would no longer be secure. His influence was far from negligible, firstly on Churchill, later on Conservative governments after 1951, and even today on the party's right wing. In the field we are concerned with in the present study, it is particularly worthy of note that his criticism led to the development of a neo-liberal body of thought associated with the Institute of Economic Affairs, which continues to campaign for non-interventionist economic policies.

The Liberal Empiricism of John Jewkes[25]

Jewkes's *Ordeal By Planning* was less theoretical. It was essentially an indictment of the economic policies pursued during the first two years of the Labour government.[26] For Jewkes too the central issue in the debate on economic planning was the dialectic between socialism and capitalism. This would cease to be so only with the emergence of new means of planning within Western capitalist systems — mainly the French example. (For although France introduced planning in 1946 her neighbours became fully aware of what was happening there only at the end of the fifties.) In addition to this antipathy towards socialism, Jewkes criticised those who favoured planning for pursuing novelty regardless of cost, and for their readiness to sacrifice current progress for the sake of a completely problematical future. They seriously oversimplified economic problems, imagining for example that an increase in investment could be relied on to produce speedy and spectacular results. The outcome was that in their ideas consumption was practically sinful. While this owed much to the characteristic puritanism of many British socialists, with their tendency to look on concern for anything beyond the bare necessities of life as a step along the road to perdition, it was also true that where consumption was controlled and standardised, the job of the planners was made that much easier. Hence the suspicion with which supporters of planning viewed uncontrolled prices, particularly during an 'abnormal' period such as that following the war. 'More converts are brought to the planning fold through ignorance of the price system than through any other cause . . . . The price system in a free economy is not without its defects . . . . But no one has yet devised a better system for coordinating the work of very large groups of people, for shifting the emphasis of production as consumers' demands change. . . .'[27]

Another consequence of the mania for planning was the adoption into the language of politics and economics of a dubious jargon which not only meant quite different things to different people, but also hid its authors' true intentions.[28] What most infuriated Jewkes was the misuse of the term 'national interest':

> This casual use of the 'national interest' argument carries in its train many social dangers . . . [It] is a highly convenient device for justifying dictatorial action . . . [It] means that many of our economic decisions must be made in the absence of concrete and objective criteria . . . [It] leaves us open to the policies of cranks of every sort who will justify their case 'in the national interest'.[29]

Thirdly, Jewkes was angered by the readiness of so many supporters of planning to depict it as applying scientific methods to running the economy. It was nothing of the kind. Assuming that the planners prepared their plans with the appropriate degree of scientific rigour, they would have to be prepared to make compromises to take account of what the public would accept — for, in a democracy at least, all economic decisions are potentially political decisions. 'It is, indeed, ironically naive to imagine that the political leaders in a planned economy will quickly allow a group of economic and statistical experts to operate, without question, an economic system according to the latest theoretical ideas as to how goods can be produced and distributed in order to maximise total satisfaction.'[30] Whether they had to contend with the government or with private interests, the planners would have to compromise. But the way in which compromises would be arrived at would be no more scientific than the working of the market.

The Supporters of Planning

Evan Durbin and Barbara Wootton were both moderate socialists who were unquestionably committed to equality and social justice, but were no less concerned to preserve traditional political liberties. If they were advocates of planning, then, this was because, for them, there was no contradiction between planning and freedom.

Evan Durbin and the Attempt to Define Democratic Planning

Durbin was a young socialist economist who was elected to Parliament in 1945 but met a tragically early death while bathing. He wrote a number of articles advocating planning, which were collected in a volume published after his death.[31] Durbin's reply to Hayek was that socialist economists were every bit as hostile to totalitarianism as he was: 'Most of us are socialist in our economics because we are "liberal" in our philosophy and we believe that it is Prof. Hayek who has missed the road to freedom that all humanitarian "liberals" wish to find.'[32]

But Durbin's main preoccupation was with defining what he understood by planning. For Durbin planning was 'a principle of administration and not an inflexible budget of production',[33] and he was quite prepared to state that 'planning does not in the least imply the existence of a Plan'.[34] His desire to overcome his readers' reservations was understandable, but if words were to have any meaning, could one really assert baldly that planning does not imply a plan? Admittedly he went on in the very next line to resolve this apparent paradox by adding: '. . . in the sense of an arbitrary industrial budget which lays down in advance the volume of output for different industries'.[35] But in that case what did democratic socialists want? According to Durbin, 'By "economic planning" . . . we mean a change in the direction of responsibility. Instead of looking towards small and unrepresentative minorities of shareholders, the persons or corporations directing production would look upwards or towards a Central Economic Authority for guidance on the larger questions of output, prices, investments and costs.'[36] What Durbin outlined here could equally well be applied to a system of short-term intervention by the State based on a network of nationalised basic industries. Durbin himself realised this, and rounded off his analysis by saying:

> It is, of course, one of the great advantages of a 'planned economy' in my sense of the term, that it is possible to construct *statistical budgets* of production for long periods ahead. . . . One of the superiorities of a centrally directed economy will be this ability to analyse and add up, to calculate and foresee the statistical implications of any given decision — and in this sense there will be many industrial 'plans' that can be combined in order to give a statistical picture or budget of the productive activity as a whole.[37]

These plans, or rather programmes, were quite different from the arbitrary, authoritarian plans feared by Hayek. Their purpose was essentially to provide an idea of future patterns of consumer demand. Moreover, 'if . . . a change takes place later in the preferences of the consumers, then the "plans" can be altered to suit the new conditions'.[38] There could be no better description of what came to be known later as indicative planning. At the time it represented the most thoughtful attempt to reflect on and give expression to a theme that has so often been misused and so rarely defined.

As for Hayek's contention that socialism had been responsible for the rise of Nazi Germany, in Durbin's view this was quite simply contrary to the historical evidence. For the Germans were very hesitant in 1918 about adopting the democratic values of the victors. The reason they abandoned them so rapidly had less to do with socialist ideology than with the fact that these values were never fully espoused. Conversely, it seemed improbable that Britain, where there was such a strong attachment to freedom, would be prepared to allow any strengthening of the State to be at the expense of freedom. 'If we have "economic planning", it will be our own "economic planning". It will fulfil the wishes of our people. It will be the servant of our freedom and will bring another part of our common life within the control of our social wisdom.'[39]

Barbara Wootton and Planning in a Free Society

In *Freedom Under Planning*, as in her earlier work,[40] Barbara Wootton was concerned less with answering particular arguments than with analysing, from the standpoint of a vigilant committed democrat, the temptations that might lead the planner to encroach on people's freedom. Dismissing Hayek's pessimistic argument, she examined one by one the points where threats to freedom were most likely to arise. However, her definition of planning stayed rather vague. To her, it was 'the conscious and deliberate choice of economic priorities by some public authorities'.[41] It was 'a matter of degree. It is nowhere completely absent nor does it anywhere cover 100% of all economic activity'.[42] More interestingly she recalled that planning did not necessarily imply socialism — a view that had been argued by both Macmillan and Salter[43] before the war, but which seemed to have been practically forgotten in 1945:

> State planning of priorities in production, even if it covered much the greater part of our economic life, is not necessarily identical with socialism. In theory at least, it is quite possible for the State to make all major decisions about how much of what is to be produced without itself undertaking anything approaching the whole of that production. ... How far such planning without socialism would be practicable except in the special circumstances of war is a question to which experience gives as yet no clear answer.[44]

Unlike Durbin, she did not distinguish clearly between planning and governmental intervention, but while Durbin associated planning with the nationalisation of the means of production, she foresaw the advent of the type of Western capitalist planning of which France was to provide the model from the fifties onwards.

Barbara Wootton did not seek to disguise the fact that planning threatens what is commonly termed 'economic freedom'. But this had two separate aspects: the freedom of the consumer and the freedom of the producer. A compulsory plan necessarily restricts consumer choice, at least indirectly. But how serious was the loss of a freedom of which the ordinary citizen had no clear awareness, and which had already suffered so many onslaughts under the market economy? 'Liberty of consumption in this sense is a highly sophisticated concept. It can hardly be said that people greatly prize a freedom the nature of which they do not understand and the presence or absence of which they would not even recognise.'[45] The liberty of the producer was a more delicate matter. It encompassed freedom of the firm, freedom of employment and freedom in collective bargaining. Although freedom of the firm affected only a minority, it was an influential one. Barbara Wootton saw no basic incompatibility between private initiative and the collective establishing of economic priorities. Consequently she refused to join in the traditional argument between socialists and non-socialists over the ownership of the means of production, and she thought that the freedom of the firm could be restrained without being eliminated. If it were demonstrated that resistance by businessmen was seriously jeopardising the plan, then this might show that nationalisation was necessary. But it was no service to the cause of planning to declare right from the start that nationalisation was essential without any evidence from experience. Choice of employment was of course a basic liberty which had both a positive side (the choice of a particular occupation or profession) and a negative side (the possibility of rejecting any particular job). In a liberal democracy there could be no question of removing this freedom. But it had a price. Though the planner could try to attenuate the more obvious consequences by such indirect methods as manipulating wage rates, offering incentives to mobility and expanding facilities for occupational training, this was as much as he could do.

The fundamental issue was freedom of collective bargaining. Traditionally, the outcome of negotiations between employers and workers depended on the balance of power between them at any particular moment in the particular industry concerned, and no account was taken of the implications for the economy as a whole. So it was logical that planning should embody a policy for wages (and incomes generally): 'There must in fact be a plan for wages; and this planning of wage rates must, indeed, extend not only as far as the planning of production but further.'[46] But it was obvious that planning of this kind would not be well received by either side of industry. Here again, Barbara Wootton adopted an empirical approach; she did not claim to have any ready-made answer. Her merit was to point to a fundamental problem which remains as timely now as then: if incomes are uncontrolled the plan will be lopsided. A balanced plan requires control of both incomes and wage negotiations – and this will be unpopular.

Barbara Wootton was more aware than many writers of the practical limitations imposed on planning by traditional liberties. In particular, one may wonder whether there is any satisfactory solution to the problem of controlling incomes, since all forms of constraints on wages involve some infringement of rights which people have now, rightly or wrongly, come to look on as immutable. This is doubtless because certain economic freedoms – notably free collective bargaining – are thought of as being part and parcel of political freedom.

Planning and the Market: the Middle Way

There were three main strands of thought on state intervention. The first, non-interventionist, strand rested on the assumption that private initiative is in general preferable to public control, and considered that the role of the State was to have no role – or rather, as impersonally as possible, to ensure that competition continued unabated by keeping monopolies and cartels in check. The second, which was usually socialist, preferred the economy to be planned or at least directed by the State. Those holding this view almost always emphasised the flexible nature of the plan and rejected allegations that they would eventually create a 'totalitarian system' (meaning one where the State controlled the entire lives of individuals and groups). They almost invariably favoured public ownership of the means of production, but most of them were ready to admit that nationalisation of industry would not be achieved overnight.

The third, intermediate, group — which, as one might expect in Britain, was also the largest — preached moderation in all things and made a studied empiricism its guiding principle. The economists in this group refused to come down either for or against nationalisation on *a priori* grounds, preferring to judge each case on its merits. They favoured a 'mixed economy' — i.e. an economic system in which capitalism and socialism would peacefully coexist. One of the most persuasive representatives of this school was unquestionably Sir Arthur Lewis.[47] His view was that all economies are controlled, and accordingly the real issue was whether one preferred the invisible control of the market or the visible control of the State. Since either type of economy may bring some degree of welfare, could it be shown that a planned economy achieved this more quickly? If planning was to be justified the answer must be positive. Again, the debate on planning was really just a reformulation of the age-old controversy over the role of the State; while those favouring more intervention were usually on the Left, and those advocating greater economic liberalism on the Right, this has not always been so. Nor did it imply that socialism and planning are synonymous:

> Socialism ... contrary to popular belief, is not committed either by its history or by its philosophy to the glorification of the State or to the extension of its powers. ... Socialists have rather lost their perspectives of this and have sometimes seemed to welcome every extension of state powers. Perhaps this is because the two most recent influences, Lenin and Webb, were both worshippers of the State.[48]

Thus Lewis saw planning more as a technique than as an expression of an ideology. And from that point of view, 'The truth is that we are all planners now.'[49] Those who proclaimed their attachment to *laissez-faire* in fact believed in state action to impose free competition. So the problem was one of degree rather than of kind: '*Laissez-faire* can be complete or it can be modified by state action at many crucial points. Similarly, planning can be complete, or it can be combined with a market economy in various degrees.'[50] In the latter event the question was no longer one of doing away with the market economy but of modifying it piecemeal. This is what Lewis called 'planning through the market' or 'manipulating the market': 'Where planning parts company with *laissez-faire* is not in rejecting the market economy, controlled by demand, but in arguing that demand itself is not sacred, but something that should be manipulated by the State.'[51]

What Lewis was advocating was essentially the manipulation of demand by fiscal and monetary means; selective stimulation of investment; a change in the exchange rate to restore the balance of payments, and co-ordination and rationalisation of industry. If this was planning, then most governments planned without saying so, and perhaps even without realising it! Moreover, since the plan must be flexible it must be amended as often as necessary — hence Lewis's preference for 'planning through the market', since the market is highly flexible. This is why Lewis considered long-term planning impracticable:

> A five year plan cannot be more than a vague indication of aspirations. . . . One must plan five years ahead all those parts of the economy which need five-year plans — afforestation, power stations and so on — but a general five-year plan for the whole economy is no more than a game. One plans for as far ahead as one can see — and this means that even an annual plan must be subject to review.[52]

One may well wonder whether 'manipulating the market' in this way can properly be described as planning, or whether it is not simply a form of mild interventionism.

Lewis was not alone in emphasising monetary and budgetary controls. They were also favoured by Lionel Robbins (later Lord Robbins) when he spoke of 'financial planning': '[For] the avoidance of both inflation and deflation, I favour something which, if you like, you can call overall financial planning'.[53] But was this really planning? Nothing could be less certain. Even Robbins was not altogether sure:

> I am not quite sure whether a policy of this sort, which is designed to maintain overall stability of aggregate demand, while leaving the maximum flexibility between the various constituent items, is correctly described by the term planning; for in current usage that term has become more and more associated with other meanings. But on the assumption that the real meaning of the word to plan is to attempt to act with foresight and intelligence, I see no reason to refrain from staking a claim to its use.[54]

But when the first Conservative chancellor after the war (R. A. Butler) followed a very similar policy a few years later there was no suggestion that he was 'planning', firstly because he was not, and secondly the word — and the idea — were no longer fashionable.

There were other economists like Sir Roy Harrod and Professor F. W. Paish who argued along much the same lines as Robbins, while Professor J. E. Meade proposed what he called a 'liberal—socialist' solution,[55] which had much in common with the views of Lewis. He felt that whether or not one was a planner was entirely a matter of what meaning was attached to the word:

> Am I a planner? If a planner necessarily believes in a quantitative programme of output, employment and sales for particular industries, occupations and markets and the exercise of such direct controls by the State as are necessary to carry this out, I am certainly no planner. If an anti-planner necessarily denies that the State should so influence the working of the price mechanism that certain major objectives of full employment, stability, equity, freedom and the like are achieved, then I am a planner.[56]

We see here how ambiguous these terms were in 1945, even after a decade of theoretical debate. Clearly many economists and political commentators used them because they were readily to hand, but few made any attempt to define them precisely. Indeed, too many of them seem to have been guilty of that unthinking following of fashion that Jewkes attacked. Accordingly, special credit goes to Evan Durbin and Barbara Wootton, who were almost alone in trying to make the discussion less superficial and who attempted, with some success, to give us a theory of democratic planning. Like all halfway houses, democratic planning implies that a way must be found between two pitfalls — being too bold and being too timid. If it were too detailed or extensive democracy would be in danger; dilution of the basic strategy through too single-minded a preoccupation with freedom would mean the withering away of the plan. Such was the basic dilemma that hung over the Labour ministers, and which still influences attempts at planning in the West.

The Legacy of War

At the outbreak of war the British government was seriously worried at the danger of inflation generated by the enormous budgetary demands of a war economy. Had there been any likelihood of their forgetting this, then a short book by Keynes, which was published in early 1940, would have provided them with a timely reminder.[57] Thus initially the central problem appeared to be primarily financial, but it was soon apparent that the task of allocating scarce resources — not just raw materials but also labour — was even more important. This led to the introduction of machinery to co-ordinate production, allocate labour and control prices. Since the economic problems of the immediate postwar period were of roughly the same nature, in 1945 there was a great temptation for the new government to turn to the machinery it found readily to hand, particularly since it was already familiar with its working from its experience in the wartime coalition.

The central function of allocating men and materials so as to meet the needs of the armed forces, which had first priority, while ensuring that minimum civilian needs were met was carried out not by a highly centralised machine but by a system that, both nationally and regionally, was flexible and varied — though as the war extended the power of the centre tended to increase, and by the end of the war a whole network of controlling and consultative bodies had evolved, under the co-ordination of the Lord President's Committee.

The Lord President's Committee

After a number of false starts and hesitations in 1939 and 1940, the machinery of wartime government was finally established in January 1941, with responsibility for the general direction of the economy being vested in the Lord President's Committee, which had a large measure of autonomy, though the most important decisions and the settling of major disagreements were still matters for the prime minister and the War Cabinet — of which the Lord President himself was of course a member. Given the burden of his other responsibilities, Churchill had no choice but to accept this division of responsibilities.

In 1942 Churchill described the Lord President's Committee as 'a parallel cabinet concerned with Home Affairs'.[58] The phrase was apt, for under the chairmanship of Sir John Anderson the Committee exercised oversight over the production programmes of all ministries with a view to avoiding duplication and inconsistencies and detecting any gaps. This led to its settling disagreements between spending departments — which would have been a Treasury responsibility in peacetime. Also, in January 1941 the Central Economic Information Service, which had been set up at the beginning of the war, was split into the Central Statistical Office and the Economic Section.

Before 1939 there had been yawning gaps in British economic statistics, and in some areas the only available data were what had been thrown up by university economists like Colin Clark in the course of their personal research. The Central Statistical Office was given three main functions: to see that each department systematically compiled statistics in its particular field, to collect the statistical data required by the War Cabinet, and to inform the various ministries of its findings. The Economic Section was a group of economists headed by Professor Jewkes who were officially intended to assist the War Cabinet, but in practice served more as economic advisers to the Lord President's Committee. Without such a group — which few other ministers without portfolio have had at their disposal — the Lord President would have found it quite impossible to do his job for lack of information.[59]

This was not the only reason why the Lord President's Committee came to play such a central role. In D. N. Chester's view there were three more reasons for its ascendancy.[60] Firstly there was Sir John Anderson himself, a man who had not been involved in party dogfighting before the war, who was universally respected, particularly by Labour ministers, and who was intimately acquainted with the Whitehall machine. Secondly, the original complex network of committees, which reflected Churchill's determination not to give up a scrap of power if he could avoid it, was scarcely realistic. However, once he had found in Anderson someone who enjoyed his complete confidence, Churchill rapidly resigned himself to the existence of a parallel cabinet. Finally, with the creation of the Ministry of Production in 1942, the Lord President's Committee shed many of its more technical responsibilities and was able gradually to develop its planning role along two main lines: high-level co-ordination of the war economy, and national needs and desirable reforms once peace had returned.

Other Bodies

The aim of total economic mobilisation for war was something that could not be achieved through the traditional system of ministries based in London. It called for organisation at every level, and not just at the centre. This was achieved by dividing the country into regions along the lines set out in the civil defence plan before the outbreak of war, and subsequently endorsed by the Citrine Report of 1942.

Centrally, the Ministry of Production was established in 1942 and given responsibility for the entire range of civil and military production. In addition to deciding policy it had a co-ordinating and consultative role. While decision-making followed orthodox Whitehall lines, co-ordination was entrusted to the Minister of Production's Council (which included both ministers and civil servants), while consultation took place at both national and regional levels. In London there was a National Production Advisory Council with 23 members (6 employers, 6 from the unions and the 11 deputy-chairmen of regional councils). But the original feature was the regional and local organisation. Britain was divided into eleven regions (Scotland, Wales, Northern Ireland and eight English regions). In each there was a regional production controller whose job essentially was to see that as far as possible his region ran on its own resources so as to economise transport and manpower. Almost always he was a prominent industrialist on temporary loan from his firm. He was supported by a fairly small regional production office and advised by a regional production board, which included regional civil servants, representatives of seven ministries and of the unions and employers. The regional boards were important channels of communication, and as time went on they also acquired significant powers of decision – an unmistakable indication of genuine decentralisation. In addition, each region was subdivided into districts organised along similar lines. Below this there were joint production committees in individual firms, containing equal numbers from management and from the unions, and responsible for organising co-operation between the two sides of industry at shop floor level. Co-operation of this kind was new in Britain. Although British unions have not on the whole been Marxist, and have shown little inclination to preach the class struggle, until that time they had seen their role as simply one of defending the interests of their members. But it was not long before these joint committees covered several million workers, and their views carried considerable weight. They dealt with working conditions (improvement of machinery, demarcation matters, production line speeds, and so on), but not with questions that traditionally had been a matter for negotiation between employers and unions – notably wages. The creation of these joint committees was closely watched by the unions, who did their best to bring the workers' representatives (many of whom were union officials) under their control.

Mobilisation of the country would not have been complete without a parallel organisation for civilian labour. At the centre of this was Ernest Bevin, minister of labour and one of the most influential leaders of the trade union movement. He was backed by an organisation that was very similar to the one on the production side. The Minister of Production's Council was chaired by Bevin when dealing with manpower and employment problems, and there was a National Advisory Council of fifteen employers and fifteen trade unionists to advise the minister on wages and salaries. In addition a National Arbitration Tribunal had complete power to resolve labour disputes where direct negotiations had broken down. Strikes and lockouts were consequently illegal; the minister was required to submit all disputes to the tribunal within twenty-five days of being notified. At the regional level there were eleven regional labour controllers, and locally the joint production committees which belonged to both the production and labour organisations. In the management of the war economy manpower planning was to be as crucial as the allocation of raw materials and finished products. This was all the more striking because Britain had just experienced such acute underemployment that many observers had come to consider unemployment a permanent feature of the British economy. With the mobilisation of surplus manpower – in June 1943 only 60,000 people were registered as unemployed – the war confirmed Keynesian analysis, though the methods adopted were scarcely those he would have chosen.

The third concern of the wartime government was to ensure that the cost of arms and military operations did not lead to rampant inflation. The authorities attached particular importance to maintaining real wages, for this would be a major factor in the sustaining of morale on the home front. This led to the adoption of a system of universal industrial and agricultural price controls. In the industrial field there were three types of control: the conventional 'governmental' machinery of the Board of Trade, which to all intents and purposes meant the price controllers, who were civil servants; the private machinery of the trade associations; and the quasi-governmental machinery established nationally by the Central Price Regulation Committee, which comprised nine representatives of business interests, several politicians, one member from the TUC, a Co-operative representative and an accountant. This achieved a considerable degree of autonomy. Below this were regional price regulation committees with between eleven and twenty members – manufacturers, distributors, wholesalers and independent members (usually lawyers or accountants). Agriculture was of course vitally important in civilian food supply. At the Whitehall level co-ordination was exercised by the Food Policy Committee of the cabinet, chaired by the Lord Privy Seal (who for most of the period was Attlee). At departmental level there was a system of dual control of prices and products, one relating to the production stage and operated by the Ministry of Agriculture, and the other at the distribution stage run by the Ministry of Food. Regionally there was the same part-governmental, part-corporative organisation as for industry (though the subdivisions were different). The key bodies were the county war executive committees for agriculture, which had between eight and twelve unpaid members representing the various interests involved – landowners, farmers and farmworkers – appointed by the minister.

This new system of state control was notable less for the expansion of state intervention and the rise in the numbers of civil servants than for the arrival in force in Whitehall of professional economists, and for the close involvement of the producers, including managers, workers, farmers and traders, at every level, especially regionally and locally.

Governments can use professional economists in one of two main ways. They can be banded together in a special unit which is consulted from time to time and asked to report on specific problems. The danger in this approach is that they will become rather isolated and their proposals will be somewhat out of touch with reality. Alternatively, they can be absorbed into the normal organisation of the department and given responsibility for advising on policy and executing it in some specific field. But then the economist, just like a conventional administrator, becomes so submerged in day-to-day problems that he has no time to think about the longer term. As D. N. Chester notes, a pragmatic compromise was gradually worked out during the war.[61] While most of the economists stayed concentrated in the Economic Section or the Central Statistical Office, they were rapidly enlisted to provide expert advice to a variety of departmental and other committees that were responsible for the co-ordination of economic policy. In this way they were brought into almost continuous contact with regular civil servants. These contacts were strengthened by the peculiar circumstances of wartime life; the long hours at the office, meals taken together — some civil servants even had camp beds in their offices. This had two advantages. The dons rapidly gained an understanding of practical administrative problems, and could no longer be suspected of being mere ivory tower intellectuals; this made their advice more acceptable. Also, their influence was now no longer confined to official reports or discussions with ministers, but could be brought to bear continuously and informally as the need arose. Their influence was lasting, and continued long after most of them had returned to their universities, for the civil servants with whom they had worked, argued, and thought through so many problems together remained in Whitehall and often were in more senior positions.

The second main characteristic of the war economy was the gradual introduction of corporate forms of organisation. During the thirties the State had encouraged attempts to rationalise a number of industries which had experienced severe difficulties, notably mining and textiles, through schemes resting essentially on self-discipline by the industry itself. Basically these schemes involved limiting production to the most profitable firms in order to prevent a complete collapse of prices. During the war the problem became one of organising the conversion of firms that had little relevance to the war effort or of securing the necessary manpower from elsewhere. Needless to say this did not meet with universal enthusiasm. But the conversion or closure of factories was made easier in 1941 by the establishment of a compensation fund financed by firms on war work. This corporative pooling of financial responsibilities was a further infringement of the principle of free enterprise. The same was true of the emergence of a large number of trade associations and agreements, some of which were little less than monopolies. They not only had a representative function but also regulated both production and prices. Admittedly there were precedents for this sort of development, and it took place with the encouragement of the State and under its supervision. Nevertheless, the State frequently vested responsibility for the general interest in sectional interests, which is always a dangerous thing to do, and the running of a public service by people who were not civil servants played a not inconsiderable part in the working of the war economy. The organisation of the Ministry of Production varied according to level. Centrally it was more or less conventional; the regional level was a mixture of public and private, and the local level was almost completely corporative. Add to this the fact that many of the civil service posts which were specially created during the war, such as the regional production controllers, were held by people seconded from their normal jobs in the private sector, and one can see why British industry so readily accepted this governmental intervention, and why some trade associations were even in favour of continuing it after the war had ended, by creating professional or corporate bodies with compulsory membership, which would have co-operated closely with the government in the preparation of plans for the economy and scientific development, the fixing of import and export quotas and targets, and in ensuring that the labour market worked in a more satisfactory way than before the war. Some people felt that this created a danger of a corporate system along fascist lines; others, on the contrary, saw it as a possible transitional stage towards socialism.

However that may be, it was clear that, when Labour came to power in 1945, in their attempt to introduce democratic socialism they had this wide range of machinery of government control and intervention at their disposal. It is noteworthy that they made relatively few changes in the committees of the regional and local organisations, either in the field of production or prices or manpower. The most important changes were therefore at the central level in the government sector, and as a consequence of nationalisation in the private sector. In going on to consider what happened under Labour, it should not be forgotten that they took over the wartime system almost intact — which is why this survey, rapid though it has been, makes a useful introduction to what happened later.

CHAPTER 2

Planning Under Labour
1945–1951

The 1945 election not only brought Labour to office, but for the first time there was a clear majority in Parliament favourable to a socialist programme. Many leading members of the new government had left the wartime coalition only a few weeks earlier, and in common with the other party leaders an aura of victory still clung to them. Consequently there were no major difficulties over the transition. Churchill returned to the opposition benches with dignity, though with some bitterness, making way for his former deputy, whose views – if not his personality – he respected. While a few newspapers perorated on this 'turning point in the history of Britain', the only immediately obvious change was in individuals, for the new prime minister made few alterations to the machinery of government. Indeed, there were only two changes of real note. First the cabinet was increased to seventeen members from the wartime level of between five and nine. This represented both a return to its normal peacetime size and a way of emphasising the collective nature of the new leadership. More important, in terms of this present study, the Ministry of Production was abolished. Some of its functions were discontinued, but most, together with its regional organisation, were transferred to the Board of Trade, which thus became responsible for most sectors of industry. The Ministry of Production might well have developed after the war into the main economic co-ordinating ministry with responsibility for planning. Having rejected this possibility Labour would have to find some other solution.

It is worth noting that Labour still had no clear and coherent policy on planning. The party's programme seemed to treat planning as of secondary importance, just one among several methods of achieving the party's aims. These were well established: to transform society, by way of more equal distribution of wealth and incomes and greater equality of opportunity. At first glance these objectives were not so very different from those of the other parties. For all the partners in the wartime coalition had committed themselves to the policies set out in the series of White Papers that followed in the wake of the Beveridge Report, dealing with social insurance,[1] industrial injuries,[2] a National Health Service[3] and full employment.[4] But these commitments could be looked on as no more than the essential basic minimum. Beveridge, for instance, considered the White Paper on employment quite inadequate, and in 1944 he had published his own more far-reaching proposals on employment policy.[5] Labour was even more firmly bound to implement at least this minimum programme because one of its main arguments during the election was that, while all parties paid lip-service to these proposals for social welfare, Labour alone could and would carry them through. In addition, the new government had to find the money to implement the Butler Education Act of 1944. In doing this it drew heavily on the experience of its wartime predecessor, with a policy of cheap money, high rates of income tax and death duties and a full panoply of physical controls, while also adding such fresh weapons to its armoury as the extension of public investment and a reorganisation of industry, in which nationalisation was only one aspect. The influence of Keynes on all this was evident, particularly while Hugh Dalton, the first Labour chancellor, was at the Exchequer.

In 1945 it was by no means clear what role planning had to play in this — whether there would simply be a continuation of wartime controls, or whether a completely fresh approach would be developed. New ideas did emerge gradually later, but initially it was evident that the main emphasis was to be on relying as far as possible on wartime machinery and experience. The early speeches by the minister with overall responsibility for economic policy, Herbert Morrison, are particularly revealing in this respect. They show that Morrison, who was then Lord President of the Council, still had no clearly formed views on the matter. In a speech to the Institute of Public Administration he took refuge in generalities: 'Planning is a very large and complicated business, and Britain is the first great nation to attempt to combine large-scale economic and social planning with a full measure of individual rights and liberties.'[6] Planning must go through five stages. The first was 'making up one's mind to plan and grasping what planning means' (sic); the next was 'assembling the necessary facts and forecasts to make sure that the plan can be put on a sound practical basis'.[7] The third stage was devising 'alternative plans', and the fourth was to choose between these. The fifth, and 'by far the most extensive, is carrying out the plans in practice'.[8] Morrison's conclusion was that 'after all, planning, though big and complicated, is not much more than applied common sense'.[9] Clearly, he was unlikely to embark on any rash innovations!

The First Phase (August 1945—July 1947)

The first phase, running from August 1945 to July 1947, roughly corresponds to the period of demobilisation, when Labour's greatest fear was of being unable to honour its pledges on full employment. This was understandable. Even then British governments were still haunted by the memory of the vast army of the unemployed between the wars, more than a million strong even in a good year. Now millions of men had to be reabsorbed into civilian life. At the same time there was an urgent need to reconstruct and modernise productive industry. The government was to embark on a huge investment programme which, consistent with Keynesian theory, had a dual aim: to ensure industrial reconstruction and to generate such a high level of economic activity that men would immediately be absorbed into civil employment on their release from the armed forces. Accordingly the Attlee government tackled the most urgent problems first, and it was to be some time before it realised that the central machinery of economic policy-making was not really adequate for the task in hand.

The Central Organisation of the Economy

The retention of most of the wartime machinery was in itself an innovation. In 1919 the controls that had been introduced during the First World War were rapidly abandoned — unlike the situation in Germany, where in 1919 the Socialists retained the wartime machinery for government intervention and employed it to make a modest start with planning, though this was soon abandoned.

The war economy had been run from outside the Treasury. In 1945 it was the Lord President, Morrison, who was responsible for co-ordinating the economic departments and presenting important proposals to the cabinet. However, the balance of the Lord President's Committee had been altered by the abolition of the Ministry of Production and the transfer to many of its responsibilities to the Board of Trade.[10] The committee was now dominated by three men: Morrison, Dalton and Cripps. Thus responsibility was shared between the chancellor, who was responsible for financial and budgetary policy, the president of the Board of Trade (Cripps), who was in charge of most aspects of physical planning, such as the various controls on industry, and the Lord President, who had overall responsibility for economic co-ordination and was the chief spokesman on economic affairs in cabinet, in the House and in the country generally. As in wartime there was a parallel Steering Committee of senior civil servants, chaired by the permanent secretary to the Treasury, which prepared the meetings of the Lord President's Committee. A number of other specialised committees of civil servants were established, with responsibility for major areas of economic policy such as manpower, capital investment, raw materials or the balance of payments.

During the first year of the Attlee government implementation of the Labour programme proceeded without major incident. Both ministers and civil servants were apparently reasonably satisfied with the system — yet, although it had the virtue of flexibility, it was not particularly efficient, for it failed to foresee the fuel crisis of February 1947. This was clear from the economic debate in the Commons in February 1946. Frank Byers, the Liberal MP, complained of a lack of clarity about the government's intentions:

> If we are to get true economic development, three things are obviously required. The first is a comprehensive plan to guide the resources of private and public enterprise to serve the best interests of the community. The beginning of that plan was explained by the Prime Minister today. The relationship which has to exist between private and public enterprise must be

more adequately defined in the near future . . . . Secondly, we must have adequate and flexible machinery for this coordination, execution and development of the plan. I do not believe we have it. Thirdly, we must have adequate administrative machinery which will be entrusted with the development and execution of the decisions of the government's administrative machinery where the responsibility for decision is delegated to a relatively low level.[11]

The following day Morrison replied, 'We now have a . . . piece of organisation . . . coordinating, advising, looking ahead, forecasting, putting all its economic, statistical and administrative knowledge at the disposal of the separate Departments of State.'[12] He refused to contemplate any change in the existing set-up and explicitly rejected the idea that an economic general staff should prepare the plan, guide it through Parliament and then implement it, on the ground that such an arrangement would raise dangers of both duplication and internal friction: 'I think this is a mistaken conception. Such an organisation would become almost as big as the government itself . . . . It would not work and there would be friction all round.'[13] Yet within a year the view Morrison rejected prevailed. But before that there was to be the fuel crisis and a number of other setbacks, which the government, if not outside observers, quite failed to foresee. However, before moving on to consider these developments, it is useful to consider the financial powers at the Attlee government's disposal in running its economic policy.

Control over Credit and Financial Institutions

No party wanted a recurrence of 1919, when a brief inflationary boom led to a long and painful recession. Moreover, Labour did not want to revive the economy by stimulating personal consumption; the government was more concerned with restoring and modernising basic industry, sections of which were to be taken into public ownership, and with making a start on its promised programme of social welfare. Consequently public expenditure was maintained at a high level (with industry and the social services taking up the slack left by the decline in defence spending), and this was accompanied by a policy of encouraging investment in both the public and private sectors of basic industry. Accordingly there was no question of reducing taxation, which stayed at over 35 per cent of national income throughout Labour's period of office. Neither was there any question of using interest rates as a means of controlling consumption or channelling investment. Rather, Dalton pursued a resolutely Keynesian line, determined that reconstruction and full employment should not be hampered by high interest rates. Consequently bank rate was held at a very low level, while rates in the money market during 1946 hovered at around 0.5 per cent over bank rate.[14] With such a policy there was obviously a risk of a disorderly scramble for credit provoking inflation. In reality, however, in 1945 the risk of this occurring was small, for the government was armed, or was about to arm itself, with two weapons, which were at the same time offensive and defensive: on the one hand there was a whole range of statutory controls over production and prices, and on the other a variety of bodies responsible for seeing that the available funds for investment were allocated according to needs.

Labour's proposals for financial institutions had never been set out systematically in a single document; they had emerged piecemeal in a large number of speeches and statements by a wide variety of spokesmen of varying standing. Like the party's general line they had moved from the outright hostility of the thirties to wartime acceptance of 'co-operation between the classes'. The earlier attitude, which was more in line with the traditional view of European social democrats on such matters, was that the banks and other financial institutions were integral parts of the capitalist system and consequently should be nationalised, together with the means of production. Apart from the Bank of England itself the chief targets were the 'Big Five' clearing banks, which were accused of having established a 'private credit and banking monopoly'.[15] While many members of the party must still have thought in such terms in 1945, the leadership's position was more complex. For, given the paramount importance attached to maintaining full employment, they realised that the banks held such a central position in the economy that any upheaval there might well have harmful repercussions throughout the entire system, and precipitate the very unemployment the party was so committed to avoiding. Consequently, pragmatism prevailed. In this, as in so many matters, Keynes was a powerful influence. Labour gave up any idea of nationalising the whole of the banking system and instead confined their attention to the central bank, which passed into public ownership at the beginning of 1946.

Socialists had long felt a special sense of grievance towards the Bank of England. They were particularly critical of the degree of independence enjoyed by the governor, and with some justification accused Montagu Norman (governor from 1920 to 1944) of having pursued a personal policy regardless of the wishes of successive chancellors. Looking back on the nationalisation debate in his *Memoirs*, Dalton recalled the main criticisms of the Bank and the formidable figure who ran it for so long.[16] The first complaint was that in 1925 the Bank had brought pressure on the then chancellor, Winston Churchill, to return to the prewar gold standard, with disastrous consequences. The second was that Norman had thrown his weight behind a programme of sweeping industrial rationalisation heedless of social cost, particularly of the resulting unemployment. The third criticism was that the Bank had allowed the City to subscribe too heavily to German and Austrian loans, and was thus to a large extent responsible for the financial crisis of 1931. The governor was even accused of taking these risks because he was pro-German and anti-French! Finally, Norman was also attacked for his attempts between the wars to turn the Bank of International Settlements into a 'bankers' international', immune from interference by national governments, and with himself as its head. All these criticisms had some basis in reality. As a result Labour's proposal to nationalise the Bank was sure of wide public support. Even many Conservatives, Churchill himself among them, were by no means completely hostile. Consequently, the debate on the nationalisation Bill was notable for its courtesy and the absence of any bitter ideological clash. Dalton implies in his book that he expected a sharper fight, and attributes the moderation of the debate to his own parliamentary skill. But although this was doubtless a contributing factor, a far more important reason was surely the Conservatives' unwillingness to stand in the last ditch for a cause they knew to be doomed in advance not only in Parliament but with public opinion.[17] Moreover everything possible was done to make the change look as unrevolutionary as possible. The State simply bought up the Bank's entire share capital of £14,553,000, compensating the former shareholders particularly generously. In addition, the cabinet virtually committed itself to make no major changes in the board of directors which, at the chancellor's request, reappointed both the governor (Lord Catto) and deputy governor (Mr J. Cobbold). The Bank also retained formal responsibility for fixing bank rate (though in practice, under a well-established convention, the decision now lay with the government, as part of its overall financial strategy). The result was that nothing of consequence changed, and neither the City nor the Stock Exchange was unduly worried, for it was obvious that the financial community would continue to operate much as it had done in the past.

Indeed, the nationalisation of the Bank of England was to be the only such measure affecting financial institutions during the entire life of the Labour government. Its record was to seem remarkably timid in comparison with the way that, after Liberation in 1944, French provisional governments nationalised a substantial portion of the private sector, including the four largest joint-stock banks, and strengthened the existing public corporations in this sector. It is true, as will be seen, that the British government was to intervene to control investments, but here again it never went as far as France, which set up the Conseil National du Crédit which, as its first act, approved the financing of the Monnet Plan — an event of historic importance for the future of planning.[18]

In the field of borrowing for investment, then, the government was to arm itself with additional powers. The Investment (Control and Guarantees) Act of 1946 'gave the government two small but useful additions to their set of tools for economic planning'.[19] The first of these gave the Treasury standing authority to control new capital issues. According to Dalton the sole criterion in determining priorities was to be the national interest. The second was that the Treasury was authorised to underwrite loans of up to £50,000,000 in any year for rebuilding or modernising factories or other industrial establishments. For the most part the chancellor entrusted the implementation of these policies to existing institutions. The Act specifically confirmed the Capital Issues Committee, which had been established by the Conservatives in 1939. This was an advisory body of seven experts from industry, commerce and finance, which reported on all sizeable share issues or loans for periods exceeding six months (i.e., it was not concerned with short-term loans). Its rulings had to be within general guidelines laid down for it from time to time by the chancellor — who in turn was greatly influenced by the Committee's advice. The system had worked well during the war, and this was why Dalton continued to hold it in high regard even though it was now being asked to cope with a quite radically different set of problems. While in both cases 'the national interest' was the paramount criterion, a notion that had been relatively easy to interpret in wartime had become considerably more ambiguous once peace was restored. With the best will in the world there was ground for disagreement over priorities even once the government had indicated that the main aims were to modernise industry and stimulate exports.[20] The Act also confirmed the Public Works Loan Board, and the chancellor also decided to maintain two non-governmental financial agencies which had been set up under the Churchill government early in 1945 on the initiative of the then governor of the Bank of England, Lord Catto. The first, the Industrial and Commercial Finance Corporation (ICFC), was established in February 1945 by a group of bankers to help small companies that were unable to raise capital through traditional financial channels. The second, the Finance Corporation for Industry (FCI), was formed in May 1945 as a public company with the Bank of England as a minority shareholder. Its purpose was to help reconstruct or reorganise large and medium-sized firms. These two corporations met genuine, urgent needs, and it was not surprising that the Labour government decided to retain them. What was surprising was that it did nothing to bring them under its direct control. It merely set up the National Investment Council to co-ordinate existing bodies and lay down guidelines for investment and savings policy. According to Dalton, the Council would 'advise and assist the government in organising, and when necessary stimulating investment so as to promote full employment'.[21] The chancellor himself was its chairman, and the members included the governor of the Bank, the chairmen of the CIC, PWLB, ICFC and FCI and the chairman of the Stock Exchange, all *ex-officio*, and five or six others selected for their personal qualities and relevant experience. The Council was to meet monthly. It might well have developed as the main agency for drawing up the investment programme for projects of national importance.[22] Unfortunately, it was never very active, and even before Dalton left the Exchequer it had ceased to meet regularly. It is clear, then, that in this crucially important area Labour's policy was cautious, not to say timid. The desire to avoid further disturbing an economy that had already suffered so many shocks prevailed over hopes of change and, some would say, over the party's declared policy. One may well feel that a major asset in creating effective planning was virtually thrown away.

The Beginnings of the Labour Government

Dalton and Morrison were on the whole content to leave the machinery of government more or less as they found it. Both were basically pragmatists who preferred to stick to the methods that had proved themselves during the war rather than to innovate for innovation's sake. But in any case the pressure of events was such that they had little time for looking beyond the immediate crisis. This was to be a permanent problem in managing the British economy: the policy-makers were constantly caught between the insistent demands of the short term, over some of the external factors in which they had little control, and what they had hoped to achieve in the medium or long term. For example, even before coming to power the Labour leaders were well aware that one of their immediate problems would be overseas trade and the balance of payments, where the situation was little short of catastrophic.

Britain emerged from the war victorious but ruined. She had been forced to sell off overseas assets worth over £1,000 million; her reserves were around £500 million while her liabilities (including the sterling balances) were over £3,500 million. Britain had survived, financially speaking, only thanks to American lend-lease, 'the most unsordid act in the history of any nation' as Churchill called it. Such a situation could not be remedied overnight. According to a memorandum Keynes (who was at this time a highly influential adviser to the Treasury) submitted to the cabinet when it came to office, with external financial aid Britain could run a balance of payments deficit of £2,100 million. He estimated it would take four years to restore foreign trade to balance, providing imports were strictly controlled, exports greatly expanded and foreign spending cut back sharply. The overall deficit for the period would amount to some £1,700 million. One can readily imagine the alarm with which the new cabinet learned of the abrupt ending of lend-lease within a week of the Japanese surrender. This was something Britain had come to look on as her moral due, and she had been expecting it to continue for some considerable time after the war.

On 6 December 1945, after three months of humiliating negotiations, Keynes (the chief British negotiator) signed a new agreement with the Americans providing for a loan of £4,400 million (rather than the £6,000 million which Britain had hoped to receive), repayable over fifty years with interest at two per cent. In addition, Britain pledged herself to ratify the Bretton Woods agreement, although she was distinctly unhappy about a number of its provisions, and, more important, to restore the convertibility of sterling within fifteen months – a requirement that was to prove disastrous when implemented. The agreement was ratified by large majorities in the Commons on 13 December and the Lords four days later, but there was much criticism, often in very bitter terms. To rub salt in the wound, Congress took over six months to decide whether to grant the loan. At the end of the Commons debate Dalton noted in his diary that some day the Americans would have to agree to modifications in the agreement, possibly sooner than they expected. He could not know how truly he spoke.

One reason for the American attitude was a simple failure to grasp how much the war had cost Britain. It has also been suggested that they might have behaved differently had Churchill remained prime minister, and there could be some truth in this. The new rulers, who had been concerned mainly with internal questions during the war, were almost unknown in the United States; they were labelled as 'socialists', and, even more important, they were thought to be intent on spending large sums on social welfare. It was vital that the American taxpayer should not have the impression he was being asked to mop up another country's budget deficit, particularly if this arose from expenditure on social welfare. The support of Keynes, who was well-known and respected in the United States, was apparently insufficient to persuade the American leaders to abandon their 'realism'. But this attitude did not last long, and Britain later benefited from the Marshall Plan on an equal footing with other European countries.

Without being unduly perturbed by difficulties abroad and the threat of inflation at home, Labour was embarking on the implementation of its plans for social reform and reconstruction. In 1946 the pace of reform was particularly rapid. During the year most of the legislation that was to bring the welfare state into being was either enacted or in an advanced stage of preparation: the National Insurance Act, the National Insurance (Industrial Injuries) Act and the National Health Service Act. The first two, together with the Family Allowances Act adopted under the 1945 caretaker government and the National Assistance Act of 1948, organised or reorganised the entire range of social service provision: unemployment, pensions, sickness insurance, industrial injuries and family allowances. The Bank of England had already been brought into public ownership; nationalisation of the mines followed in July 1946, and other major nationalisation measures were well advanced. Work was also under way on the Town and Country Planning Bill, which was to be the major legislation in the field for many years. All this reforming activity took place in a heady atmosphere in which the government radiated optimism and confidence. Looking back in 1962, Hugh Dalton recalled this as a time of great enthusiasm among ministers and others involved in politics:

> It is difficult now, more than fifteen years later, to convey the intense sensation which many of us felt in those first days and held through the first years of that new chapter of British history: Labour in power. . . . That first sensation, tingling and triumphant, was of a new society to be built, and we had the power to build it. We felt exalted, dedicated, walking on air, walking with destiny . . .[23]

This atmosphere lasted until 1947, when it was brutally shattered by the fuel crisis.

It seems that no one, not even the minister of fuel and power, Emmanuel Shinwell, saw this coming. Coal was still by far the most important source of energy, and the combination of inadequate supplies and an unusually bitter winter led to a crisis that not only had the whole country shivering, but interrupted production in many factories at a time when any loss of production was little short of a disaster. Thanks to even more stringent rationing and improvements in organisation, the crisis was over in a few weeks. But the morale of both the government and the country had been deeply shaken. Where unemployment had previously been the main fear, now it was realised that there was actually a shortage of labour in such key sectors as mining and agriculture. Moreover, despite controls, there was a danger of inflation, for demand was outstripping supply for almost everything. Throughout 1946 this had been concealed from the consumer by price controls; retail food prices bore less and less relationship to true production costs, with the ever-widening gap being closed by ever-increasing subsidies.

On top of this, from March 1947 there was a deepening balance of payments crisis. Exports had been increasing rapidly in 1946, and imports had been kept in check. At the end of the year the situation seemed reasonably satisfactory, particularly in light of the fact that since July Britain had been able to draw on the American loan. Against this, though, was the decision to restore the convertibility of sterling at the beginning of 1947, despite the fact that the government had been unable to persuade holders of sterling balances to sign consolidating agreements. The consequences were soon felt. By March it was clear that the American loan would soon run out. On 20 August the government was obliged to suspend convertibility. The atmosphere was now very different. From the fuel crisis to the autumn budget nothing seemed to go right for Labour. In fact, at the beginning things had run so smoothly for the government that it had over-reached itself. The prime minister tacitly admitted this by claiming whenever he defended the government's record that its problems were caused by having tried to do too much too quickly.[24]

This was also the burden of the mounting wave of criticism of the government during 1947, much of it very sharply expressed. Professor Jewkes spoke of a 'new ordeal by planning', while Roy Harrod asked whether 'all these hardships' were really necessary.[25] Both criticised the government for setting export targets unrealistically high; for embarking on an over-ambitious investment programme and for holding the exchange rate too high;

Not surprisingly, the government felt there had to be a change of course. In November 1946 it promised a full-scale Commons debate on economic policy after the publication of the *Economic Survey for 1947*.[26] This appeared at the end of February 1947, and the Commons debated it a fortnight later. The survey did more than simply outline and defend the government's economic strategy; its opening section offered a lengthy exposition of the case for planning in a democratic society.[27] Doubtless the government was mainly concerned to emphasise that in a democracy it could not do everything, particularly in the area of manpower and distribution — for instance, the fuel crisis was due in large measure to a shortage of miners. Nevertheless, the *Survey* was a notable attempt to communicate and defend official policy.[28] In the words of its introduction, the aim of economic planning was to 'use the national resources in the best interests of the nation as a whole'.[29] This is obviously a very general way of looking at the matter. However, the *Survey* was more precise about the type of plan it was hoped to develop and the kind of balance that was intended. For its authors[30] the basic difference between totalitarian and democratic planning was **that the** former

... subordinates all individual desires and preferences to the demands of the State. For this purpose, it uses various methods of compulsion upon the individual which deprive him of the freedom of choice. Such methods may be necessary even in a democratic country during the extreme urgency of a great war. Thus the British people gave their wartime Government the power to direct labour. But in normal times, the people of a democratic country will not give up their freedom of choice to their Government. A democratic Government must therefore conduct its economic planning in a manner which preserves the maximum possible freedom of choice to the individual citizen.[31]

In the light of the limitations this implied, the *Survey* proposed a system of planning which was as supple as possible so as not to rob the economy of its flexibility. Its three salient elements were:

(i)   An organisation with enough knowledge and reliable information to assess our national resources and to formulate the national needs.
(ii) A set of economic 'budgets' which relate these needs to our resources, and which enable the Government to say what is the best use for the resources in the national interest.
(iii) A number of methods, the combined effect of which will enable the Government to influence the use of resources in the desired direction, without interfering with democratic freedoms.[32]

The *Survey* made it clear that the authorities intended to rely on 'much the same techniques as were used for allocating resources' during the war, adapting them to the new circumstances. It went on to explain why the government's commitment to planning had not led it to produce a plan rather sooner. During the period now drawing to a close, dominated by the problems of demobil-isation and putting the economy back on its feet, the emphasis had had to be on relatively short-term measures: 'It is too early yet to formulate the national needs over, say, a five-year period with enough precision to permit the announcement of a plan in sufficient detail to be a useful practical guide to industry and the public. There are still too many major uncertainties, especially in the international economic field.'[33]

The *Survey* moved from this apologia to an explanation of how planning would proceed. The main approach was to prepare 'economic budgets' setting out requirements and resources in terms of both manpower and national income and expenditure. These 'budgets' were prepared by a central staff working with representatives of the appropriate government departments in an official committee. The reason advanced for proceeding in this way was the gap between requirements and resources. While in the end a number of proposals would have to be sacrificed in order to close this gap, at least allocations would be based on full knowledge of the situation and would not be left to chance. 'The economic budgets must balance themselves ultimately, for it is impossible to consume more than is produced; the real question is how the balance is brought about.... [They] have a considerable bearing upon the Chancellor's Budget, but the two forms of national account are entirely different and should not be confused.'[34]

The central problem, then, was of how the balance was to be achieved. The White Paper recognised that the 'control apparatus' at the disposal of the government could not by itself bring about very rapid changes or make very fine adjustments. Success would therefore be dependent on a large measure of co-operation, particularly from employers and workers: 'Events can be directed in the way that is desired in the national interest only if the Government, both sides of industry and the people accept the objectives and then work together to achieve the end.'[35]

This was the first time the Labour government had laid such an emphasis on the need for co-operation with private industry, and this clearly owed much to Cripps, whose powerful personality was to dominate economic policy during the period ahead. It was Cripps, as president of the Board of Trade, who declared, in presenting the *Economic Survey* in the House, 'We shall work out our own method of planning in the empirical way that suits our temperament as a people. Hence the somewhat tentative nature of the machinery that we have so far set up . . . . It is of the essence of democratic planning that it is, to a very considerable extent, dependent for its implementation upon the willingness of employers and employees to join in working out the plan.'[36]

The Second Period (July 1947–October 1951)

When he presented the *Economic Survey* Cripps indicated he was considering a number of administrative changes to improve economic co-ordination, and the possible creation of a special office to prepare and implement the 'economic budgets'. In fact, 1947 proved to be a notable year for political and administrative innovation in these areas.

On 27 March the prime minister announced in the Commons the creation of a Central Economic Planning Staff (CEPS), headed by a chief planning officer (the first CPO being Sir Edwin Plowden), assisted by an industrial adviser, Sir Robert Sinclair. The CEPS only came into being effectively in May 1947. Initially it was an interdepartmental body whose 'primary task . . . under the supervision of the Chief Planning Officer will be to develop the long term plan for the use of the country's manpower and resources. They will also follow through the implications of the *Survey* set out by the White Paper, keeping in touch with all Departments so as to coordinate their action under the Plan'.[37] The chief planning officer's responsibilities were defined by the prime minister as follows: '[He] will work directly under the Lord President and will have access to all Ministers concerned with production matters.'[38] But he would not be able to act independently. Attlee left no doubt on that score: 'All decisions on planning policy will be made by the Cabinet, and not by the Chief Planning Officer.

Responsibility for these decisions must of course reside wholly with Ministers.'[39] Thus, although the cabinet wanted to show its desire to improve its working methods, the creation of the CEPS and the appointment of the chief planning officer involved no major changes. It should not be forgotten that the proposal had been rejected by Morrison only a little over a year earlier. Moreover, the creation of an economic planning staff was an old Liberal idea which had been advocated by both Keynes and Beveridge well before the war. At bottom CEPS was to be what in later years would have been called a 'think tank', suggesting an overall economic strategy to the government and indicating in terms of logistics and resources how it might be implemented. But it had no autonomous power. Consequently it was important only to the extent that it could influence ministers. In essence it was much more concerned with advising on general economic policy than with promoting any particular form of detailed planning — which in any case it lacked the resources to undertake. As Brady remarked at the time:

> It seems almost wholly accurate to say that operational planning is felt by the Economic Planning Staff either not to be necessary at all or at best something that will take care of itself more or less spontaneously once the proper analyses of needs have been made, the goals have been set, and the appropriate advisory, technical and (on occasion) monetary aids have been supplied by the government to the otherwise self-initiating entrepreneurial system.[40]

In his statement of 27 March the prime minister also announced his intention of establishing an Economic Planning Board, but the details of the actual membership and functions of the Board were not revealed until 7 July, when the Lord President made a further statement in the House. The chairman of the Board would be the chief planning officer (or, on occasion, the minister himself) and it would have 13 members: 3 from the FBI or British Employers' Confederation (BEC), 3 from the TUC, 3 civil servants from the ministries most directly concerned, and 4 members of the CEPS.[41] The Board accordingly was an attempt to involve both sides of industry in economic decision-making at the highest level, though of course only in an advisory role. As the Lord President put it, 'The principal task of this body will be to advise His Majesty's Government on the best use of our economic resources, both for the realisation of a long-term plan and for remedial measures against our immediate difficulties.'[42] Since the Board was to meet fortnightly it was well placed to play a role of some consequence, particularly since it was also linked with the regional organisation, which had survived the abolition of the Ministry of Production. Each regional industry council also had a tripartite composition and met monthly.

There remained one other central advisory body, which to some degree overlapped with the Economic Planning Board. This was the National Production Advisory Council, another survivor of the war. Its meetings were usually attended by representatives of the main departments concerned with production matters: the Board of Trade, the Ministries of Labour, Food, and Fuel and Power.[43] Its role was to brief ministers on the industrial situation, to give advice on a wide range of production problems and to relay any complaints from the regional councils. It was not concerned with relations between workers and employers which, on the national level, were the concern of the National Joint Advisory Council, which was also a survivor of the war but which was linked to the Ministry of Labour. These two bodies were the best possible link between government and industry. Unfortunately the government seems to have failed to make the most of the opportunities which they offered it, while the relationship between these two bodies and the Economic Planning Board was never clearly defined.

But the most marked changes were those in the machinery of government itself. While these were intentional, their actual introduction was facilitated by a number of accidental personal considerations. Early in 1947 Morrison had a heart attack and his place was temporarily taken by Cripps, who presented the *Economic Survey* in his stead. When Morrison resumed work his load had to be eased. A few months later came the dollar crisis and the suspension of convertibility. The prime minister announced that a new economic plan was in preparation, and that its aims would include a still further expansion of exports and bigger cuts in imports. In such a situation the government was naturally tempted to look for some sort of reassuring gesture. Among those dealing with economic affairs the man who was steadily coming to the fore at the time was Cripps. His air of austere integrity inspired confidence, while at the Board of Trade he had done much to increase exports and he had won the respect of industry. The time had therefore come to increase his responsibilities.

After some weeks of uncertainty and anxiety, on 29 September the prime minister announced Cripps' appointment as minister for economic affairs. He added that the new minister would have a small personal staff and the assistance of the CEPS, the Economic Information Unit and the Economic Section. He took over from the lord president responsibility for co-ordinating economic policy. The Lord President's Committee was disbanded and replaced by two new ones. The first was the Economic Policy Committee, which was chaired by the prime minister and also included the minister of economic affairs, the Lord President and the chancellor. This dealt with major issues of internal and external economic policy. The other was a ministerial Steering Committee, dealing with day-to-day co-ordination and forwarding of the government's economic programme. Cripps was chairman; it also included the president of the Board of Trade and the ministers of agriculture, fuel and power, transport and supply. There was also an interdepartmental committee of civil servants from the same ministries. This system required no alteration when the last stage in the reorganisation was reached with the appointment of Cripps as chancellor.

It is interesting to speculate how the relationship between Cripps and Dalton would have developed. In the event, however, Dalton was to resign only six weeks later, on 13 November, and Cripps was his natural successor at the

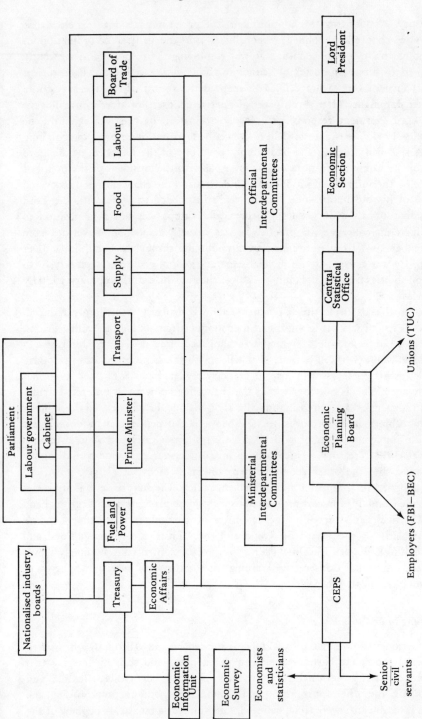

Figure 2.1. Organisation of government management of the economy in 1947.

Treasury. Announcing the appointment, the prime minister made it clear that the new chancellor retained responsibility for the general co-ordination of economic policy – which meant he was combining the responsibilities recently assigned to him as minister of economic affairs with the traditional powers of the chancellor (see figure 2.1). This marked the return of the Treasury to its former dominance after seven years of relative eclipse. For after Churchill gave the Lord President responsibility for co-ordination of the war economy in January 1941, the chancellor had no longer been *primus inter pares* in economic matters. During the war he had simply been one of the members of the Lord President's Committee, more or less on a par with the president of the Board of Trade or the minister of production. Under Dalton the chancellor had recovered some of his old importance, but he was still obliged to work with the Lord President on all major issues. Theoretically Cripps was not in a position to dominate his colleagues; in practice he was virtually an economic overlord from December 1947 to his retirement from public life through ill health in October 1950. He was assisted by a financial secretary and an economic secretary, with responsibilities including planning – a post that was held until February 1950 by Douglas Jay.

After the 1950 election, at which Labour's majority was sharply reduced, Hugh Gaitskell was made minister for economic affairs to help the ailing Cripps. The post of economic secretary was abolished, but it was re-established in October when Gaitskell became chancellor with the same powers and responsibilities as his predecessor. Thus the Treasury regained and confirmed its former ascendancy. This is not to say that the chancellor's power was unlimited. While he no longer had to share economic decision-making, he still needed the support of the cabinet on important issues, and he was still dependent on other ministers for the implementation of policy. Table 2.1 shows clearly the basic difference between the Treasury, which was primarily a source of ideas and policy initiative, and the other economic departments, which were larger, unwieldly and designed to administer and implement policy. The staff of several ministries expanded rapidly, for two main reasons: firstly the proliferation of regional and local offices, and secondly the retention of a number of wartime controls (particularly at the Board of Trade and the Ministries of Supply, Food and Agriculture), despite Harold Wilson's 'bonfire of controls'. Accordingly it was not surprising that Conservative warnings of the threat of bureaucracy began to fall on increasingly receptive ears.

Planning in Practice

The period was dominated by Cripps. Although he and Dalton always insisted there was complete harmony between them, one could scarcely imagine two more contrasting personalities; the one optimistic, expansive, flexible and pragmatic, the other apparently dogmatic, unbending and uncompromising, and even, if his enemies were to be believed, something of a fanatic. A nephew of the

Table 2.1.   Coverage of the main economic departments in 1951

Department	Concerned with	Numbers employed
Treasury	Central economic planning; taxation; budgetary and monetary policy; balance of payments; investment; control of expenditure and of the civil service	1,639
Admiralty	Navy shipbuilding and ship repairing	30,777
Agriculture	Agriculture and fisheries	15,276
Food	Food imports, food rationing, and food manufacture, animal feeding stuffs	25,761
Fuel and Power	Coal, electricity, gas and oil	4,023
Labour	Labour supply, industrial conciliation and labour relations generally, including general policy re wages and conditions; employment exchanges and appointments offices	27,731
Supply	Military supplies and government dealings with the aircraft, engineering, iron and steel, metal and radio industries; atomic energy	34,367
Trade	External trade relations; location of industry; retail price control; distribution of consumer goods; insurance; company law; supplies of certain raw materials; government dealings with the textile and certain other industries	9,973
Transport	Shipping, docks, inland transport, roads	6,240
Works	Building and civil engineering and most building materials	16,233

Source: D. N. Chester in Worswick and Ady, *The British War Economy.*

Webbs, part Christian socialist and part near-Marxist economist, Cripps derived from the one a puritanical leaning towards austerity and from the other a strong antipathy towards capitalism — though this did not prevent him establishing a highly successful practice as a business lawyer.

Yet he was not a man of fixed ideas. Expelled from the Labour Party before the war for advocating a popular front and opposing rearmament, like Laski he harboured strong doubts about the capacity of the British parliamentary system to carry socialism through without sweeping constitutional reforms. After the war he retained his ascetic fervour but had no hesitation in accepting Attlee's offer of a place in the government, and threw himself behind the most traditional ideas with all his customary energy. At the Board of Trade he initiated a policy of co-operation between the 'three partners' — government, unions and employers — in a vast area still remaining to private enterprise. Under Cripps the economy was to be guided and planned chiefly by verbal means — argument, persuasion and exhortation. Proclaiming that God was his copilot, he persuaded the unions to accept a virtual freeze on wages (the increase was held down to five per cent over two and a half years) and encouraged industry to sell an even higher proportion of its production abroad. (Exports rose twenty-five per cent between the end of 1947 and 1948.) After a little relaxation during the previous two years, under Cripps Britain experienced a period of renewed austerity. After 1948 the budget was balanced but tax rates remained extremely high and rationing was as strict as at the height of the war.

There was a return to the 'Dunkirk spirit' throughout the country. Cripps tirelessly preached harder work and higher productivity. Despite weariness from a prolonged war effort and understandable hopes for some relaxation, this strategy was successful for three years. When Cripps resigned in October 1950 he had had to concede a thirty per cent devaluation of the pound in September 1949, but industrial plant had been rebuilt and partially modernised, while industrial and agricultural production and exports had soared.

But the time had come for the nation's rulers to offer new policies with a greater appeal to the man in the street. Indeed, electorally speaking at least, it was already a trifle late. The Korean War, which led to rearmament and prevented the new chancellor, Gaitskell, from presenting a budget that would give greater freedom to the consumer, together with defeat in the election of October 1951, robbed Labour of the fruits of their efforts to rebuild the economy.

The New Institutions: Methods of Approach

Under Cripps the new institutions for planning and economic co-ordination continued to employ the 'budgeting' approach that had been outlined in the *Economic Survey for 1947*. They were also to attempt to develop a medium-term programme.

Short-Term Allocation of Resources

Under Dalton and Morrison the 'budgeting' approach had been employed very approximately, but the Economic Planning Board was to use it more rigorously. Basically it was an empirical approach, the aim of which was to secure the optimum allocation of scarce resources. Very roughly there were five stages in the allocation processes.

1. The first was to establish in as much detail as possible just what the current situation was. This required a major effort to collect and collate statistical data by both the departments and the Central Statistical Office.

2. The second stage was to use the information thus gathered as a basis for estimating what resources would be available for, say, the year ahead. This was done by the CEPS.

3. The third stage was to establish global requirements. One difficulty here was that this could only be done by those who would use the resources; thus responsibility for reporting the needs of the aircraft industry lay with the Production Directorate of the Ministry of Supply. But the sponsoring department (which ostensibly was responsible for particular industries but far too often became their advocate within the government) tended to act as a pressure

group on behalf of the industries for which it had responsibility, and consequently to inflate their requirements, particularly since it was well aware that owing to shortages they would obtain only a limited proportion of what they had requested. However, at least in the early part of this period disputes were more easily resolved because of the slack arising from the running down of arms production.

4. In the fourth stage the sponsoring department submitted and defended its estimates with the CEPS. Then the official list of each department's requirements was finally drawn up, generally incorporating a number of cuts, and sent with the CEPS's covering recommendations to the chairman of the interdepartmental committee on raw materials (who in Cripps's time was Douglas Jay).

5. The final stage therefore was the resolution of outstanding differences by the chairman — for, since the other members of the committee were civil servants, he alone had the power to take final decisions. He did so on the basis of three documents: an inventory of resources drawn up by the CEPS; the list of requirements submitted by departments after consultation with the CEPS, and a list of recommendations prepared by the CEPS. Thus, although the CEPS itself did not formally take any decisions, it was clearly in a position to exercise considerable influence over the final choice. If the economic secretary was unable to find a solution, then the final decision rested with the interdepartmental Economic Committee chaired by the chancellor. The more important of these were later announced in Parliament, and sometimes were the subject of a White Paper.

Manpower raised very special problems. As the *Economic Survey for 1947* emphasised repeatedly, it is impossible to allocate manpower in exactly the same way as raw materials, particularly in peacetime. At the end of the war there was a widespread demand that all controls over labour should be removed, despite the difficult problems of reconstruction that lay ahead, and this was conceded in 1945. But as men were demobilised they did not automatically assign themselves to jobs in accordance with the urgency of needs for labour; this was particularly true with mining and agriculture, as the 1947 fuel crisis was to show only too clearly. During the preparation of the *Economic Survey* four ministers argued for more stringent measures but they were outvoted in cabinet.[44] But this was only a temporary setback. After the dollar crisis the government had to resign itself to extending powers to allocate and direct labour in certain specified circumstances, through the Control of Engagements Order of 1947, which remained in force until March 1950. Men were allowed to move out of a number of 'essential' occupations only with the consent of the Ministry of Labour, which was also empowered to direct men to particular jobs in key sectors of the economy.

The main justification for these measures was obviously that a number of production targets would never be achieved without them. Nevertheless, this was an extremely serious decision to take in peacetime, and despite the various safeguards that hedged it about, it was bound to be seen as a breach of personal freedom. Opponents of the government, some of whom had been greatly influenced by Hayek's prophecies of doom, were quick to protest and to emphasise how well founded their fears had been. But it was soon clear that the government had no intention of making extensive use of its powers, but saw them more as a line of defence if the situation deteriorated. But the situation did not deteriorate – or rather it was tackled by other methods. The Control of Engagements Order had a mainly deterrent effect, preventing the situation in the key sectors of the economy becoming any worse; resort to outright direction of workers was rare. Employment exchange officials were able to persuade some hesitant workers to let themselves be steered towards essential industry. Doubtless their powers of persuasion would have been less effective had they not been able to employ compulsion as a last resort. Over almost three years (August 1947 to March 1950) only seven hundred 'directives' were issued. In most cases these required workers to stay in the two key industries of agriculture and mining. Only twenty-nine people were officially directed to new jobs.

There was another way of achieving the desired transfer of labour: devising a wages policy that would not simply hold wages down but would discriminate in favour of the undermanned industries. This was the approach advocated by Barbara Wootton. It had the advantage of entailing only an indirect limitation on the freedom of labour. But the TUC had gone on record against such a policy in 1943. Moreover, the government was so anxious not to lose the co-operation of the unions that, as the *Economic Survey for 1947* made clear, it very rapidly dismissed any idea of legislating along such lines. It preferred to negotiate, but could only obtain a mild degree of voluntary restraint on wage claims – and even this commitment could be secured only by substantial concessions.

In February 1948 the government published a White Paper setting out its policy on prices and incomes,[45] but there remained the problem of obtaining the support of employers and workers. The employers' organisations persuaded their members to agree to voluntary restraint on prices and dividends. In return for this, and for the government's promise to impose a special capital levy (estimated to yield £50 million for the budgetary year 1948–9) and to increase food subsidies, the unions agreed at a special conference of trade union executives to exercise wage restraint. Both sides kept these promises remarkably faithfully until the spring of 1950 when irresistible inflationary pressures arising from the devaluation of the autumn of 1949 brought this 'gentlemen's agreement' to an end.

In the end the unions preferred to accept government direction of labour or wage restraint rather than contemplate adjusting wage rates in accordance with the needs of the economy. One of the most perceptive observers of contemporary Britain, Samuel Beer, sees the unions' hostility as the main reason for the subsequent decline of planning. There were other reasons, yet there can be no doubt that failure to take energetic action over the 'manpower budgets' often resulted in their remaining mere pious aspirations, with a consequential failure to meet production targets.

In this way the unions took the risk of compromising the implementation of the plan, even though this was the method by which the Socialist Commonwealth, to which the TUC, like the Labour Party, officially subscribed, was eventually to be achieved. No doubt this was due to the persistence of attitudes that had originally been fostered by operating within a capitalist society, or it sprang from the feeling that as yet there had not been a significant enough advance towards socialism for the unions to accept any change in their social role. Whatever their reasons, the unions contributed to delaying that advance.

Attempts to Programme

When the CEPS was founded, in addition to drawing up the 'economic budgets', it was made jointly responsible with the Economic Section for preparing the annual *Economic Survey*, and it was thought that it might subsequently draw up a more ambitious medium-term plan. But at the end of the summer of 1947 there were two problems requiring immediate attention: short-term action was needed in the wake of the August monetary crisis (sterling convertibility had been suspended on 20 August), and preparations had to be made for receiving Marshall Aid. A start was made on the first problem in the autumn budget, which Dalton presented on 12 November, in which he bravely raised taxation by a further £250 million. The second problem was entrusted to the CEPS. In setting up OEEC and giving it responsibility for allocating Marshall Aid, the countries involved agreed to draw up long-term programmes showing how they proposed to use such aid as they received. It is striking to note that the country which at home was the most hostile to restraints on free enterprise actually encouraged the countries of Western Europe to prepare *programmes*, if not full-blooded *plans* — both terms being tarred with the same interventionist brush within the United States itself.

At the end of 1947 the CEPS embarked on the preparation of a 'long-term programme', which was eventually published in a White Paper in December 1948.[46] In the circumstances it was not easy to tell whether this was a genuine plan or merely a dutiful exercise to meet the requirements of OEEC. One way of deciding this is to see whether it met two minimum criteria: did it serve as the yardstick for short-term planning; to what extent was it actually implemented? On the first point, the programme itself had fairly modest ambitions. While it noted that government had a wide range of direct control over basic industry, which it could use to secure implementation of its policy, it was in fact purely indicative: 'Any programme of economic planning must be in the nature of a broad strategical plan . . . not intended as a detailed forecast of what will actually happen. The United Kingdom's national programme sets out to define the general objectives which the country will seek to follow.'[47] What happened in practice was that the programme was rapidly 'forgotten'. Politicians scarcely ever mentioned it in their speeches, nor was it referred to in any subsequent official publication, except the *Economic Survey for 1949* which appeared only a few months later and which repeated some of its analysis.[48] Overall, then, it cannot be said to have served as a continuing frame of reference to the authorities. Nevertheless, were its targets attained? We should note that those who drafted the programme took account of a number of existing plans for particular industries or sectors of the economy, to the extent that these were considered realistic. Consequently it is scarcely surprising that they were concordant at a number of points. The document in fact fell into three sections, corresponding closely to the concerns of the moment, covering the balance of payments, production and investment.

The first of these was interesting in the way it genuinely sought to correct 'natural' trends by stimulating exports and holding imports down to the absolute minimum. The outcome is shown in Table 2.2. There is a considerable measure of agreement between forecasts and results. While the figures appear much higher than had been anticipated, allowance must be made for the world inflation that developed after the outbreak of the Korean War. The actual increase in the *volume* of trade was much as predicted. How far the credit for this can be taken by the planners is another matter, for the thirty per cent devaluation of September 1949 must have made a considerable contribution to the steady improvement of exports. Indeed, there is every reason to consider it decisive. Moreover, this was the area in which, spurred on by Cripps, the government had made its greatest effort. A special interdepartmental committee had been set up in 1947 under Harold Wilson (then secretary for overseas trade) to co-ordinate and stimulate the export drive. In addition, the Treasury, through its general responsibility for economic matters, and most particularly the running of exchange controls, maintained a tight grip on import licences. In these ways the 'natural' operation of the economy was considerably modified.

There was a comparable harmony between the forecast and the out-turn in the area of domestic production, too. The programme forecast an increase of more than a third over prewar figures, and this level was reached during 1952–3.

Table 2.2. Outcome of the long-term programme

	1948 (Jan.–June) (Annual rate, revised)	Forecast (revised)	1952–3 Outcome Current prices	Corrected prices
	(£m.)	(£m.)	(£m.)	(£m.)
Imports	1,834	1,960	2,801	2,020
Exports	1,508	1,740	2,613	2,005
Trade balance	− 326	− 220	− 188	− 15
Invisibles	+ 130	+ 359	+ 265	+ 265
Balance of payments (Current account)	− 196	+ 139	+ 77	+ 250

Source: Joan Mitchell, *Groundwork to Economic Planning* (London, 1966), pp. 79 and 81.

However, within this general outcome there were some significant variations. While a number of expanding industries like cars, chemicals and petroleum comfortably exceeded the target, transport and coal lagged far behind.

The same held true of the investment programme. Here again the overall result was satisfactory. The programme had forecast investments totalling £1,480 million and the sum actually spent amounted to £1,600 million. But agriculture failed to reach the expected level, and while industry as a whole did so, this was no thanks to transport or the energy industries, which fell behind despite the fact they were supposed to have priority, but was due largely to engineering which had grown beyond all expectations. The building and construction industry also exceeded its target, but for reasons owing nothing to Labour planning. Immediately they returned to power in 1951 the Conservatives embarked on an ambitious housing programme with an annual target of 300,000 in place of 200,000, in keeping with their election pledges. The overall result therefore concealed the fact that the investment policy adopted in 1948 had been virtually abandoned.

But was the relative harmony between the programme and what had been achieved by 1952–3 a proof of success or a mere coincidence? According to Joan Mitchell there were:

> ... broadly three possibilities: (1) The programme might have been merely a forecast of what would happen in four years time, given actual data available in 1948 and really containing no element of purposeful direction on policy to achieve the result shown ... all that can be concluded is that the forecast was remarkably accurate. This is in itself of some interest .... (2) The whole thing may be a coincidence. The original plan did set out what it was intended to achieve using the best forecast that could be made as a basis .... That performance turned out close to the programme has no significance at all .... (3) The plan may have 'worked'. The policies adopted may have succeeded in directing the economy enough to achieve the stated purpose.[49]

For this last hypothesis to be confirmed one would have to show that the supporting measures set out in the programme, such as co-operation with the unions and industry, taxation policy, voluntary restraint on wages and other incomes, redistribution of labour, productivity incentives, restraints on consumer spending and controls on external trade, would not have been introduced had there been no programme. But measures of this kind were envisaged long before the programme itself. Some went back to the war, while the others were conceived in the latter half of 1947 by Cripps, as minister for economic affairs or chancellor, and by the young economist–politicians assisting him such as Harold Wilson, Hugh Gaitskell and Douglas Jay. We may reasonably conclude therefore that, had there been no long-term programme, economic policy would not have been very different overall — and consequently that the outcome would also have been very much along the lines of what actually occurred.

While the 'long-term programme' covered the whole period, the government also continued to publish the annual *Economic Surveys*, which were intended partly as reports on the year which had just ended, and partly to set out the main targets for the year ahead.[50] The *Economic Surveys* were akin to small-scale, short-term plans; this at least was one of the original intentions as set out in the introduction to the 1947 *Survey*. Despite its cautious wording and its repeated reminders of the limitations on planning in a democracy, the first *Survey* exuded the confident enthusiasm of men who were aware they were making history. The *Economic Survey for 1948* dealt at length with targets for the current year.[51] Like its predecessor it included a detailed estimate of the distribution of labour in the form of a 'tentative budget' for 1948. There was still talk of 'targets' and 'voluntary co-operation' by the public with the plan proposed by the government, and of the need to inform the public. The 1949 *Survey* repeated some of the analytical material from the long-term programme and its authors also emphasised the need for higher productivity, while emphasising that 'what government can do is mostly indirect. The problem is primarily one for industry . . . . Our recovery will never be complete unless we can develop a keen and adventurous spirit in management and a readiness to welcome new and improved methods by labour.'[52] The *Economic Survey for 1950* also offered a number of short-term projections, notably a table of 'changes in the distribution of the working population'.[53] But it now spoke of 'forecasts' rather than of 'targets'. The next year's *Survey* entirely omitted projections of manpower distribution; indeed it said very little at all about the future, preferring to hold forth at length on the current situation.[54]

Thus, between 1948 and 1951 the *Surveys* underwent a marked change. Less and less was heard of planning for the future. The first two *Surveys*, while not in the strict sense plans, were cautiously yet unmistakeably documents about planning. The same could not be said of the last two. As *The Economist* commented on the 1950 *Survey*, this was 'a humble document, meek almost to the point of being meaningless . . . . There is nothing here of the notions of "democratic economic planning" as proclaimed in earlier *Surveys* . . . . Indeed, the perplexing thing about the *Survey* for 1950 is its lack of plan.'[55] On the one hand, then, more and more space was given to discussing the year that had just elapsed, while on the other, although forecasts were still made, they were increasingly estimates of what could reasonably be expected to arise from the normal development of the economy, rather than targets to be achieved by manipulating the market mechanism. As Chester rightly notes, 'It would therefore be wrong to say that Britain had an economic plan during the period, if by economic plan is meant a set of economic objectives, integrated and consistent in their assumptions, which the government had decided to carry out.'[56]

How do we explain this retreat from planning? Firstly there was a greatly increased scepticism about its value. Neither the 1947 fuel crisis, nor the dollar crisis, nor the devaluation of the pound in 1949 was foreseen by the planners. Many people were aware of the technical and political problems the planners were experiencing, and confidence in their ability to overcome these had declined. People were also increasingly unwilling to envisage a continuation of austerity into the fifties. Indeed, a second fact in the explanation of the decline in planning was that, at least in the form engaged in by the Labour government, it was meeting growing resistance. 'Controls' were readily accepted during the war, and during the early years of peace they continued to be tolerated because the public were well aware they were still necessary because so many items were still in short supply. But as time went on consumers began to feel that controls were no longer being used to cope with problems of scarcity — which were now becoming less acute — but rather to channel production into exports and excess purchasing power into investment. There was also growing opposition from private industry. The case against retention of controls was put most effectively by Lewis and Meade who, though personally well disposed toward Labour, nevertheless argued in favour of returning to the normal working of the market for most products, and for acceptance of a mixed economy with no further changes in the ownership of industry.

Responding to these criticisms, Labour announced what Harold Wilson termed a 'bonfire of controls'. This in fact fell far short of complete abolition of government controls on the economy (even the Conservatives considered that some controls were still needed and retained them when they returned to power). Nevertheless, there was a clear trend towards a return to a market economy. Cripps was temperamentally much more disposed to try to govern by consent rather than resort to compulsion; this led him to a policy of co-operating with private industry, and he attached great importance to winning over public opinion. However, by relinquishing controls little by little the authorities were also abandoning the possibility of steering the economy by means of selective measures, leaving themselves only the more indiscriminate techniques such as budgetary policy, exchange controls, anti-monopoly legislation and so on. Labour ministers, with the possible exception of Bevan, were slow to grasp the implications of this, largely because of their rejection of any form of dogmatic ideology. By the time it was fully realised what was happening, the tide could no longer be stemmed. Planning had been virtually abandoned by Labour even before the Conservatives officially rejected it. But this did not necessarily mean that there was a resulting reduction in either the authority or the effectiveness of the State, since the administration of controls had, directly and indirectly, been largely in the hands of industrialists. Thus, paradoxically, the decline of controls was also accompanied by a decline of these corporative influences.

Relations Between Government and Industry

The Labour programme gave no clear indication of the fate the party intended for private enterprise under socialism. The party theorists had devoted much more attention to how to organise the nationalised industries than to relations between central government and the section of industry remaining in private hands. Probably it was assumed tacitly that in time the private sector would wither away, to be replaced by either public corporations in manufacturing industry or co-operatives in distribution. But in 1945 it was clear that the public was not ready for such drastic changes. Consequently, the first nationalisation programme left something over eighty per cent of industry in private hands.[57] As a result, the Attlee government was obliged to work out its industrial policy as it went along — a situation that men who prided themselves on their pragmatism may not have found wholly displeasing. It was not really possible for ministers to do nothing, for this would have run counter to the party's belief in intervention, as well as being incomprehensible in view of the urgency of problems like demobilisation, reconstruction and modernisation. In the event Labour retained the structure of controls that had been established during the war, and engaged in extensive consultation with the aim of working out in conjunction with industry new patterns of co-operation capable of carrying through the renovation of industry.

The machinery that had been established under the Ministry of Production and subsequently transferred without substantial modification to the Board of Trade was characterised by a blend of governmental and corporative elements. Nationally the machinery was almost wholly conventionally governmental; regionally it was half-governmental, half-corporative, and locally it was almost entirely corporative. It is easy to understand why Labour decided to retain machinery that was already working reasonably well, particularly as the party had no clearly worked out proposals for reform in this area. More surprisingly, though, the government was prepared to leave operation of the controls in the hands of the same men. For 'participation' and 'co-operation' were ideas that covered a wide range of circumstances. Where purely advisory bodies were concerned, it was obviously appropriate for both sides of industry to be represented in addition to the government. This was the case with the Economic Planning Board, the National Production Advisory Council, the National Joint Advisory Council and the regional production councils. But this was not the only form of co-operation with industry. Industry also supplied the State with administrators who were involved in decision-making at every level. Whether they were paid or were volunteers, the result was a close involvement of private industry in decision-making by the State itself. This was particularly dangerous because the need to meet the requirements of the State had led to a considerable strengthening of trade associations during the war. By 1945 corporatism had become a greater danger than bureaucracy. Some people in the Labour Party were very much aware of this. Even before the war the party had been highly critical of the growing involvement of business in the decisions of Conservative governments. Labour ministers in the wartime coalition seem to have expressed some concern at the trend towards corporatism but had not been able to control it directly. One might accordingly have expected that in 1945, even if they were not going to change the actual machinery, they would at least have shown more concern for safeguarding the rights of the State. Paradoxically, not only did nothing of the kind happen, but if anything the involvement of business intensified. Before attempting to explain this it may be useful to consider in more detail some of the forms this involvement took.

The usual way by which an industry tries to influence government is through the appropriate 'sponsoring department'. At this time the main departments concerned were the Board of Trade (which was responsible for textiles, the chemical industry, rubber and paper); the Ministry of Supply (which controlled iron and steel and other metals, engineering including vehicle building, and explosives); the Ministry of Food (food manufacturing); Fuel and Power (coal, gas, electricity and petroleum); Public Works (building and contracting); the Admiralty (shipbuilding and repair) and Transport.

By and large these sponsoring departments had two main responsibilities: to convey the government's instructions to the industries concerned, and to make sure they understood the implications of the government's economic policy for them. They also spoke for these industries in the appropriate economic committees and were the government's main source of information on them. Generally the former role is the more important in a centrally run economy, but in Britain during and after the war the two functions were of roughly equal importance. It could even be said that ministers were sometimes unduly concerned with their protective role and actively campaigned on behalf of industries they were supposed to control. This was largely due to the long-standing co-operation that had grown up between the two sides, but it also owed much to the fact that within the civil service itself there were many men drawn from the industries affected, to a degree where *The Economist* warned in 1944: 'The great defect of collectivism . . . is not that the bureaucrats will control industry; it is that they will *not* control it but cede their duty to the private monopolists.'[58] A number of examples from the Labour period illustrate this. Sir Edwin Plowden was doubtless chosen as chief planning officer both for his considerable personal qualities and because he was a personal friend of Cripps. But he was also a director of British Aluminium and two other companies. Sir Edwin's loyalty and integrity are not at issue, yet it seems hardly likely that on taking up this new post he was able to shed completely the attitudes he had acquired as a manager in private industry. As a result he may not have been the best man to put in charge of democratic socialist planning. Again, the Capital Issues Committee, which had a key role in the control of investment, was made up entirely of businessmen (bankers, brokers and industrialists) with the solitary exception of a Treasury official who served as its secretary. In general, the 'controllers' in the sponsoring departments (whether of raw material allocations or prices) were people who had worked in the industries they were now controlling. Unilever alone had ninety men in the Ministry of Food, twelve of them in senior grades. Through almost the entire period of Labour rule the chief industrial adviser to the president of the Board of Trade was the president of the British Rayon Federation. Moreover, the government encouraged the formation of trade associations and tended to make either these associations or one of the leading firms in an industry responsible for administering controls. For instance, the committee for newsprint supply, which was drawn entirely from the industry itself, was given sole responsibility for allocating newsprint. Again, the government delegated responsibility to the Mond Nickel Company for importing and allocating nickel.

Rogow and Shore quote many such examples. It is surprising that the government failed to realise that, without being in any way dishonest, businessmen were only too likely to be concerned more with the interests of their companies than with the national interest as seen by the government, particularly since — as Cripps put it — they were allowed to remain 'in general contact'[59] with their companies, from which in most cases they were merely on temporary secondment. In addition, at least at the higher levels of the civil service, men with Conservative or Liberal sympathies who favoured the existing economic system were perhaps not ideal people to administer controls that, on principle, they wished to see swept away. While outright sabotage was rare, involuntary sabotage was probably rather less uncommon. The deficiencies of this system were perhaps most obvious in the field of price controls. Here the Central Price Regulation Committee played a key role; it was a quasi-governmental body, most of whose members came from business. Consequently, negotiations on prices took place mainly among people drawn from industry, with only a handful of neutral voices. It is scarcely surprising that prices were often set at the levels requested by the trade associations, and based on figures of costs, turnover and profits that they themselves had prepared. In the view of Rogow and Shore, the inevitable outcome was that 'the resulting high prices were reflected in profits which were for most of the period the highest in the history of British industry'.[60]

Moreover, even where they had no links, past or present, with industry, it was difficult for ordinary civil servants to resist pressure from firms. A relatively junior civil servant might be required to decide matters of great importance to an industry, and this might lead to attempts at pressure or even actual corruption. The problem was discussed by the Committee on Intermediaries in these terms:

> Junior officials (often on low salary scales) habitually deal with, and in many cases decide, matters of great importance to the personal fortunes or amenities of applicants, and even when the decision is not in their hands their reports and recommendations have a considerable effect upon the fate of the application. There is an obvious risk (the extent of which we feel may not always be realised in the Departments themselves) that applicants may be tempted to try to influence the action of officials by improper means, and that officials may be tempted to succumb to or even to initiate such proceedings . . . .[61]

Such information as is available indicates that abuses were very rare, but as has been suggested, the danger lay in a subtle indirect influence rather than in outright corruption.

In considering why the Labour leaders acted as they did, the first thing that comes to mind is two apparently technical factors which had considerable political implications. The first was the fear of an inflated bureaucracy; the second was that there were very few people with the appropriate skills apart from those who came from private industry. Labour's fear of accusations of bureaucratism was by no means an idle one, for it was levelled from a number of different quarters at an early stage. Table 2.1 shows the strength of a number of the main departments, swollen by the need to operate a system of controls at national, regional and local levels. But this was not the only consequence of a managed economy. In the face of the torrent of forms, questionnaires and statistical returns companies had to recruit additional office staff. Small firms turned to their trade associations for help, and in consequence they too had to take on more staff. The Census of Employment showed that the ratio of clerical staff to production workers, which had been 13 per cent in 1935, had risen to 17 per cent in 1948. Many firms complained bitterly of the administrative complications and higher overheads that resulted. This is almost certainly one reason why Labour was reluctant to introduce major changes that would have swelled the bureaucracy still further and made administration even more cumbersome. The second 'technical' explanation is that in 1945 the business world was really the only source of people with the appropriate knowledge and skills. For the most part senior civil servants were men with an arts background and with neither the talent nor the desire to control the economy. Even if they had it would have made little difference because they and the men running industry came from very similar backgrounds; they had been to the same schools and the same universities. They shared this sort of background with a majority of the Labour ministers who, despite their differing political views, were members of that same political, economic, financial and cultural élite that became known as the Establishment. It is really not surprising, therefore, that everyone concerned was content to leave things as they were.

On the other hand, it is more surprising that there was no attempt to alter this situation and train young civil servants, and even more young trade unionists, to take up key positions. And yet in 1946 the government had established the Administrative Staff College 'for young executives in private enterprise and officials of the public services and trade unions'.[62] Again, the British Institute of Management was established with government backing in 1947. No trade unionist followed up these opportunities. It was a pity that these two bodies failed to produce sufficient young managers to meet the needs of the civil service and other public services, and it was even more regrettable that the government took no steps to provide new management for the nationalised industries.

Hugh Dalton, for instance, lost no time in maintaining almost the entire top management of the Bank of England in their posts. Taking the nationalised boards, we find that, in 1951, 9 of the 47 full-time members and 7 of the 48 part-time members were trade unionists sitting in a personal capacity rather than as representatives of their unions; most of the others were prominent businessmen. Apart from Lord Citrine, the former general secretary of the TUC, at the Central Electricity Authority all the chairmen came from industry or private banking. Lord Hyndley, the first chairman of the National Coal Board, had been a leading figure in the coal industry before nationalisation. Once again, there was no real transfer of power.[63]

A third and more ideological element in the explanation was the attitude of the unions. During the twenties the guild socialism of Cole[64] and Tawney had exercised a considerable influence over the trade union movement. They believed that factories should be owned by the producers rather than by the State; basically they wanted power in industry to be decentralised to autonomous workshops run by the workers themselves. This idea, which had much in common with more recent demands for 'self-management' and 'workers' control', was rejected by supporters of state socialism like the Webbs who, while favouring substantial decentralisation in political matters, none-theless favoured centralism in economic matters, though with a number of democratic safeguards such as a Social—Economic Parliament. They were highly suspicious of 'producer socialism'. The eclipse of the soviets in the USSR lent weight to their views, and after about 1930 guild socialism ceased to be a significant force at either TUC congresses or Labour Party conferences; though the faithful still sent in their resolutions, this was more an act of piety than because they had any real hope of being adopted. At the 1933 Congress, by approving a Memorandum negotiated with the 'political wing', the unions not only rejected workers' control but even defeated the less radical policy of workers' participation.[65] Morrison — who incidentally had never been a union leader — strongly approved of this 'non-participationist' mood because it was in keeping with his preference for autonomous public corporations run by non-political specialists — a first, sombre step towards technocracy. In fact, during the 1929—31 Labour government Morrison and Bevin had clashed on trade union representation when nationalisation of London Transport was under discussion. But by 1933 Bevin's position had to some extent changed (probably as a result of grass-roots reticence) and he eventually approved the Memorandum because, in so doing, the unions retained complete freedom over the timing and substance of their demands. The 1944 and 1945 congresses showed no change in the unions' views on the matter, and at the 1948 Labour Party conference a resolution calling for union participation in the management of the nationalised industries was withdrawn in the face of opposition from most of the union leaders, notably the president of the National Union of Mineworkers, Will Lawther, who declared, 'We . . . do not want to have people in the ridiculous position that we see on the continent, where the president or secretary of a miners' organisation is also on the Coal Board running the industry, so that he has on occasion to pass a resolution to ask himself to give himself something.'[66] Obviously this was a gross oversimplification — but Labour leaders were nevertheless forced to take this attitude into account. It partly explains — with Morrison's personal hostility — why so few trade unionists were appointed to posts in the public sector, and why those who were had either retired or had to resign their union posts.

The Search for a New Industrial Strategy

A final explanation of the government's policy was its desire to find ways in which, once the shortages of the moment were things of the past, the State and the two sides of industry could work together to expand production and make preparations for the future.

From the moment he arrived at the Board of Trade in September 1945, Cripps was considering ways of reorganising industry, but at the same time he was determined to do nothing that would prejudge the final decision. This led him to set up a number of working parties. There were seventeen of these in all, covering a wide range of industries,[67] but most of them producing consumer goods, especially textiles. Most of the industries involved had a large number of small firms, many of which were rather backward technically. While the government never officially gave reasons for its choice, there are reasons to think that it deliberately chose industries that it had no intention of nationalising in the foreseeable future, and that the industries selected were among those where extensive rationalisation and concentration were possible without undermining competition, for innovation depended less on financial and technical resources than on ideas. Each working party included representatives of employers and the unions and a number of independent experts. A typical group had twelve members, four from each of the categories mentioned, with an independent member serving as chairman. Each was instructed to 'examine and enquire into the various schemes put forward for improvements in organisation, production and distribution methods and processes, and to report as to the steps which should be taken in the national interest to strengthen the industry and render it more capable of meeting competition in both the home and foreign markets'.[68] A succession of reports of varying length and calibre appeared up to 1948. Those on cotton and wool textiles, the most important industries considered in this way, were substantial and authoritative documents, but this was not true in all cases. Some were damning, reporting great variations in productivity not just in comparison with foreign companies (of the order of 50—100 per cent in relation to American levels), but between firms in Britain of comparable size, turnover and location. They all revealed how much scope there was for improving productivity, quality, the share of production going for export and so on. The government did not wait for all the reports to come in to introduce the necessary legislation; the Industrial Organisation and Development Act was carried in July 1947.

The aim of the Act was best described by Cripps, its initiator. During the second reading debate he indicated that the Bill was 'designed to provide methods for enabling private enterprise industries to make themselves as highly efficient in the production and distribution of their products as possible'.[69] Essentially the Act empowered the government to establish development councils in any industry or group of industries. As with the working parties, the development councils were to include employers, workers and independent experts, and would be appointed by the minister. The Act provided that before creating a council the minister should satisfy himself that it was 'desired by a substantial number of the persons engaged in the industry'. The range of powers and activities assigned to the councils included scientific and technical research, recruitment and training of personnel, improvement of working conditions, the collection of statistics, improvement of accounting methods and advice to ministers.

As this list shows, there was no question of giving the councils power to make any fundamental alteration in the structure of the industry concerned; they were really confined to increasing the efficiency of individual firms through the provision of ancillary services — much as any trade association might have done. Consequently, there seemed no need for Cripps's assurance:

> There may still be some people who fear that this Bill is in some occult way an introduction of nationalisation of industry. It is, of course, nothing of the sort. If and when we believe it to be in the national interest to bring other industries under national control or ownership, we shall act directly and not by some ingenious subterfuge.[70]

The reason he emphasised this was that the Conservatives were by no means convinced of the need for the Bill to leave so much to the discretion of the minister; in their view each industry should receive individual treatment according to the needs of the situation. Cripps argued in reply that any action he took required the agreement of the industries concerned: 'to do things by compulsion is far less effective than to do them by agreement'. Cripps himself, therefore, restricted the potential scope of the Act; there was to be no question of the councils acting as Trojan horses for nationalisation, and the government had no intention of imposing its will on industry. State intervention was accordingly reduced to a minimum.

More striking than the apprehensions of Conservatives was the total absence of criticism from the Labour back benches, considering that the Act was giving full legal status to the corporatist practices that had grown up during the war. This silence was particularly remarkable because, when the FBI had advocated similar measures at the end of 1946 after the publication of the first of the working party reports, it had immediately been accused of encouraging a further development of corporatism, not just by Labour people but by much of the press, including the *Financial Times*. There was widespread concern over the under-representation of consumers on these bodies in which employers and workers would be likely to join forces in ways which might well be prejudicial to the wider public interest.

Yet, even though the government proceeded with such caution, the policy was a failure. Only three development councils ever saw the light of day (four if one counts the old Cotton Board, which was converted into a development council in 1948). These were in furniture, jewellery and silverware and clothing; and it was by no means easy to get even these set up. The reason was that between the publication of the first working party reports in 1946 and the implementation of the Act (between 1948 and 1951) the political climate had changed. In 1945—6 it had seemed that Labour might be in power for many years, and many private employers felt it would be prudent to try and find some acceptable *modus vivendi* with the government. But by 1948 the economic setbacks outlined earlier had turned the tide of opinion against Labour. While it regained some of the lost ground in 1948 and 1949, the party never recovered its 1945 strength; by-elections and local elections confirmed its political vulnerability. The resulting prospect of a change in the parliamentary majority encouraged industry to drag its feet or even resort to open defiance. Moreover, most of the original reports had recommended the setting up of a non-governmental national organisation in which only the independent members would have been official appointees. The Act itself was rather more 'governmental'. The third reason for the employers' *volte face* was economic. In 1945—6 there was still a widespread fear of a recurrence of the old prewar economic difficulties. Many employers felt that, by agreeing to a reorganisation of their industries under state auspices, if there was subsequently a problem of overproduction, then the existence of this link with the State would increase the likelihood of the State coming to their aid. In any case a central organisation would be better placed to arrange restrictions on output than would individual firms which were in competition with one another. But by 1948—9 the problems were completely different — principally how to expand output as rapidly as possible.

For all these reasons the Act was almost ineffective and the councils had only a minor influence. Labour's policy must be considered a failure, particularly since, despite the moderation of the government's policies, by the time it left office in 1951 its relationship with industry had seriously deteriorated. Yet Labour had worked hard to conciliate the private sector. The operation of controls was very largely in the hands of men brought in from industry; the bodies established to modernise industry very largely reflected the wishes of industrialists themselves and certainly did not attempt to attack them in any way, while the new Monopolies Commission was no great threat.[71] It is hard to account for the deterioration of relationships in anything other than strictly political terms — the prospect that the Conservatives would return to power sooner than anyone had expected in 1945. It may also be that, as many on the Left argued at the time, the Labour leaders were rather naive in their assessment of the extent to which employers had been 'converted' to their views. While intelligent employers were attracted by the Labour government's moderation in 1946, the idea — so dear to Cripps and his followers — that the interests of employers and workers could be reconciled at no cost to either and still also be in 'the public interest' made very little progress. Equally, the idea of transforming the relationship between producers through co-partnership raised little enthusiasm from either side of industry.

One major factor in increasing industry's suspicion of the government's intentions was the continuing fear of nationalisation – though this had very little real foundation. The Labour leaders had always made it clear that once the 1945 programme of nationalisation had been carried through they would consider what should follow, but that those affected by any further nationalisation proposals would receive adequate public notice of their intentions. Yet although Labour kept its word, this did not prevent many industrialists harbouring the deepest suspicions. The main cause of this was the long struggle over iron and steel nationalisation, which was finally approved in November 1949.

The reason there was such a battle over iron and steel, unlike the other industries Labour had taken over, was that this measure introduced a radical change in the nature of nationalisation. Earlier measures had been restricted to industries like fuel and power and transport where the need for reorganisation was beyond question and, since they were losing money, this could only be undertaken by the State. Iron and steel was completely different. The industry had a respectable record both before and since the war. Although it featured in Labour's first nationalisation programme, in 1946 the government had confined itself to setting up the Iron and Steel Board (comprising two representatives of the employers, two trade unionists, one representative of the consumers, a civil servant from the Treasury and an independent chairman) with general powers to control the industry and co-ordinate its investment plans. This arrangement had worked well and the industry made a major contribution to the economic recovery of 1948–9. Consequently, when the Attlee government decided to press on with nationalisation, it seemed to opponents to be motivated purely by doctrinaire socialism. From the beginning Conservatives and Liberals pledged themselves to denationalise the industry at the first opportunity. Moreover, Labour ministers were unwilling to impose a thoroughgoing solution: after nationalisation the various parts of the industry were neither merged nor regrouped – which made it much easier to restore them to the former owners. The powerful Steel Federation was also allowed to survive. Thanks to these two concessions the leaders of the industry never despaired and fought nationalisation from both within and without.

Finally, in January 1950 a list of proposals for further nationalisation was published. It was a modest one, including non-ferrous metals, sugar, cement, water, wholesale meat trading and life insurance, totalling about three per cent of trade and industry. Nevertheless, there was an outburst of rage from the industries concerned, which immediately launched a campaign against both nationalisation and the Labour Party. While mostly fought by the industries which felt directly threatened, with the blessing of the courts[72] the campaign became something of a crusade by private industry against a socialist state, particularly after Labour's near-defeat in the 1950 election when it looked as if the Attlee government would be unable to last a full five years because of the smallness of its majority and the growing rifts within its own ranks. The 'collusion' between industry and the Conservative Party has never been more obvious. One could almost say that private industry fought the Conservatives' campaign for them, instead of confining itself to its customary role of providing financial support. In the face of this alliance the Attlee government seemed indecisive. By 1949, despite a considerable measure of economic success, the impetus of 1945 had been lost. The prime minister was a good co-ordinator but no leader; he was incapable of revitalising the party in the way that was needed. Morrison, Bevin and Cripps were ailing, and the last two were to die shortly afterwards. There was a feeling that Labour had done what it had set out to do, and that it should either find a new programme or give way. As Paul Foot aptly puts it:

> The Labour Party had reached the crossroads. The nationalisation of basic industries and much of the promised welfare measures ... had been accomplished .... They [the leaders] chose, in the event, to *announce* that they were proceeding with a radical programme, to abandon many of their controls and to rely on what they had already done .... [The] effect of the announcement was to unleash a stream of propaganda in favour of private enterprise and against the government.... The Tories leapt on the bandwagon and harried the government relentlessly.[73]

Thus the tacit consensus of 1945 on which the Labour leaders had based their policy had broken down:

> As far as the FBI was concerned, the Labour government had reached the point of maximum reform. Further taxation, further nationalisation, further welfare measures might ... upset the delicate balance of class power .... A consensus, they argued, though useful in periods of crisis like 1931 and 1945, can never be permanent between those who possess power and wealth and their dispossessors.[74]

While perhaps not everyone would agree with the way Paul Foot formulates the problem, he catches the reaction of private industry accurately enough. But the impact was so great only because the Labour government seemed incapable of rallying the public behind it. Yet it should have been encouraged by the success of the popular version of the *Economic Surveys for 1947* and *1948*. While there is no proof these popular accounts were fully understood, their success might well have been followed up. However, just as the role of government was steadily increasing, the official information services were being run down. Maybe the Attlee government thought there was no need for it to defend its social welfare achievements because the record spoke for itself. But this was not the case with nationalisation. Most of the nationalised industries were declining, and they raised a wide range of intractable problems; consequently there could be no rapid or striking benefits. This made the task of their opponents considerably easier.

The failure of Labour's industrial policy and the abandoning of controls naturally had repercussions on every aspect of economic policy and planning. The latter, as conceived by Cripps, rested on co-operation between the State and producers – for the most part in private industry. The refusal of private industry to co-operate therefore spelled the failure of Labour planning.

The Labour Record

Before and during the war there were endless arguments among socialist theorists and politicians such as the Webbs, Shaw,[75] Laski and Cripps over whether it was possible to achieve a socialist society without sweeping reforms in traditional democratic institutions. Anti-socialists had argued in return that, whatever the original intentions, socialist planning would lead ineluctably to authoritarianism. Looking back over Labour's years in office it can at least be said that there was no infringement of traditional civil liberties or interference with the normal working of Parliament – where, admittedly, the Attlee government had the loyal support of some four hundred MPs. There are two possible explanations of this record of respect for democratic procedures. One may agree with most observers that this 'silent revolution' demonstrated unambiguously that socialist planning was possible in a constitutionalist–pluralist political system. And yet, looking back on the period, it could reasonably be argued that the fact that Labour ministers stuck to democratic procedures forced them to observe the limits set by a consensus outside Parliament – limits that were in considerable measure set by what private interests considered tolerable.

Naturally enough Labour leaders prefer the former view. Attlee's account of his premiership reaches a modestly optimistic verdict. He had no doubt this was a period of genuine advance towards socialism rather than mere social reformism:

> Our policy was not a reformed capitalism but progress towards a democratic socialism . . . . The legislative programme on which the 1945 Labour government embarked was much more extensive than that launched by any peacetime government, and it undoubtedly made a heavy demand on the House of Commons. . . . [The] verdict of the electors had, however, been sufficiently decisive to prevent the opposition from indulging in obstruction . . . . There was also not much real opposition to our nationalisation policy . . . . Only iron and steel roused much feeling, perhaps because hopes of profit were greater here than elsewhere. In fact, during these years a peaceful revolution has taken place. Broadly speaking there has been a great levelling up of conditions. The great mass of abject poverty has disappeared.[76]

Not everyone would accept Attlee's optimistic conclusion. Some of those who have written about the period, particularly Americans, have seen it as simply a British equivalent of the New Deal, differing little from periods of social reform in other European countries. In Brady's view there was really no fundamental social change: 'The general structure of British society has not been seriously altered. In a few respects, primarily where long, slow disintegration of the old order had been evident since before the First World War, various measures of the Labour government may somewhat have hastened the process. But ... it has done relatively little to alter the structure, to redistribute the burdens....'[77] Rogow in turn wonders whether 'the transition from the Welfare State to the Socialist Commonwealth can be accomplished without violence being done to the traditions and customs of British democracy. The steel dispute, at least, suggests that some of the effective limits of planning are determined not at the ballot box or by the planners themselves, but by the power interests of affected groups.'[78] In the face of such diverging judgements, it may be helpful to summarise Labour's economic achievements before attempting an assessment.

There can be no doubt that, despite the vicissitudes of 1947 and the devaluation of 1949, reconstruction went ahead rapidly, and the British economy was considerably stronger. GNP fell 4.1 per cent in 1947, but then it rose steadily between 1948 and 1951 (by 3.19 per cent, 2.82 per cent and 2.66 per cent per annum respectively).[79] Industrial production also increased at an average rate of 6.1 per cent over the period of Labour rule, despite demobilisation and reconstruction.[80] Two further comments are in order; firstly that production increased considerably more slowly after 1951 (the average was 3.3 per cent for 1952—9 and 3.5 per cent for 1960—4[81]), and also that the rate of postwar recovery was roughly in line with what was achieved by other European countries, with the exception of West Germany, where growth was more rapid, but from a far lower base. The 1937 level of output was regained by about the end of 1947 — though this was not a good year in Britain — while France did not return to 1937 production until around the middle of 1948.[82] The lag in British economic growth relative to other European countries, which was to be so widely commented on in the early sixties, is therefore of relatively recent origin, and did not begin in the Labour period. On the other hand, Shonfield is probably right in criticising ministers for sacrificing the future by failing to assign a high enough proportion of the national income to investment: 'The Labour leaders, especially Sir Stafford Cripps, were peculiarly complacent over this whole issue. Partly it was because they got the relevant figures consistently wrong.'[83] Not all economists would share this view; many felt at the time that the government's investment plans were over-ambitious. Indeed, at the time of the dollar crisis in 1947, on the advice of such experts as Harrod, Meade, Lewis and Jewkes, the Attlee government cut back proposed investment. Moreover, economic growth depends at least as much on the quality of investment as on the quantity. And Shonfield acknowledges that on the whole Labour allocated available resources wisely: 'Their real success consisted in one thing only, in pushing a much larger proportion of a smaller total of investment into industrial plant and machinery. The volume of this kind of investment was well above prewar.'[84]

Unemployment remained consistently very low, falling from 3.1 per cent in

1947 to 1.2 per cent in 1951. When one recalls that full employment was the paramount aim of postwar policy, and that it was considered a peculiarly difficult one to attain, then this was a particularly satisfactory outcome. Events were to show that the real intractable problem in the area of employment was no longer the danger of mass unemployment but the chronic imbalance between supply and demand, which required improved provision for occupational training and a better geographical distribution of investment in the backward areas.

It is hard to be sure just how far the good results were due to favourable world conditions, and how far they can be credited to Labour's economic policies, and in particular to planning. On the whole, though, the external factors were not particularly favourable, apart from the existence of a high level of demand for consumer and capital goods, which particularly helped Britain during the early years after the war, because many of her competitors – most notably Germany and Japan – were still in ruins. But Britain herself had such difficulty in securing supplies of raw materials that the extent to which she could benefit from these favourable circumstances was limited.

In the short term planning was undoubtedly effective. But its greatest successes were essentially restrictive, that is in ensuring fair allocation of scarce resources.[85] On the more positive side, the priorities Labour laid down were on the whole observed, despite considerable problems arising from the inadequate labour mobility and the government's reluctance to use its powers to control labour. But short-term planning by means of controls was cumbersome, and after 1948 it was gradually reduced. Moreover, as an inheritance from the war, it could scarcely be considered a 'new technique of ruling'.[86] The Attlee government was slow to grasp the dilemma in which it placed itself. For if scarce resources were to be allocated, then there had to be controls, but these controls became the symbol of restraints on consumer freedom. So far as food was concerned, thanks to controls everyone was able to receive equal shares at subsidised prices, which was very much in keeping with the socialist ideal of fair shares for all. But by 1948–9 the average consumer had ceased to see it in this light. Consequently, nobody on the Labour side dreamt of continuing with rationing a moment longer than was absolutely necessary. Yet it was obvious that these controls were essential to any continuation of short-term planning, and were the reason why Britain was held up as a model to other European countries, since they ensured that everyone's basic needs could be met in an orderly manner and without undue waste. The abolition of some of these controls therefore severely impaired planning, particularly since there was no attempt to replace them by a more detailed medium-term plan which was less dependent on the methods appropriate to wartime production. But the secondary role assigned to the long-term programme, and the declining belief in the sort of forecasts that had been attempted in the *Economic Surveys*, showed how limited the attempt was.

Thus, the technique of planning was in decline even before Labour left office. Cripps's 'planning by persuasion' had been a success, but like all attempts at government by persuasion it lasted only as long as its initiator, and it could only briefly conceal the government's lack of imagination at the level of both policy and administration. Their inaction over food rationing is a particularly striking case in point. While their stewardship of the economy was laying the basis for an eventual abolition of rationing, ministers remained convinced to the very end that if rationing were ended there would be a grave danger of fresh shortages, which in turn would provoke a rapid rise in prices. While the rationing of basic necessities had its positive side, it was quite clear (and the failure to grasp this was a grave psychological error) that the party that restored even partial freedom to the housewife would reap enormous popularity.

If one looks at Labour's record from a political angle, it is clear that the government set out to be both socialist and democratic. The ultimate objective was to build a socialist society, or at the very least to lay its foundations. As Attlee's remarks show, the Labour leaders were firmly convinced that this is what they achieved. But for this to be the case, Labour planning would have had to bring about a transfer of both wealth and power. That there was some redistribution of incomes is quite clear. At the end of 1947 wages (in terms of constant prices) were estimated to have risen 16 per cent compared with 1938, salaries by 19 per cent and profits by 4 per cent. There can be no doubt that working-class living standards improved over this period, particularly as from 1948 there were the additional benefits of the new social services. Nor can there be any doubt that this was at the expense of the middle and upper classes; the former lost its domestic servants, and the latter had to begin opening their houses or castles to visitors to pay for the maintenance of their property or to meet death duties. But great inequalities of wealth remained. Death duties were severe, but their effect was felt only once in a generation — if then — and their contribution to greater equality was less than that of income tax. But the 1947 Town and Country Planning Act paved the way for an improvement in the quality of other aspects of life, the establishment of new towns and the renovation of the decaying industrial areas. Thus it seemed that Disraeli's 'two nations' were perhaps on the way to becoming one. This trend was accepted by all parties, but Labour was clearly better placed to carry it through, and it is quite possible that, had another party been in power, the redistribution of incomes would not have gone quite so far.

However, for this transfer of wealth to have been durable there would have had to be a transfer of power within society. No such transfer took place. The industrial and commercial Establishment was left virtually intact. Whether one looks at the administration of controls or the management of publicly owned industry, most of the jobs were filled by men from private industry. Moreover, the Labour leaders quite failed to see the possibilities of using the new public sector as a way of steering the whole economy in the direction they desired. They behaved as if, while carrying through their plans for nationalisation, they had no understanding of the real meaning of what they had done. Ownership changed; power did not. It had long since ceased to be true, if indeed it ever was, that the shareholders in industries like the mines and railways exercised any real power over them. Admittedly people were sometimes both managers and shareholders, but if, on nationalisation, they remained managers though no longer owners, the reality of power changed little if at all. This was a cause of some disappointment in several industries, particularly on the union side, at finding that the same old gang were still in the same old seats of power. But, to be fair, the situation was partly due to the attitude of most of the big unions, which refused to become involved in management. Thus, in the battle over iron and steel the issue was not, as Attlee thought, one of who should get the profits, but of who should control such a key industry. The general picture was little different. As Rogow emphasises:

> It was also significant that the non-cooperation of industry with Labour government policies was largely confined to areas in which questions of control formed the substance of controversy. Of the three major disputes between government and industry, comprising Development Councils, the nationalisation of steel, and the proposal to restrict dividends, the first two, it is worth noting, involved essentially control rather than property-rights issues . . . . Indeed, a remarkable feature of the entire period was that the most notable concessions made by industry to government or organised labour were invariably those which disadvantaged shareholders.[87]

Rogow and Shore both see the postwar welfare state as only an unsatisfactory compromise between the political power of a Labour government and the economic power of private industry, the one inherently temporary and incomplete, the other scarcely impaired by nationalisation. But are they right in maintaining that all Labour did was bring to fruition the old 'radical' programme of the early years of the century – to which business was by now resigned – rather than lay the bases of a new socialist Commonwealth, to which these sectional interests were so deeply hostile? They saw confirmation of their views in the fact that the Conservatives reversed so little of Labour's legislation after their return to power. But here they surely misunderstand one of the traditions of British democracy, that one government's legislation is rarely overturned by its successor, for it is considered to have enjoyed majority support at a particular point in time, and therefore to have become part of the national consensus. The Conservatives observed this convention by denationalising iron and steel[88] – to which they had always held the majority of the public were hostile – while leaving intact a whole range of other legislation that they had earlier contested. In this respect Rogow and Brady take the argument too far. It is not the only one.

If one really wants to trace the ancestry of what Labour accomplished in 1945–51, one should look not only to the radical reformers of the turn of the century, but even more to the Fabian programme as expounded in the work of the Webbs, most concretely in the 1909 minority report on the poor law, which was almost wholly the work of Beatrice Webb. Its central argument was that the causes as well as the consequences of the imperfect operation of capitalist society had to be attacked. Under Labour the 'step by step' socialism of the

Fabians in fact took a giant's stride forward. In addition, the public sector, which now amounted to some twenty per cent of productive capacity, was now universally accepted, and future governments would have the possibility of using it as an instrument in achieving their general economic aims, as French governments, even of a professedly 'liberal' hue, have never hesitated to do. This was a situation that even the Conservatives would be able to use to their advantage, though without openly admitting it.

Thus the Beveridge Report, which in some respects had been the swan song of the earlier radical tradition, had now been overtaken by events. But to follow what it had begun right through to its final conclusion, the Labour government would have had to display far greater imagination and determination. Unfortunately, this was just what the cabinet Attlee formed after the 1950 election most lacked. Several of the party's leading figures had died; Attlee himself was deeply shaken at being rejected by a sizeable part of the electorate; a bitter dispute over policy was to break out among the younger ministers who were to ensure the succession, and the government was so aware of its own precarious position that it could obviously not survive for a full term. Obviously, a government that was to restore confidence in democratic socialism could not afford to give such an impression. Many voters must have thought that, if the time had come to do away with wartime controls and call a halt to nationalisation, then it was better that this should be done by the opposition. All this explains the atmosphere of disillusionment that hung over the government during its last year in office. It was more the feeling that the government was exhausted than partial failure of its policies that led to the change of majority in 1951. Or, rather, the combination of those who thought that Labour had made too many changes, and those who thought it had made too few, was less conclusive than the impression the party gave of being no longer capable of carrying on with its reform policies. But the almost total abandoning of economic planning without making any real attempt to turn it into an effective method, despite the fact that the Labour leaders held there was such a close connection between planning and their attempt to create social democracy, contributed in no small measure to the public's disillusionment.

PART II

Planning Between 1951 and 1964

CHAPTER 3

The Conversion of the Conservatives

At the time they returned to power in October 1951, the Conservatives' thinking on economic matters could almost be boiled down to two phrases: preserve the welfare state, and restore free enterprise. During the election they had promised to abolish the remaining controls — notably food rationing — and to build more houses than Labour, whom (with some justice) they accused of neglecting the matter. Although they did not question the need for the State to intervene in the economy, they clearly thought that it should confine itself to short-term adjustments. These would rely on a mixture of monetary policy (mainly the use of bank rate) and fiscal policy (varying taxes according to the desired level of demand). The Conservatives were firmly opposed to any idea of planning. That, in their minds and in those of a large section of the public, remained inextricably associated with Labour controls and austerity. Yet the government had no desire to leave itself open to allegations of leading a dogmatic return to *laissez-faire*, or of being set on giving the upper and middle classes their revenge over the working class. Consequently it was at pains to demonstrate its concern for social welfare, and at least initially it was very cautious in its dealings with the unions. In the event, too, it did not immediately sweep away all controls but waited for an opportune moment to abolish them one by one.

As a result it became fashionable to suggest that there was almost no difference between the policies followed by Labour's last chancellor, Hugh Gaitskell, and those of the first Conservative chancellor, R. A. Butler — hence the success of the term 'Butskellism'.[1] Yet there were some significant differences; Gaitskell still displayed some of Cripps's preference for austerity, while Butler was by nature more optimistic and took an expansionist line. Early in 1952 the threat of inflation and a lack of confidence in the pound added up to a serious economic situation. Nevertheless, Butler produced a balanced budget, confounding the wiseacres who confidently expected it to be severely deflationary.[2] The trick worked; his three remaining budgets were also moderately expansionist. The two salient features of Butler's economic policy were gradual restoration of the normal working of the market in three key areas (food, building and the raising of capital), and a mild annual stimulus to demand by reduction of direct taxes. Food rationing, which some on the Labour side considered the touchstone of egalitarianism, was gradually ended; ration books finally disappeared in 1954, thanks to the abolition of import quotas. And this was done without the disastrous price increases that had been predicted, even though it was accompanied by the progressive withdrawal of food subsidies. The success of this policy was a major factor in the government's popularity and the electoral victories of 1955 and 1959.

More generally the Conservatives set out to run the welfare state as well as possible, thus challenging Labour in a field which they knew the public felt strongly about. While proclaiming their belief in a free economy, they had no hesitation about retaining controls temporarily where they felt it necessary. They could do this all the more readily because there had always been two bodies of thought within the party, first one and then the other predominating at different periods. There was the paternalist view that the State should intervene to protect people from the harsher consequences of the remorseless working through of economic laws; and there was the economic — liberal belief in leaving things to the market. The original feature of the policy pursued by Butler and the younger reforming-minded ministers associated with him (Rab's boys, as they were known) was that he demonstrated that these two approaches were not incompatible and he had a considerable degree of success in attempting to reconcile them. Nevertheless, planning — however interpreted — continued to be anathema. After a few years of Conservative rule, what remained from the Labour period was something midway between the Welfare State and the Affluent Society — a kind of 'welfare-capitalism', which won for the Conservatives the relative neutrality of the trade unions (though this also owed much to the willingness of Sir Walter Monckton at the Ministry of Labour to compromise all along the line). It also produced increased majorities in the House of Commons and a divided opposition. Slogans like Butler's 'Invest in Success' in 1955 and Macmillan's 1959 'You've never had it so good' (which was, strictly, a misquotation but nevertheless a symptomatic one) catch the ebullient optimism of the Conservative leaders, which found a responsive echo among the public. In fact Britain was expanding at a rate that compared not unfavourably with what was happening among her European neighbours. It was only around 1956[3] that a relative decline set in, which took several years to become generally recognised. Indeed the lesson did not fully sink home until after the 1959 election.

Butler has usually been considered the best of the Conservative chancellors; he was certainly the luckiest. Once the Korean boom ended the cost of imported raw materials fell by around a quarter. (The same good fortune was to ensure the success of M. Pinay in France at around the same time.) This made it the ideal moment for ending quotas and subsidies without triggering off an alarming increase in domestic prices. But in 1955 the terms of trade once again turned against Britain — which is one reason why Butler's successors were less successful. Nevertheless, Butler deserves credit for grasping a favourable situation in such a way as to fulfil his party's election promises. The less impressive record of his successors obviously owed much to a less favourable world situation, but it was also the result of serious mistakes.

The Conservatives' later resort to economic planning was to be the product of a widespread mood of uncertainty and introspection about Britain's role in the world, and how best to play it. This was to give rise to a widespread feeling that it was time for an *aggiornamento* in both foreign and domestic policy.[4] In external policy there was a growing tendency to wonder whether perhaps Britain had not made a mistake in standing aloof from the construction of Europe, and the first voices were beginning to be heard questioning the need for a continued presence East of Suez. At home the short-term economic remedies favoured by Conservative chancellors were beginning to look increasingly inadequate. However, there was as yet little disposition to challenge existing orthodoxies about the objectives of economic policy; few queried the desirability of maintaining the international role of sterling, with all this implied for the balance of payments, or the need to avoid inflation or ensure full employment and increase personal disposable incomes as rapidly as possible. Some people, mostly Conservatives, argued that more incentives were needed to encourage scientific and technical management to greater efforts. Others, mostly Labour, placed greater emphasis on fairer distribution of incomes. But both sides were aware that, on the one hand, if egalitarianism were pushed too far it might stifle innovation and technical progress, while on the other those who were unable to benefit from expansion could not simply be abandoned by the wayside. Thus there was really no basic disagreement about the aims of economic policy, even though it seemed difficult to reconcile them all simultaneously. The debate accordingly was about means rather than ends, and at the end of the fifties it became very much concerned with the need to break away from the stop–go cycle, the effects of which had become progressively clearer since 1955.[5]

Basically, stop–go, like Butskellism, rested on deliberate governmental manipulation of domestic demand. But really it was a 'deviation' from both Butskellism and the Keynesian ideas that underlay it. The main criticism of stop–go was not that monetary and budgetary methods were used to steer the economy, but that this involved sudden switches from inflation to deflation, or vice-versa, which, unlike previous economic fluctuations, were deliberately induced by those running the economy. The phases of the cycle went roughly as follows.

1. The economy is gradually expanding, the balance of payments reasonably healthy, but stocks of raw materials begin to drop.

2. Expansion continues, apparently accelerating, owing to the rapid increase of imports because industry is replenishing its depleted stocks of raw materials. This leads to a deterioration of the balance of payments.

3. The balance of payments continues to deteriorate; speculation against the pound gathers pace; hot money leaves the country. The government becomes alarmed and introduces several deflationary measures just when stocks have returned to their normal levels, and purchases are accordingly beginning to taper off.

4. Some time later the measures begin to bite. Production is cut back, and demand begins falling on the home market, but without a proportionate increase

in exports. Imports fall sharply. Thus the object of the exercise appears to have been at least partially achieved — though as stocks had been replenished during the previous phase this would probably have happened anyway.

5. Stalemate. Unemployment has risen and output fallen. The reduction in imports has restored the balance of payments to surplus; hot money returns. A new equilibrium appears to have been attained. Despite the restraints on consumer spending the first signs of economic recovery appear.

6. Encouraged by the improvement in the pound but alarmed at rising unemployment, the government hastily removes the brakes and gives a sharp boost to private consumption just as it was about to improve in any case. Thus the cycle begins again.

The main weakness of stop—go was the way in which the economy was suddenly and repeatedly thrown into a different gear. But also the inevitable delay between the moment decisions were taken and the time their effects worked through (and in some cases the hamhandedness of chancellors and those advising them) meant that time and time again production was cut back just as it was beginning to show signs of turning down. Or alternatively it was stimulated just as the upswing was beginning. The reason why stop—go policies were pursued was that the Treasury was trying to steer the economy between the twin reefs of mass unemployment and a flight from the pound, which were viewed as equally disastrous. As Sam Brittan explains:

> In the 1950s and early 1960s the Treasury behaved like a simple Pavlovian dog responding to two main stimuli: one is a 'run on the reserves' and the other is '500,000 unemployed'. On the whole (although not invariably), it was officials who panicked at the first stimulus, and ministers on the second.[6]

Consequently, the fatal flaw in stop—go was that it crippled both long-term and short-term expansion. It very soon became clear that the firms that suffered most from restrictions on domestic consumption were often those that were doing the most to generate expansion and stimulate exports. Thus periods of 'stop' did little for exports. This created the impression (which seemed increasingly justified) that the goal of a balance of payments surplus was being pursued at the cost of the expansion of Britain's world trade. It also meant that industrialists were increasingly hesitant about investing in new productive capacity. Not surprisingly, industrialists were among the most vocal in calling for a change in policy.

Their arguments gained force from the growing number of works on the British economy that were comparing Britain's economic performance unfavourably with those of the European Common Market. The lagging growth rate was particularly alarming. Between 1950 and 1960 the average annual growth in GNP was 2.2 per cent for Britain; Germany achieved 6.5 per cent, Italy 5.3 per cent and France 3.5 per cent. The relatively low proportion going to capital investment (10 per cent at the beginning of the fifties and 13 per cent between 1958 and 1960, compared with 14 and 16 per cent for the same periods in the

Six) was a clear indication that unless something was done the decline would continue. Last but not least, the continuing fall in Britain's share of world trade was further proof of the industrial decline of the country that had been 'the workshop of the world' in the nineteenth century. While none of this was new, it lent force to those who were not prepared to accept such a decline and who were calling for a more expansionist policy. For the return to favour of planning was really an indirect consequence of this desire for a policy of stimulating more rapid growth. Many of those advocating planning in the fifties were by no means uncritical devotees of state intervention. They came round to the idea of planning because they saw it as the only way of achieving growth. Thus 'planning' no longer had quite the same meaning as under the 1945—51 Labour government; it came to mean 'indicative planning' along French lines.

As PEP put it, 'The term "planning" became inextricably associated with the use of direct controls. . . . French economic planning has been done in a different spirit. . . . It is a matter not of directions but of a voluntary coordination of plans in which all those party to it concur.'[7] One of the main aims of the campaign for planning was to convince sceptics just how important this difference was.

The greatest readiness to agree that an *aggiornamento* of some kind was needed was to be found among employers. And, however paradoxical it may have seemed at the time, it was they who marshalled the case for planning the most effectively. Yet given the widespread restiveness and dissatisfaction in a number of industries, that was perhaps not so surprising as it seems at first sight. However, as usual it required a few far-sighted individuals, 'a tiny minority of intellectuals', as Brittan calls them,[8] to launch the idea, which then snowballed with remarkable rapidity.

It all began, as so often in Britain, with a dining club, which began meeting early in 1960, bringing together industrialists and economists to discuss a wide range of economic problems relating to growth. The guiding spirit of these private, almost clandestine, gatherings was Hugh Weeks, who was then chairman of the FBI's Economic Policy Committee.[9] Weeks, 'whose mild manner conceals a good many rumbling heresies',[10] was the ideal man for this kind of undertaking. An economist by training, he had been both a temporary civil servant and a director of several companies, while for some years he had given most of his working time to the Industrial and Commercial Finance Corporation, which had been set up in 1945 to help finance small firms. In addition, he had 'acquired in the course of his work a way of talking about national business problems that [was] equally comprehensible to industrialists, officials and economists'.[11] However, it was his wish that the dining club should be quite separate from the FBI's Economic Committee. But although the group therefore had no official standing whatever, it was to pave the way for what Brittan terms 'the Brighton revolution'.

A few months after the club was formed, in November 1960, the FBI met in conference at Brighton. The theme to be discussed by the 121 leading industrialists and 31 guests was 'the next five years'. Among the guests were the permanent secretaries to the Treasury and the Board of Trade, the chairmen of the nationalised boards, the chairman of Lloyds and a few economists. The opening speech, by Mr Heathcoat Amory,[12] who had left the Treasury in July, received a fairly cool reception, for the conference was expecting something more than a routine defence of official policy, however polished the presentation. The conference divided into five groups; most of Weeks's club were assigned to group III and asked to present their views on economic growth in Britain under the chairmanship of Sir Hugh Beaver, managing director of Guinness, who had the reputation of being something of an industrial radical. The innovators were reinforced by Mr Reay Geddes, managing director of Dunlop, who had made a speech earlier in the year which foreshadowed what was eventually to become the NEDC. In presenting the group's report at the end of the conference, Sir Hugh Beaver went out of his way to express disagreement with the ex-chancellor's opening remarks. Amory had contended that stable prices and a favourable balance of payments were essential conditions for expansion; Beaver argued that the achievement of a faster rate of growth might be the best way of attaining stable prices and a healthy balance of payments. The group also called on the major industries to make 'a more conscious attempt to assess plans and demands in particular industries for five or even ten years ahead',[13] as had already happened with steel. This of course would take place entirely within industry itself. But the group also suggested, after a severe condemnation of stop—go, that government and industry might meet to consider 'whether it would be possible to agree on an assessment of expectations and intentions which should be before the country for the next five years'.[14] This amounted to suggesting, albeit in a rather roundabout manner, the introduction of a five-year indicative plan. At that time very few people held such views, but they very rapidly became more or less the official FBI line, which naturally meant that they were listened to with respect in official circles. Moreover, other leading businessmen were taking up the issue. The stir created by the Brighton conference had scarcely died down when *The Times* published (on 5 January 1961) a letter from a prominent banker and City financier, Lionel Fraser, attacking the government's economic policy and calling for the preparation of a five-year economic plan. This showed that even quarters that had never been as given to expansionism as industry, and that were more concerned with the role of sterling as a world currency, might well support indicative planning.

The discussion of planning focused around two main approaches, one British and one French. In Britain, since the denationalisation of steel in 1953, supervision and co-ordination of the industry had been the responsibility of the Iron and Steel Board. For the Conservatives had no wish to be accused of hindering the rationalisation of the industry; nor were they prepared to relinquish all the powers the State had enjoyed during nationalisation. Thus, although the industry was no longer in public ownership, the State was still in a position to exercise considerable policy guidance and supervision through the

Board. The Board controlled prices and supplies of raw material, provided the companies with a wide range of services, including research and technical training facilities and, most important, drew up the investment programme. This involved it in the preparation of a five-year development programme. The Board worked closely with the individual companies and also retained a considerable degree of autonomy from the government (it reported directly to Parliament). Although concerned with a single industry, its experience offered a relevant and successful 'native' model for other industries, and the modest degree of governmental intervention it entailed appeared acceptable.

This was all very well, but something larger-scale was needed. It was around this time that interest in the merits of French planning began to develop in Britain. Among the leading advocates were OEEC, which had been making discreet attempts to get Britain to break out of the vicious stop—go cycle and join the virtuous cycle of countries like Germany, Japan and France. In addition research institutes such as Political and Economic Planning (PEP) and the National Institute for Economic and Social Research (NIESR), whose *Economic Reviews* were awaited with some apprehension by governments of either hue, had been campaigning for growth for years; they were delighted that they were no longer voices crying in the wilderness. But the main burden of explaining what indicative planning involved naturally fell on the French themselves. Around this time there was a steady stream of visits by businessmen and civil servants between the rue de Rivoli and the rue de Martignac (the respective Paris homes of the Ministry of Finance and the Plan) on the one hand, and the Treasury and the FBI headquarters in Tothill Street on the other. The organisation of a three-day conference on planning in France at Easter 1961 in London provided clear evidence of the 'complicity' between these various bodies. The initiative for the conference came from a British official at OEEC; it was organised by NIESR; the chief French participants came from the Planning Commissariat, and the conference report appeared in *Planning*, the organ of PEP.

But before coming to the conference itself, one might well ask why French civil servants showed such enthusiasm for converting the British. It had been obvious for some time that Britain would shortly apply for membership of the Common Market. The French planners may well have thought that if they wanted to have a chance of persuading the other Common Market countries to adopt indicative planning, despite the firm opposition of the Germans, there would be no harm in winning over an important potential recruit to the Community, for this would alter the whole balance of forces in favour of France. Events were to show that, if such a strategy existed, it was to say the least somewhat premature.

Apart from the commissioner-general of the Plan, Pierre Massé, the French delegation included M. Claude Gruson, head of the Service d'Études Économiques et Financières (SEEF) at the Ministry of Finance, and other senior officials from the SEEF and 'the Plan'. There was also, and this was a wise move given that the main problem was one of winning over industrialists, a strong contingent of French businessmen from the Plan's modernisation committees, including M. Landucci, chairman of the Chemical Industries Committee, M. Latourte, chairman of the Steel Committee, and M. Gouri, secretary of the Energy Committee. The British participants were mostly academic economists and economic journalists, but they also included Sir Robert Shone, chairman of the Iron and Steel Board.

The opening address outlining the French conception of planning was naturally given by Massé. Very diplomatically, he showed that he was aware of the dangers his audience had in mind and tried to anticipate their questions on such problems as the danger of bureaucracy and the risks to free enterprise involved in implementing a plan. He laid great stress on the smallness of the Commissariat's staff, which numbered only 140 in all, from the commissioner-general himself down to the chauffeurs, despite the incorporation of the former Commissariat à la Productivité: 'Officials in charge of planning in the true sense have not increased in number despite the very large extension of the field they have to cover — one of the rare exceptions to Parkinson's law.'[15] He also described the exact duties of the Commissariat au Plan: 'The role of the Commissariat-General inside the administrative and governmental machinery is confined to that of proposing, advising and estimating. It takes part in discussions and prepares decisions, but it manages no funds and has itself no power of economic intervention.'[16] In addition, by French standards the Plan enjoyed a considerable degree of autonomy, and this made it an ideal meeting ground for civil servants and businessmen. Turning to the implementation of the Plan, Massé laid great emphasis on the plan as a 'reducer of uncertainties', and on the 'powerful psychological factors', which meant that, as the Plan had been accepted by all concerned, it could be implemented without any need to resort to compulsion. 'The agreement achieved while the Plan is being drawn up tends spontaneously to extend itself when it comes to implementing the Plan. If the real forces of the country have been associated with making the Plan, they are more likely to stand together in action.'[17] This was more than a little ingenuous. Indeed, when Massé went on to portray the Plan as being essentially a piece of market research on a national scale, the elements of compulsion involved in French planning were, if not actually denied, very considerably soft-pedalled:

A modern economy requires considerable investments; and the return on these investments is greatly affected by the evolution of their environment — an evolution which is rapid and difficult to forecast. . . . The logic of 'indicative planning' consists in integrating all these interdependent effects, thus extending to a nation-wide scale the market surveys made by each single firm. The Plan gives to each branch of society some reassurance that it can obtain its supplies and dispose of its products without running into shortages or gluts. . . . [It] is not binding on anybody. Firms are not relieved from making their own calculations, and forming their own assessments of the risks. But because of the Plan they are better informed when making their own plans.[18]

Naturally Massé noted that implementation of the Plan did not depend on psychological factors alone, but in his view such 'practical means of influence' as tax rebates, extended credit, reduced interest rates, refundable subsidies, equipment premiums and suchlike should be considered 'incentives' rather than 'coercive methods'. Finally, he emphasised that the Plan was not only an instrument for achieving growth and a piece of nation-wide market research, but it was also a way of improving the quality of life. Nevertheless, his speech concentrated mainly on the 'indicative' aspects of the French Plan, and he gave the impression that he was particularly concerned with allaying the fears of his listeners.

However, the ensuing discussion showed that some of the English members of the conference had not been entirely convinced. Two concerns were also widely voiced. Many participants wondered what effect planning would have on competition. Massé's reply was that, firstly, there had always been agreements between companies and there always would be, plan or no plan. Consequently it was better for this to happen under the auspices of the Plan and in a context of economic growth. Secondly, although competition is excellent it must not be taken to excess, as this could give rise to surplus capacity, which entailed a waste of resources. Some of his listeners may well have found this reply rather less than completely convincing. It remained for Sir Robert Shone to put the fundamental question for those who wanted Britain to achieve a rate of growth comparable to her European neighbours: how far was France's rapid growth attributable to planning? At the close of the conference he himself provided a rather qualified answer: there seemed no doubt that the procedure gave rise to a climate of confidence in expansion, but French growth appeared to rest on considerably more concrete bases than that, notably on an investment policy which, though of course integrated with the Plan, could also be pursued quite independently. His conclusion was that: 'the French Plan is in the main an attempt to guide the investment policy of the country. . . . The French experience in bringing these plans [i.e. those of private industry] as well of those of the public sector together, and determining national policy on the basis of a four-year investment plan, throws up possibilities for this country.'[19]

The rather rosy picture of French planning that was held up for the British on this occasion may explain the sequel: they drew up two sound plans but gave little thought to how to implement them. In part they did this because they had been led to expect too much of the 'psychological factors' they had been told would be so important — the 'spontaneous execution' Massé had led them to expect.

When Mr Selwyn Lloyd succeeded Heathcoat Amory as chancellor on his resignation for reasons of health in July 1960, the Treasury was deep in consideration of how its working methods might be improved. At the time a committee under Lord Plowden (the former chief planning officer until the abolition of the post in 1953) was examining the control of public expenditure.

While its report was not actually published until July 1961,[20] and thus could not as yet have any direct impact on ministers' attitudes to planning, its main outlines were known in the higher reaches of Whitehall considerably earlier. One of its four main proposals was that programmes for public expenditure should be drawn up several years in advance. This recommendation started from the obvious proposition that the traditional annual budget provided no way of considering possible long-term developments. However, there was already a long-term capital programme in education, and there were also five- or ten-year plans in the nationalised industries. What was new in the Plowden Report was the proposal that these rather isolated efforts should be brought together in a single document. The chancellor immediately gave this proposal his backing, and beginning in 1961 the Treasury adopted the practice of preparing an annual report on public expenditure, though the first to be actually published did not appear until 1963.[21] Nevertheless, as far as the 'planners' were concerned this was very much a step in the right direction, for without it indicative planning was scarcely conceivable. The Report also implied a considerable change in the role of the Treasury — a body that had no great reputation for relishing change. And yet, from around 1960, forward-looking men in the Treasury, as in industry, were giving the matter very serious consideration, though they worked independently of one another and their conclusions were by no means identical. In fact, while the businessmen were criticising stop-go, and the Treasury's whole handling of the situation, the Treasury itself was coming round to the view that the real need for reform lay with employers and unions! Moreover, although some were attracted to planning, this was largely because they saw a need for a forum where government, employers and trade unionists could discuss national economic policy in complete candour. They had it in mind to breathe fresh life into the old Planning Board, which had been more or less in suspended animation since the abolition of the post of chief planning officer in 1953.[22] Furthermore, a number of civil servants who were really more interested in finding a way of controlling incomes than in planning as such thought a tripartite body of the kind envisaged might offer a way of involving the unions in the introduction of an incomes policy. Thus the Treasury had not undergone a wholehearted conversion to planning, and there were probably other reforms it would have preferred to have seen adopted, but most senior officials felt that they could go along with such a system, provided it was a way of achieving an incomes policy, and that whatever body was made responsible for planning was not independent of the government machine. But industry was flatly opposed to the new body being under the Treasury.

The minister therefore had to decide between these two diametrically opposed views. Following the FBI conference Lloyd had started taking a serious interest in planning. Lloyd was something of a pragmatist. He was not a particularly original thinker, but once he was convinced an idea had merits he was prepared to throw all his considerable energy behind it. He thought the proposal to draw up programmes for public expenditure was sound, and he rapidly gave it his full support. He was basically opposed by both background and training to undue government involvement in the economy, and left to himself he would have been most unlikely to adopt the 'socialist' idea of planning; but because so many people whom he knew to be utterly opposed to socialism, including leading businessmen, assured him that 'indicative planning' was not at all the same thing, he was prepared to move in that direction. He was also acutely aware that the public was expecting him to come up with some new policies. However, there was still the cabinet to convince.

Shortly after the FBI conference Selwyn Lloyd raised the issue with the prime minister, Harold Macmillan. Macmillan's reaction was favourable. He had long been a supporter of a non-socialist form of planning; well before the war, when he was a very junior back-bencher, he had aired his views widely in a manifesto[23] and two books,[24] which caused a certain stir at the time. It was no secret that although he had aged and risen through the ranks of the party to the leadership, his position on these matters had not varied. However, at that particular moment he was deeply engrossed in foreign affairs, particularly with Anglo-American relations and the problem of Europe, and despite the impression some observers[25] have received he seems to have done no more than encourage Lloyd without actually intervening personally.

The same was not true of Lloyd's colleagues. Most ministers were hostile to the idea of an independent planning council — as were many people in the Treasury. Among the opponents of the proposal was Mr Maudling, president of the Board of Trade — the minister who was most involved in industrial matters, and who would therefore be most affected by 'competition' from any new body. Maudling argued that the existing links between government and industry were quite adequate, and that an independent council would be a threat to the authority of the cabinet. But this was precisely the point on which Selwyn Lloyd could not give way. For it was all too likely that if the new council were attached to the Treasury it would be unable to command full support from outside, and would rapidly turn into yet another traditional piece of administrative machinery. He was also not unaware of the value of having a channel of information independent of that supplied by the Treasury, and one that would be quite prepared to challenge the Treasury's priorities.

The extent of cabinet opposition was all the more surprising since the Conservative Party was not in general hostile to adopting a fresh economic policy. Since its return to power the party had been changing; there were fewer and fewer of the old diehards, while many of the new generation of back-benchers tended to see themselves as spokesmen for a new middle class of technicians and engineers. They had just won a great victory over the 1961 budget by persuading the chancellor to raise the threshold of surtax from £2,000 to £5,000. This new middle class, and some of the younger Conservative ministers, wanted a more rapid rate of growth, as a way of achieving a faster improvement in the standard of living; they had no objection to a planned form of expansion provided it rested on the consent of the groups affected rather than on compulsion.

During that summer of 1961 the cabinet was to change course on Europe.

There were only a few days between the government's announcements of its decision to set up a national planning council and of its intention to seek membership of the Common Market. This has led some people to discern a cause-and-effect relationship, the decision to plan being intended as a way of preparing the country for competition within EEC (just as in France the concepts of planning and European integration merged in the person of Jean Monnet, creator of the former and promoter of the latter). But in fact this seems to have been no more than a coincidence. For the decision to plan was chiefly related to economic factors and pressure from industry, while – initially at least – the reasons for entering Europe were primarily political. What clinched the matter for the prime minister – and the decision was fairly clearly his – was much more the collapse of the May 1960 summit conference on which he had been counting very heavily, and the relative isolation for Britain that resulted from it. While the 'planners' and the 'Europeans' were often the same people, this shows no more than that both decisions tended to challenge established attitudes and policies, and they had a similar aim: to rouse Britain from her lethargy. Nevertheless the conclusion arose from quite different lines of thought, conducted by different men. The best indication of the tenuous nature of the connection between the two was that the dashing of hopes of early membership of the Common Market had no adverse effect on the development of planning in 1963–5. Conversely, a year or so later the prospect of a second application for membership did nothing to prevent the decline of planning.

To return to 1961, it is likely that the establishment of a planning council would have been considerably delayed by the cabinet had not Selwyn Lloyd been forced by a fresh run on the pound and a loss of nerve by the Treasury and the Bank of England to present a special 'crisis budget' on 25 July 1961. This imposed a new round of deflationary measures, and, most importantly, a highly unpopular 'pay pause'. The decision to set up Neddy[26] should therefore be seen as a last despairing effort by the chancellor to show that the government did have a long-term strategy despite the note of panic in the measures he was announcing. (The corridors of Whitehall were buzzing with rumours that the currency reserves would run out before the end of the year unless drastic action were taken.) The cabinet had not been consulted about this section of Lloyd's speech and this subsequently gave rise to some acrimonious exchanges. A fortnight later Macmillan, who considered Lloyd's statement to have committed the government, agreed to the chancellor opening negotiations on the setting up of Neddy with the main bodies representing employers and workers. But although talks began it was some months before the cabinet resigned itself to the creation of Neddy.

In his budget speech the chancellor reached the subject of planning at the end of a long series of short-term measures. He practically smuggled it through in the middle of a paragraph: 'I shall deal, first, with growth in the economy . . . . The controversial question of planning also arises. I am not frightened of the word . . . . I intend to discuss urgently with both sides of industry procedures for pulling together the various processes of consultation and forecasting with a view to better coordination of ideas and plans.'[27] Pressed for further details, the following day he attempted to be more precise without committing himself too far: 'I envisage a joint examination of the economic prospects of the country stretching for five or more years into the future. It would cover the growth of national production and distribution of our resources between the main uses, consumption, government expenditure, investment, and so on.'[28] Answering criticism that he had been too vague on the proposed planning council, the chancellor added, 'for the government to lay that down beforehand is not, I think, the best way to get full cooperation'.[29] But eventually he stated that he was 'certainly not limiting [himself] to the idea of some planning board within the Treasury'.[30] From the opposition benches Messrs Wilson, Gunter and Grimond expressed satisfaction at the government's conversion to planning, but were sceptical about its determination to carry its intentions through. Parliament heard a further report on the progress of the negotiations during a debate on 18 December; this gave both sides an opportunity to clarify their positions, but the real negotiations were taking place elsewhere.

In August Mr Lloyd had contacted the TUC and the employers' organisations. The FBI gave his scheme a warm reception. This was scarcely surprising in view of the fact that he was falling into line with the FBI's own suggestions. The FBI made just two conditions; that the new council should be completely independent of the Treasury, and that the employers' representatives should serve in a purely personal capacity, because of the difficulty of committing three different and rather loosely knit bodies. The first point was in line with the minister's own views, and probably those of the unions too, and was not even raised in the ensuing negotiations. The second was bound to detract from the council's standing, but the minister felt he had no choice but to accept it. The situation would only alter with the merger of the three main employers' organisations to form the CBI in 1965.

Negotiations with the TUC were rather more delicate, and took more than six months. The unions and the Labour movement generally were of course favourable to planning in principle. Their hesitation was not due to ideological opposition but because they did not fully trust the government. All the same, the Labour view of planning had also been changing since the party had gone into opposition. The mid-fifties were years of furious arguments over policy within the Labour Party. Should the party shed the fading trappings of early twentieth-century social democracy, with its sweeping condemnation of capitalism and its belief in nationalisation of the entire economy which was so unpopular with the middle class, and had yet to prove itself workable, let alone ideal? Those who wanted to drop such policies failed to carry the day in formal terms, for their attempts to amend Clause IV of the party's constitution, with its traditional commitment to nationalise the means of production, distribution and exchange, were unsuccessful. But in practice there was a considerable watering down of the party's economic policy. The programme published by the party in

1953[31] was completely in harmony with the policies the Labour government had followed between 1945 and 1951, and it attacked the Tories' 'systematic dismantling' of the 'planning apparatus' and controls that Labour had established. A year or so later there was a considerable change in tone. The idea of widespread state intervention had completely vanished; the party committed itself to nationalising only those industries that were found to be 'failing the nation'.[32] The party also gave ground on planning. In a policy statement issued in 1958[33] much was made of the benefits of planning, but by now planning had come to mean something rather different. There was no question now of a return to the compulsion of the immediately postwar years: 'Planning does not mean a return to detailed controls',[34] not because the party was turning its back on what had been done in the past but because times had changed. Thus, 'day to day decisions can be best left to industry and the consumer . . . . The object of planning will be to provide a broad framework within which . . . the detailed decisions of industry do not come into conflict with national objectives.'[35] The statement added that 'a partnership between the State and both sides of industry is essential to democratic planning.'[36] Consequently, Labour should have been delighted at the Conservatives' conversion to their own ideas. That their initial reaction was one of suspicion arose from a feeling that the Conservatives were simply clutching at straws and would abandon planning as soon as the economic situation improved — and there may also have been a certain amount of pique at finding someone else exploiting one of the party's cherished ideas.

However, it was not the Labour Party but the TUC that was most immediately affected. Throughout the earlier debate the unions had remained very reserved, because of their general opposition to the Conservative government's policies. However, the day after Selwyn Lloyd's statement the TUC, though protesting at the pay pause, indicated it was interested in the minister's proposition and was prepared to take part in any talks that might be held on them. In fact the TUC was in two minds. It was attracted by Lloyd's idea because this offered them an opportunity to influence economic policy,[37] but it was worried that its acceptance might be seen as condoning the pay pause or any subsequent introduction of an incomes policy.

After a long meeting with Selwyn Lloyd in August the TUC seemed on the point of agreeing — on three conditions: that the council should be free to draw up its own agenda; that the TUC should have full control over its representatives; and that an incomes policy would not be introduced for the time being. After several months of uncertainty, talks almost broke down in November after the prime minister sharply rebuked the Electricity Council for granting excessive wage increases to some of its employees. Selwyn Lloyd met the TUC again, but apparently little progress was made. However, early in December the distance between the two sides narrowed, possibly on the prompting of the Labour Party, which argued that the unions would lay themselves open to severe public criticism if they appeared to be evading their responsibilities. Selwyn Lloyd was accordingly in a position to give more details in a Commons debate on 18

December on the new council's responsibilities and organisation. After regretting that he was still not in a position to announce that the unions had agreed to take part, he stated clearly, 'I certainly do not regard this body as one whose duty is to negotiate about wages or to seek to enforce a wages policy. Its primary task is to tackle the obstacles to sound growth . . . . I have decided that it would be wrong for me to delay any longer the setting up of the staff . . . . I accordingly propose to appoint a Director General and proceed with the recruiting of the staff.'[38] The director-general was to be Sir Robert Shone. The ensuing exchanges between the chancellor and Ray Gunter, the opposition spokesman, showed a general desire to secure agreement.[39] On 20 December 1961 the TUC agreed to meet the chancellor again. While this fresh interview did not produce complete agreement, on 10 January 1962 Mr Lloyd wrote in very conciliatory terms to Mr Woodcock, the general secretary of the TUC, and on 25 January the General Council decided by 27 votes to 8 to take part in Neddy.[40] (One of the eight was Frank Cousins, who was nevertheless to be an influential member of Neddy.) All the obstacles had finally been removed; Neddy could at last come into existence.

CHAPTER 4

The National Economic Development Council

The birth of Neddy spelled the demise of several other consultative bodies. These included the Economic Planning Board (EPB) and the National Production Advisory Council (NPAC), both of which had been more or less moribund for several years, and the Council on Prices, Productivity and Incomes which had led a somewhat ambivalent existence since 1957. However, unlike the EPB and the NPAC, the Council had met regularly over the previous four years. It had been founded with three members, each of whom was an expert in his particular field – Lord Cohen in law, Sir Harold Howitt in accountancy and Sir Dennis Robertson in economics. The date when the Council was appointed was of some significance. For it was around 1957 that the Conservatives began to show the first signs of uncertainty over their commitment to a 'free economy'. As a result the 'three wise men' were asked to study what was seen as the root cause of the recurrent balance of payments crises – the persistent tendency for prices and incomes to rise more rapidly than production. They were to report regularly on trends in prices, productivity and incomes.

The Council published four reports.[1] A comparison of the first and last reports sheds a revealing light on the way its views developed over the four years.[2] The first report emphasised the discrepancy between the rate of increase of production and of wages and other incomes – the latter being almost double the former. It advocated vigorous measures, not just to slow down the rate of inflation but to stop it completely, and it favoured the most traditional of all remedies – cutting back demand. It made clear its approval of the various measures that had been taken since 1958 to promote a freer and more competitive economy and stoutly opposed any restoration of price controls and subsidies. Accordingly the Council's recommendations were largely of a limited, technical nature, and in no way ran counter to prevailing orthodoxies about managing the economy. But the fourth report, published at the end of July 1961, displayed quite a different attitude, reflecting the changing attitude among both economists and politicians. For now the Council added its voice to the chorus favouring planning. Recalling its opposition to price controls and support for action against restrictive trade practices, the Council emphasised the desirability of promoting growth and of securing the requisite volume of investment by means of a national projection of investment intentions; it advocated a policy for wages and profits based on projections of increases in production, which would be related to the national investment programme and to forward assessment of manpower needs and resources. All this would require greater government leadership and co-operation with both sides of industry. This really amounted to an indirect plea for indicative planning. Finally, it suggested that it should be replaced by a larger and more representative body better suited to the task of planning it felt should now be undertaken.

The Organisation of Neddy

Since Neddy was intended to be independent of the regular Whitehall machine it had to have its own staff to provide its Council with an independent channel of information, and to put the organisation on a permanent basis, for the Council itself was to meet only once a month. The Council's autonomy in relation to the Treasury was emphasised when the Office found its home in the Millbank Tower, sufficiently distant from Whitehall in general and from the Treasury in Great George Street in particular.

The membership of NEDC was officially announced just a few days before its first meeting. It had a total of twenty members, four of whom served *ex-officio* (the chancellor, who was also chairman, the president of the Board of Trade, the minister of labour and the director-general of NEDO) and sixteen ordinary members sitting in a personal capacity, two from the nationalised industries, six from private industry, six from the TUC and two independent experts.[3] Officially these sixteen members were appointed by the chancellor. In fact the selection of employers' and union representatives was preceded by lengthy consultations with both the FBI and the TUC. The TUC members — who were the general secretary and the leaders of five of the most important unions — considered themselves delegates and in consequence reserved their right to consult the General Council before approving any of the Council's reports. They were accountable to the TUC, and accordingly any line they took on the Council committed the TUC at least morally. However, the employers' representatives could only speak for themselves rather than for the CBI — and this detracted from both the value of their contribution and the Council's standing.

As even a quick glance shows, the Council was by no means fully representative of the main economic interests. Remarkably, there was no spokesman for the City or agriculture, or unions outside the TUC. This was because the primary emphasis was on industrial development, and consequently the main object was to secure *concertation** between government, industrial

---

* *Concertation* and *économie concertée* are again terms that have no exact English equivalents, and so are left in French in the text. The best definition of them was that given by M. François Bloch-Lainé, one of the senior officials who, together with Jean Monnet, Pierre Massé and Claude Gruson — to mention only four — were the authors of the economic regeneration of France after the Second World War. *L'économie concertée* is 'a system in which representatives of the State (or other public bodies) and those of companies

employers and unions. But the result was that the scope of planning in Britain was to be considerably narrower than in France.[4]

The National Economic Development Office

The first director-general of Neddy was Sir Robert Shone, who was appointed in December 1961. As a former chairman of the Iron and Steel Board for some seven years, Sir Robert was one of the few people in Britain at the time with experience of drawing up an investment programme. As director-general he was responsible to both the Council and its chairman, the chancellor. He was the chief link between the Council and the Office — the staff of which he personally recruited. At first the staff numbered 75; by 1964 it had reached 100. Initially it was in a unique position as regards both composition and terms of service, though others — notably the Prices and Incomes Board — later followed the precedent in some respects. But at the time it included the highest concentration of economists and statisticians ever seen in British government. About three-quarters of the staff were drawn from industry, mostly from the management side because the unions employed very few such experts, with the remainder coming from the universities and the civil service. Most were recruited by the director-general himself on fairly long-term contracts. Others were seconded for two or three years and their salaries continued to be made up by the normal employers; this was a useful way of securing an adequate turnover of staff. Apart from those seconded from government departments, the staff were not, technically, civil servants, though in practice the rules relating to job security, holidays and so on were very similar. As Joan Mitchell aptly puts it, they 'are public servants in a general way. But they are not the servants of the government'.[5]

Initially NEDO had three divisions:

1. An Administrative Division. This served as a secretariat to the Council, and handled personnel matters and the routine operation of the Office. This division had the highest proportion of seconded civil servants, mostly from the Ministry of Labour. It was headed by a secretary acting as secretary to the Council itself.

2. An Economic Division, responsible for planning and for examining all

---

(public or private) meet in an organised way to exchange information, to compare their forecasts and either to reach decisions or to make recommendations for consideration by the government' (F. Bloch-Lainé, *A la recherche d'une Economie Concertée* (Paris, 1961), pp. 5–6). Such a system implies complete openness in the exchange of information, and an adequate degree of planning, producing a sort of moral contract between all the main economic actors — in other words, a basic consensus on economic objectives. In France many people believed, at least between 1955 and 1965, that this difficult consensus had been achieved. Since 1968 we know that this was an illusion among men who, in all good faith, believed rather too rapidly that 'the end of ideology' had arrived.

aspects of economic growth, and for preparing studies of the economy for consideration by the Council. This division had the highest concentration of economists and statisticians. It was headed by an economic director and two deputy directors. The first economic director was Sir Robert MacDougall, an Oxford economist who held the post until the end of 1964.

3. An Industrial Division, dealing with the problems and plans of specific industries. It was this division that proposed the establishment of economic development committees in 1963. It was also Neddy's main means of contact with industry, avoiding the need to work through government departments. It was headed by an industrial director, with two assistant directors; the first director was Mr T. C. Fraser, formerly with the Board of Trade and the Wool Textile Employers' Council.

The founders of Neddy were, initially at least, trying to create a forum for discussion by the chief interests concerned, rather than to invent yet another piece of decision-making machinery. Consequently considerable stress was laid on obtaining membership at the highest possible level. In France the Conseil Supérieur du Plan fell rapidly into abeyance (though an attempt was made to revive it shortly before the British decisions in July 1961), partly because it duplicated the Conseil Économique et Social, and partly because its membership of fifty-eight after 1961 made it too big to be anything but a talking shop. Lloyd was quite determined that NEDC should not be a talking shop. Consequently it was better placed than its French counterpart to survive and retain a leading role.

NEDO differed from the Commissariat-Général au Plan, however, in both its basic nature and the source of its authority. It was firmly intended that NEDO should not be a conventional governmental body, both because employers and unions would not have as much confidence in its independence if its staff were ordinary civil servants, and because the existing departments would in any case have found it almost impossible to provide NEDO with the economists and statisticians it needed without seriously undermining their own efficiency. Since the Office was completely independent of Whitehall its authority derived from the Council. By contrast, the Commissariat-Général au Plan was in all practical respects part of the ordinary administrative machine and the French civil service was in a position to supply it with all the expert assistance it needed. Its authority was not derived from a council, but from being part of the regular machinery of state (by training and terms of service the staff of the Commissariat-General were no different from their colleagues in the economic ministries), and from its close relationship with the Ministry of Finance, particularly the Service des Études Économiques et Financières and the Institut National de la Statistique et des Études Économiques — bodies that had a major role in both inspiring and implementing the Plan. Thus for all the apparent similarities the two bodies were really very different. This is scarcely surprising in view of the profoundly differing conceptions of government and adminis-tration in the two countries.

Neddy's Responsibilities

At the time of NEDC's first meeting in March 1962, the only indication of what was expected of Neddy lay in Mr Lloyd's speeches, which were neither full nor explicit. Thus the task of defining its brief and order of business was left very largely to the Council itself. These were worked out over the first few meetings. However, the employers and trade unionists were for the most part prepared to leave the initiative to the chancellor, and his suggestions on the Council's terms of reference were agreed, after a certain amount of debate and the adoption of a number of amendments. In their final form the terms of reference were:

> (a) Examine the economic performance of the nation with particular concern to plans for the future in both the private and public sectors of industry;
> (b) to consider together what are the obstacles to quicker growth, what can be done to improve efficiency and whether the best use is being made of resources;
> (c) to seek agreement upon ways of improving economic performance, competitive power and efficience [sic] — in other words to increase the rate of sound growth.[6]

This brief was to remain unaltered. The accent was therefore on growth, but whether this was to be achieved through more competition or more planning was not clearly spelled out. This ambiguity was the outcome of an internal contradiction in the new style of planning. If *dirigisme* were unacceptable as a way of stimulating more rapid growth, the only alternative was to fall back on the traditional 'liberal' weapons of enhancing competition and vigorous action to combat restrictive practices. Although point (c) was left ambiguous, in the event preference was given to planning through *concertation*. That at least was the conclusion the Council itself drew, for at its next meeting it agreed that its first main task would be to prepare a report 'studying the implications of an annual average growth rate of 4% for the period 1961–1967, or nearly 22% over the whole period', and gave the Office two assignments. It was to discuss with a cross-section of industries in both the public and private sectors the consequences for them of such a growth rate and it was also to study the general implications of more rapid growth for the main elements in the economy — manpower, savings, investment, exports, the balance of payments and so on. Thus, although there is much that might be said about the method of inquiry chosen, it was clear the Council had embarked on planning — or, to be precise, that it was engaged in the first, preparatory phase of planning. For neither the Office nor the Council was competent to embark on the second phase of implementing a plan; that was the business of ministers and the departments of state, as well as of public and private industry. So the measure of Neddy's success would be the extent to which it could influence those who actually took the economic decisions.

Neddy in Relation to Political and Economic Institutions

The New Organisation of the Treasury: November 1962

Since before the war the only major changes at the Treasury had been the administrative reform of 1956. But this was only a very tentative first step. It was not until November 1962 that, following the Plowden Report, reorganisation was carried through to its logical conclusion.

The Treasury was divided into two 'sides'. The Pay and Management side dealt with wages and salaries in the public services, recruitment, promotion, civil service manpower policies and the general organisation of Whitehall. In France and a number of other countries in Western Europe these functions are assigned to a separate department, often attached to the prime minister's office. (And indeed, in 1968 the Pay and Management side was hived off to become the Civil Service Department.) The responsibilities of the Finance and Economic side roughly corresponded to those of the Ministry of Finance in most other countries.

Up to 1956 there had been a single permanent secretary, as in other departments. But on the retirement of Sir Edward Bridges (later Lord Bridges) the permanent secretary's job was split in two. One joint permanent secretary became head of the Home Civil Service and secretary to the cabinet, while the other was put in charge of the Finance and Economic side.[7]

In 1962 reorganisation disentangled the three separate jobs of head of the civil service, head of the Finance and Economic side of the Treasury and secretary to the cabinet, assigning them to different people. The three branches thereafter worked on a much more autonomous basis. After reorganisation the organisation of the Treasury was as shown in figure 4.1. (It was slightly modified in October 1964 but then remained substantially unchanged until 1970.)

Neddy was chiefly involved with the Finance and Economic side, which was divided into three groups:

1. The Finance group had three divisions with a total of twelve sections. Its chief concern was the defence of the pound sterling. For that reason it was the most conservative influence in the Treasury. Its own traditionalist outlook was bolstered by its close relations with the Bank of England – which was the main channel by which the views of the City reached Whitehall and Westminster, where they were very influential. This group had the unenviable task of acting as the main link between the chancellor and the Bank.

2. Though only having two divisions with five sections, the Public Sector group had the largest staff of the three groups and could be considered the central group in the Treasury. 'Public sector' is to be understood in its widest sense, for the group had responsibility for the Treasury's oldest and most central role of controlling public expenditure. Not surprisingly, it often seemed very

Figure 4.1. The Treasury in 1962

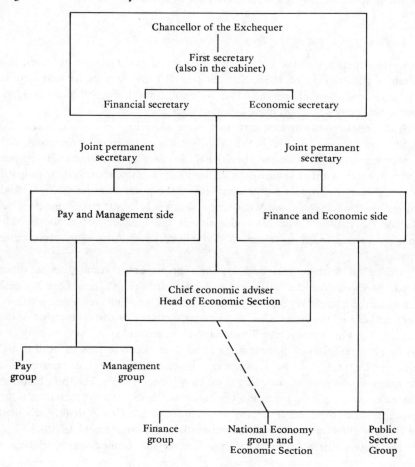

traditional, and it had the reputation of keeping a tight hold on the public purse strings. The Plowden Committee expressed the hope that it would develop a greater interest in good management generally rather than simply in economising. One section of this group became responsible for preparing the annual five-year forward surveys of public expenditure recommended by Plowden. It also kept Neddy informed of forecasts of public expenditure.

3. On the whole, though, Neddy was more involved with the National Economy group, the smallest and newest of the three, which was a product of the 1962 reform. It was responsible for the co-ordination of national economic policy, working in conjunction with the Economic Section (which to all intents and purposes formed an integral part of the group) and the Central Statistical Office, which supplied primary statistical data required by the other two. The Economic Section, under the government's chief economic adviser, who was at

this time Professor Cairncross, had around a dozen economists, most of them on contracts of four or five years. Its main function, which it had had for some time, was the preparation of studies of the main problems in managing the economy. It was particularly concerned with monitoring the impact of public expenditure and taxation, and consequently it was constantly consulted by the other two groups.

The National Economy group was headed by a third secretary (the other two groups being in charge of second secretaries), and had only two sections. The first section, under the assistant director of the Economic Section, assisted by a senior economic adviser, was staffed largely by professional economists. Its main task was the preparation of short- and long-term forecasts.[8] It also drafted reports for OECD and NATO. Its short-term forecasts were intended to keep the chancellor and his colleagues fully informed about trends in the economy. Its work on long-term forecasts brought it into close contact with Neddy's Economic Division. The second section, under a deputy secretary and an assistant secretary, was staffed largely by administrators. It was responsible for co-ordinating matters relating to economic growth and for relations between the Treasury and NEDC. It also had responsibility within the Treasury for measures to control monopolies and restrictive practices, the prices and incomes policy and manpower questions.

According to Lord Bridges, the 1962 reorganisation brought the structure of the Treasury more into line with the responsibilities it was actually exercising.[9] But he argued that it would be naive to conclude that because the old structure was rather less coherent a number of functions were not carried out at all. However, he agreed that the reform was beneficial if only because it led to the setting up of the second section of the National Economy group. This meant that there was now a considerably greater emphasis on the co-ordination of economic policy than there had been previously — and the setting up of Neddy had made this even more essential than in the past. This section was later to form the nucleus of Labour's Department of Economic Affairs.

The reorganisation raised the question whether administrative changes alone were sufficient to change the role of the Treasury; whether or not the real need was for fresh thinking by Treasury officials, and in particular for a rethinking of priorities. Relations between Neddy and the Treasury over the next two years were to shed much light on these problems.

Neddy and the Treasury

During the discussion preceding the birth of Neddy, many people in the Treasury were highly sceptical about planning; others were resigned to accepting it as the only way of securing union agreement to an incomes policy. But there was general agreement that the Council must be part of the Treasury itself. Thus the outcome of the battle on this point was unquestionably a defeat for the Treasury mandarins.[10]

In Neddy's early days its independence was constantly underlined.[11] Some observers even went so far as to see Neddy as a rival to the Treasury itself, a competing source of information and ideas for the chancellor, the cabinet, and even the general public.[12] Rightly or wrongly, the Treasury was considered as a stronghold of conservatism and caution which was happier as watchdog of the public purse at home and guardian of the pound abroad than acting as the spearhead of modernisation. Consequently Neddy must take completely the opposite tack to counter Treasury influence. Michael Shanks, who for several years had been campaigning for modernisation, argued that:

> One of Neddy's main functions must be . . . to provide a rival source of expertise and policy-making on economic matters to the Treasury; to put the case for growth as the mainspring of economic policy in season and out . . . . By the creation of Neddy, the government has introduced an element of conflict into the central decision-making mechanism of economic policy and it is important that this conflict should not be too unequal.[13]

Brittan argued that:

> The great gap in Britain during much of the postwar period was an institution that would promote the claims of growth as against those of sterling, or as against those of a quiet life for existing producers. The real significance of Neddy was that it was a potential group for growth . . . . This, rather than detailed planning of individual industries, is its ultimate justification.[14]

Yet it was surely the height of optimism to expect the confrontation of Neddy's proposals with the policy the Treasury was actually pursuing to either illuminate or even accelerate the growth of the economy. Moreover, Neddy's autonomy was not an unmixed blessing. For if its relations with the Treasury were bad it might be reduced to impotence, while if they were too close autonomy would be purely theoretical. Also Neddy would be dependent on the economic departments, particularly the Treasury and the Board of Trade, for its statistical data. In principle it had right of access to all information available to the government; nevertheless there was a risk that it would only get this information at a price[15] — at the very least it would not be completely free to publish it. So if Neddy was to be something more than an advisory committee supported by a state-aided research institute, it was absolutely vital for it to gain the support of the chancellor. While the few successes obtained early in its existence doubtless owed a lot to the energy and determination of the director-general and his economic director, what was really conclusive was the readiness of the chancellor to adapt his short-term management of the economy to some extent to fit the medium-term policies advocated by Neddy.

Neddy, the Treasury and the Chancellor

One of the first tasks the Council assigned itself was to prepare a medium-term economic plan. At its second meeting in May 1962 it took as a working hypothesis a growth rate of 4 per cent — 'a reasonably ambitious figure likely to bring out problems that have to be solved if faster growth is to be achieved'.[16] At this time Mr Lloyd was still chancellor – though not for long. (He was abruptly replaced by Mr Reginald Maudling in July.) His last important act at the Treasury was the April budget – dubbed by Brittan 'the unfortunate budget'. The chancellor's advisers had warned him of the danger of over-heating in the economy when in fact the cycle had already begun to turn downward. The result was a drab, cautious budget which, on top of the curbs of demand previously introduced in July 1961, actually had a deflationary impact. But at that time Neddy had held only one meeting, and whatever else Lloyd can be criticised for, it cannot reasonably be for failing to take Neddy's views into account.

His successor, Maudling, was no great friend of Neddy. In cabinet he had opposed it, fearing that Neddy would encroach on the prerogatives of the Board of Trade (of which he was then president). However, Neddy's thinking about growth was very much in harmony with his own – though the Treasury thought them unduly ambitious. The decision to opt for 4 per cent was to show just how far Neddy's influence depended on getting the chancellor on its side.

Why 4 per cent? (Initially this was simply a figure plucked out of the air and advanced as a working hypothesis in the industrial inquiry undertaken by NEDO, but it was generally taken to be an official target well before it was formally adopted.) It was not without economic justification. There was ample statistical evidence that the productive capacity of British industry was increasing by an average of 3 per cent per year. Allowing for some unused capacity and improvements in productivity, Neddy concluded that it was reasonable to assume an annual average growth rate of 4 per cent – though one gets the impression that even if it had been impracticable this figure might have been chosen anyway for a mixture of internal and external political consider- ations. Compared with what was being achieved elsewhere in Europe the figure was modest enough. After all, on taking office the Kennedy administration had talked in terms of a target of 50 per cent over ten years for the West as a whole, and this worked out at just about 4 per cent compound. Consequently, although in economic terms the target may have been a trifle ambitious, politically it was the minimum acceptable if the government was not to give the impression that, here again, it was resigned to Britain's continued economic decline.

The new chancellor was quick to grasp the significance of the choice he had to make, and he was not the man to lose any sleep over arguments based on 'statistical theology' – to employ Brittan's phrase – that were being deployed by the two sides.[17] Thus, well before Neddy officially adopted its plan with the magic figure of 4 per cent, the chancellor had begun referring to it as a target in his speeches.[18] So the eventual adoption of 4 per cent owed less to collaboration between the two centres responsible for economic policy than to the fact that the chancellor had in large measure accepted NEDC's optimistic proposals for essentially political reasons.

This outcome to the debate over the growth rate was in fact Neddy's greatest victory. It is a clear indication of the role Neddy played in the period up to 1964. It emerged as a formidable rival to the Treasury — always providing it had the chancellor on its side. In other words, thanks to NEDC the chancellor increased his ability to command events. On the one hand he could use contrary advice from Neddy to challenge what his own civil servants were telling him, or policies urged on him by other ministers. On the other hand, he could easily ignore Neddy's advice when it was inconvenient or unacceptable — in which case Neddy's influence could be almost nil. The advent of NEDC probably strengthened the chancellor's hand in dealing with the Treasury. It remained to be seen whether this was also true of his relations with his cabinet colleagues.

Neddy, the Chancellor and the Cabinet

In theory there were two stages between NEDC's deliberations and a cabinet decision. Firstly, the Council had to agree on a particular line, on the basis of a report prepared by the Office. Then, subsequently, the chancellor might if he wished put all or part of its report before the cabinet. Obviously the prime minister would not be prepared to allow matters of such importance as the level of demand, the balance of payments and the working out of an incomes policy to be settled by the chancellor and NEDC alone without reference to Parliament, the cabinet or himself. Consequently, NEDC simply became yet another stage in the decision-making process. The readiness of the government to accept mid-term commitments was thus wholly a question of how far the chancellor and the cabinet were willing to join wholeheartedly in an *économie concertée*.

Initially, as we have seen, there was such a desire, at least on the chancellor's part. Moreover, in 1963 the chancellor went out of his way a number of times to defend his short-term measures in terms of the need to keep to the medium-term plan drawn up by NEDC. The most striking example of this was in his 1963 budget speech. This was an avowedly expansionist budget which cut taxation by something of the order of £250 million. According to Maudling, 'The purpose of the budget . . . is to do the government's part in achieving the rate of growth . . . which we have already accepted in the NEDC.'[19] He went on to indicate that the government was hoping to limit wage increases to between 3½ and 4 per cent, which was fully in line with Neddy's targets. Maudling's attitude was interesting as it showed that he and the government considered themselves bound by their acceptance of the aims set out by NEDC. As Joan Mitchell notes, 'commitment in these terms apparently established NEDC in influence if not in power. NEDC's calculations and projections were actually accepted as the framework for fiscal policy'.[20] To crown it all, at the end of the year the government published its first five-year investment programme for the public sector (it ran from the 1963–4 budget year to 1967–8), and this foresaw a growth in public expenditure that was in keeping with a growth rate of 4 per cent.

So 1963 was a good year for Neddy. At the beginning of the year its plan had been accepted by the government, and on several occasions the chancellor had treated it as authoritative. But this state of affairs did not last long. In the following year there was a widening gap between Mr Maudling and NEDC. There were several reasons for this. In 1963 it had been very much in Maudling's interest to be on good terms with Neddy, particularly with its trade union members, since he was hoping to win their support for the incomes policy he hoped to introduce. The 1963 budget was in fact well received by the TUC's Economic Committee. Also, in the stop—go cycle, 1963 came after a deflationary year and a rather sombre one, and it was time again for a spell of optimism and expansion. During this 'go' phase it was relatively easy for the chancellor to give the impression that he was conscientiously following NEDC's recommendations. Unfortunately, by the end of 1963 there were fresh signs of overheating, with GNP rising at an annual rate of 7 per cent. This meant that the brakes would have to be applied again. Moreover NEDC had proved incapable of agreeing on incomes policy, and the chancellor no longer had the same need to take the feelings of NEDC and its union members quite so fully into account. But the 1964 budget was only mildly deflationary (increasing taxation by around £100 million), because the chancellor had sufficient nous to realise that the boom in production was beginning to peter out of its own accord. But there was a significant change in his general attitude to Neddy. During the debate on the 1964 Finance Bill he defined the relationship between the government and NEDC in much more restrictive terms than his actions over the previous year had implied: 'It would be wrong for me, as Chancellor, to try to exercise a veto over consideration by NEDC of any matter . . . . It is well understood that neither the government, nor the unions, nor the employers, are bound by every word in a report made by the Council, unless they specifically say so. Otherwise NEDC would make no progress.'[21]

Admittedly, this was said in the rather special context of a reply to an opposition motion on the possibility of a wealth tax, which NEDC had endorsed in its first report. This partly explains why Maudling took such a negative line. Moreover, though Maudling was still at the Treasury, Mr Macmillan had by now been succeeded by Sir Alec Douglas-Home, who may well not have shared Macmillan's enthusiasm for a close relationship between Neddy and the cabinet. At all events, the change in Maudling's attitude is hard to explain except in terms of the political context.

On reflection, this was not a surprising development. Relations between NEDC and the government had never been spelled out clearly. Neddy was the product of an agreement between the chancellor and the prime minister in which the cabinet had little or no part. It was not — and is not — a statutory body. So it was all too easy for the government to adopt Neddy's recommendations when they suited its purpose and to ignore them when they did not. The chancellor was the only sure line of communication between Neddy and the cabinet. Not surprisingly, therefore, apart from the chancellor, even ministers like the president of the Board of Trade and the minister of labour who attended meetings of the Council were not disposed to attach a great deal of importance to its recommendations. In the end Neddy's autonomy and the rather unconventional way in which it was set up rebounded against it. This is why, well before the October 1964 transition to Labour rule, many observers, not all of whom were on the Labour side, felt the time had come to strengthen the ties between the planners and the Whitehall machine.

Neddy and Industry

Neddy had a free hand in developing its contacts with industry. These took a variety of forms, ranging from occasional reports on specific industries and problems to permanent links like the development committees.

On being instructed by the Council to prepare a development plan, NEDO decided to consult a number of industries on the advisability of taking a 4 per cent growth rate as a working hypothesis. But speed was essential. There could be no question of setting up modernisation committees along the lines of the French Plan, because it would have taken too long to set them up, and it would have been many months before they would have been able to make any recommendations. Consequently, NEDO limited itself to an 'industrial inquiry' involving seventeen industries. Unquestionably this involved putting the cart before the horse. Their haste, which was hardly conducive to scientific accuracy, was justified by the Council's determination to deliver its report as rapidly as possible. All the same, it was unfortunate that this first stage in preparing the plan was carried out with fewer safeguards and consultations than were really needed.

The inquiry was conducted during the summer of 1962. It was directed to seventeen industries covering 'nearly half of industrial production, something approaching two-fifths of visible exports and nearly half of total expenditure on fixed investment other than in dwellings'.[22] It in fact covered agriculture (in relation to fuel requirements), coal, petroleum, electricity, gas, chocolate and sugar confectionery, chemicals, iron and steel, machine tools, heavy electrical engineering, electronics, motor vehicles, wool textiles, paper and board, construction, the post office and distribution. Though the list included one public service and several nationalised industries, it related mostly to the private sector.

Because of the need for speed, NEDO proceeded very much by rule of thumb and worked through existing machinery, which for the most part meant the trade associations: 'In general, the main discussions have been with trade associations, supplemented where practicable with help from individual companies, trade unions, government departments directly concerned, and individuals with special knowledge of particular industries.'[23] NEDO was concerned, firstly, to discover what figures were available about existing plans for each industry, and what the outcome of these plans was expected to be; the implications for each industry of a growth rate of 4 per cent between 1961 and

1966 and, finally, any special problems that were foreseen and suggestions for resolving these. Replies were to be based on a number of assumptions:

1. that the development of the remainder of the economy would be fully compatible with achieving 4 per cent growth;

2. that the estimates would refer to particular industries without any attempt to take into account the impact on the supply of capital goods, raw materials and manpower across the economy as a whole of 4 per cent growth;

3. that there would be no significant variation in the terms of trade between primary producers and industrialised countries;

4. that the rate of industrial expansion in the rest of the world would be stable at around the level of recent years;

5. that Britain would join the Common Market about halfway through the period.[24]

On the basis of the replies it received, NEDO calculated that the industries consulted could achieve a growth rate of 4.8 per cent for 1961–6 (as compared with 3 per cent in the preceding five years), with an increase of only 0.7 per cent in the labour force — equivalent to an increase in productivity of 4.1 per cent. Consequently, since the assumption for the economy as a whole was below this, the growth of the rest of industry was put at the lower level of 3.5 per cent with an increase of 0.9 per cent in manpower, giving an improvement of 2.6 per cent in productivity. The Treasury considered these estimates of the likely improvement in productivity unduly optimistic.

This approach was open to error because there is no limit to the manpower and capital a given industry can command to reach a particular target, once one ignores the fact that it will be in competition with the rest of the economy for these scarce resources.[25] Nevertheless, the inquiry was an advance on the way in which British economic policy-making had been conducted up to then. Joan Mitchell notes:

> The industrial inquiries were, at any rate in principle, more systematic than the piecemeal collection of information through industrial divisions of government departments in the postwar period. The outline of the economy at the end of the plan, for all its defects, was more firmly based on a reasonable analysis of past information, current trends and future possibilities of structure than previous attempts.[26]

Its first task completed, NEDC embarked on giving a more permanent form to its links with industry. In December 1963 the Council announced its intention of setting up development committees for a number of industries. The role of these committees was — and still is — defined as follows:

. . . each Committee will:

1. Examine the economic performance and plans of the industry, and assess from time to time the industry's progress in relation to the national growth objectives, and provide information and forecasts to the Council on these matters;

2. Consider ways of improving the industry's economic performance, competitive power and efficiency and formulate reports and recommendations of these matters as appropriate.[27]

Like NEDC itself, the development committees had a tripartite structure, though their membership was not as strictly balanced as the Council's; the employers were over-represented and the government under-represented. For instance, the Machine Tools Committee, which was set up in April 1964, had eight representatives from management (including the chairman), four from the unions, two civil servants, an independent expert and a member of the Office. The over-representation of the employers was due to the fact that the work of the committees was mainly technical and only the management side was in a position to supply the necessary expertise. Moreover, as with NEDC itself, the main purpose of the committees was to provide a forum where representatives of the industry could discuss their problems across the table in the presence of government and NEDC representatives. Basically the committees were more like Cripps's development councils of 1947 than the modernisation committees of the French Plan. Civil servants also had a much more modest place than the officials of the Commissariat-Général au Plan. The latter were expected to steer their committees in the direction desired by the Commissariat, while the staff of NEDO were, on the contrary, expected to be strictly neutral, acting essentially as secretaries and honest brokers.

The development committees were welcomed by both employers and unions. This represented a marked change in employers' attitudes from 1947; faith in free enterprise no longer burned quite as brightly, while it was felt there was little to fear in the way of backdoor nationalisation from a Conservative government. The TUC was glad to be entering more fully into the process of *concertation*. By the close of 1964 eight development committees had been set up,[28] but as yet it was too early to assess how important a role they were likely to play.[29]

CHAPTER 5

The Conservative Record

Arising from its preparation of the development plan between May 1962 and January 1963, NEDC published three reports. The first was modestly entitled *Growth of the United Kingdom Economy to 1966.*[1] After outlining how Neddy had conducted the industrial inquiry, a second section, headed 'Economic Implications of a 4% Growth Rate', presented the results of the inquiry and concluded that 'the achievement of an average growth rate of 4% between 1961 and 1966 should not prove impossible'.[2] Apart from the overall figure of 4 per cent for growth, which had been widely publicised well before the report actually appeared, it suggested that personal consumption and government expenditure would both increase by 3.5 per cent, investment by 5.3 per cent, exports by 5.0 per cent, but imports by only 4.0 per cent.

Curiously, although the report called for the rate of growth to be almost doubled, it gave the impression that this could be achieved at the cost of little additional effort. Admittedly NEDC later published another report which considered the problems of achieving growth in much greater detail. Nevertheless, there seemed far too great a readiness to skate rapidly over awkward problems and painful choices. This was only too likely to store up trouble for later. One important example will suffice to illustrate this tendency. Within its overall assumption of 4 per cent growth, the paper estimated that personal consumption would rise at an annual rate of 3.5 per cent, which implied a rise of 2.9 per cent per head compared with 2.1 per cent in the recent past. Yet in the past personal consumption had consistently risen a trifle more rapidly than GDP; now Neddy's projections were clearly implying that henceforth it would fall *behind* the increase in GDP. If this did in fact happen it would mean a major change in the share of personal incomes going to consumption and saving – and the early introduction of an incomes policy. But the report carefully refrained from spelling this out because at the time trade unionists were not prepared to contemplate any infringement of free collective bargaining.

The targets proposed for overseas trade also looked a little rash, and NEDC admitted they would be hard to achieve. The plan provided for imports to rise exactly in line with GDP, by 4 per cent per year, though in the past they had always risen by more than GDP. There was similar optimism over exports. They had been rising by an average of 3 per cent per year; the plan forecast an increase of 5 per cent. Admittedly, as has already been noted, NEDC was counting on British entry into the Common Market about halfway through the period. It expected that this would give Britain a 'Salutary shock',[3] which would speed up economic modernisation and lead to Britain becoming more competitive in international markets thus giving rise to higher exports and fewer imports. But it was extremely optimistic to expect changes of such magnitude in so short a time. In any case the assumption was shattered the following year by the breakdown in negotiations with the Six, and the targets for overseas trade had to be revised. Thus, while the paper was full of laudable intentions, translating them into reality was likely to be quite another matter.

With its next report on *Conditions Favourable to Faster Growth*,[4] NEDC made a start on the second of its three main tasks, 'to consider . . . what are the obstacles to quicker growth'. This also gave it the opportunity to suggest how the growth rate it proposed in its previous report might be achieved. Unfortunately, the remedies it suggested were all extremely orthodox, and had been aired on many past occasions – without being adopted.[5] They included a number of well-meaning but ineffectual platitudes along such lines as 'Success in achieving a higher rate of growth will depend, to a large extent, on the way in which government, management and the unions carry out their respective functions and on a new spirit of cooperation between them to make a reality of the agreed common objective.'[6] Pious exhortations of this kind had become all too familiar since the time of Cripps. However, there was more substance in the report's emphasis on the pre-conditions for growth and modernisation: development of science and education, which should become more relevant to the needs of industry; better vocational training; and more technological research – and in this it heralded the themes on which Mr Wilson was to base his campaign in the 1964 election.

The third paper, published at the beginning of 1964, was essentially a report on the condition of the economy a year after the launching of the plan.[7] The Council remained resolutely optimistic. However, it thought some figures needed revising; the average annual increase in personal consumption was raised from 3.5 to 3.6 per cent, and in investment from 5.2 to 5.3 per cent. More important, the import target was raised from 4 to 4.7 per cent, which amounted to an admission that the government would be unable to keep imports down to the level suggested earlier, particularly in the light of the breakdown in negotiations with the Six. Moreover, the report did not dismiss the possibility of a renewed overseas trade deficit, though it seems not to have allowed fully for either its imminence or its size.

These three reports, all of which were primarily concerned with problems of growth, constitute NEDC's contribution to planning.[8] Thus NEDC did what it had been asked to do, in a way that did not disappoint those in economic and financial circles who had been watching its first efforts with sympathy.

The reception the announcement of a 4 per cent growth target received was particularly striking. Initially it had been put forward simply as a working assumption, but it had been met with such enthusiasm that the government had almost no alternative but to make it official. For instance, after the Council's second meeting *The Economist* wrote, 'It [the Council] launched itself down the slipway this week in precisely the form which *The Economist* has long advocated .... [It will] examine the implications of, and get statistical projections for, achieving an entirely new and specific objective for British economic policy.'[9] Earlier Sam Brittan had spoken of 'a first-class start'.[10] The main reason for this enthusiasm was the hope of breaking out of the stop–go cycle. Even those like Professor Alan Day, who considered the 4 per cent target a 'myth',[11] thought it might not be entirely useless, since the psychological benefits might be considerable. Consequently the discomforture of Neddy's supporters was to be all the greater when the first plan was a relative failure. And their dismay was intensified by the inability of the government and the two sides of industry to reach agreement on an incomes policy.

First Steps Towards an Incomes Policy

The government did not really wake up to the danger of allowing wages to rise twice as rapidly as production until about 1957. Then the realisation was a major factor in the setting up of the Council on Prices, Productivity and Incomes, which was intended to keep the government fully informed of developments on all three fronts. But its 'three wise men' were confined to supplying information and advice; there was nothing they could do to get a prices and incomes policy under way.

The idea of a policy for controlling prices and incomes really dates from the 'pay pause' of July 1961, though the government's attention had been drawn to the need for energetic action rather earlier, in a memorandum for OEEC, which had shown that, while there was undoubtedly a problem of demand inflation, cost inflation – which was due mainly to wage increases – could not be ignored.[12] Also, the Bank of England was repeatedly warning that the outcome of current wage negotiations at the beginning of 1961 might well lead to the pound being overvalued, particularly since already in the second half of 1960 wages were running 6.5 per cent above the level of a year earlier. In those days nothing was more calculated to strike dread in a prime minister's heart than the prospect of devaluation. Mr Macmillan was no exception, particularly since even then a devaluation of the pound was likely to cause difficulties for the Americans, because the dollar would then find itself in the front line against the international speculators. And a close relationship with the United States was one of the main pillars of Macmillan's foreign policy. Consequently, the prime minister was doubly anxious to avoid devaluation.[13]

Nevertheless the 1961 budget seemed singularly unconcerned with such problems. Mr Lloyd took the opportunity to raise the threshold of surtax from £2,000 to £5,000. While this was in theory perfectly justifiable, as a way of providing people in the upper income brackets with an incentive to pioneer and work harder, a worse moment could scarcely have been chosen. It came just three months before the introduction of the 'pay pause', and the two measures taken together inevitably gave the impression that the Conservatives were pursuing a 'class policy'. Certainly Labour lost no time in portraying the situation in those terms, though in fact the chancellor had been inept rather than deliberately provocative. But in politics appearances can often count as much as true intentions. It is true that the chancellor also announced the introduction of a new tax on speculative capital gains, but this would only apply from his next budget, and at the time it was impossible to tell what it would amount to At all events, the unions denounced his decisions as unfair and discriminatory. The TUC took the 'pay pause' particularly badly because it had not even been informed, much less consulted. While it was difficult for the chancellor to take them fully into his confidence because of the secrecy that must inevitably surround his fiscal and monetary proposals until they had been officially announced in Parliament, there was nothing to prevent him from proceeding in two stages. The unions' anger, which was a major factor in the delay in securing their agreement to NEDC, was heightened by the rigidity with which the freeze was enforced. This ill-feeling annoyed the prime minister, and was one of the reasons for the way he sacked Mr Lloyd the following July. Despite its disastrous psychological effect, the pause did succeed in slowing slightly the rate of wage increases; there was only one clear breach of it – in the settlement with the electricity workers in November 1961. But its real success lay in focusing attention on the need for a consistent incomes policy. When the pause ended, in April 1962, after testing the ground the Treasury began exploratory talks with the TUC in the hope of persuading it to join in an agreed policy for wages. But these various comings and goings were brought to an abrupt halt by the departure of Mr Lloyd and the establishment of the National Incomes Commission.

In February 1962 the Treasury published a White Paper that represented its first public attempt to outline a possible incomes policy.[14] It was in fact the final version of a draft that had been going the rounds of Whitehall for almost five years. Not surprisingly, the successive drafts through which it had passed in the search for an agreed compromise had improved neither the quality of its prose nor the clarity of its proposals. However, the White Paper announced the introduction of an annual 'guiding light' for wage increases. This was new; it was intended to provide guidance for arbitration tribunals. The 'guiding light' norm for 1962 was 2.5 per cent. The White Paper set out more clearly than before the view that wage increases must be related to increases in productivity and the general state of the economy.

But the White Paper was not enough to satisfy the impatient Macmillan. In his view the Treasury had been both hesitant and inept. He wanted rapid action to establish an arbitration tribunal that could lay down priorities for wage increases, according to the type of income and the specific circumstances of each claim. The cabinet was indecisive, while Selwyn Lloyd, who was preoccupied with trying to gain the agreement of the TUC, was also hesitant. So Macmillan himself summoned a meeting of senior civil servants, including the permanent secretary at the Ministry of Labour, Sir Laurence Helsby, who helped him to draw up the proposal for a National Incomes Commission (NIC).[15] The creation of the Commission was announced at the time of Mr Lloyd's replacement by Mr Maudling in July 1962. But it was only in November that final details were published of its functions and membership. Since the TUC and the employers had both refused to have any part in it, the Commission was made up entirely of independent members.[16] It had the powers of a royal commission. Matters could be referred to it by the government itself or by employers or unions. The government could ask it to consider wage settlements that appeared to be unduly inflationary or seek its views on claims that were currently being negotiated; employers and unions could come before the Commission only if they had been unable to reach agreement. NIC was barred from dealing with disputes in the nationalised industries or from acting where there was existing arbitration machinery. It sat in public, like a court, and had the power to compel the attendance of witnesses. But its judgements did not have the force of law; they were simply recommendations to the government. The main criterion NIC was required to consider was the relationship between higher wages or incomes and improvements in productivity, but it was also enjoined to give particular attention to the problem of the lower paid and to bear in mind the special needs of particular industries. To try and avoid the impression that it was concerned only with wages, the government announced that it would deal with any excessive increases in dividends or incomes other than those arising from wages or salaries by means of higher taxation. While the Commission did its best in its various reports to give every appearance of fairness, its influence was in fact minimal. It was eventually abolished early in 1965 by the new Labour government.

This was largely due to the fact that it was boycotted by the unions. The general secretary of the TUC, George Woodcock, took the establishing of NIC as a personal insult, since during the talks that preceded the setting up of NEDC Selwyn Lloyd had promised him he would take no action about incomes policy without the agreement of the unions. There had in fact been discussions during the spring and summer but these had been inconclusive. The TUC also thought NIC to be too exclusively concerned with holding back wages; in its view similar machinery for controlling prices should have been introduced at the same time. The unions remained unwaveringly hostile to NIC to the very end. Macmillan's unilateral action had clearly had unfortunate effects. It would have been better to wait for NEDC to take up the problem and then to try to find a solution. This had probably been Selwyn Lloyd's view. But also, as events were to show later, it was easier for Labour than for the Conservatives to secure at least the appearance of concessions from the unions in this area.

Within a few months of the setting up of NIC it was clear that, politically at least, it was a failure. The government was therefore forced to cast about for other ways of securing the co-operation of both sides of industry in the preparation of an incomes policy. This could only be done through Neddy. This was why Mr Maudling paid such close attention to the Council throughout 1963. As noted earlier, his interest was at its height around the time of his April budget, which raised the 'norm' for wage increases from 2.5 per cent for 1962 to between 3 and 3.5 per cent — a figure that was in line with the plan's estimate of 3.5 per cent for increases in personal disposable incomes. Consequently the budget was well received by the TUC. This was accordingly an opportune moment to persuade NEDC to involve itself in controlling incomes. In fact the Council had already indicated that it thought the issue fell within its brief. In *Conditions Favourable to Faster Growth* it had stated:

> Success in achieving a higher rate of growth will depend, to a large extent, on the way in which government, management and unions carry out their respective functions and on a new spirit of cooperation between them to make a reality of the agreed common objective. In the last resort the government has the responsibility for ensuring that limited sectional interests do not frustrate the achievement of an agreed growth objective.[17]

This seemed a hopeful augury. But after several long discussions NEDC was in the end unable to reach agreement on an incomes policy, even though, towards the end of the year, there were growing signs of overheating in the economy. Despite all the chancellor's efforts, the representatives of unions and employers were unwilling to endorse a call for wage settlements to be kept within the norm for 1964. This failure was eloquent evidence of the hostility of both sides to even the slightest encroachment on their freedom in such crucial areas as wage agreements and the fixing of dividends.[18] But, more generally, it also confirmed the extent of the erosion in the authority of the Conservative government after twelve years in office.

Neddy's complete inability to agree on a workable policy for controlling incomes was probably a major factor in the decline in its standing even before the Conservatives left office. Certainly it accounts for the disfavour into which it fell with the chancellor in 1964. In February Mr Maudling remarked in an interview in the *Financial Times* that 'it would be a pity if Neddy came to be regarded as an organisation which produced blueprints of a possible economy but did nothing to make it happen in practice'.[19]

The failure was due to the attitude of the trade unionists on the Council — but they could not go beyond what their members would accept, and they were in a particularly delicate position because they were split. Their disagreements mirrored the divisions within the trade union movement as a whole over what line to take on wages policy: whether to persist with the existing situation, with its anarchic wage negotiations where the outcome was entirely dependent on the bargaining strength of the two sides, and there was little thought for the implications for the economy as a whole, or to accept the principle of a national incomes policy by which there would be a norm for wage increases that would be decided after discussions between the government, the employers and the unions — at the same time insisting on comparable controls over prices and incomes other than wages or salaries. There was a long debate at the 1963 TUC. But Congress was deeply divided and failed to reach any clear decision; in fact it ended by facing both ways by adopting two quite contradictory resolutions. The Left, led by Frank Cousins, was really not prepared to contemplate any form of restraint whatever. The Centre and Right would probably have been prepared to shoulder their responsibilities, as George Woodcock put it, had they not been so opposed to the Conservative government on more general grounds.

The government's clumsy handling of the matter also explains the basic misunderstanding between it and the unions. For Maudling, more for opportunistic than doctrinal reasons, 'incomes policy' was synonymous with 'wages policy', and consequently he thought that all that was needed was to secure the unions' agreement on a norm or a ceiling for wage increases; this explains why he tried so hard to get the unions to subscribe to some sort of declaration of intent. A more resolute government might have deployed other weapons: it might have stepped in to prevent excessively generous wage increases being reflected in prices, made a special attack on monopoly profits, and cut tariffs as a way of forcing industrialists to keep their prices down. Above all, it could have resisted unjustified strikes.[20] But by now the government's authority in Parliament and the country as a whole had eroded too far for it to act with the necessary energy and determination. This was only too obvious from the battle over the abolition of retail price maintenance.[21] The Act opened a large breach in the traditional relationship between suppliers and retailers; previously this had been regulated by the law of contract, with retailers required to sell goods at the price specified in the contract. Mr Heath (who was then president of the Board of Trade)[22] saw the repeal of retail price maintenance as just one aspect of a wider policy of making the economy more competitive, and since it would make it more difficult for manufacturers to pass increased costs on automatically to the public it had an important part to play in tackling the problem of the cost of living. It would never have stirred so much antagonism from the government's own supporters (even a number of ministers made no secret of their dislike for it) had not the imminence of an election and the toll of the party's long years in office made the government particularly vulnerable and its supporters particularly restive. Probably election fever was the main reason why Labour adopted a scornfully non-committal attitude to a Bill of such importance to consumers. Their behaviour certainly did not enhance Labour's reputation as a responsible opposition, and may well have contributed to the way the Bill was watered down during its passage through the Commons.

This parliamentary battle was not the only sign of a tired government. When the employers suggested establishing a watchdog body for prices to investigate and report on controversial price increases, the government should have accepted the proposal on the spot. Instead it havered and wavered, and in the end agreed only after the TUC had rejected the idea and there was no prospect of the decision being reversed. Moreover, anyone who had not actually been told that an official incomes policy was supposed to be in force and that there was a 'norm' for wage settlements would never have guessed.[23] For virtually every settlement in the public sector broke the norm, with very little public reaction from Mr Maudling. And when the engineering employers granted a 5 per cent increase in basic wages, announcing that this would inevitably lead to higher prices, there was no reaction from the government. It was now patently obvious that the government had no intention of fighting for its policies. In more general terms, it showed it was impossible for any government to operate a consistent incomes policy during the run-up to a general election – unless it wished to commit political suicide. This view was to receive eloquent confirmation in the behaviour of the Labour government in 1969–70.

The Economic Record

NEDC set out to achieve three main aims: to speed up the growth of the British economy; to bring about a lasting improvement in the balance of payments situation; and, secondly but no less important from a psychological viewpoint, to avoid any return to the stop–go cycle. The best yardstick of Neddy's achievement is to compare intentions and performance in these three areas.

Neddy's target for the economy as a whole was 4 per cent, and it suggested a number of secondary targets for demand, investment, the balance of payments and so forth which were in keeping with this general aim. Table 5.1 shows that none of these aims was wholly attained by 1966. GDP grew by only 2.9 per cent per annum – or 16 per cent for the period as a whole in place of 22 per cent. GDP per head rose 2.2 per cent per year instead of 3.2 per cent. In 1961 NEDC itself had assessed the 'natural' growth of the economy at 2.7 per cent between

Table 5.1.   NEDC's main growth targets and actual outcome, 1961–6 (Average annual percentage increase)

	NEDC projection	Actual
	(%)	(%)
Gross Domestic Product (GDP)	4.0	2.9
GDP per worker	3.2	2.2
Total fixed investment	5.3	4.4
of which: investment in manufacturing	3.3	0.2
public investment	7.0	6.4
Consumer expenditure	3.5	2.8
Public sector consumption	3.5	2.7
Exports	5.0	3.6
Imports	4.0	3.6

Source: George Polanyi, *Planning in Britain: the Experience of the 1960s* (London, IEA, 1967), p. 58.

1956 and 1961, with GDP per head rising by around 2.2 per cent (between 1952–4 and 1959–61). While this seemed at first glance to represent a slight overall increase, after allowing for the rise in the employed population, GDP per head appeared in fact to have been virtually stationary.

Further consideration of the table shows that the gap between the projections and the outcome was almost uniform with the exception of investment, where the rise of 4.4 per cent (compared with the forecast of 5.3 per cent) was relatively better than the others. NEDC had hoped to push up the share of GDP going to investment. In the event it rose a little, from 17.6 per cent in 1961 to 18.8 per cent in 1969. Here at least the planners might claim a measure of success. However, the improvement was almost entirely due to the public sector; investment by private industry scarcely rose at all. Yet this was precisely the area of the economy where investment would contribute most directly to increased production.

Two lessons can be drawn from this. Firstly, contrary to popular belief, an increase in investment does not automatically lead to an equal increase in output. Next, although the fact that the State almost fully met its commitments in the public sector was a necessary condition for growth, it was not in itself a sufficient condition: it was equally vital to create a climate in which industry would be prepared to invest. Firms would not be likely to make any special effort to meet targets simply because Whitehall considered them 'reasonable' and 'attainable'; they needed the more tangible evidence of higher demand in their own sector of the economy.

Variations in the pace of growth in various industries are probably rather less significant. However, the serious errors in the forecasts for a number of basic industries does merit comment. If the growth of each industry had conformed fully to the overall development of the economy, this would have implied their reaching about 75 per cent of the target (since between 1961 and 1966 GNP rose by only 16 per cent rather than the expected 22 per cent). But only the car industry, which, with a growth of 6.6 rather than 11 per cent, reached 60 per cent of its target, and electricity supply, with 7 instead of 10 per cent (i.e. 70 per cent of the target), came anywhere near this result. (Ironically, electricity's achievement, coupled with the failure of the rest of the economy to expand as rapidly as expected, meant that by the end of the sixties capacity in electricity generating considerably outstripped needs. Over-investment is of course as much a planning failure as under-investment.) Petrol and the paper and board industries grew at the rate predicted by the plan (respectively 7.8 per cent against an estimated 7.5 per cent and 2.5 per cent compared with 2.6 per cent). Steel lagged far behind with an average annual growth of 1.9 instead of 5.5 per cent – which was only about 35 per cent of what had been expected. At the other end of the scale gas grew almost twice as fast as had been forecast (6.8 per cent as against 2.8 per cent). In itself these variations were not particularly serious, for this was, after all, only 'indicative planning'. The French Plan has never yet been able to attain complete uniformity of fulfilment in every industry. However, in France the variations have usually been rather smaller, and 'underfulfilling' and 'overfulfilling' industries have tended to cancel one another out, with the overall result roughly in line with the initial forecast. In the NEDC plan, on the contrary, apart from the special case of gas — where no one foresaw the enormous expansion of natural gas — every projection was in the end over-optimistic. It is not surprising that the growth of the economy as a whole was as unimpressive as in the past. The plan, therefore, did not even succeed in accelerating the 'natural' development of the British economy, much less in significantly altering it.

The results for overseas trade were particularly crucial, since a favourable balance on current account was essential if expansion was to continue. What was important here was that domestic consumption and investment should not rise by more than GDP. But in the event they did, and the vicious circle continued. For, as indicated earlier, the plan assumed a 4 per cent annual rise in imports and 5 per cent in exports (or 22 and 28 per cent respectively for 1961–6). If this could be done, then the pattern of recurrent balance of payments crises would be a thing of the past; the deficit of £77 million on current account for 1961 would become a surplus of £300 million (at 1961 prices) in 1966. But the outcome was very different. Exports and imports both rose by 3.6 per cent per annum. While imports were a little below the level forecast, the great leap forward in exports simply never happened, though there was a slight overall improvement since in the fifties imports had risen on average by 5 per cent each year. Nevertheless, the result was that by 1966 the balance of payments was still ailing, and the trading deficit for the year was £61 million (at 1966 prices) despite some improvement towards the end of the year. Apart from the general sluggishness of growth, the most unhappy aspect was the continuation of the decline in Britain's share of world trade. It had already fallen from 19 to 16 per cent between 1956 and 1961; by 1966 it was down to 13 per cent — though one of the main aims of the NEDC plan had been to halt this decline. From 1964 the weary battle to 'save the pound' had to be fought yet again. It was to be continued by the new Labour government, most notably by the introduction of a temporary surcharge of 15 per cent on manufactured goods, until in July 1966, exactly five years after the Selwyn Lloyd 'stop', there had to be yet another sudden change of course.

The planners had also hoped to maintain a fairly even rate of growth and avoid the stop–go cycle. In the event, the near-stagnation of 1961–2 was followed by two years of rapid expansion. By the end of 1963 production was rising at an annual rate of 7 per cent which, in view of the imbalance between the various regions, meant that there was overheating in the more prosperous areas. This rate was sustained for several months. Nevertheless, the 1964 budget was only mildly deflationary, since Mr Maudling had realised that the economy was beginning to cool down — and after all, it was an election year. By the time the Labour government came to office in October, the currency reserves were running down at such a rate that restrictions were inevitable. The measures adopted by the new administration were flexible enough to slow expansion without stopping it dead; Labour clearly made a determined effort to cope with the immediate crisis without jeopardising the longer-run requirements of the plan, at least until the sudden 'stop' of July 1966. This effort can be seen in the 1961–6 line in figure 5.1(a). In 1965–6 the line continues to rise slightly. The same is true of employment (figure 5.1(b)), which rose, but at by no means as sharp an angle as in the corresponding stage of the 1957–62 cycle. Investments (figure 5.1(c)) grew less rapidly but at least did not decline. The concomitant of this was a smaller improvement in the balance of payments (figure 5.1(d)). Here the situation was clearly more serious than in 1957–62. Indeed, the 1961–6 curve provides a clear indication of the need for devaluation; the slow rise after 1961, which was the result of the Selwyn Lloyd deflation and the pay pause, and even more the inadequate improvement of 1965–6 showed the pound was overvalued.

The striking similarity between the two sets of graph lines shows that, not only was there no fundamental change in the way the economy was developing, but there was not even any significant alteration in it. The reason expansion came to a halt in 1966 was exactly the same as in 1961: the balance of payments had to be righted by cutting back imports because exports had failed to expand as expected. This was the consequence of the refusal to contemplate the only solution capable of restoring the trade balance for a considerable time without at the same time halting the economy in its tracks — devaluation. The restrictions of July 1966, which were hastily decided during the summer recess, bear all too striking a resemblance to Mr Lloyd's 'little budget' of July 1961 not to give the impression that, despite Neddy's expectations, history was repeating itself. The stop–go cycle was by no means dead.[24]

The Record to 1964

At the end of 1964 the failure of planning under the Conservatives could only be a matter of conjecture, since it was as yet too early for the full facts to be known and assessed. Nevertheless, there was already a widespread feeling of disappointment about the new approach to planning. This was probably because the deficiencies in the system were apparent at a very early stage. The criticisms can be summarised under three headings: the NEDC did not do what it had been expected to do; its autonomy had proved a handicap; and it had too little share in the actual execution of the plan.

If the NEDC economists were to work really effectively they needed some form of close, continuing link with industry. Yet the first development committees were not set up until 1964, more than a year after the publication of the plan. Consequently, unlike the modernisation committees associated with the French Plan, they were in no position to serve as a link between the planners

Figure 5.1. Comparison of trends before and after planning

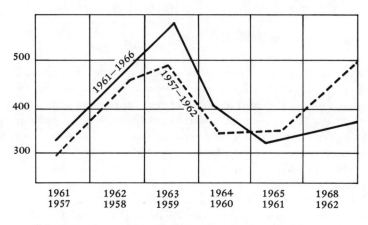

(a) Gross National Product (1958 market prices)

(b) Unemployment (monthly average in thousands)

Source: Polanyi, op. cit.

(£ million)

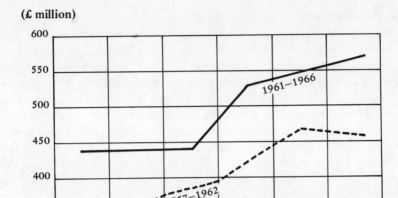

1961	1962	1963	1964	1965—	1966
1957	1958	1959	1960	1961	1962

(c) Investment (gross capital formation at 1958 prices)

(£ million)

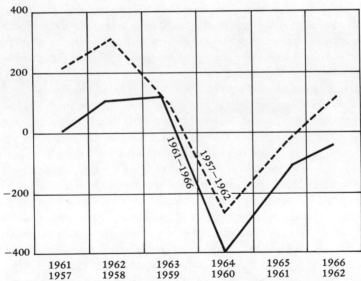

1961	1962	1963	1964	1965	1966
1957	1958	1959	1960	1961	1962

(d) Balance of payments (current account)

and the industries concerned, with the vital role of bringing the rather abstract approach of the experts into constant contact with everyday realities. This was particularly regrettable because the British planners were far more isolated than their French counterparts, and consequently much more dependent on their own sources of information. The explanation of why NEDO acted in the way it did is essentially that it was under pressure from the Council, which wanted to justify its existence as rapidly as possible, and which was in turn under pressure from an impatient government and others concerned with the economy. In comparison with the gradual process by which French Plans come to fruition one can only be disagreeably surprised by the rapidity — under a year — with which the NEDC document was prepared. A striking achievement — but a suspect one. It was evident that the 1962 industrial inquiry, which bore signs of haste and improvisation, could not be taken as seriously as the work of the modernisation committees, but it was called on to play the same role. Again, NEDO was obliged to devote much of its energies to preparing working documents for Council meetings and to the long and ultimately unsuccessful search for agreement on incomes policy. It is hardly surprising that it scarcely embarked on the really crucial task of carrying through a thoroughgoing transformation of the British economy. The need to supply a striking new backdrop for the government's short-term economic policy was allowed to prevail over the planners' preoccupation with long-term development.

Neddy's position outside the conventional machinery of Whitehall was both an asset and a liability. It was an asset in that it had a measure of freedom to express and publish its views, and this allowed it to challenge the Treasury. It was a liability in that it consequently could have no part in the preparation of the short-term measures on which the success of the plan very largely depended. By the end of 1964 there was general agreement that the disadvantages outweighed the advantages.

Observers like Andrew Shonfield, who wanted Britain to follow the French example in the letter as well as the spirit, were disappointed at how little influence NEDO had over the Council. For NEDO behaved more like the head office staff of a private firm than like the Commissariat-Général au Plan. Its prime function was to prepare working documents for the Council, and without prior approval from the Council it could not publish anything or express any view. Also, the NEDO staff acted more as secretaries and intermediaries rather than providing leadership or positive guidance. This must be seen as the product of the characteristic British suspicion of the expert, which was as widespread among civil servants as politicians, and among employers as trade unionists. Both employers and unions had insisted on NEDC having as few independent members — and as large a representation of sectional interests — as possible. Both were equally insistent that NEDO experts must be clearly subordinate to the Council, and according to Shonfield a leading trade unionist one day described NEDO's activity as 'lad's work'. From such a viewpoint planning was less an exact science than 'a bargain between interest groups, that is given a formal shape in terms of national economic policy and occasionally tidied up by the professional staff'.[25]

But in that case, with an autonomous planning body and the role of uncommitted experts reduced to an absolute minimum, surely this would give an excessive degree of power to private interests? This was a danger, and although there was not time for things to develop along these lines, it was real enough. But the Conservatives deliberately ran this risk because they judged it was the only way of gaining the wholehearted co-operation of industry. As Sam Brittan remarked, 'The confidence with which both sides of industry treat NEDC at present is in large part due to the feeling that it is their own organisation and not just a creature of the government.'[26] If planning in a capitalist society is to have any prospect of success, private interests must feel that the plan is their concern, and this means that they must be fully involved in its preparation. But while this is essential for success it is certainly not sufficient to guarantee success, for the problem of implementing the plan has yet to be solved.

Mr Maudling clearly made a great effort in his budgets to consider the requirements of the plan. This was undeniably important. Public investment was almost wholly in conformity with the projections for public expenditure included in the plan. It cannot be reasonably claimed that the government failed to keep its share of the bargain. Its good will was all the more striking because the birth of Neddy was coolly received by a number of ministers, and because it came after French governments had taken considerable liberties with the provisions of their own Plan — especially in the field of public expenditure! However,. this was obviously not enough to guarantee that others would equally play their part. This was an area where NEDC itself had no powers, and the plan itself contained no injunctions to the various economic actors that would promote its implementation. There was only Neddy's second report that offered a series of proposals for stimulating growth, but these took the form of rather general advice and could just as well have been made if there had been no plan. This was not surprising, because the Conservative government's philosophy led it to reject categorically any form of control or compulsion, and to rely on persuasion alone for the execution of the plan. This persuasion was to operate at two levels; nationally the government would persuade the unions and employers' associations; locally the unions and employers' associations were to persuade their members, though it was obvious that such an approach was bound to be uncertain and incomplete. According to Shonfield,

> The NEDC system depends ultimately on moral pressures. Each party offers something which is conditional on certain actions by the others . . . . But the truth is that there is no natural place in the British system, as it has developed to date, for the contractual relationships between the government and the individual private firms covering the objectives of the plan, which have from the beginning been a feature of French planning.[27]

In other words the Conservatives were attempting to plan without increasing the capacity of the State to intervene in the economy: the machinery they established took over the 'indicative' approach of French planning, but not the 'encouragements' that made it work, and by 1964 it had a corporative rather than a governmental air to it. However, looking back after a decade, one can see that the main reason for the relative success of French planning and the failure of British planning lay in the differing views of investment held in the two countries. Apart from the fact that investment consistently represented a higher proportion of GNP in France than in Britain, when French governments ran into economic difficulties their reaction was usually to cut back investment which was not immediately productive, such as school building, hospitals and recreational facilities, and to spare industrial expansion as far as possible. In Britain, in comparison, while governments met their targets for public investment fairly well (at least up to the March 1968 budget), the resort to a deflationary policy almost constantly after 1964 was fatal to industrial investment. While the French approach was a source of repeated bottlenecks (roads and telephones) and political acrimony (hospitals and schools), it did at least avoid sacrificing the Plan's targets for growth, unlike the British solution. In fact, the two responses reflected quite different political aims: where British ministers were simply looking (without any great conviction) for ways of halting the country's decline, successive governments of the Fifth Republic (which in this respect differed relatively little from their Fourth Republic predecessors) were intent on transforming France into a major industrial power for the first time in her history.

In 1964 the people who wished to strengthen planning in Britain favoured two main changes: the partial incorporation of the machinery of planning into the government machine, and a strengthening of the State's powers of economic intervention. Varied though they were, the proposals for reform all tended to strengthen the role of the State. Very few people wanted to see Neddy completely absorbed by the Treasury. Most preferred the establishment of a new ministry with responsibility for planning and medium-term economic policy (while fully recognising the territorial disputes with the Treasury this would entail), with NEDC remaining independent and retaining most of its existing functions.[28] Others, like Brittan, wanted the Treasury to divest itself of jobs that were not directly related to running the economy, such as running the civil service and collecting taxes, because they thought that responsibility for short-term measures and long-term planning should be concentrated in a single ministry — the Treasury — rather than divided between rival departments.

Apart from these structural reforms, some observers were prepared to argue that since there was bound to be an increase in state intervention, it was preferable for this to be in the hands of politicians who genuinely believed in it. Consequently they looked to a Labour victory in the forthcoming elections. This was the line followed, for example, by *The Economist*. In the event it seems to have been the view of most voters too.

PART III

Labour
and Planning
1964–1970

INTRODUCTION

By setting up Neddy, Selwyn Lloyd robbed Labour of one of its longest-running lines of attack on the Conservatives' handling of the economy. Ever since 1951 the party had repeatedly criticised the Conservatives' 'doctrinaire refusal to assume responsibility for planning our natural resources'.[1] The birth of Neddy therefore left Labour at something of a loss, and there were some months of rather embarrassed hesitation before the party took up the theme of the scientific and technological revolution (which was to dominate Mr Wilson's campaign speeches in 1964), all the while making every effort to emphasise that there was all the difference in the world between Mr Lloyd's tinkering and genuine 'socialist planning'. From 1963 Mr Wilson called repeatedly for 'purposive' and 'effective' planning, while George Brown, who was to be given responsibility for planning in the 1964 government, was emphatic during 1963 and 1964 that planning under Labour would 'have to have teeth in it somewhere',[2] and that 'the great thing the next government must achieve is to introduce planning into every area of national life'.[3] Mr Wilson even rashly held out the possibility of an 8 per cent growth rate – double the NEDC target. Not surprisingly, nothing more was heard of this after October 1964. Labour was clearly looking to planning to speed up growth, and it was counting on the fruits of growth to meet all the promises in its election programme, some of which were extremely expensive. It is no exaggeration to say that the entire economic and social strategy of the Labour leadership turned on their success in planning.

The ways in which Labour's methods would differ from those of the Conservatives were also becoming clear. Firstly the planners were to be incorporated fully into the normal machinery of government by means of a separate planning ministry, and secondly the economic departments should have more and better ways of encouraging, and even compelling, implementation of the plan. In their different ways both these changes implied a strengthening of the State's powers of economic intervention.

In assessing these proposals it is preferable to look beyond remarks made in the heat of an election campaign or the run-up to it, to the rather more carefully considered views of men who had a considerable influence on the movement's thinking about such matters – men like Mr Thomas Balogh (now Lord Balogh),[4] who subsequently became an economic adviser to Mr Wilson, and Michael Stewart, the economist.[5] While they disagreed on many points, the general tenor of their argument was very similar, and was to be reflected to a large degree in the reforms that the Labour government subsequently adopted. Balogh was highly critical of NEDC, arguing that its powers were quite inadequate to the task in hand. Stewart was more optimistic, pointing to the finding of NIESR's 1963 industrial inquiry that 17 per cent of firms replying reported that they had been influenced by the target of 4 per cent growth, and that 8 per cent had taken it into account when they were preparing their own production and investment programmes. He remarked that 'without wishing to be needlessly cynical ... this seems an encouragingly high proportion'.[6] Both men argued that, given that Britain would continue to have a mixed economy, the State must have more and stronger powers to intervene in the economy. However, there was no point in blindly aping the French; the administrative and institutional differences between the two countries were too wide for that. All the same, French planning in fact remained the basic model for Labour as it had been for the Conservatives — and after all it was characterised by a particularly varied range of techniques of intervention.

There were four ways of strengthening the plan while retaining its essentially voluntary character: bringing the planners into the regular machinery of government and investing them with some of the authority of government; improving links with industry; a determined search for incentives to secure fuller implementation of the plan; and introduction of a strict prices and incomes policy. Balogh, who was on the whole more *dirigiste* than Stewart, particularly emphasised the last two points. He argued that the strongest 'encouragements' would be provided by the taxation system, but that obviously other methods should be considered, such as controls of investments, imports and profit margins, and even the introduction of a 'sharp negative allowance' to penalise wasteful investment.

These proposals were to provide a fairly accurate preview of the changes Labour was to introduce in the letter and the spirit of British planning — though the State was to prove considerably less interventionist than Balogh at least would have wished.[7]

CHAPTER 6

The Department of Economic Affairs

The first act of the 1964 Labour government was to establish an independent Department of Economic Affairs. It would have been perfectly feasible to put the new ministry under the wing of the Treasury, with the chancellor as its spokesman in the cabinet. But Mr Wilson decided otherwise. Apart from his desire to find an appropriate post for Mr Brown,[1] he wanted to emphasise the importance of the new economic policy. Mr Brown was accordingly made first secretary of state and minister for economic affairs, ranking second to Mr Wilson in the ministerial hierarchy, which in terms of protocol at least placed him slightly above the chancellor, Mr Callaghan. The new ministry was given a wider brief than had been expected: to take general responsibility for economic co-ordination; to prepare a five-year plan, and to work out an industrial policy, a regional policy and an incomes policy.

All this was to be done with a staff that never exceeded six hundred,[2] though of course the DEA had few of the managerial or executive responsibilities that require a large staff. Consequently the department had a considerably lower proportion of its staff in the junior grades than most other Whitehall departments, while its economists, industrial and scientific advisers, statisticians and programmers formed the highest concentration of expertise anywhere in Whitehall.

The main role of the DEA was to co-ordinate the work of the other economic departments, including the Treasury. The setting up of the DEA was a further indication of the government's desire to see that the requirements and priorities of an overall medium-term economic policy were fully taken into account. This had previously been the job of the Treasury, which still retained responsibility for short-term management of the economy. The danger of friction or even outright conflict between the two departments was only too obvious, unless they reached some sort of *modus vivendi* providing for constant close co-operation.

The DEA's Structure and Functions

The DEA's structure was basically functional. That is, its organisation corresponded reasonably closely to the tasks it was called on to perform — which was by no means always true in the older ministries.

The appointment of Mr Brown gave this energetic and highly committed man a role to match his energy and experience. The task of co-ordinating economic policy at cabinet level would call for all his ability as a negotiator and conciliator, and all his skill in public relations. He threw himself into the job with his characteristic blend of uncomplicated ebullience, overbearing enthusiasm and warm-heartedness. He had the support of a powerful ministerial team. Initially there was Mr Crosland, who was appointed jointly as minister of state at the DEA and economic secretary to the Treasury. He would have been well placed to link the two ministries. However, he held the post for only a few weeks, and his successor, Mr Austen Albu, was appointed to the DEA only and not to the Treasury. There was also an under-secretary with special responsibility for regional planning, as well as four PPSs. This was a sizeable ministerial team by the standards of the day, because the DEA had to liaise and co-ordinate so widely with other departments, and it was felt that this was a job for politicians rather than civil servants. The team also included two men who were neither politicians nor permanent civil servants, but who nevertheless had important responsibilities: the director-general, who served both as chief economic adviser to the minister and as director of planning (this post was held by Sir Donald MacDougall, who had already supervised the preparation of the first plan while economic director of NEDO); and the chief industrial adviser, who was initially Mr Fred Catherwood, who headed a panel of industrial advisers. Since Mr Catherwood came originally from British Aluminium he was well placed to serve as an intermediary between the minister and industry.

On the civil service side, the DEA was treated as an ordinary department. Unlike the Treasury, with its two joint permanent secretaries and two second secretaries, the DEA's highest ranking civil servant was the (single) permanent secretary, initially Sir Eric Roll, and later Sir Douglas Allen.

In its early years the DEA had five divisions, two dealing with co-ordination of domestic and external economic policy, and the others handling planning, industrial policy and regional policy.

The Internal Economic Co-ordination Division was responsible for analysing the economic effects of fiscal policy, the expansion of agriculture and, most important, the preparation of the programme for public expenditure, a job in which it worked in close co-operation with the Public Sector group of the Treasury. Thanks to the energy of George Brown, it was able to bring into effect the incomes policy the government was committed to introducing.

The External Economic Co-ordination Division was set up in recognition of the fact that future development of the economy would largely turn on success or failure in foreign trade. This division was concerned with the United Kingdom's long-term trading interests with Europe, the Commonwealth and the rest of the world, including EFTA, and with the prospects for eventual membership of the Common Market. Theoretically its work was quite distinct from that of the Finance group of the Treasury, which retained responsibility for the short-term balance of payments and the defence of the pound. In practice, the two were bound to follow very similar policies.

The Economic Planning Division, which was headed by Sir Donald MacDougall, contained most of DEA's twenty-four professional economists, a majority of whom had previously worked in the economic section of NEDO. Its main job was to prepare the national plan, with which the Wilson government intended to replace the NEDC document, even though it still had a couple more years to run. In the event this meant that almost the same team as had prepared the original NEDC proposals was now being asked to rework what it had done three years previously. So it was no coincidence that there was such a similarity between the way the new plan and its predecessor were prepared. In this as in other fields, close co-operation with the Treasury's Public Sector group was essential. This was one way in which the DEA was better placed than Neddy had been; it had full access to the Treasury's thinking on public expenditure, an area where Neddy had experienced some difficulty. At all events, 'much of this work is done in the closest consultation with the Treasury. It depends for its success on the reconciliation of the short and long term development of the economy, and a continuous dialogue − or perhaps better, a joint operation − between the Department of Economic Affairs and the Treasury.'[3] The Division also benefited from assistance by the Department of Applied Economics at Cambridge.

The Industrial Policy Division was the most novel feature. The co-ordinator was chief industrial adviser to the government, with direct access to the prime minister and the cabinet, but he was also attached to the DEA, where he headed a panel of between five and seven industrial advisers. This group's task was to improve industrial efficiency and productivity − in short, to work out an industrial policy that would be acceptable to both the CBI and the TUC.

The Regional Policy Division had its origins in the Regional Development Division of the Board of Trade, which had been set up under Mr Heath in 1963−4. Within the DEA, initially under Mr William Rodgers, its job was to work out a form of regional organisation that would give economic planning a new dimension. The new structure was to be a regional extension of both the DEA and NEDC. According to Mr Brown it was to do two things: 'First, to provide for a full and balanced development of the country's economic and social resources; and secondly, to ensure that the regional implications of growth are clearly understood and taken into account in the planning of land, of development − in particular of industrial development − and of services.'[4]

It should not be thought Labour inherited a *tabula rasa*. The Conservatives had given a lot of thought to regional development, though with very limited success. Indeed, attempts to improve the position of the less prosperous regions had begun back in the thirties. But the Labour government of 1964−70 was the first to treat regional development as an extension of central planning, forming a coherent whole with it and meeting the same criteria.

The DEA's organisation seemed to a marked extent inspired by the example of the wartime Ministry of Production. The job of planning and co-ordination was basically similar, though co-ordination was rather more straightforward between 1942 and 1944, given the relatively uncomplicated aim of maximising war production, than the job that now lay ahead of the DEA. Also, by the end of the war the Treasury had dropped into a subordinate position; now it was at least the DEA's equal. Again, the old Ministry of Production also had its panel of industrial advisers whose functions were very similar to those the DEA was now recruiting. The regional organisation also drew heavily on wartime experience. There was the same number of regions (eleven, including Scotland, Wales and Northern Ireland) and the boundaries were in many instances the same. Each region had both a system of regular meetings between the regional officers of the various economic departments and a council with representatives of the employers and the trade unions. (The great difference was that the new councils had to take their place in the existing structure of local government, though they included many local politicians and had to be careful not to compete with existing bodies.)

It was not long before a number of changes were made in the organisation of the DEA. It was soon realised that economic co-ordination and planning could not readily be separated, and consequently the two functions were merged in a single division. At the same time prices and incomes policy was transferred to the Industrial Division. Thereafter the DEA was organised in four groups: economic planning and public expenditure (which was headed by Sir Donald MacDougall until the end of 1968); regional planning (under Mr Rodgers); industrial policy and prices and incomes (headed by Mr Michael Shanks, who became co-ordinator in the spring of 1967 on Mr Catherwood's appointment as director-general of Neddy); and external policy.

The DEA therefore embarked on two experiments: in co-ordinating industry through a system of industrial advisers, and in co-ordinating the economy in conjunction with the Treasury.

The Industrial Advisers

The industrial advisers were perhaps the most original feature of DEA. They were drawn from private industry, where most had twenty years or so of managerial experience behind them, which meant that they were mostly between forty and fifty years of age. Most were seconded to DEA for a couple of years, and returned to their firms at the end of that period. Each could claim an intimate knowledge of his industry, and so could advise the government of the likely reaction to any measure it was contemplating. Also, because they were in constant contact with their industry, they would be asked to sound people out at any time.

They had three main responsibilities. The first was obviously to advise the government both as experts and as representatives of their industry. They might be called in to meetings of civil servants or ministers at any level in addition to sitting on a large number of official committees both inside and outside the

DEA.[5] They were also responsible for liaison and co-ordination. They naturally took a hand in the work of the Little Neddies as part of the general strengthening of the role of the State which the Labour government wished to promote. Just as Mr Brown now chaired NEDC, and the DEA took over supervision of Neddy from the Treasury, so the industrial advisers were to keep an eye on the Little Neddies; each represented the DEA on several of the economic development committees. The combination of their official status and their detailed knowledge of industry made them a most valuable source of advice to the chairman and members of these committees. Finally, they had a public relations role in relation to other departments, public and private industry, and the wider public. This was particularly important in the early months of DEA's existence. In private conversations and public speeches they were constantly explaining what the DEA was and what it was trying to achieve. The reactions they gathered on these occasions in turn increased the value of their advice.

The chief industrial adviser or co-ordinator of industrial policy was the spokesman for the panel to the government. He recruited the panel and chaired its weekly meetings. He worked very closely with the director-general of the DEA, the deputy permanent secretary and the director-general and economic director of NEDC. With the latter he was joint chairman of the committee that co-ordinated the Little Neddies. He was the official go-between between Whitehall and the economic development committees.

Initially it looked as if the industrial advisers might tend to duplicate the work of the Industrial Division of NEDO, and it was far from clear what sort of reception they would get from industry. In the event there was clearly some coolness, and even a measure of suspicion. For both the employers and the unions by now looked on NEDC (particularly the Little Neddies) as their private stamping ground, or at least a neutral terrain where they could speak to the government without being overwhelmed by it. Consequently they tended to look on these intruders, even where they were former members of the industry, as tools of the government, which would use them as a means of emptying Neddy's autonomy of all meaning. While Neddy did indeed take a back seat around this time this was less because of the industrial advisers than because it had lost responsibility for national planning. The subsequent appointment of Mr Campbell Adamson, who had been an industrial adviser with DEA and then co-ordinator of industrial policy from 1966 to 1969, as director-general of the CBI on the departure of Mr Davies seemed a good indication that such suspicions had faded on the employers' side.

The outcome seems to have been most successful within the government machine itself. The advisers' views were sought from every side. Some were later appointed to senior posts in the nationalised industries or other public bodies, while several other departments followed the example of the DEA and appointed their own industrial advisers. However, their role appears to have been largely negative: they could much more readily nip ill-advised measures in the bud than promote any positive improvements of consequence.

Neddy and the Treasury

R. W. B. Clarke once described the Treasury's central responsibility as follows:

> [It has] responsibility for the management of the national economy as a whole. It must formulate the general objectives of economic policy in its totality and act as coordinator of the policies of individual departments towards the achievement of these objectives. It, therefore, must be able:
>
> 1. To relate each department's activities and requirements to the general objectives of national economic policy, to the prospective availability of economic resources, and to the total of claims upon them;
> 2. To provide informed advice to departments as partners in a joint enterprise on all aspects of economic policy and to help them to fulfil their departmental responsibilities efficiently and economically.[6]

In the view of Sir Eric Roll, who was the first permanent under-secretary at the DEA, there could be no better description of the job the DEA had been assigned. However, he added:

> Let me say at once, that using these same words, I am not making a 'takeover bid'! They happen to be extremely well chosen to define the function of overall economic management, in so far as it is carried out by the Whitehall machine. Of course, neither the DEA today, nor the Treasury three years ago could do this job by itself. . . . All the economic departments . . . are also involved.[7]

All the same, the DEA did in fact deprive the Treasury of its role in co-ordinating economic policy, which it had won back when Cripps went to the Treasury, and had managed to hold on to throughout the period of Conservative rule.

But despite Mr Brown's title as first secretary of state, it would be wrong to conclude that the Treasury had become subordinated, however briefly, to the DEA. What emerges from documents and speeches of the time is that the DEA and the Treasury were equals – and rivals. This rivalry was no accident. It arose from a notion dear to the hearts of the theorists of growth, which had already had its influence on the birth of Neddy, that growth would somehow emerge from the 'creative tension' between competing centres of economic power. The Conservatives had sought to turn Neddy into a pressure group for growth. Neddy had only achieved this to a limited degree because its political influence was too dependent on the chancellor's good will. When Labour set up the DEA it attempted to do the same thing in a different way. This time, on paper at least, the DEA seemed in a better position to act as the expansionist challenger to an overcautious Treasury. It was headed by the deputy leader of the ruling party; it had recruited an impressive array of experts; the chancellor was well disposed towards expansion, and the entire Labour programme depended on being able to speed up growth.

A number of journalists took great delight in depicting the situation as a contest between two teams, one of which was much more experienced, knew the ground intimately, was thoroughly familiar with the game but was getting a little long in the tooth; the other young, spirited, inexperienced but determined to win the championship at its first attempt. But if sportsmen tend to consider sport too grave a matter to be left to the politicians,[8] economists may reasonably feel that the economy is too serious to be so crudely reduced by journalists to cricketing clichés. There is no denying that there was some rivalry and that at times the differences were severe, but the long-term dilemma of the British economy — how to achieve a healthy balance of payments at the same time as rapid growth — cannot be reduced to a mere tug of war between rival ministries. This was not, of course, how the problem was seen by most civil servants, economists and politicians involved; they preferred to emphasise the importance of the closest possible co-operation between the two departments.

In principle the division of labour was that the DEA dealt with the long-term aspects of economic policy, the emphasis being on the allocation of 'physical resources', as Mr Brown called them — in other words, planning. The Treasury remained responsible for short-term management of the economy with an emphasis on the financial aspects. Sir Douglas Allen, who followed Sir Eric Roll as permanent under-secretary at the DEA, advanced the following reasons for this division of responsibilities:

> It is clearly desirable that, if a different choice has to be made between short-term and longer-term objectives, the full implications of the choice should be brought out for Ministers collectively; with the best will in the world this is difficult to achieve if both kinds of responsibility are carried by a single department grappling with the short-term crisis.[9]

The argument is by no means devoid of merit; in the past the cabinet had heard only the Treasury view and more or less had to take it or leave it. Between 1964 and 1969 the cabinet could judge between two competing presentations. But since it almost always came down on the same side — the Treasury's — it is hard to see how the quality of decisions benefited.

However, apart from those problems that had to be referred to the cabinet for decision, the two ministries were meant to co-operate closely. When DEA was first established it was thought necessary to link it with the Treasury at ministerial level, but the link was discontinued after only a few weeks when Mr Austen Albu replaced Mr Crosland early in 1965, and in consequence the links with the Treasury seem to have weakened. This was apparent in decision-making. The Treasury had very little part in preparing the new national plan, which was issued in September 1965, apart from the five-year programme for public expenditure. This probably reflected the prime minister's determination that the chancellor should not be involved in the planning process; for several years the chancellor was even denied a place on NEDC, to the great annoyance of the employers and the unions. Yet was it reasonable to make decisions without hearing from the man who controlled the purse strings? Again, it was clear that during the sterling crises of 1964 and 1966 drastically deflationary measures were adopted without taking into account DEA's strategy for growth, which was based on an increase in both domestic and foreign demand. The abandoning of the national plan in 1966 was a particular indication of how weak the DEA's position had become. However, it is not particularly illuminating to describe these events as a struggle between two powerful hierarchies which ended in victory for the Treasury. At least as far as the crucial decisions in July 1966 are concerned – and these were to leave their mark on British planning for years thereafter – it seems reasonably clear that the choice between devaluation and abandoning the national plan was fully argued out in cabinet, and it was the prime minister's determination to avoid devaluation which tilted the balance in favour of an all-out defence of the pound.

The DEA and Government Economic Organisation, 1964–1969

Since Sir Stafford Cripps had gone to the Treasury in 1947 the government's economic organisation had changed little. The creation of Neddy and the reorganisation of the Treasury had entailed a few minor alterations. In addition, when Mr Heath was at the Board of Trade in 1963, it was given a wider brief which included responsibility for regional development. But none of these modifications had entailed any really fundamental changes in a system that still gravitated round the Treasury. As we have seen, Neddy had in the end tended to add to the Treasury's already considerable power.

However, the creation of the DEA did entail a major disruption of the traditional pattern. As figure 6.1 shows, the focal point of the new structure was now the DEA, which was in direct contact with all the other economic departments – indeed, it was theoretically their channel to the prime minister, though in practice most of them had direct representation in the cabinet.

It was obviously vital for DEA to be on good terms with these other departments since they had the responsibility for overseeing large sections of industry, and consequently for achieving the aims of the plan in so far as these related to their particular section of the economy. The other departments apparently accepted the 'technocratic' sway of DEA much as they accepted the financial sway of the Treasury. The DEA even had one advantage over the Treasury; while Treasury financial control tended to cramp initiative, the DEA was trying to rally the other departments behind its expansionist policies, and they tended to reason that if they conformed to the DEA line there might be some chance of securing additional funds. The role of three ministries in particular, Labour, Technology and the Board of Trade, was by no means wholly executive in character, and had they been unwilling to co-operate with the DEA it would have been severely hampered.

Figure 6.1. Government economic machinery after the 1964 reform

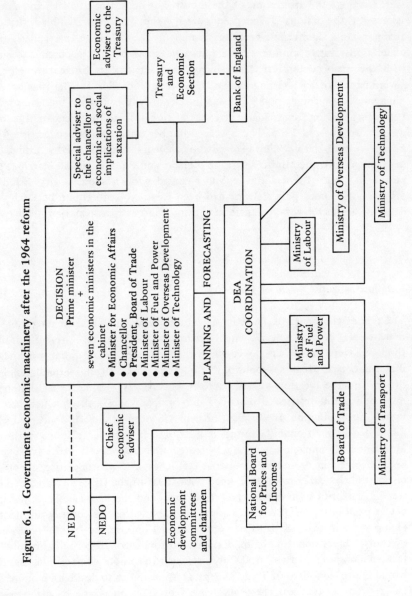

Relations with the Ministry of Labour[10]

Traditionally the Ministry of Labour had tended to see itself and to be seen as the workingman's friend in Whitehall. Many an industrial dispute had been settled there, through the arbitration of the minister or his senior officials, and almost always in the unions' favour. Periodically the Treasury grumbled that its actions were a significant element in fanning inflation. This was particularly true under Conservative ministers of labour, who showed little inclination to clash with the major unions. In 1964 many wage settlements broke through the government's official ceiling. Since DEA was responsible for drawing up and implementing incomes policy, it was bound to take issue with the Ministry of Labour's behaviour, particularly after the National Board for Prices and Incomes was set up in April 1965. There were a number of squabbles between the two ministries until Harold Wilson solved the problem in typical style by turning the department into the Ministry of Employment and Productivity in March 1969, putting it under Barbara Castle, and giving it wider responsibilities including prices and incomes policy. What had been a bone of contention between two departments therefore was transformed into an intra-departmental problem.

Relations with the Board of Trade[11]

The role of the Board of Trade in regulating the economy and the operations of industry was even more important than that of the Treasury.[12] Its staff of nine thousand were mostly employed on a wide range of detailed, but nonetheless important, tasks. It was responsible for operating the controls on the building of offices and the location of new factories; it was responsible for legislation on monopolies and restrictive practices and company law — all of which had an impact on production. It was also the department most directly concerned with many sections of manufacturing industry; it had close relations with the Monopolies Commission, which was reorganised in 1965. It had traditionally been involved in promoting industrial efficiency and in stimulating exports — responsibilities that obviously chimed with those of the DEA; increased exports were a first priority in raising the growth rate, and the Board of Trade was in a better position than DEA to do something about this. Its contribution to the export drive in Cripps's day had been of crucial importance. The DEA was also of course responsible for the modernisation of industry. This could, broadly, be tackled along one of two lines. One way was to promote competition, and this would fall to the Board of Trade under its responsibility to deal with monopolies and restrictive practices. The other was to encourage mergers even at the risk of creating new monopolies. The DEA leaned towards the second approach because planning was considerably less complicated if it had to deal with only a small number of firms in each industry. The establishing of the Industrial Reorganisation Corporation (IRC) at the end of 1966 showed that the DEA had come down in favour of the second course.

These problems were so important that there should have been some attempt to foster particularly close relationships between the two departments. Yet although the president of the Board of Trade was a member of both the cabinet and NEDC, and representatives of the DEA and the Board of Trade sat side by side on several Little Neddies (but only those dealing with industries for which the Board of Trade was responsible), there was no established machinery for consultation among senior officials, which might have brought the viewpoints of the two departments rather closer together and avoided the adoption of contradictory policies. The Board of Trade might have become, in a manner of speaking, the 'secular arm' of the DEA. One of the lessons that should be noted in any future reorganisation of British planning procedures is that the department that will be mainly responsible for carrying out the plan must be fully involved in its preparation.

Relations with the Ministry of Technology[13]

The Ministry of Technology (or Mintech) and the DEA were set up at the same time, and with the same aim of modernising and developing the economy by exploiting scientific and technical advance. Their relations were accordingly not hampered by engrained administrative traditions of the kind that had developed in the Treasury or the Board of Trade. However, it was essential that Mintech should take the priorities laid down by DEA into account, since in 1965 alone it distributed some £200 million for scientific and technical research, through subsidies to universities, learned societies and research institutes working on both pure and applied research, in addition to research on aviation matters and the Atomic Energy Authority. It was also responsible for four high-technology industries — machine tools, electronics, telecommunications and computers — which might be expected to be among the spearheads of economic expansion. It was therefore particularly important that Mintech should see their aims were in keeping with the plan.

In the event, apart perhaps for the first few months, the DEA and the other economic departments never gave any impression of having a common mind; nor did they ever seem to work together to hammer out a concerted policy. Consequently the DEA rarely played the pilot role that the old Ministry of Production filled so effectively during the war.

CHAPTER 7

Neddy's New Role

In the period immediately before the 1964 general election Neddy's fate was uncertain. The Conservatives no longer looked on it with any great favour. Labour was divided. There were some on the Left who were worried about giving so much rein to private interests in a semi-independent body of this kind. Others, such as Balogh, thought that at best NEDC was useless, since it had no real power over the implementation of the plan.[1] However, more moderate leaders like Harold Wilson implied that, although they would make major changes in the machinery of economic management, they would retain NEDC. Also the TUC, where moderates were still very much in control, preferred to see Neddy continue because they thought it an ideal meeting ground for the government, the employers and the unions. It seems that the attitude of the TUC and the desire not to begin by a quite unnecessary and avoidable clash with private industry tipped the balance in favour of retaining Neddy. But it was obvious that, when the preparation of the plan and the working out of an industrial policy were assigned to a separate ministry, the roles of NEDC, and even more of the Office, were bound to change and become less important.

Changes in Membership and Organisation

The new government added two members to the Council's original twenty: the minister of technology and the co-ordinator of industrial policy, Mr Catherwood. While these changes strengthened the government's position they were less important than the decision to exclude the chancellor. Although it was natural that the chairmanship of the Council should pass to the new minister for economic affairs, it was surely also necessary for the chancellor to remain on the Council. The reason advanced for the decision at the time was that the balance of the Council could not be tilted in the government's favour. This was a bad reason because it would have been easy to maintain the balance in some other way. It was also widely suggested, by way of explanation, that the Council was concerned with physical planning while the chancellor dealt with financial policy. Sam Brittan rightly dismisses this decision as an 'economic howler'. At all events, despite protests from the CBI (the eviction of the chancellor was one reason for the poor relations between the employers and the DEA during 1965 and 1966), as well as from the TUC and a number of newspapers, the Labour government refused for some considerable time to reverse the decision.

During the six years of Labour rule the composition of the Council changed little. When Mr Catherwood became director-general of NEDO in the spring of 1966 he naturally continued on the Council in this capacity, but his successor as co-ordinator, Mr Michael Shanks, was not given a seat on the Council. However, Mr Aubrey Jones became a member when the National Board for Prices and Incomes was established. But the most important change came in August 1967, when Mr Wilson himself took the DEA in hand.[2] However, in practice the department was run by Mr Peter Shore (who was given the title of secretary of state, unlike his predecessors, Mr Brown and Mr Stewart, who had both been first secretaries). The really significant outcome of the change was that the prime minister now became chairman of NEDC and the chancellor was restored to membership of the Council, which now contained no fewer than six ministers, with its total membership raised from twenty-two to twenty-four.

The fact that it was now chaired by the prime minister meant that the Council returned more to the public eye, and little by little it was able to recover some of the authority and status the DEA was losing. So when the DEA was swept away in the cabinet reshuffle of October 1969, not only was there no question of abolishing the Council, but it remained attached to the cabinet office (and has remained so under later Conservative and Labour governments).

Changes in NEDO

The Office continued to have three divisions (economic, industrial and administrative), and to be run by a director-general who was responsible only to the Council, thus ensuring the Office a measure of independence. Sir Robert Shone was director-general until he retired in the spring of 1966 and was succeeded by Mr Fred Catherwood.[3] Staff continued to be recruited in the somewhat informal manner adopted in 1962, with between seventy and eighty per cent coming from private industry on fairly short-term contract or secondment, and the rest from the civil service, the nationalised industries and the universities. Sir Robert Shone has commented on the complexities of attempting to run a permanent organisation with such a high rate of turnover. Also in 1964, NEDO lost as many members to the DEA and Mintech as it had received from Whitehall over the previous two years. The staff of the Office was 110 in 1965, rising to about 200 in October 1969.

The Economic Division was the hardest hit. When Sir Donald MacDougall became director-general at the DEA he took with him almost all his team of economists and statisticians, leaving only a handful behind him at Neddy, and a considerable time elapsed before the new economic director was appointed. Having lost its main function of preparing the plan, the section was reduced to drafting reports or studies of long-term growth prospects and any other working papers the Council required for its meetings. It also supplied facts and statistical data to the economic development committees. In October 1969 it had a staff of about twenty-five.

By contrast, the Industrial Division grew steadily as the Little Neddies and working parties proliferated, despite the advent of the DEA's industrial advisers. Although it no longer had responsibility for defining a national policy for industry, it still had one very important job – provision of expert assistance to the development committees, and co-ordination of their work. This task was carried out in conjunction with the Industrial Policy Division of the DEA, under the guidance of an informal steering committee chaired jointly by the industrial director of NEDO and the co-ordinator of industrial policy from the DEA. In addition each development committee included a representative of the Industrial Section of NEDO and an industrial adviser from DEA. Though there was a considerable danger of friction in this system, it seems to have worked fairly well. This was due in no small measure to NEDO's first industrial director, Mr Tom Fraser. In October 1969 the section had a staff of around 120.[4]

The responsibilities of the Administrative Division varied very little. With a staff of about sixty in October 1969 it ran the Office, acted as the Council secretariat and dealt with personnel matters. The cost of Neddy – including the Council, the Office and the development committees – was put at £912,000 in the DEA estimates for 1969–70. This does not seem excessive. One can also say that neither financially nor bureaucratically did Neddy swell to excessive size. All the same, there were some who thought the cost too high, because the results were so small.

Neddy's Role Between 1964 and 1969

While Neddy's organisation changed relatively little, its role did. Instead of preparing plans it was now merely 'discussing their formulation'. Instead of recommending to the government 'measures of such a kind as to bring about expansion', it could now only give its views on proposals originating with the DEA and the other economic departments. The extent to which it should be involved in planning was expressed in extremely vague terms: 'to examine the economic performance of the nation with particular concern to plans for the future in both the private and public sectors of industry'. With Mr Lloyd's blessing the Council had initially chosen to give that passage an extremely wide interpretation, treating it practically as an instruction to draw up a plan. But without in any way twisting the original wording it would be perfectly possible to limit the Council to a minor consultative role. However, in 1966 Sir Robert Shone felt that, 'the prime function of the Council is to consider whether, looking at the draft Plan as a whole, it is reasonable, whether its objectives can be supported, and whether the policies designed to secure the objectives are appropriate. If the Council considers further developments of policy are needed to secure the improved performance aimed at, then it has a duty to contribute to the formulation of such policies.'[5] On this view something more than mere consultation was involved; though Neddy no longer drew up the documents on which the plan would be based, this should not prevent it from bringing forward new ideas, not just about the plan but about economic policy generally.

How this worked out in practice is not wholly clear. Of the preparation of the 1965 plan a document issued by NEDO offers only this vague account: 'The DEA consulted the Council throughout the preparation of the plan and made extensive use of the industrial structure that had been built up since the establishment of the Council .... This examination led to the choice of a provisional growth rate .... The Council's conclusions are summarised in a statement which is included in the national plan.'[6]

This cannot be said to provide a very clear picture of the extent of consultations or of how far the Council's opinions were accepted. However, the non-governmental members of the Council (particularly those from the CBI) were far from happy about the new procedure and the weakness of NEDC in relation to the DEA. The employers' representatives, who were already annoyed at the exclusion of the chancellor, complained that they had not been paid proper consideration; 'although the present government paid lip service to the NEDC it has used it primarily as a means of trying to screw a reluctant commitment from industry to a national plan about which industry has serious reservations, and which the Council was given very little time to consider'.[7]

In 1965 and 1966 this dissatisfaction led to a number of clashes between Mr Brown and the employers which ended only with his departure from the ministry in August 1966, despite the undoubted good will of the director-general of the CBI, Mr John Davies.[8] In December 1965, spurred by a 'grass roots' revolt of his members, who were accusing him of passively accepting the government's proposals, Mr Davies sent Mr Brown a memorandum on the government's economic policy generally, and its attitude to Neddy in particular. It listed the CBI's criticisms and called for a number of improvements. Among these were: that the chancellor should attend meetings of NEDC (it was rumoured that Mr Brown was hostile to this; admittedly, if he had agreed that this would be useful, he would have been recognising that the influence of the DEA was not as great in Whitehall as it was supposed to be); a strengthening of NEDO to increase its independence and capacity to conduct its own investigations; a promise that the government would pay greater attention to the views of the Council, which was in danger, Mr Davies alleged, of becoming little more than a 'rubber-stamping device'; and an assurance that the supervision of the economic development committees would remain with the Council.

The CBI's complaints also had the tacit support of the TUC. Its impatience may also have owed something to the approach of a general election and the fact that it was about to appoint a new director-general. When the 1966 election resulted in Labour being returned with an increased majority, the employers resigned themselves to continuing working with the Wilson government. Also the fact that Sir Robert Shone's successor, Mr Catherwood, came from industry (though he had his critics among people in the private sector) was the kind of measure that was likely to disarm critics to some extent. Particularly as the new director-general immediately declared that he intended to turn Neddy into a spokesman for industry in Whitehall, much as the Bank of England spoke for the City. Finally, later that year the departure of Mr Brown and the abandoning of the national plan threw the DEA into a period of painful introspection. While Neddy was bound to suffer to some extent from the crisis, it was also able to profit from the situation to regain some of its lost independence.

In any event, the employers were never so unhappy that they seriously contemplated abandoning the policy of *concertation* they had accepted in 1962. The CBI document quoted earlier concluded:

> Only the NEDC provides an opportunity of discussing major national problems in an atmosphere comparatively free from departmental pressures and in a wider economic context . . . . Thus although the NEDC's influence on events in the last two years has been negligible, there is still a strong case for preserving it . . . at the same time endeavouring to make it an effective influence in the sphere of national policy.[9]

CHAPTER 8

The Little Neddies

The economic development committees, or Little Neddies, were set up to provide a way for those responsible for making economic decisions to meet working industrialists and trade unionists.[1] For genuine *concertation* had to go beyond the consultations with the general staffs of the CBI and the TUC that the government was developing through NEDC. It also required that workers and management should meet industry by industry to discuss ways of improving output and efficiency in their particular industry, within the general provisions of the national plan. The change of government in 1964 made little difference in the principles on which the committees were established and operated, though Labour did try to improve co-ordination between the various committees and their communications with the government, by appointing a representative of the DEA to each of them.[2]

An essentially empirical approach presided over the establishment of the committees. This flexibility was the main reason why they achieved such a wide measure of acceptance by industry. For the confidence that each committee would be flexible enough to cater for industry's special needs and circumstances encouraged the leaders of the two sides of industry to take part and give the experiment a trial. Also the need to develop permanent links between the planners, the board room and the shop floor through committees of this kind was inherent in the introduction of the system of indicative planning on which Neddy had embarked in 1962. Consequently, by the end of 1964 there were nine committees: for machine tools, chemicals, electronics, mechanical engineering, wool textiles, heavy electrical engineering, the distributive trades and paper and board.

It might have been expected that the advent of a Labour government would make private employers more reluctant to take part. But this apparently was not the case, since four more committees were set up in 1965 (for building, civil engineering, movement of exports, and rubber), seven more in 1966 (agriculture, clothing, hats and knitwear, hotels and catering, motor vehicle distribution and repair, the Post Office and printing and publishing), and a final two (food processing and the car industry) were established in 1967. Thereafter no further committees were set up and the number stayed stable at twenty-one (after the food processing and chocolate and sugar confectionery committees had merged).[3]

Membership of the committees followed a more or less standard pattern (see table 8.1): 45 per cent of the members were from management, mostly the private sector, and 20 per cent from the unions, while 23 per cent were

Table 8.1.   Composition of the economic development committees in June 1969

Origin of members	Agriculture	Building	Chemicals	Civil Engineering	Clothing	Distributive Trades	Electrical Engineering	Electronics	Food Manufacturing	Hosiery and Knitwear	Hotels and Catering	Machine Tools	Mechanical Engineering	Cars	Motor Vehicle Distribution and Repair	Movement of Exports	Paper and Board	Post Office[d]	Printing and Publishing	Rubber	Wool Textiles	Total
Industry	9	11	9	9	9	9	9	9	11	9	7	7	9	10	7	9	7	5	10	9	9	183
Unions	4	4	4	3	4	4	4	4	4	4	4	4	5	5	4	4	5	5	6	3	4	88
Independent experts[a]	3	3	1	3	1	3	3	3	3	2	3	2	1	3	3	3	3	5	2	3	2	55
NEDO representatives[b]	2	2	2	2	2	2	2	2	2	2	2	2	3	2	3	2	2	2	3	2	2	45
State representatives[c]	4	4	2	3	2	3	2	2	2	2	3	2	2	3	3	4	2	1	2	2	2	52
Total	22	24	18	20	18	21	20	20	22	19	19	17	20	23	20	22	19	18	23	19	19	423

Note: Although the exact economic origin of members is not always easy to identify exactly, the picture emerging from the table above is accurate enough for all working purposes.

  (a) Includes chairmen and current or former members of the management of companies outside the industry covered by the committee.

  (b) Members of NEDO are counted separately. They include a secretary (or in two instances two secretaries).

  (c) Including a DEA representative in all cases.

  (d) The five 'management' members of this committee were all senior officials in the Post Office.

independent experts (including NEDO representatives) and 12 per cent represented the State (one of them being an industrial adviser from the DEA). NEDO supplied both an independent expert, who was a senior official of the Office and also represented the director-general, the industrial director and, indirectly, the Council, and also one (or occasionally two) junior officials to act as secretaries and see to the general running of the committee. The advantage of this arrangement, combined with the fact that meetings were held at NEDO itself, was that it made members (including government representatives) feel – quite justifiably – that they were meeting on neutral ground and could engage in a completely frank exchange of views without being under pressure from either the State or sectional interests. The need for neutral ground, which also holds true at Council level, is of considerable psychological importance in relations between government and industry in Britain.

The government had at least two representatives on each committee, an industrial adviser from DEA and a representative of the sponsoring department for the industry concerned. Where the industry spread over the fields of more than one department there were additional government representatives: the construction committee had four – one from DEA, two from Public Building and Works and one from Housing and Local Government. The same was true in the 'horizontal committees', to employ French terminology; for example, the export industries committee had one member from DEA, one from the Ministry of Transport, one from the Board of Trade and one from the Treasury (acting for the Customs and Excise).

The original initiative for setting up a committee came from the Council, which then left full responsibility for implementing the decision to NEDO. So the Office had a crucial role to play. It was the Office (which in practice meant the director-general and the industrial director) that held unofficial talks with the interested parties about the scope of each committee and the names of possible members. Even after the DEA was formed, the scope of each committee was resolved by persuasion and compromise. The apparently haphazard order in which the committees were set up was in fact the consequence of this commitment to securing everyone's agreement before proceeding further. One outcome of operating in this way was that some committees covered a very broad field and others quite a narrow one. It would in any case have been difficult to lay down with any confidence an 'optimum' coverage for each committee. The procedure adopted also explains why at first there was a confectionery committee which later merged with the food processing committee. Drawing on earlier experience, the ground covered by the later committees tended to become progressively wider. A danger here was that, the wider a committee's brief, the harder it became for members to find common interests and problems.

Recruitment was carried out in a highly informal way. It had to satisfy several different and potentially contradictory requirements. It was essential to obtain members who would inspire confidence while securing the widest possible representational spread. But membership had to be held down to a reasonable size (the largest committee had twenty-four members) if the effectiveness of the committees was not to be impaired. This created some tricky problems in a number of industries, where as many as fifty bodies might lay some sort of claim to representation and there were only seven or eight places. The approach adopted was to let employers and unions work out their list of nominees among themselves. The selection of the chairman and the independent members was rather more delicate since they had to be acceptable to all concerned. Also it was felt that the chairman ought to have some say in the choice of the other members, particularly the independent experts who, together with himself, would hold the balance on the committee. So everything had to be negotiated at the same time; a possible chairman had to be discovered and consulted on the appointment of the other members, while the unions and employers were being consulted both about their own nominees and the chairmanship. To do this successfully required a real *tour de force*, not only calling on all Mr Fraser's long experience of industry and the unions, but also requiring great diplomatic skill. (He also had some help from the co-ordinator and his industrial advisers at DEA.) The choice of chairman was particularly delicate. He had to be acceptable to both sides, but he must not be directly involved in the industry concerned. Usually the choice was a prominent industrialist who either had retired or was associated with some other industry.

Once there was sufficient agreement on coverage and membership, the committee could be officially established. The secretary of state for economic affairs, as chairman of NEDC, officially appointed the chairman, and the director-general of NEDC issued invitations to the other members to join the committee. The State could scarcely be accused of acting in an authoritarian way.

Acceptance of a place on one of the committees amounted tacitly to an agreement to conform to the general aims the Council had laid down for the committees in 1963. Thus Hugh Scanlon of the AUEW and Lord Stokes of BLMC, though differing passionately on a whole range of issues, agreed when they became members of the economic development committee for the car industry to co-operate to improve 'the industry's economic performance, competitive power and efficiency'. This was why, although they were not expected to divorce themselves completely from the organisations to which they belonged, they sat as individuals rather than as representatives of their respective bodies, which were in no way committed by what they said within the context of the committee.

Initially the committees were set up to constitute a form of continuing inquiry intended to improve the calibre of industries' forecasts, within the general targets of the national plan. But if the only idea had been to provide as much data as possible as rapidly as possible about a particular industry, it would obviously have been quicker simply to set up an expert working party. The reason members of the committee were selected with such care was that the gathering of information and the preparation of forecasts were in a sense only preliminaries to their real function; all this information would have been of little value had it not been gathered with the intention of considering subsequently where the industry's main problems lay and what could be done about them.

The work of the committees therefore went through four stages: examination (the search for information), diagnosis (detection of shortcomings), prescription (reports to NEDC and discussion by NEDC), and treatment (implementation by persuasion, influence or government action). As might be suspected, each stage was a little more complicated than the previous one. Since the first involved simply gathering facts, the only problems were organisational; at the second stage it was still relatively easy to secure agreement since this involved detecting the shortcomings the facts revealed; but the last two stages were trickier because subjective considerations were bound to bear more heavily on people's judgements. It is always more difficult to agree on the causes of any inadequacy than on how it can be remedied. Thus the committee could really be considered to have completed its work only when the industry (or the government) had adopted its recommendations. Such recommendations were naturally not binding, but through its participation in the committee and acceptance of the proposals contained in its reports, subsequently endorsed by NEDC, the industry committed itself to profit from the experience and, in general terms, to be receptive to any changes that might be desirable. These necessary consequences of the committee's discussions depended very largely on the calibre and influence of the members. Those initially responsible for launching the committees hoped that little by little their work would lead to both workers and management taking a completely fresh look at some of the engrained attitudes and the custom and practice which had been such a brake on the even development of British industry. We will see below how this worked in practice.

A New Development in Relations Between Government and Industry?[4]

The question arises at this stage of the ways in which the committees broke new ground compared with, say, Cripps's development councils or the traditional links between industry and the sponsoring departments in Whitehall.

With a few exceptions, such as the Cotton Development Council (which had had a previous existence), the development councils were a failure. They were not sufficiently flexible, and the political circumstances of the time were such that they could not hope to prosper. Yet they brought the two sides of industry together, with a few independent members; there were no government representatives. Such a system should have seemed less dangerous to industry than the Little Neddies. On the other hand, the structure and functioning of the 1947 councils were prescribed by law, and consequently they might well have been seen as the product of state intervention, though in the event they proved to be purely corporatist bodies. The Little Neddies were much less corporatist, but they owed their existence to a body (NEDC) that had the confidence of both employers and unions. At all events, although the 1947 councils were able to impose reorganisation and major structural reforms on the firms concerned, their composition was such that they could not develop into a forum between the State and the two sides of industry because the State was not represented on them.

The system of 'sponsoring departments' originated with the *dirigisme* of running the wartime economy. At a period when every industry was totally dependent on the State for raw materials, labour and orders, it was desirable to provide means by which they could be in touch with government departments without delay and as often as necessary. In time departments acquired a measure of technical skill in dealing with the industry. After the ending of controls, established practices lingered on because they were of use to both government and industry. While 'sponsoring department' was an appropriate term as long as controls were in force, it was no less accurate after the Conservatives returned to power, when ministries tended increasingly to act as 'sponsor' for their industries within Whitehall, particularly in relation to the Treasury. The danger was obvious: the department's information about an industry was drawn largely from its contact with the trade association concerned and, to a lesser extent, from its direct relations with individual companies. Even when it was completely accurate the information was invariably to some extent biased, and reflected the industry's interests and concerns. So it is not surprising that sponsoring departments came to view such industries with a benevolent eye and to act as spokesmen on their behalf throughout Whitehall.

There was another serious weakness: the views of the unions were almost completely squeezed out. While the problems raised were not directly related to pay, working conditions and organisation of production, if there was to be any hope of the unions accepting a responsibility in relation to the development of the economy as a whole, they would obviously have to have their say on the problems of the particular industry in which their members were earning their livelihood – and the unions were beginning to argue increasingly forcefully in these terms. There was a further limitation in this system. It related almost entirely to situations where the industry wanted something from the government, since, apart from informal contacts, it was only on such occasions that the industry sent a delegation to the ministry. Under such a system, then, contact was bound to be intermittent unless the department also had an advisory committee – but advisory committees were widely viewed as mere talking shops, an opportunity to submit demands, rather than a body where policies could really be hammered out round a table.

In the light of this analysis the virtues of the development committees can be seen more clearly. They offered relatively permanent machinery, limited to the three parties involved in industrial development and economic progress, who could by this means hold regular discussions about the whole range of problems confronting the industry. They could scarcely have been less under the government's thumb. Meetings were not called by the government side, nor were they held under the auspices of a government department. Instead they were called by the chairman, who was completely independent of the government, and held at the NEDC headquarters — a neutral ground with a neutral secretariat. Moreover, the development committees in no way prejudiced the working of existing machinery. On the contrary, if a trade association had the backing of the appropriate development committee on a particular point, it would consider itself in that much stronger a position when it called on the ministry to make a speedy decision in its favour.

On the whole the two sides of industry were very willing to take part, as the number of committees eventually established demonstrates. The trade unionists found them an excellent opportunity to discuss problems on which their views had rarely been sought in the past, and to show by the calibre of their contribution that they were fully capable of considering the national interest. The whole undertaking would have been impossible without the favourable attitude of the employers' associations (and the CBI after 1965). The CBI paper quoted earlier listed four conditions for the committees to work successfully:

> Firstly, the industry must have absolute confidence in the chairman ... Secondly, the field of work must be clear and precise. Thirdly, as many people as possible in the industry must be involved in the committee's work. Finally ... the committee must be able to look to a competent trade association for information and advice as the main channel of information with firms.[5]

The CBI also showed its hostility to any 'takeover' by the government: 'Any attempts by government departments to reduce them to the role of departmental advisory committees should be strenuously resisted.'[6] However, there is no evidence of any attempt to do this.

Thus the committees were created to meet the requirements of all concerned. Those who took part could accept responsibility without forfeiting their independence and freedom of action in other areas. It was clearly understood by everyone involved, for instance, that they did not deal with labour relations. It was accordingly possible, in theory at least, for a trade association and a union that were in other respects at loggerheads to work together peaceably in the committees.

The question then was whether, since so many precautions had been taken to avoid conflict, the committees might not find themselves condemned to a cautious immobility.

CHAPTER 9

From Regional Development to Regional Planning

There are two complementary strands to the argument for having a regional development policy, one social and the other economic: on the one hand the fight to reduce the high unemployment in the backward areas; on the other the desire to avoid the waste of productive potential that arises when manpower is unemployed, under-employed or ill-employed. Thus in June 1962, when nationally unemployment stood at the highly satisfactory level of 1.8 per cent, in the North East it was a much less impressive 3.2 per cent. But in February 1963, when the national level had risen to a dismal 3.9 per cent, it had soared to a dismaying 7.1 per cent in the North East. As tables 9.1 and 9.2 show, the variations in Scotland, Wales and Northern Ireland were even greater.

For a long time governments saw regional policy solely in social terms. The recognition of the economic waste involved emerged clearly only with the new thinking of the sixties, with its emphasis on the inadequate rate of growth. The credit for stating the problem of the regions in economic terms goes to Neddy, which calculated in its second report that if the difference between national and regional rates of unemployment could be cut by half, this would produce a by no means negligible increase of 1.3 per cent in the rate of economic growth.[1] A further economic argument was that the imbalance between regions made it particularly difficult to deploy monetary and budgetary weapons against inflation because deflationary measures that might be needed to check the unduly rapid growth of one region might have a disastrous impact on more backward areas. Conversely, an incautious stimulus to demand to help the poorer areas might have an inflationary effect in a region where unemployment was low. However, the report still viewed the problem mainly in terms of justifying greater assistance to regions that were being left behind.

In introducing the idea of regional planning Labour added a further dimension to regional policy. Their point of departure was the recognition that in any country what happens in one region necessarily affects all the others, and consequently there was a need for regional planning even in the most prosperous regions. It might be asked why it was necessary to plan in regions that were already doing very well without the intervention of the government. There were two answers to this. The first was that distribution of investment had to be co-ordinated by central government and there had to be some way of knowing total requirements. The second was that this was the only way of maintaining a degree of balance, since experience has shown that, if the backward areas are assisted while the others are allowed to continue their unco-ordinated development, the aid has often been a waste of effort. With regions as with individuals, *laissez-faire* profits only the rich. The most striking example of this has been Italy, where the State has spent huge sums on developing the Mezzogiorno but has done little to control the development of the North. The

Table 9.1. Unemployment rates in the regions (averages of monthly figures, per cent)

	1960	1961	1962	1963	1964	1965	1966	1967	1968	1969	1970
South East	1.0	1.0	1.3	1.6	1.0	0.9	1.0	1.7	1.6	1.6	1.6
East Anglia						1.3	1.4	2.1	2.0	1.9	2.2
South West	1.7	1.4	1.7	2.1	1.5	1.6	1.8	2.5	2.5	2.7	2.9
East Midlands	1.0	1.1	1.6	2.0	1.0	0.9	1.1	1.8	1.9	2.0	2.3
West Midlands						0.9	1.3	2.5	2.2	2.0	2.3
Yorkshire and Humberside						1.1	1.2	2.1	2.6	2.6	2.9
North West	1.9	1.6	2.5	3.1	2.1	1.6	1.5	2.5	2.5	2.5	2.7
North	2.9	2.5	3.7	5.0	3.3	2.6	2.6	4.0	4.7	4.8	4.8
Wales	2.7	2.6	3.1	3.6	2.6	2.6	2.9	4.1	4.0	4.1	4.0
Scotland	3.6	3.1	3.8	4.8	3.6	3.0	2.9	3.9	3.8	3.7	4.3
Northern Ireland	6.7	7.5	7.5	7.9	6.6	6.1	6.1	7.7	7.2	7.3	7.0
United Kingdom	1.7	1.6	2.1	2.6	1.7	1.5	1.6	2.5	2.5	2.5	2.7

Source: Department of Employment *Gazette,* via Sant, op. cit., p. 8.

Table 9.2. Activity rates, standard regions, June 1968*

New standard regions	Male and female	Male	Female
South East	59.7	77.9	43.4
East Anglia	48.5	64.6	33.1
South West	47.0	63.5	32.2
West Midlands	60.2	78.4	42.6
East Midlands	56.3	74.1	39.3
Yorks and Humberside	56.1	74.7	38.8
North West	58.1	75.9	40.1
North	51.8	70.0	34.8
Wales	47.1	65.6	30.1
Scotland	56.4	74.5	40.4
Northern Ireland	48.9	64.0	35.2
United Kingdom	56.2	74.1	39.8

* Employees as a percentage of the home population aged fifteen years and over. See *Abstract of Regional Statistics* (1969), no. 5.

Source: M. Sant (ed.), *Regional Policy and Planning for Europe*, Farnborough, Saxon House (1974), p. 10.

outcome has been that, while the South has unquestionably made considerable progress, the North has developed even more rapidly and the gap between the two has widened.

A Resumé of the Development of Regional Policy

As in so many matters, it was the Fabian Society that first grasped what should be done,[2] and it was the economic crisis between the wars that brought about the first positive action. The beginnings of regional policy go back to the thirties, with the decision of a number of government departments to set up regional offices (though this was done in a quite unco-ordinated way), and the introduction of the first measure to plan the location of industry, the Special Areas (Development and Improvement) Act of 1934. Two commissioners were appointed with special responsibility for the development of the 'special areas', one for Scotland (Clydeside) and the other for England and Wales (the North East, West Cumberland and South Wales).

But the first truly regional structure dates from the Second World War, when eleven regions were set up under the government's wartime powers, initially for defence purposes and subsequently for production. This organisation soon proved its worth and gradually other departments adopted the same regional pattern. But in 1945 the system was dismantled in the face of the hostility of the local authorities who had had no part in it and saw it as a possible threat to their own powers. Some departments closed all their regional offices; most others reverted to their prewar organisation, which did not provide full national coverage. The exceptions were the Ministry of Labour and the Board of Trade. The latter retained its regional controllers throughout the country (though the special area commissioners were abolished), and the 1945 Distribution of Industry Act gave them powers over the location of factories. The Act also designated development areas, which were basically the old special areas plus Deeside, Southern Lancashire, Merseyside, North-East Lancashire and the Highlands. To encourage the installation of new industries the Board of Trade was empowered to buy land and construct factories which would be let to industrialists at specially low rents.

But at the same time as the idea of development was making headway, the Town and Country Planning Act of 1947 was introducing another line of attack. The new approach reflected both a social and an aesthetic concern. The social concern was to see that people lived in decent conditions; the aesthetic concern was to do something about the ugliness of the industrial regions. It is scarcely surprising that such concerns came to the forefront first in Britain, where the haphazard growth of industry in the nineteenth and early twentieth century had devastated large parts of the country, leaving their inhabitants living in surroundings that were as squalid as they were unhealthy. Between the wars some Labour leaders, particularly Lansbury,[3] laid great emphasis on this aspect of social advance, promising that a Labour government would make an all-out attack on the problem. It was not surprising, therefore, that the 1947 Act required local authorities to draw up development plans covering the next ten years under the general oversight of the Ministry of Town and Country Planning, and that the Board of Trade was given greater powers over the location of industry, through a new system of 'industrial development certificates'. The basic strategic appreciation on which the new Act rested was that if old abuses could be stopped, then the expenditure of sufficiently large sums of money would eventually produce a desirable environment. But this implied that British society was static, and specifically that population was stable. In the light of experience hopes have become more modest, and it is now realised that there is a continuing problem which can never be finally and permanently resolved.

After Labour left power in 1951 there was a period of hostility to everything that smacked of the interventionism of the postwar years. The town planning activities of the local authorities continued, but the Local Employment Act of 1960 which replaced the old Distribution of Industry Act was, as its title implied, concerned mainly with unemployment – the social aspect of the regional problem. It tried to refine regional development policy by replacing the development areas, which were considered unduly extensive, with a larger number of 'development districts' which were designated on the basis of their high rates of unemployment (4.5 per cent and over compared with 2.0 per cent nationally at the time). The practical difference was small.

The rethinking of the sixties was felt in regional planning, and indeed may be said to have given birth to it. In 1962 an attempt was made to renovate it. What made the Conservatives act was the alarmingly high unemployment of the winter of 1962–3.[4] The government was also influenced by criticisms of its approach to regional policy, particularly those levelled at it by the various regional committees that had been set up through private initiative over the previous few years, the most active of which was in the North East. The Conservatives' first response in 1963 was to make Lord Hailsham responsible for the development of the North East. In October 1963, when Mr Heath went to the Board of Trade, he was given the title of secretary of state for industry, trade and regional development. Thus the need was recognised for a fully coherent regional policy linked – as NEDC had recommended – with the general conduct of national economic policy. As a result during 1963 and 1964 a series of White Papers was published on the development of particular areas.[5] Their most striking feature was the emphasis they laid on the economic aspects of regional policy, and the need to set up machinery in the regions that would be in constant contact with central government. The White Papers were research papers rather than plans. Most offered a useful analysis of the problems of the region in question and outlined prospects for the future, though without any commitment by either local or central government. They were outlining a regional policy without regions, for as yet no boundaries had been set for the regions.

The Structure of Regional Planning

In December 1964 George Brown outlined in the Commons a new regional structure, involving the division of the country into regions and the establishment of new regional institutions.

The DEA was careful not to impose regional boundaries without consultation. They were eventually published after long consultation with the local authorities. There were of course no problems in relation to Scotland, Wales and Northern Ireland, but the same difficulties were experienced in England as in France, and there was some discussion about the optimum size for a region. If the regions were small they would be more coherent administratively but too small in economic terms; if they were very large they would simply be incohate with varying, perhaps even divergent, economic interests and they would be difficult to administer. It was nearly a year before the final details of the boundaries could be published. England was divided into eight regions (see figure 9.1): North, Yorkshire—Humberside, East Midlands, East Anglia, South East, South West, West Midlands and the North West. The South East region, which included London, was among the largest and also contained about one in three of the population.

It was not easy to relate these new institutions successfully to the existing structure of local government, which has traditionally enjoyed greater powers than in France. Also they had to meet two requirements: to shift decisions from Whitehall to the regional offices, and to ensure that national economic policy took full account of the needs of the regions. To meet these requirements the Labour government set up two bodies in each region, a regional economic planning board and a regional economic planning council.

The regional economic planning boards were composed of the regional officers of the various departments dealing with the various aspects of regional planning, with the DEA's regional officer as chairman. Apart from the DEA the main departments represented (in 1965) were: Board of Trade, Agriculture, Defence, Education and Science, Home Office, Health, Housing and Local Government, Labour, Fuel and Power, Public Building and Works, Technology and Transport, plus the Central Office of Information and the Post Office. It is remarkable that the Treasury was not represented; this would have been unthinkable in France.

The boards' main job was co-ordination of the work of the various departments and co-operation with the councils in the preparation of a medium-term economic plan within the terms of the national plan. Co-ordination was facilitated by housing regional offices either in the same building or very close to one another.[6] In addition, the regional office of the DEA provided the secretariat for both the board and the council, and operated a research section which co-operated with the regional offices of other departments, universities and local authorities.

The regional economic planning councils had thirty or so part-time members

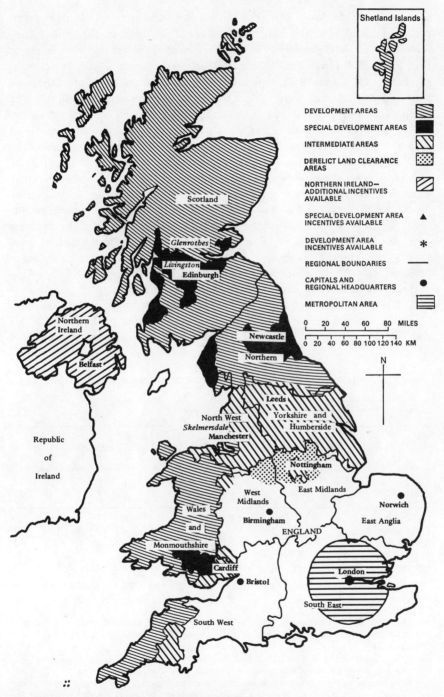

Figure 9.1.   Assisted Areas in the UK, 1973

(the largest, in the South East, had thirty-eight), who were appointed for their special knowledge of the economic and social problems of the region. They served in a personal capacity. The way they were appointed was very similar to that followed for the Little Neddies. Most were people who were active in companies and unions in the region, or were local councillors or officials; there were also some from universities, the social services and agriculture. The composition varied considerably from one region to another, as table 9.3 shows.

The councils were in a rather weak position in relation to both the local authorities and the regional officers of the government departments. Unlike the local authorities, their members were appointed rather than elected; unlike the civil servants they had a purely advisory role and no power to take decisions. Their function was to prepare a list of the region's requirements, to evaluate its productive potential, and to work out a strategy for its long-term development. With this in view each council undertook a study of its region; the resulting series was completed with the East Anglia study in 1968.[7] On the basis of these studies the councils suggested growth targets for the region, and made projections of the distribution of population, industry and employment, taking into account the national targets contained in the 1965 plan.

The councils were also to be consulted by the central government on those aspects of national economic policy that affected regional development. To this end they were allowed to communicate directly with the departments concerned

Table 9.3.   Membership of regional economic planning councils* in 1969

Category	North	Yorkshire–Humberside	East Midlands	East Anglia	South East	South West	West Midlands	North West	Scotland[a]	Wales[b]	All
					Region						
Local authorities	9	12	11	9	14	11	10	11	6	13	106
Trade and Industry	11	11	8	11	11	7	6	13	11	9	98
Agriculture[c]	2	0	0	1	1	2	0	0	1	2	9
Trade unions	4	3	4	3	4	4	5	5	5	4	41
Independent members	4	4	4	4	8	4	4	5	2	10	49
TOTAL	30	30	27	28	38	28	25	34	25	38	303

* Excluding Northern Ireland.
(a) The chairman of this council is the secretary of state for Scotland. He is not included below since he does not fit into any of the categories. The council's full membership is therefore 26.
(b) Refers to the Welsh Council, which replaced the Welsh EDC in April 1969. Its membership is larger and less homogeneous because it has a much broader brief.
(c) This should not be taken to show that agriculture is under-represented. Many local authority members indirectly represent farming interests; however, representatives of the agricultural unions are included here rather than in the trade union category.

without going through the normal administrative channels. From time to time there were meetings in London of the chairmen of the boards and regional councils to co-ordinate regional policy. Most councils set up committees and sub-committees to carry out specific tasks, for example dealing with transport, distribution of industry, mobility of labour and land use.

The chairmen of the councils were men of some standing in their home region. In 1968 five chairmen were drawn from public or private industry or commerce, while the three others were, respectively, a vice-chancellor (York-shire—Humberside), a local politician (West Midlands) and a chairman of a regional hospital board (South East).[8]

Scotland[9]

With a number of exceptions both Scotland and Wales were ruled directly from Westminster and Whitehall. The Scottish Economic Planning Council and its accompanying Board both met at the Scottish Office in Edinburgh, which after successive measures of devolution houses a sufficiently large staff of officials to constitute an embryonic autonomous government. The Council's chairman was the secretary of state for Scotland, assisted by a deputy chairman, who was a prominent local figure, like the chairman of the English councils. The Board was chaired by the assistant under-secretary of state at the Scottish Office rather than by a regional official of the DEA. Accordingly the Board and the Council had to work, if not under the thumb of the Scottish Office, at least in close liaison with it. This had one advantage and one disadvantage; on the one hand the fact of having a minister as chairman gave the Council a degree of prestige not enjoyed by its English counterparts; on the other, it was politically and administratively more dependent. Thus it was to 'draw up and implement' proposals for development in keeping with the terms of the White Paper on the Scottish Economy,[10] which had been drafted by officials and economists in the Scottish Office rather than prepared by the Council itself.

Another special feature in Scotland was the setting up of a number of local advisory committees to help in the implementation of the development plan, in the North East, Tayside, the South West and the Borders. These bodies, which had no equivalent elsewhere, included leading figures from the area, local authorities, trade unionists and employers. They were close enough to the people to constitute a useful channel of communication between them and those responsible for the development of the region.

There was also the Highlands and Islands Development Board. This was set up in 1965, and it was assisted by an advisory committee. Its chairman sat on the Scottish Economic Planning Council. It had three main functions: to consider any question relevant to the development of the Highlands; to make proposals to the secretary of state; and to monitor the implementation of any resulting decisions. The trouble with the Board was that it was not subject to any form of democratic control, apart from the very indirect control exercised by the House of Commons through the secretary of state, and there were considerable risks of friction with the local authorities.

Wales

Until 1968 Wales was treated very much like Scotland. One of the ministers of state for Wales acted as chairman of the Welsh Economic Planning Council, and the two deputy chairmen were prominent figures in the Principality. The chairman of the Planning Board was an assistant under-secretary of state at the Welsh Office. In April 1969 the Council was replaced by a Council for Wales, which was assigned a rather wider brief. It has thirty-eight members under the chairmanship of Professor Brindley Thomas, head of the Department of Economics at University College, Cardiff. The chairman and members are appointed by the secretary of state. In addition to exercising the same functions as the English regional planning councils, the Council for Wales watches over the Development Corporation for Wales, the Wales Tourist Board, the Welsh Arts Council and a number of similar bodies. The Board remains under the chairmanship of an assistant under-secretary of state from the Welsh Office.

Some Problems

According to Mr A. W. Peterson, deputy under-secretary of state in charge of regional policy at the DEA between 1964 and 1966, the councils and boards contributed in two ways, 'first, by assessing the economic potential of each region, and the measures which are needed to realise it fully . . . and secondly, by ensuring that full weight is given to the regional implications of national policies'.[11]

As might be expected, good relations between councils and boards were of the greatest importance to their effectiveness. To foster the relationship, the chairmen of the boards usually attended council meetings; other regional officers would be present when there were appropriate matters on the agenda. If the councils were to carry weight in Whitehall they needed the help of the boards; conversely, if government directives were to be fully taken into account at the local level, regional civil servants needed to carry the council with them.

But the real problem was raised by the existence of local authorities who had long had an important role in town and country planning. In announcing the setting up of the new regional economic planning councils, Mr Brown was careful to make it clear that there was no question of encroaching on the powers of the local authorities. While the councils were operating at a different level from the local authorities, they were to some extent engaged in defining the economic context within which the local authorities would act. Again, economic development inherently implies using additional land to create the necessary infrastructure, and there was accordingly some danger that the councils would interfere with the work of the local authorities. In other words, it was very difficult to maintain a clean separation between economic planning and town and country planning. If they are dealt with by different authorities the result is only too likely to be friction and even serious conflict. The sizeable representation of the local authorities on the regional councils was meant to eliminate such difficulties, though it may perhaps have been envisaged at one time as a transitional arrangement until such time as new regional authorities could bring the two functions together.[12]

The success of regional planning councils would therefore depend to a very large extent on how much influence they could exercise over the government's regional policy on the one hand, and over the local authorities' decisions on town and country planning on the other.

CHAPTER 10

The Birth of the Prices and Incomes Board

When Labour came to power in October 1964 it inherited a moribund National Incomes Commission which it was pledged to abolish. But it had also promised to introduce an incomes policy that would be acceptable to the unions. The party had long been aware that there was a problem of cost inflation, and Mr Gaitskell, who was both an economist by training and resolutely hostile to all forms of demagogy, had ever since the fifties been familiarising party conferences with the idea that wage claims could not go on being settled in an anarchic fashion, in total disregard of the general state of the economy.

Thus Labour's position was unambiguous and ministers were determined to show results quickly. They could also profit from the Conservatives' experience, and whenever incomes were mentioned they made a point of adding immediately that it was just as necessary to control profits as to control wages and salaries, and that the best way of exercising this control was a combination of specific measures of taxation and special machinery to keep prices under constant scrutiny. So where the Conservatives had officially had an 'incomes policy' (which in practice was a 'wages policy'), Labour now offered a 'prices and incomes policy'.

The Statement of Intent

Events moved quickly once Mr Brown took up his post at the DEA. The introduction of an effective policy was a matter of urgency because the country was once more in the midst of a balance of payments crisis, and Mr Wilson had rashly pledged that there would be no devaluation of the pound within twenty-four hours of forming his cabinet. Also the introduction of a prices and incomes policy was just the kind of thing that many of the middle-of-the-road voters, who had swung to the party in the election, were expecting Labour to achieve. By December 1964 Mr Brown succeeded in persuading the employers and the unions to sign a joint statement of intent on productivity, prices and incomes.[1] The signing of this document was in its way a historic event, for it was the first time that the employers and the unions had ever been prepared to subscribe to a joint statement on the problem, and to recognise their respective responsibilities in relation to prices, incomes and productivity. Although the commitments were cast in general terms, and the document did not contain a single figure, they were nevertheless quite unambiguous. The government pledged itself to create the conditions needed to achieve and sustain 'a rapid increase in output and real incomes combined with full employment'.[2] With this aim in view it promised to 'prepare and implement a general plan for economic development, in consultation with both sides of industry through the National Economic Development Council',[3] and that greater emphasis would be given to increasing productivity, particularly through encouraging technological advance;[4] to getting rid of restrictive practices; to preventing the abuse of monopoly power and to facilitating the mobility of labour by introducing 'essential social improvements such as a system of earnings-related benefits in addition to the improvement in national insurance benefits already announced'.[5] Finally, the government announced its intention of setting up 'machinery to keep a continuous watch on the general movement of prices and of money incomes of all kinds',[6] and of using its 'fiscal powers or other appropriate means to correct any excessive growth in aggregate profits as compared with the growth of total wages and salaries, after allowing for short-term fluctuations'.[7]

The representatives of the employers' associations and the trade union movement agreed that:

> . . . major objectives of national policy must be:
>
> — to ensure that British industry is dynamic and that its prices are competitive;
> — to raise productivity and efficiency so that real national output can increase, and to keep increases in wages, salaries and other forms of incomes in line with this increase;
> — to keep the general level of prices stable.[8]

Accordingly, on behalf of their members they undertook:

> . . . to encourage and lead a sustained attack on the obstacles to efficiency, whether on the part of management or of workers, and to strive for the adoption of more rigorous standards of performance at all levels; to cooperate with the government in endeavouring in the face of practical problems, to give effective shape to the machinery that the government intend to establish for the following purposes:
>
> (i) to keep under review the general movement of prices and of money incomes of all kinds;
> (ii) to examine particular cases in order to advise whether or not the behaviour of prices or of wages, salaries, or other money incomes is in the national interest as defined by the government after consultation with the management and unions.[9]

This commitment was accepted by Mr George Woodcock on behalf of the TUC, and by representatives of the FBI, BEC and NABM (which had not as yet merged to form the CBI) and of the Association of British Chambers of Commerce. The most important feature was the commitment by the TUC not to oppose improvements in productivity and to accept the need for 'more rigorous standards of performance'. However, it remained to be seen what the TUC's constituent unions would make of these statements in practice. The immediate sequel was that the general secretary's action in signing the Statement of Intent on behalf of the TUC was endorsed by an impressive majority of 6,000,000 votes to 1,800,000 at a special conference of union executives in April 1965. The only large union opposing the agreement was the TGWU, whose general secretary, Frank Cousins, had never made any secret of his total opposition to any form of control of free collective bargaining, but who also happened at the time to be minister of technology and, as such, a member of NEDC![10]

The National Board for Prices and Incomes (PIB)[11]

In putting their signatures to the Statement of Intent unions and employers had agreed to the setting up of machinery to 'keep a continuous watch on the general movement of prices and money incomes of all kinds'. This represented a step forward for the unions, which had refused to have anything to do with NIC. The way was accordingly clear for the establishment of the PIB.

In February 1965 the DEA issued a White Paper on the setting up of this new machinery. It had been approved by the NEDC, the TUC and the employers' associations before it appeared. It indicated that NEDC would continue as before to monitor changes in prices and incomes regularly, while a National Board for Prices and Incomes would 'advise whether or not the behaviour of prices or of wages, salaries or other money incomes is in the national interest as defined by the government after consultation with management and unions'.[12] But the Board only came into being effectively after publication of a further White Paper in April 1965 specifying its membership and laying down the criteria to which the Board should refer in making its rulings.[13] The annual average increase in productivity was estimated at 3.5 per cent, and accordingly the norm for wage increases was 3.0–3.5 per cent.

The Board had fifteen members, only five of them full-time (see figure 10.1). They were drawn from industry, the unions, the professions and the universities. The five full-time members in September 1969 were, respectively, a business-man and former minister (the chairman, Mr Aubrey Jones), a former director of the CWS (Lord Peddie, deputy chairman), an economist who had earlier worked in nationalised industry (R. Turvey, deputy chairman), and two former trade unionists (Mr W. L. Heywood and Mr J. E. Mortimer). The ten part-timers included five businessmen, three academics, a former senior civil servant and a former trade union official. Members were appointed by the government after consulting the chairman and the various interested parties. As a leaflet issued by the PIB put it, 'Their diversity of background and experience ensure that collectively they reach independent and unbiased conclusions although individu-ally they are drawn from many aspects of British society.'[14]

Figure 10.1. Organisation of the Prices and Incomes Board

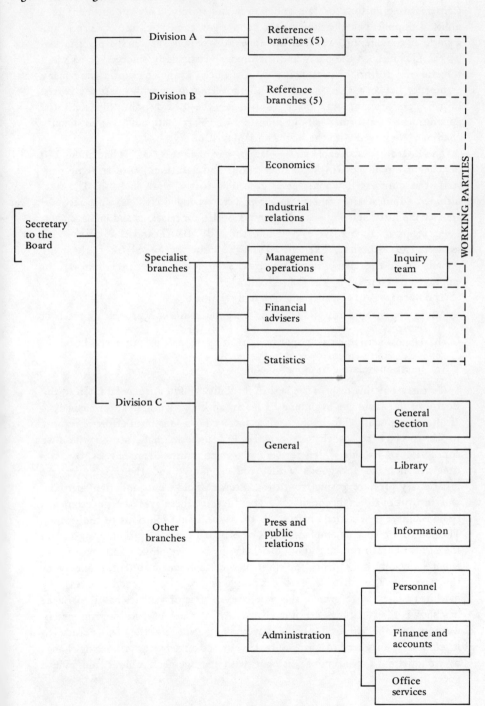

Throughout its existence the chairman was Mr Aubrey Jones, formerly Conservative minister for fuel and power and supply. This appointment of a political opponent, while showing the Labour government's sense of fairness and a spirit of conciliation, was far from universally popular: it was sharply attacked by the Left in both the party and the unions, particularly since Mr Jones was a forceful and forthright personality who had been in the thick of a good many arguments between the unions and the government over the past few years. Initially an attempt was made to balance the Board politically with the appointment of a former Labour minister, Mr Hilary Marquand, as joint deputy chairman. He stayed with the Board until May 1968.

The Board had a sizeable staff — larger than that of NEDC. It had about 240 permanent employees (in September 1969) and a further 40 or so temporary staff, the number of whom varied according to the work in hand. The staff included administrators, most of whom were seconded civil servants, accountants, economists, statisticians and advisers on labour relations and management. Their terms of service were very like those of NEDO, and thus of the civil service. The PIB staff, like NEDO's, were either seconded for fairly short periods from the civil service, universities or public or private industry, or employed on contract by the Board itself.[15]

The Board was to consider any question relating to:

(a) prices charged for goods or for the application of a process to goods or for services;
(b) claims, settlements or questions relating to pay or other conditions of service or employment;
(c) questions relating to money incomes.[16]

To carry out this task to the best of its ability and in the general interest, the Board set out from the beginning to act as 'an impartial catalyst for change',[17] as Mr Jones put it. Thus it saw itself as involved in a long-term effort of reform. In the preface to its first report the PIB unhesitatingly set out its own conception of its role.[18] There were two main causes of price rises. One was excessive demand for goods within the economy, and the other was 'the inflationary pressure arising from the existence of old habits, inherited attitudes and institutional arrangements'.[19] The first of these was the government's responsibility; it was the Board's job to try and find solutions to the second. This led to a recurrent emphasis in its reports on improving productivity and on the need for fresh thinking about efficiency by both employers and unions — an emphasis wholly in line with the spirit of the Statement of Intent. Linked with this was the view that, while legislation was doubtless needed and existing machinery must be reformed, this would not by itself be sufficient: 'Experience has shown that attitudes are not changed by the use of fiscal and monetary weapons at the disposal of the government. Nor are they susceptible to legislation. Habits are not changed by law; we see ourselves as promoting change by conducting a continuing dialogue with management, unions and indeed government. . . .'[20]

The three aspects of this dialogue in a way defined the three functions of the Board — educative, advisory and quasi-judicial. In its educative role, the PIB felt it had a duty to confront the various parties involved fairly and squarely with the implications of their actions for the community as a whole. This is why most of its reports had such a didactic tone; in ruling on a specific case it would try as far as possible to frame its judgements and recommendations in such a way that they had a wider application. The Board's advisory function followed naturally from its general brief, and made it particularly important that the PIB was independent of both the government and private interests. The quasi-judicial function was related to the powers that required it to make decisions by reference to the criteria laid down by the government in the White Paper,[21] but its position as an independent arbitrator allowed it to apply the criteria flexibly, and to take into account efficiency and productivity — to which it always attached the highest importance.

It was clear that the Board had more relish for the long-term reform side of its work than for its job of arbitration. However, while the government did nothing to stop it taking the long-term view, it also wanted the PIB to be an instrument of its short-term policies.[22] There was accordingly a great risk that, in trying to go too far too fast and by conducting too restrictive a policy, the fragile consensus that had been built up with such difficulty would be shattered.

CHAPTER 11

The National Plan of 1965

Within weeks of taking power the new Labour government made it clear that it intended to replace the NEDC plan before it had run its full term to 1966. It had at least two main reasons for doing so. Firstly, the Wilson government wanted to show that Labour planning marked a major national turning point, and this required a completely fresh start. Secondly, on taking office Labour found itself grappling with an overheated economy and a balance of payments crisis; it was clearly impossible to stick to NEDC's original targets and also achieve a healthy balance of payments unless there was a change in the parity of sterling. But within forty-eight hours of arriving at Number 10 the prime minister had ruled out devaluation. This meant that the targets that had been set for growth in 1963 would have to be scaled down. However, during the run-up to the election Labour had rashly claimed that NEDC's target of 4 per cent was only a minimum, and that full implementation of Labour's social programme would require a growth rate of between 5 and 6 per cent. Now it was clear they would have to renege on election promises that had been made far too lightly, and to face harsh economic realities. The new government could argue (and did) that it was only when it had 'seen the books' that it discovered how serious the situation was. This was doubtless true. Nevertheless, it now fell to the planners to extricate the politicians from this situation, and to find some form of presentation that came to terms with reality while sparing ministers too great a loss of face. The outcome was that the National Plan was devised to cover six years (rather than the NEDC plan's five), with an overall growth of 25 per cent (or about 3.8 per cent a year), compared with NEDC's 22 per cent (which was equivalent to 4 per cent a year).

So in September 1965, a bare eleven months after Labour's return to power, the National Plan was published with no little ceremony in the form of a White Paper of 475 pages – thus stamped as government policy, unlike its predecessor, which appeared on the sole responsibility of NEDC.[1] On the evening it appeared Mr Brown presented it on radio in these terms: 'This is a national plan, drawn up after the closest cooperation between the government and every section of the community . . . . The National Council for Economic Development has said that it is within our capacity to carry out this plan, and has agreed to undertake the responsibilities which will fall to it under the terms of the White Paper.'[2] In fact, NEDC had been extremely hesitant about endorsing the aims of a document it had had to consider piecemeal over several meetings. The statement issued by NEDC after its meeting on 5 August 1965, when the Council discussed the Plan as a whole, indicates clearly enough to anyone who can read between the lines that the Council's approval was secured only after long and difficult discussion: 'The Council considered that the Plan was a valuable analysis of the problems to be considered in achieving a 25% growth rate between 1964 and 1970. While considering that such an increase was within the nation's capacity, the Council pointed out that its achievement would require a major national effort.'[3]

The Preparation of the National Plan

The National Plan was prepared in very much the same way as the Economic Division of NEDO had drawn up the 1962 plan. This is scarcely surprising since to all practical intents and purposes it was prepared by the same team, doing the same jobs, under the same man, Sir Donald MacDougall. (However, on transferring to the DEA they were now able to draw on the assistance of the Economic Section and National Economy group at the Treasury.) Not surprisingly, then, they embarked on another industrial inquiry along much the same lines as the one they conducted in 1962, only this time instead of sending it to only seventeen industries their questionnaire was intended to cover all sections of industry. The crucial question was what the implications would be for the industry if the economy as a whole grew by 25 per cent for the period 1964–70. Usually the questionnaire was sent to trade associations – who were to ask their members in turn – but some were sent directly to the largest firms in an industry. If the industry concerned had a Little Neddy, it discussed the replies (which was a useful improvement on the way the earlier inquiry was conducted); where there was no Little Neddy unofficial working parties were set up with representatives of the industry, NEDO and the departments concerned.

Like its predecessor, the 1965 industrial inquiry had virtues and short-comings. It allowed the plan to be prepared more rapidly. Most of the questionnaires had been returned within a few months (and by then it was clear that the very few firms that had not replied had no intention of replying). An inquiry of this kind could not, of course, hope to achieve complete accuracy. Moreover, it had the inherent failing of any such survey in that those replying felt in no way bound to act in conformity with their replies. But the real weakness arose from the way in which the central question was put. Industries were not asked for their views on the likely development of their particular sector of the economy; instead they were asked how it would be affected if the economy as a whole grew by 25 per cent. This tended to bias the replies. For it is obvious that, subject to any special circumstances in the particular industry, the industry would immediately tend to think that demand for its products would increase by that amount. In short, its estimates of the increase in its own production would be strongly influenced by the initial premiss. The planners were aware that this criticism might be levelled at them and tried to rebut it in advance:

> Although industry was asked to assume an increase of this amount in gross domestic product there is no reason why their independently calculated estimates should add to this figure and in fact the original estimates by industry gave a significantly lower increase in total output and showed a different pattern from that finally put forward . . . .[4]

This explanation is unconvincing on two accounts. Firstly, if the estimates for each industry singly were unlikely to reach the level desired, since the capacity for expansion would vary from industry to industry, there was no reason why the sum of the individual estimates should not produce an overall figure close to the figure suggested. Consequently — and this is the second objection — if 'the original estimates by industry gave a significantly lower increase in total output', that meant both that industry as a whole had not taken the DEA's premise very seriously, and that the DEA had taken little account of the results of the inquiry during the final preparation of the Plan — and had in fact simply stuck to the original quite arbitrary figure of 25 per cent. As *The Banker* said at the time, 'it is hard to repress a suspicion that the planners have at times been tempted to tailor the figures to fit the pattern of their own model'.[5] It is of course entirely natural for planners to attempt to alter the general picture of the economy that emerges from a study of the market, but if they wish to do so they must be sure they have the powers and resources to carry those modifications through — and that the modifications are attainable.

The Plan as a Strategy for Growth

Like all previous documents on planning that had appeared in Britain, the National Plan could not resist the temptation to be didactic, and its opening chapter contained a whole section on 'the nature and purpose of planning'.[6] Recalling the rather ambiguous nature of planning in a capitalist society, it went on to contrast the public sector, where the State takes the initiative and has direct responsibility, with the private sector, which it can influence directly only through legislation and taxation. In place of this traditional, one might even say trite, distinction one would have preferred it to have explained the nature of the Plan itself rather more clearly, indicating how far it could simultaneously be a 'statement of government policy',[7] a 'commitment to action by the government'[8] and a 'guide to action',[9] as Mr Brown claimed it to be. Though the Plan contains a pertinent 'check list of action required',[10] a considerable number of the measures suggested were never in fact introduced. In addition, words like 'target', 'forecast' and 'projection' were employed quite indiscriminately, possibly because the planners themselves were unsure exactly what kind of operation they were involved in. This is probably a result of the fact that the politicians responsible for the Plan could not make up their minds whether it was merely an indicative plan or something more. Nevertheless, most of the targets set out in the Plan gave every appearance of being official government targets.

The White Paper had two sections. The first contained the Plan itself, comprising a summary of the main aims, an analysis of the national sectorial targets for manpower, industrial efficiency, investment, prices and incomes, the balance of payments and regional planning, consideration of the same factors industry by industry and estimates of the use of resources under the headings of consumer expenditure, housing, public expenditure, defence, health and welfare, education and benefits and assistance. The second part contained appendices based on the answers to the industrial inquiry. Obviously, though, the main political interest lay in the targets for the economy as a whole.

As we have seen, the target of 25 per cent growth rested only on an industrial inquiry that had been considerably 'adjusted'. In the light of previous experience the authors of the Plan had nevertheless slightly reduced the overall target. Even so they were well aware how great a gamble this involved, particularly since it was clear that measures taken to restore the balance of payments in 1965 were bound to cast a shadow over the first year or so of the new plan. This led them to press the idea of catching up — which had already made its appearance in relation to the first plan. 'The plan is designed to achieve a 25% increase in national output between 1964 and 1970. This objective . . . involves achieving a 4% annual growth rate of output well before 1970 and an annual average of 3.8% between 1964 and 1970.'[11] In plain language this meant that the planners were fully aware that for the first year or so there would be little growth. They went on to explain a little further on: 'The measures that have been taken to redress the balance of payments will inevitably lead to less growth within the next year or so than would be possible if the balance of payments weakness had already been overcome. This will make the 25% objective more difficult to achieve.'[12]

The average rate of 3.8 per cent rested on three basic objectives: a rise in productivity of 3.4 per cent (the labour force would increase by only 0.5 per cent), a rise in fixed investment of 5.5 per cent and, most important of all, an increase of 5.25 per cent in exports as against only 4 per cent in imports.

The estimates made by companies of their manpower requirements in 1970, assuming overall growth of 25 per cent, led the planners to conclude that the economy would require some 800,000 more workers (after allowing for an improvement of 3.4 per cent a year in productivity). Projections suggested that the work force would in fact increase by 400,000 by 1970. The planners also calculated that an energetically conducted regional policy would lead to the redeployment of some 200,000 workers. Thus there was a shortfall of about 200,000 people. The Plan was sharply criticised for this gap. It really arose from a presentational device, by which the planners drew attention to the fact that productivity would have to increase by an extra 0.1 to 0.2 per cent a year, failing which growth would only be about 23 per cent over the six years. If this had occurred it would have been unfair to say the Plan had 'failed', since a straight extrapolation of the experience of the past few years indicated growth of only about 15 per cent. (But as figure 11.1 shows, real growth has been lower still.)

The target for the growth of all forms of fixed investment was set at 5.5 per cent a year, and within this industrial investment would rise by an annual average of 7.0 per cent. This figure emerged from the industrial inquiry and discussions with representatives of the various industries. Nevertheless one doubts whether it was attainable, in view of the fact that, as figure 5.1 (p. 123) shows, industrial investment rose by only 2.4 per cent a year on average between 1960 and 1964. These doubts were increased by the state of the economy at the time the Plan was published and by forecasts for 1966. Alarm was expressed that any attempt to catch up subsequently would simply trigger off an inflationary boom.

Figure 11.1. Targets and achievements of the policy of stimulating growth.

Index of GDP (1958 prices, 1958 = 100)

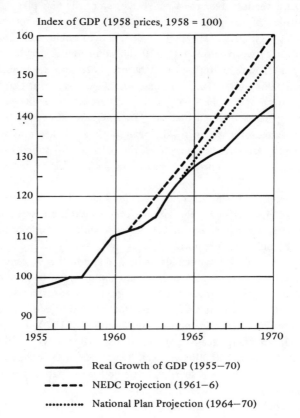

——— Real Growth of GDP (1955–70)

– – – • NEDC Projection (1961–6)

•••••••••• National Plan Projection (1964–70)

As *The Banker* put it: 'Such large investment is surely inconceivable in 1966, when entrepreneurial expectations will hardly be cheered by the general business climate. . . . If all the required investment really takes place and is concentrated in the period from some time in 1967, the result will be a powerful boom operating in a labour market which is forecast to become increasingly tight.'[13]

But this was not the biggest gamble. Unlike the NEDC plan, which had to some extent glossed over the difficulty in fixing a target of 5 per cent a year as the increase in exports, the National Plan noted in its opening lines:

> For too long the United Kingdom has suffered from a weak balance of payments . . . . It is the government's aim to break out of this vicious circle and to introduce and maintain policies which will enable us to enjoy more rapid and sustained economic growth . . . . The task of correcting the balance of payments and achieving the surplus necessary to repay our debts, while at the same time fostering the rapid growth of the economy, is the central challenge.[14]

Regrettably, the target of 5.25 per cent for exports (and 4 per cent for imports) appears to have been arrived at by much the same questionable means as were used to fix the target for growth. Between 1954 and 1964 exports had in fact risen about 3 per cent a year on average. The National Plan expected a rise to 4 per cent, for which it offered this justification: 'An extrapolation of previous trends allows us to reckon on an increase of very near to 4% per annum in the future.'[15] But there was no real explanation of the reasons leading the planners to expect the additional one per cent a year. Yet the planners were not content with this progression, which made the other aims of the plan appear very unrealistic. Accordingly they added that some further improvement should be possible, and adopted the target 5.25 per cent. How had 4 per cent become 5.25 per cent? This was where the industrial inquiry came in. Each industry was asked what it expected to be able to achieve by way of increased exports, assuming again that production was increasing by 3.8 per cent a year. 'Perhaps the most encouraging result of the enquiry was in the field of exports. The replies from industry suggested that these could grow by about 5½% a year in volume.'[16] It could perhaps be argued that by setting a target of 5.25 per cent the planners were in fact showing a proper professional caution. However, the more likely reason is that this was a sufficient level to support their overall figure for growth. In addition, the way in which the figure of 5.50 per cent had been obtained from industry raised questions about its accuracy. As Alan Day noted in *The Observer*, the questionnaire was accompanied by a note indicating that exports would have to rise at twice the existing rate if the overall target for growth was to be achieved. Once more, it is not surprising that industry tried to conform, particularly since it had nothing to lose by being agreeable!

While the Plan made a number of proposals that might improve the balance of payments in the long run, it was hard to see how their impact could produce a large enough change soon enough. In fact, the projection for exports assumed two conditions would be met, and one of these was not within the government's control: that world trade would continue growing at the same rate or faster than in recent years, and that the prices and incomes policy would succeed – though its attempt to improve the competitiveness of British manufactured goods could not hope to bear fruit for some time. Contrary to its protestations, the Plan had in fact nothing new to contribute to the solution of the problem of external trade. Yet it was only too likely that a slight deficiency in the requisite rate of growth in exports would gravely compromise the success of the Plan as a whole, since a slight deterioration in the balance of payments tended to lead to a run on the pound, which in turn could be stemmed only by deflationary measures quite out of proportion with the actual size of the deficit. So the entire structure rested on a solution being found to this problem: 'Thus the technique used in "solving" the future balance of payments problem . . . was . . . in the first place to assume a desired rate of progress, then to send out a questionnaire to industry which induces it to forecast a rate of growth of the same order and finally to announce that the national forecast has been confirmed by the forecasts of industry'.[17] Not surprisingly there was severe criticism, by no means all of it from opponents of planning.

The Reception of the Plan

Only the credulous could believe that such a nice round figure was the invention of science.[18]

The 1965 Plan unquestionably received a cooler reception than the NEDC document. Equally unquestionably this was due in large measure to the disappointing outcome of the earlier plan. Admittedly Labour had set up new machinery and generally attempted to give planning a new look. But the move from NEDO to the DEA seemed to make little difference in the way in which the planners went about their job. As a result economists and political observers had a strong feeling of *déjà vu*. The general public were quite indifferent. A Research Services poll taken four days after publication of the Plan showed that more than half the men and seventy per cent of the women had heard nothing about it.[19] For all Mr Brown's efforts, the man in the street did not feel in the least involved. And yet the Plan had been prominently reported and discussed by the press. Even *The Times* managed a kindly greeting, saying it 'deserves a warm welcome', and describing it as 'a first-class analysis of the British economy'[20] which involved 'a greater commitment to long-term planning than has ever been accepted before except in time of war'[21] – though that particular remark of course implied no judgement on the merits. The rest of the article was more critical. *The Financial Times* and most of the weeklies were even more sceptical. Under the heading 'National Platitudes', *The Economist* commented, 'It is much easier to poke fun at the National Plan than to echo Mr. George Brown's hosannas for it.'[22] *The Observer* ran a scathing article by Alan Day.[23] It is worth noting that all these papers had supported indicative planning and had given Neddy and the NEDC plan a sympathetic welcome. In the host of commentaries that were published during the ensuing weeks and months in the more specialised journals, the same expressions or criticisms recurred: 'optimistic'; 'unrealistic'; 'an upward bias dictated by political considerations';[24] 'more a pipedream or reverie'.[25] The planners were accused of taking their wishes for realities and even, occasionally, of intellectual dishonesty.[26] The PEP study regretted that 'it offers arguments to those who are hostile to national plans and raises doubts in the minds of those who are favourable'.[27] PEP was also particularly critical of the ambiguity of the Plan: 'The National Plan is thus in part a national market forecast, in part indicative or target planning, partly a feasibility study, and has some elements of a directive or action programme. Because these roles are insufficiently distinguished, it is unsatisfactory when judged in terms of one or the other of them.'[28] However, it also attacked those 'obscurantists' who opposed all forms of planning, particularly when they questioned whether there was any point at all in national forecasts. But it admitted that by setting an unduly ambitious rate of growth the credibility of the Plan had been undermined:

> Of course, the acceptance that demand expectations have some part to play in faster growth implies that the target must be ambitious; it must be a target for a faster rate than would probably have been achieved without the Plan. But if the target is too far above what is feasible, it will either fail to be credible or lead the economy into a short-lived boom followed by yet another stop.[29]

The Economist shared the same fear and was also doubtful about timing:

> It has been introduced at just the wrong moment, when Labour, because of its external fears for sterling and internal fears for its majority, cannot plan to do the things that it would really like to do. It talks of growth and great social reform, but it does not set down even on white paper the proposals to achieve them, not with all those foreign bankers looking on.[30]

In fact, the Plan was to have a political role of some importance — though this should only have been a secondary consideration — since it served as a basis for the Labour election manifesto in the March 1966 election,[31] from which Mr Wilson emerged with a considerably increased majority. For the National Plan allowed the manifesto to count on a probable improvement of 25 per cent in the standard of living in the course of the next Parliament, and to promise handsome increases in social benefits with every appearance of behaving responsibly. Where President de Gaulle had termed the French Plan a 'burning obligation', Mr Wilson spoke of 'a central strategy set out for all the nation to see'.[32] To his opponents, and even to some independent observers, this operation was very close to moral fraud, since the experts were already doubtful whether, in the light of expenditure cuts announced by the chancellor in June and July 1965, there was any longer any real chance of the targets being met.

The Abandoning of the Plan

> *On July 20 1966 the demise of the National Plan was announced. It had of course been suspected dead for a long time past. The doctors had diagnosed congenital defects as soon as the infant was born; and its chances of survival were never rated very highly even before its birth in September 1965.*[33]

This mock-heroic epitaph came from the pen of one of the men who had pinned his hopes on 'growth through planning' in the early sixties. But disillusionment had begun to set in well before July 1966. Apart from the doubts about the Plan itself, the short-term management of the economy since October 1964 had given the 'growth lobby' little ground for hope. When Labour returned to power the balance of payments crisis was at its peak and there were some, like John Brunner, who felt that this had happened because Mr Maudling had shown too much respect for the NEDC plan. But it might equally be felt that the main reason for the crisis was that the pound was overvalued. In October 1964 the deficit for the year was estimated at £800 million. (In the event it proved to be rather less.) At that time this was the worst figure since immediately after the war. At first the Wilson government, which saw no need for devaluation, tried to avoid resorting to traditional measures for cutting back consumption. Instead it imposed a temporary import surcharge on manufactured goods (which accounted for a third of imports). The advantage of this course was that it did not check internal expansion, and might even encourage it by reducing competition from imports. But it was deeply resented by Britain's trading partners, particularly the other members of EFTA, and to head off reprisals Mr Wilson had to cut the surcharge by a third in February 1965. Also, since it was a purely temporary measure (it was eventually abolished in November 1966), it led to stocks being run down as importers waited for the opportunity to replenish their stocks at lower prices. Its psychological consequences were more serious; for international financial circles took the measure as heralding a forthcoming devaluation of sterling.[34] This fanned speculation and forced the government to seek international assistance following a week of panic between 20 and 25 November 1964, despite raising the bank rate to 7 per cent – which at the period was considered to be a crisis level – which ought to have brought hot money flowing back to London. This operation to save the pound was the first on such a scale but by no means the last; it put something in the region of $3,000 million at the disposal of the Bank of England to cope with the situation – in return for a categoric assurance that the pound would not be devalued.

This was the start of a financial policy in which the government eventually lost all freedom of action. It was its determination to defend the 1949 parity of the pound at all costs that led to this inglorious dead end. Indeed, it was soon apparent that there was a contradiction between the aims of the DEA, which was responsible for drawing up a plan for expansion, and those of the chancellor who was forced to fight every inch of the way with the traditional deflationary weapons, since devaluation was ruled out. This provoked Mr Iain Macleod's biting remark that 'we have a minister of long-term "go" and a minister of short-term "stop" '.[35] This situation led to the widespread journalistic impression, noted earlier, that there was a tug-of-war between rival departments or ministers. But this was an oversimplification which seriously distorted the real situation; though there was a clash it was less between two ministries than between contradictory commitments entered into by the cabinet and, indeed, the prime minister alone.[36]

Over the months Mr Callaghan announced a series of measures designed to restrain demand, amid continuing speculation and a steady rise in the external debt (arising from swap agreements and longer-term loans from IMF and central banks). As the government's measures bit harder they threatened to bring expansion to a complete halt; as John and Anne-Marie Hackett noted at the beginning of 1966, 'In the end . . . the cumulative effect of the succession of restrictions imposed between October 1964 and July 1965 was of much the same order of severity as during the previous "stop" of July 1961.'[37] The stop—go cycle lived on. Only the fact that the government's measures were spread out prevented expansion being stopped abruptly in its tracks as it had been during earlier crises. More serious in terms of the eventual success of the Plan were the cuts in public investment announced in June 1965 and the restrictions on private investment introduced in July. Thus, even before the Plan had been officially published, the statistical basis underpinning it was in danger of being undermined.

But the real turning point came only after the election of March 1966, when the cabinet was forced to introduce 'draconian measures' to meet a fresh sterling crisis. After several days during which rumour was rife, the prime minister told a tense House of Commons that once more the international financial community had rallied to 'save the pound'; a fresh line of credit, amounting to some £413 million, mostly under swap agreements, would be available to the Bank of England to check speculation; there would be fresh measures of austerity; bank rate (which had fallen since 1965) would go back to 7 per cent; there would be further cuts in public expenditure; and wages would be frozen. It could no longer be pretended that the bid for rapid growth had not been abandoned. Speaking in the Commons on the consequences of the government's measures, Mr Brown admitted that the Plan was effectively dead: 'How does this affect the National Plan? I will be absolutely frank with the House; it means that the rate of growth we intended to set, and on the basis of which we predicted all other things for 1970, is no longer available.'[38] In the light of this failure Mr Brown offered to resign. The prime minister, who had just accepted the resignation of Mr Cousins (who was utterly opposed to the introduction of the wage freeze), persuaded the deputy-leader to stay on for a little while, and then in August moved him to the Foreign Office, sending Mr Stewart to the DEA.

Yet again, as under the Conservatives but in even more striking fashion, the defence of the pound was put before expansion; in other words short-term management of the economy was not a means of implementing the Plan, as it should have been if the Plan had indeed been the 'central strategy' for the nation that Mr Wilson had said it was. This would not have meant meeting every last dot and comma of the Plan, but it would have meant respecting its general outlines and spirit. One does not have to talk to former members of the DEA for long before they will admit that the Plan was less than honest in refraining from recommending a change in the parity of the pound. Obviously no country can afford the luxury of announcing in an official document that it intends to devalue. Probably the planners, most of whom considered devaluation as inevitable, thought the politicians would be able to read between the lines and not allow themselves to be satisfied with the Plan's 'solution' of the balance of payments problem. For, to be credible, an increase in exports of 5.25 per cent implied a sharp turnabout that could only be achieved through devaluation. But ministers appear not to have asked themselves the question in such clear terms. They saw the problem as an international rather than an internal one, and at every crisis what counted most with them was whether the deflationary measures they were contemplating would be adequate to damp down specula-tion and convince 'the gnomes of Zurich' of their determination not to devalue. Despite what he says in his autobiography, it is not even sure that in July 1966 Mr Brown was in any position to propose to his colleagues an alternative strategy based on devaluation, because the DEA had never been able to give this alternative serious consideration owing to Mr Wilson's instructions that this was taboo.[39]

Thus the period between November 1964 and November 1967 produced a series of missed opportunities by Labour. In November 1964 devaluation would have been politically astute; it would have been only too easy to justify it by pointing to the state in which the Conservatives had left the economy. By confining himself to repeated complaints over the size of the balance of payments deficit the Conservatives had bequeathed to him, Mr Wilson inevitably fanned speculation without in any way contributing to a solution to the problem. In November 1965 devaluation would have been politically honest; the Plan had just been launched and we have already noted its implications for sterling. Before campaigning on expansion and 'Labour Government Works' the government should at least have removed this obstacle from its path. Even in July 1966, a 'hot' devaluation would have avoided struggling on fruitlessly for a further fifteen months and allowed ministers to give the appearance of having a coherent economic policy. There can be no doubt that this obstinacy in the face of the inevitable during three crucial years cost Mr Wilson his third electoral victory in 1970 (for although by then there had been a belated improvement in the situation it was widely thought to be purely ephemeral). As Paul Foot notes, the call for 'the Dunkirk spirit' in peacetime stirs less and less response, particularly when sacrifices seem pointless.[40] This is not to say that all Britain's problems would have been resolved by a substantial devaluation in 1964.[41] But there can be no doubt that ministers would have been in a position to envisage implementation of their economic and social proposals with greater confidence.

But how can one explain the behaviour of Mr Wilson, who has so often been accused of being the arch political opportunist? At that time the mere word 'devaluation' stirred panic among British politicians, most particularly on the Labour side, both for valid technical considerations and for more direct and less excusable political reasons.

Technically the pound sterling had two international roles: as a medium of exchange and as a reserve currency. On the whole the former role was an asset, producing a useful contribution to invisible earnings. The second was more of a liability. For although the sterling balances were held in central and local government securities and industrial stock, and thus benefited public and private investment (while being advantageous to the holders because of the high rates of interest they could earn on the British money market), they were subject to sudden and violent fluctuations because the holders (both states and private individuals) became nervous not only when Britain was running a balance of payments deficit, but whenever there was any major political upheaval anywhere in the world. Thus, there was a constant risk of very large sums being suddenly switched out of London. Devaluation would obviously reduce the value of the sterling balances and consequently undermine the City of London's standing in the financial world. This is why the City, which drew much of its livelihood from sterling's international role, was such a potent pressure group for the existing parity, not just for reasons of commercial ethics, but because it feared that the loss of confidence among holders of sterling would produce a gradual decline in its role as an international currency.[42] The Bank and the Treasury were understandably receptive to such arguments. However, in the last analysis, these considerations probably weighed less heavily than others of a more purely political kind.

The main political motive was the fear, whether founded or not, of embarrassing the United States. For if the pound were devalued it was widely expected that the dollar would find itself in the front line, as President Johnson's Secretary to the Treasury put it. In those days British leaders, whether Labour or Conservative, were still hoping to preserve the 'special relationship' with the United States and would do nothing that might displease the Americans, particularly since the United States had always been the first to help the pound. (They tried to do so once more in November 1967, but apparently too late.)

The second consideration was Labour's special complex about devaluation. There had been two previous devaluations — in 1931 and 1949 — and both had been under Labour prime ministers and chancellors (MacDonald and Snowden in 1931, and Attlee and Cripps in 1949). Mr Wilson and Mr Callaghan had no desire to be the third pair of Labour leaders to have their names linked to the dreaded spectre of devaluation. It would be naive to say this was the main reason, but equally it would show little understanding of human nature in general and politicians in particular to suggest it had nothing whatever to do with the obstinacy of the prime minister and the chancellor. As we have seen, the charge of obstinacy should be aimed mainly at Mr Wilson, whose narrow nationalism was in Paul Foot's view unworthy of a genuine socialist.[43] He may well have feared that the Conservatives would accuse him of being unpatriotic. This was also a reason why he decided to withdraw from east of Suez only when financial pressures compelled him to do so, rather than as part of any carefully considered policy. It might well be thought that in 1964, and still more later when Britain was in even deeper economic difficulties, any accusation of scuttling vital British interests would have seemed grossly overdrawn, particularly if there had been any real prospect of an improvement in the economy. Nevertheless, whenever possible Mr Wilson preferred to wait, fearing he might cause irreparable harm; but in such matters inaction can. actually lead to the irreparable. For the July 1966 measures meant not abandoning a particular plan, whose passing few would mourn, but the torpedoing of the entire policy of indicative planning set up in 1962. For in the wake of this failure neither the public nor the civil service would be ready to give much weight to the planners for a long while to come.

CHAPTER 12

The Consequences of the Failure of the Plan

The DEA had been so closely identified with the Plan that the failure of the Plan was bound to affect both its influence and its organisation. While the department had many other responsibilities which it continued to discharge normally, Mr Brown's departure in August 1966 marked the beginning of its decline, less than two years after its creation. Mr Brown's successor, Michael Stewart, was not a man to launch bold new policies. In any case, given the difficulties of the pound, the DEA had to take a back seat to the Treasury in economic policy-making. Moreover, with the cabinet reshuffle of August 1967 the minister for economic affairs ceased to be chairman of NEDC; Mr Wilson himself became officially responsible for the department, and consequently chairman of Neddy. He was assisted at the DEA by Mr Peter Shore. The intention was to restore a little much-needed lustre to the DEA and NEDC and to make it clear that planning had not been abandoned. So far as NEDC was concerned the gambit was reasonably successful, and Neddy regained a measure of prestige with both the CBI and the TUC, which were also pleased that the chancellor had been restored to membership. But it did almost nothing for the DEA, since it was soon clear that Mr Wilson was not in fact running the department. The DEA's responsibilities were gradually being whittled away; in August 1967 it lost its responsibility for external economic policy to the Board of Trade, and then in March 1968 it had to hand over the running of the prices and incomes policy to the new Department of Employment and Productivity under Mrs Castle.

Thus the DEA was run down, and eventually it was abolished in the reshuffle of October 1969. This was no surprise to either the public or Whitehall — except, perhaps, for those senior officials, including the secretary of state himself, who had been planning to mark their department's fifth birthday in an appropriate manner! In fact some of the leading lights had already left the DEA. From 1 January 1969 Sir Donald MacDougall had become chief economic adviser at the Treasury, in succession to Sir Alec Cairncross, and in August 1969 Mr John Jukes,[1] the deputy under-secretary, was transferred to the Ministry of Transport and not replaced, even though the DEA had returned to the field of medium-term planning in February 1969 by publishing what it modestly referred to as a 'planning document'.[2]

The Crisis in National Planning

When indicative planning became fashionable in the early sixties, it was clear that most of those advocating planning had only a limited commitment to it. They fell into two main groups. The first, and larger, group seemed to expect planning to banish both deflation and devaluation by some sort of exorcism — in other words it was an expedient that avoided difficult choices. The second group were expansionists who supported planning for strictly pragmatic reasons. They saw the preparation of a plan for growth as the surest way of bringing to light the basic contradiction between the short-term policies that had been pursued until then and the need for expansion, and they thought that when they ran up against the constraints the balance of payments was imposing on the economy, the planners would be able to force the political leaders to tackle head-on the continuing impediment to growth constituted by a fixed exchange rate. Most of them expected the planning apparatus to become a powerful pressure group for growth, challenging the prevailing Treasury orthodoxy.

In July 1966 both groups had to change their tune, the first because it was quite clear that planning had not prevented either deflation or devaluation and that in the period ahead Britain would experience both; the second because they were now aware that to the politicians planning was simply a pretext not to tackle the really basic problems, and if forced to a choice they would prefer to fall back into the same old rut. Hence those who had advocated planning in 1962 were disappointed, particularly those in the second group who were now regretting that they had not campaigned for their views directly and openly, rather than trying to achieve them indirectly through planning. Sam Brittan, who may be included with the second group, put the problem in these terms:

> Those who challenged the sterling-first doctrines and put forward the claims of expansion have no reason to be repentant — not even about the goal of a 4% growth rate. But they should have concentrated on policies for making such a growth rate possible . . . instead of getting involved in the diversions of the planning exercises . . . . The planning movement has thus delayed for at least five years the real debate on policy, and is more likely to have hindered than to have helped the radical reassessment of national priorities desired by many of its adherents.[3]

Brittan concluded that it was useless to persevere with planning and that it would be better to press directly for expansionist policies. He took his argument to its logical conclusion in January 1967 by advocating that there should be an immediate devaluation after which sterling should be allowed to float. His analysis was shared by a number of other observers who had advocated planning a few years earlier.

Until the 1967 devaluation the government exhausted itself in a series of rearguard actions to defend the pound. Little was heard from Mr Stewart at the DEA, though in October 1966 he did suggest that, instead of redrafting the Plan, which everyone agreed had been completely overtaken by events, it should be extended beyond 1970.[4] In this way sooner or later its targets would be achieved! But a rolling plan is only fruitful when accompanied by reasonably clear rules. In any case, Mr Stewart only threw this out as a vague suggestion, and nothing more was heard of it subsequently. The DEA's morale and influence had suffered seriously, and little was heard officially about medium-term planning until early in 1969.

The CBI was now taking a very cautious line. The view of planning endorsed by its Eastbourne conference in early 1965[5] and subsequently worked out in fuller detail was clearly less ambitious than at the Brighton conference which, as we have seen, marked the beginning of the revival of planning: 'The adoption of a 4% growth rate now appears to have been based on an overoptimistic assessment of our ability to maintain a favourable balance of payments . . . . So long as this imbalance persists it will be necessary for the government to modify the rate of growth of the economy by appropriate fiscal or monetary methods'.[6] So by 1965 the CBI was resigned to a return to the old policy of deliberate stagnation; this to a large extent explains its scepticism about the National Plan even though it was slightly less expansionist than the NEDC plan. This attitude was confirmed at the end of 1966 in an internal memorandum which concluded that 'the first task of the NEDC is to consider how best to make progress with the solution of long-term structural problems. It is well placed to act as a watchdog over the level of government expenditure'.[7] So Neddy was no longer seen as a pressure group for growth but as a device for holding down government expenditure. The CBI had come a long way since Brighton!

Not all members of NEDC shared this attitude. Following devaluation, its patience exhausted by more than a year of recession, the TUC began to call increasingly vociferously for a resolutely expansionist policy. This was to be a continuous source of friction between the unions and the government over the next two years, on top of the other major disagreements on incomes policy and industrial relations reform. In the TUC's view, the recession caused by the July 1966 measures, as well as the effort many companies had made to modernise at the government's behest since 1965,[8] had led to a considerable rise in unemployment.[9] Consequently it called for the introduction of a plan based on the maintenance of full employment:

> There is a danger at the present time that Britain's potential for economic growth may once again be under-estimated . . . . Far too many men and women have found themselves without jobs in the past twelve months. Higher productivity has been achieved but the new jobs promised as part of the programme for redeployment are not yet there . . . . If the new approach to productivity proves, in the eyes of the workpeople, to have been at their expense, there will only be an inevitable tendency for them to protect themselves in the only way they know how — by restricting output and productivity and by sharing work. This would be a tragedy.[10]

The TUC's comment was very much to the point. In a country that has suffered so much from unemployment, and where working-class reactions are still conditioned by the fear of being under-employed, expansion is the only way of winning acceptance for improving productivity. This was one reason why the TUC favoured more rapid growth, but it was not the only one. It also believed growth was economically feasible since increased productivity should make it possible not only to produce more with the same workforce, but to produce even more so that both men and machinery would be employed as fully as possible:

> There is no reason why, after an initial period of adjustment, the GDP should not be expanding rapidly. The rate of expansion can be put at 6 per cent in the year from mid-1968 to mid-1969. Of this total, in broad terms 4 per cent will come from an increase in hourly productivity, 1 per cent from extra hours per man and 1 per cent from increased employment.[11]

Unfortunately, the TUC's faith in a high growth rate and its desire to put forward a constructive policy of detailed and coherent proposals was not to have its reward. Though in a speech to the Parliamentary Labour Party a few days after devaluation Mr Wilson did mention the possibility of a growth rate of 6 per cent, this was only a slip of the tongue and nothing more was heard of it. On the contrary the government's approach — with the new chancellor, Mr Roy Jenkins, well to the fore — was resolutely pessimistic. Actually, 1968 was not a bad year for growth; GNP rose by 3.8 per cent, which was one of the best figures for years, and productivity by 4.6 per cent, which was very good by British standards. But employment fell by 0.7 per cent, which justified the TUC's fears and their desire to see expansion speeded up.[12] But would it really have been possible to do better still, in view of the fact that the effects of devaluation would take some time to work through and as yet, at least, there was little improvement in the balance of payments? The government thought not. In March 1968 Mr Jenkins presented another austerity budget aimed at cutting back internal demand, which was still vigorous, hoping that exports would take up the slack and thus allow some small amount of growth. These contradictory assessments of the situation almost led to open hostilities between the TUC and the government in 1968 — a war in which the stake was the growth rate and the victim looked like being *concertation*.

To some extent NEDC became the battleground, since from the summer of 1968 the Council was involved in the gestation of a new medium-term plan for the period up to 1972, which was under preparation by the DEA. This envisaged a much lower rate of growth than the TUC was demanding. Having burned its fingers over the National Plan the DEA, in keeping with the government's general approach, decided to be cautious and suggest 'flexible' targets. Most members of the Council (government, CBI and independent members) were sympathetic to this approach, and when by the end of the summer it had become increasingly obvious that the TUC would be unable to bring the other members round to its way of thinking, it reached the point of threatening, if only obliquely, to withdraw because membership of NEDC was not producing the slightest impact on the government's economic policy. It was obviously difficult for the TUC to appear, by continuing its membership of the Council, to be approving an economic policy that had led to unemployment being over the half million mark since the second quarter of 1967. But the unions' unhappiness was in line with the longer-standing discontent of the CBI, which had felt ever since the establishment of the DEA that the Council was no longer as influential as it had been when Mr Maudling was at the Treasury and it was NEDC itself which decided the main targets for the plan.

Yet NEDC continued with its monthly meetings, and from 1967 Mr Wilson himself was in the chair. These meetings were a way for him to keep in touch with the development of the economic situation, to discuss many of the major policy issues, such as the consequences of devaluation, a new overseas trade policy, overseas investment, improvements in productivity, prices and incomes and restrictive trade agreements, and to consider the recommendations contained in the reports of the Little Neddies. Also, in 1966 and 1967 NEDC organised several 'prime minister's productivity conferences' which examined the problems of raising productivity across the economy as a whole. While these conferences produced little in the way of tangible results, they were not without their political importance, since they were the prime minister's last attempt to tackle Britain's economic problems by 'physical planning' — that is by structural reform — as an alternative to devaluation and deflation. But it became evident that, even if these efforts had been successful, the results would have been felt only in the very long term. Thus members of NEDC felt that they were having no influence on events, that they were holding endless discussions at which nothing was ever really settled, and they were merely setting their seal on measures that Whitehall had every intention of introducing anyway. The TUC's annoyance was therefore due to a feeling that the government was failing to display sufficient determination in pressing forward with expansion, and to the latent dissatisfaction felt by almost all members of NEDC as well as by members of the regional economic development councils. Here again, it would have been surprising if the failure of the National Plan had not had repercussions on the working of these bodies whose prime task was precisely to translate its objectives into regional terms.

The Crisis in Regional Planning

The Industrial Development Act of 1966 authorised the government to designate development areas, to which the government hoped to attract industries by offering a variety of inducements. The areas were mapped out on the basis of several criteria; as in the past the level of long-term unemployment was the main consideration. However, other specifically economic factors were also taken into account, such as a particularly high proportion of young people who were or would be entering employment, or a well-developed but under-used system of public transport. The development areas covered nearly the whole of Scotland, much of the North of England and Wales, North Devon and Cornwall and Merseyside. As in the past the State's attempt to promote industrial development in these areas rested on a combination of the carrot and the stick — financial inducements to move to where more industry was needed and controls to deter industrialists going anywhere else.

The financial assistance to companies included both aid to build new factories and subsidies to operate them. Firms new to an area could claim investment allowances of 40 per cent, while existing firms could claim up to 25 per cent of the cost of new plant, depending on the number of fresh jobs that would be created. Thereafter they might qualify for a variety of special allowances, the most notable of which was the regional employment premium which was introduced in 1967 and paid in respect of all full-time employees in manufacturing industries for all firms whether new or established. In 1968 the annual cost of assistance to development areas was running at about £250 million — a huge sum in comparison to, say, France, which allocated about £14 million to comparable activities in the 1970 budget, or an annual average of £30 million during 1968–9 when there was particularly heavy expenditure on major projects in the mining areas of the north.[13] On the administrative side the system of industrial development certificates was tightened up, and while these were readily available for development areas, they were increasingly difficult to obtain for regions where there was full employment.

In addition, the government soon realised something must be done for those parts of the country that, though not requiring help on the same scale as the development areas, nevertheless had considerable social and economic difficulties. Following the report of the Hunt Committee in 1969 it designated a number of 'intermediate areas' which qualified for assistance at about half the level of the development areas.[14] Initially much of Yorkshire and Lancashire were designated intermediate areas with further smaller areas being added in 1971 and 1972. At the same time, the extra aid that had been extended in 1967 to localities with a particularly persistent problem of high unemployment within the original development areas was more formally established in 1971 by the creation of a number of special development areas qualifying for higher scales of assistance. Thus the range of state aid became more diversified and graduated over the years, and the system was confirmed and extended by the Conservatives' Industry Act of 1972.[15]

The earlier discussion of the regional economic planning councils showed that their success would depend in large measure on their ability to influence government decisions on regional policy on the one hand and the planning decisions of local authorities on the other. The danger was that, sandwiched between the regional directors and the local councils, they would be reduced to a dispiriting immobility.

Their first job was to work out a long-term strategy for the development of their region. In doing this they had to prepare projections for the future rather than analyses of the current situation (which had been the case with the various studies that had appeared before that time). The two White Papers that appeared under DEA auspices in 1965 were still 'studies' prepared by civil servants on the instructions of the outgoing government.[16] The first papers that can really be said to have come from the regional councils were published in 1966 and 1967,[17] with East Anglia completing the series in 1968.[18] These papers did not claim to be regional economic plans; they supplied a great amount of information on the region, provided a detailed analysis of its problems and suggested a large number of ways in which the social and economic conditions of those who lived there could be improved. But, having no previous experience, or even adequate statistics, they did not set precise targets or even venture detailed projections; the report of the South West Economic Planning Council showed clearly the difference between a study of this kind and a genuine economic plan:

> It is too soon in the experience of regional planning to aim at achieving a set of government-approved plans for all regions which will neatly dovetail with each other and which, in numbers of population, distribution of manpower, growth and location of industry, scale and disposition of public investment, etc., will in aggregate coincide with the forecasts, intentions and capabilities envisaged by the government for the economy as a whole.[19]

While in the light of the novelty of the undertaking there was doubtless considerable justification for this view, it had a disadvantage as well as an advantage. The advantage was that the councils were left a great deal of initiative; the disadvantage was that their reports in no way committed the government. Admittedly cynics were prompt to point out that the fact that the government was not bound by them mattered little, since even if it had been — as with the National Plan — this would have meant very little in practical terms. But it was patently obvious that the work of the councils was futile unless Whitehall took some notice of what they said.

The situation was a trifle different in Scotland and Wales (until the 1968 reform), where the councils were directly under the respective ministers. Their special position could have had either of two consequences; either the work of these councils would gain prestige and influence, or on the contrary they would be inhibited by being obliged to keep within the confines of government policy. It looks as if the former prevailed in Scotland and the latter in Wales — though it is only fair to add that the Scottish 'Plan' appeared in January 1966,[20] when the National Plan was still applicable, while the Welsh 'Plan' was published in July 1967 at the height of the crisis over national planning.[21] Perhaps, then, it is not surprising that the former suggested ambitious targets for 1970 in keeping with the National Plan, while the Welsh paper refrained from suggesting any target for growth at a time when the economy was in recession.

In the view of Gavin McCrone, an authority on regional planning in general and the Scottish economy in particular, the Scottish 'Plan' was much the most original of all the regional planning papers. It was the only one to include the word 'Plan' in its title – and the only one that really merited the name. According to McCrone it was both a study and a plan; as a study it was good, as a plan it was poor. 'The techniques of planning, however, take time to build up and the rudimentary state of Scottish statistics only permitted a crude attempt.'[22] However, it can be argued that the growth rate chosen was useful in itself, not because it was particularly 'credible', but because of the way it illustrated the significance that should be given to regional planning: the target for the growth of industrial production was 4.8 per cent per year, which was more than the national target of 4.5 per cent, but this was not surprising because Scotland was a development area. However, the plan failed to demonstrate that its targets were plausible, and it must be admitted, as McCrone concedes, that it did not succeed in 'tracing the effects of British expansion, as foreseen in the National Plan, on Scotland'.[23] The weaknesses of the Scottish plan at least had the merit of revealing the difficulties inherent in regional planning in three ways:

> In the first place, the regional plan must rely on the assumptions of the national plan. If these are unrealistic and the national plan's targets are abandoned, the regional target must fail also. Secondly, the preparation of meaningful targets, if it is to be done properly, requires the development of sophisticated forecasting techniques. Over and above this, there ought to be some reconciliation at national level of the claims of the competing regions, to ensure that when all their targets and forecasts are put together they are within the capability of the nation.[24]

Whether they were plans or not, the papers published by the regional planning councils attempted to indicate the broad outlines of a suitable strategy for the development of the region. Feeling that they had completed one part of their job successfully, the members of the councils looked to the government to act rapidly on their proposals. This hope was in part disappointed. A year after the report on the North was published the council had still not had any reaction from the government. In addition, the abandoning of the National Plan in 1966 was a severe blow to planning in general. With no national plan to establish a general framework, regional planning was in danger of drifting aimlessly. This was the feeling among most members of the regional councils in 1967, and many either resigned or declined to serve for a further term when their three years expired. The malaise was felt first in the North of England, where the need for action was probably the most urgent, but it spread rapidly to the other councils, even in the more prosperous regions. This suggests that the dissatisfaction of councillors was related less to the importance of the issues they were being asked to discuss than to the conditions on which they dealt with them.

According to Alan Day, who served for three years on the South East Economic Planning Council, the greatest ground of discontent was the feeling among councillors that it was all a waste of time, because nothing they did had the slightest impact on regional policy.[25] 'In spite of the glossily produced South East study which came from the Council, the truth is that practically none of the planning proposals or decisions for the region has been the slightest bit different from those which would have been made if the Council had never existed.'[26] Though Day's verdict is so sweepingly dismissive there is no reason to think it was anything other than carefully considered. The explanation of the councils' near-failure seems to have been that, as might have been feared, they could not tackle major issues because these were normally reserved for national government, and they could not tackle lesser ones because the local authorities jealously guarded their prerogatives from these bodies that were non-elected, had a rather motley membership and were purely advisory. If the councils were to do a worthwhile job they were left to discover for themselves how. According to Day, the answer to the problem was not necessarily to have elected councillors, but to define the scope of the councils more clearly, allowing them to act as watchdogs over the decisions of regional civil servants, with the assistance of their own research staffs. For it was difficult for the councils to detect questionable decisions by the civil service unless they had some independent specialist source of information.

This is certainly not to say that regional planning was a complete failure. It must be remembered that the councils were not the only regional institutions, and that we have been considering a transitional period leading, it was hoped, to more solid achievement. On the whole the boards seem to have been successful in carrying out their responsibilities in relation to devolution and co-ordination. Britain, after all, has nothing like the French system of regional prefects to co-ordinate the work of the regional offices of the various departments. The boards therefore met a real need, and according to Mr Philip Chantler, chairman of the North West Regional Board from 1965 to 1969, they had a number of achievements to their credit,[27] in the areas of transport, building, location of factories and improvement of amenities. While, like the councils, the boards had no powers, they could bring influence to bear: 'What influence? The answer to this lies in what regional planning is all about. It is really a process of study and discussion of the factors, problems and possibilities of each region, and of co-operation with bodies which do exercise power.'[28] The potential influence of the boards was by no means negligible, since they represented the central government, which was the source of the funds required to implement policy in the region. In other words, while the boards as such had no power, they had an influence derived from the powers held by their individual members as representatives of the central government. The councils were of course not in the same enviable situation.

It was clear from the beginning that the structure of regional planning was only a tentative experiment which implied the subsequent development of some new form of regional political organisation. The government was only too well aware that the existing local authorities were ill-adapted to running a country that was experiencing rapid change. Consequently it set up the Royal Commission on Local Government; following its report in 1969[29] the Labour government proposed a major reorganisation of the structure and powers of local government, but was unable to complete this before leaving office. It was accordingly left to the Heath government to bring the reform to fruition. It published three White Papers in 1971[30] which, while broadly derived from the proposals of the Royal Commission and the Labour government, also introduced a number of major modifications. It subsequently carried two Acts reorganising local government, one covering England and Wales (which came into effect in 1974, with the councillors being elected a year earlier), and the other for Scotland (which was to take effect from May 1975). The reform was based on the two-tier system, which was logical enough in relation to the tasks that had to be carried out, but meant that if the regional councils were included there were three levels between the citizen and the central government. However, so far as the issues that most directly concern us here are concerned, although the regional boundaries underwent some minor changes to bring them into line with the new local authority boundaries,[31] there were no major alterations in the structure of regional planning, at least until the government indicated what action, if any, it intended to take on the report of the Royal Commission on the Constitution.

The Commission produced both a majority report signed by eleven of its thirteen members,[32] and a Memorandum of Dissent from the remaining two.[33] Not surprisingly there was considerable division over the extent of devolution that should be envisaged. But there was also a clear division, less frequently discussed, between those who were ready to give a certain degree of autonomy to Scotland and Wales while leaving things much as they were in England, and those who believed that the basic uniformity of the politico-administrative structure of the country should be maintained, and were consequently prepared to see the eight English regions receive the same measure of devolution as Scotland and Wales. (The essential ambiguity of the Commission's report reflected the rather contradictory task assigned to it of meeting the challenge of Scottish and Welsh nationalism and of recommending an improved form of regional organisation.) One course led to preserving the English regional councils with a rather wider brief covering not only regional planning but also co-ordination of local policies, with members either nominated or indirectly elected by the local authorities, and a strictly advisory status. The second course led to the existing councils being replaced by directly elected regional parliaments with wider responsibilities and substantial powers of decision. One supposes, though this was not directly discussed, that their responsibilities would include regional planning. However, the Commission's proposals appeared to be largely stillborn, in so far at least as they related to the English regions. Confronted by the rising electoral fortunes of the Scottish nationalists, the two big parties realised that they could scarcely stand still, but equally they were prepared to advance only with the greatest prudence and deliberation.[34]

To return to the period 1964–70, there was certainly a regional policy, and it was actively pursued, if only in the sense that the central government spent a great deal of money in the regions; but the setting up of really substantial regional economic institutions remained — and remains — to be achieved.

The DEA's Swan Song

The new plan was originally intended to appear in the autumn of 1968, but as a result of disagreements within the cabinet and heated discussions within NEDC it was not published until February 1969. The first question that had to be resolved was whether, like its predecessor, it would appear as a White Paper. Eventually it was decided that it would appear as a Green Paper published by the DEA.[35] It took the form of a rough draft, rather than a fully worked out plan, which was to be sent to the regional councils for comment and revised subsequently in the light of their reports and the general state of the economy at the time. This way of doing it had the two-fold advantage of being acceptable to those ministers who were not convinced there was any need to publish another plan until one could be built on rather firmer foundations (the uncertainties of 1965 still persisted in 1968), while it also brought into play all the machinery that had been established under the NEDC. This was likely to diminish the scepticism of the CBI, which was determined not to give its support a second time to a document as unrealistic as the National Plan, and to lessen the hostility of the TUC, which might feel that their representatives could see that fuller studies were undertaken which might bring to light possibilities for more rapid growth than the government had in mind. Nevertheless, there had to be three meetings of NEDC, including a special all-day meeting at Chequers, before the two sides of industry could be persuaded to agree to the plan. The TUC's irritation had at least one positive consequence: the discussions at NEDC were more thorough than in 1965 and more attention was paid to the members' amendments, even though the unions' proposed growth target was rejected as unrealistic.

The Task Ahead fairly and squarely presented itself as a 'planning document' rather than a plan,[36] and went on, 'The document provides a basis for a further stage in the continuing process of consultation between government and both sides of industry about major issues of economic policy.'[37] Thus it constituted only one of the stages in the planning process, whereas both its predecessors had been the culmination. Also it claimed to do no more than offer several different models of growth for consideration though it favoured a moderate growth rate. Each model was based on the assumption that an annual surplus of £300,000,000 was required on the balance of payments. Thus the point of departure was realistic. The middle model provided for a growth rate of 3.25 per cent, implying that exports would rise by 5.75 per cent and imports would be held down to 4 per cent; the pessimistic model was that GDP would rise by a little less than 3 per cent, with increases of 5.25 and 3.75 per cent respectively for exports and imports; the optimistic model was based on a growth rate of nearly 4 per cent, which would have required an increase of 6.75 per cent in exports, with the increase in imports limited to 4.75 per cent.

The level of exports envisaged by all three models might seem optimistic, given that up to then exports had only grown by about 3 per cent annually on average. However, unlike the previous plans, the new estimates took into account a factor that greatly favoured exports — devaluation, which had not yet produced the anticipated improvement. It was estimated that it would give British exports an edge of 10 per cent over those of their chief competitors. It could therefore be felt that the document was much more realistic than its predecessors because it took the constraints under which the British economy had to operate more fully into account.

The Task Ahead received a reasonably good reception. While the press had been almost unanimous that the National Plan was unrealistic and made quite unjustifiably optimistic extrapolations, it now considered the new document to be modest, realistic and flexible. Alan Day, who had been a severe critic of the National Plan, wrote under the significant headline 'Honesty Always Pays':

> If the Labour government had in those days published such a survey, the economy as a whole would by now be in a much happier state. The lesson has been learnt that while it is desirable to plan, in the sense of looking ahead to see how the economy is going and how it can be steered, it is useless to build on unrealistic expectations. . . . The most likely prospect is a continuing hard slog into the seventies. The government deserves at least one hearty cheer for saying so honestly and openly.[38]

While this was simply a hasty journalistic evaluation, Messrs Barker and Lecomber's paper for PEP was fuller and more searching.[39] After analysing at length the forecasts in *The Task Ahead* and comparing them with their own estimates, they concluded: 'No previous official assessment has been as realistic and as comprehensive. The projections are on the whole free of the optimistic, but unfounded, expectations which were characteristic of the National Plan, although there remains an unfortunate approach to the balance of payments.'[40] On this, they thought the paper did not take its analysis of different rates of growth far enough. It pointed out that more rapid growth would require higher imports, which would be balanced by increased exports 'provided the faster rate of increase in productivity was combined with a strict control of costs',[41] which in their view boils down to making one particular factor depend on the variation of another ill-defined factor: 'This is all too reminiscent of the treatment of the balance of payments in the National Plan.'[42] One could argue that the context was now very different, since instead of a single objective, as in the National Plan, there were several different models of growth. In any case the paper was only a provisional assessment, and as such did not attempt to solve all the problems raised, for which answers might be found later. Thus the DEA showed it had learned from its earlier unhappy experience with the National Plan, and the new paper offered a different approach to planning.

However, this was not the view of George and Priscilla Polanyi in *Economic Age*.[43] They argued that nothing had changed, and that as the title of their article, 'National Plan Mark III', implied, the Green Paper was a direct descendant of the earlier plans. In their view experience had made the planners more cautious but there had been no basic change in their methods. They criticised them for not taking into account the stop—go cycle, 'determined by the emergence of periodic balance of payments crises, which is quite uninfluenced by the existence of the plan targets'.[44] While not denying that the economy would benefit from devaluation, drawing on figures published by NIESR they argued that the Green Paper was unduly optimistic: 'In our view the balance of payments is tilted much more in the direction of some continuing deficit in visible trade by 1972 than in favour of a £300 million surplus',[45] and since the success of the plan – as of its predecessors – turned on the ability to achieve the target for growth and a balance of payments surplus at one and the same time, the planners were caught in the same old double bind, to which they still had no answer. Thus there was no significant change, and the Polanyis thought that the same recipe was bound to produce the same results and that consequently, like its predecessor, the new plan would fail.

Reactions to the Green Paper showed once more the split between those who still believed in planning despite all the mistakes and failures, and those who thought that however one went about it planning was undesirable, at best useless, and rather than helping solve the problems of the British economy was really only delaying a solution.

The Task Ahead outlined procedures for consulting industry. These consultations would be on the basis of the 'average' model of 3.25 per cent growth, but it was not to be taken as binding, but instead should be considered as more of a point of departure for the subsequent discussions. Particularly detailed consultations were scheduled for chemicals, heavy electrical engineering, mechanical engineering, electronics, motor vehicles, machine tools and paper and board (all of which had Little Neddies), and for shipbuilding, aircraft and iron and steel castings (which had no Little Neddy) and for steel and the fuel industries. Where there was no development committee, consultations would be conducted through trade associations for private industry, and directly with the nationalised industries. The Fuel Advisory Committee and the Iron and Steel Advisory Council would also be consulted. There would be more general discussions by the other Little Neddies. The DEA thought that this should take about eight months. Then NEDC would consider all the reports together with the latest estimates of economic prospects, with the aim of arriving at a revised provisional projection until 1973 or 1974.

Although the DEA was abolished in October the timetable was on the whole met. Discussions went on right through 1969, and the first reports were considered by NEDC at special meetings chaired by Mr Wilson and Mr Jenkins in November and December. These revealed some errors in the estimates in *The Task Ahead* – which was one of the objects of the whole exercise – but they also showed how seriously the policy of austerity was affecting productive investment. This was why, at the February 1970 meeting, NEDC decided to narrow the spread of possible growth rates from 2.9–4.0 per cent to 3.0–3.75 per cent. After the government reshuffle of October 1969 responsibility for medium-term planning was transferred to the Treasury, and so the process initiated by Mr Shore, the last minister at the DEA, was completed by Mr Jenkins.

A fresh Green Paper issued by the Treasury modified the earlier estimates for

1972 that had been drawn up at the beginning of 1969.[46] This Green Paper had only a modest 23 pages compared with the 400-odd pages of the National Plan. It finally advanced two possible models for growth between 1969 and 1972, one of 3 per cent and the other of 3.75 per cent. The pessimistic model allowed an increase in private consumption of 3 per cent, while the optimistic one suggested 3.8 per cent.

Looking back on the outcome, as we are now in a position to do, we can see that the pessimistic model, which implied that earlier trends would continue (since between 1963 and 1967 growth had averaged about 3 per cent a year),

Table 12.1. I Comparative statistics of gross national product and gross fixed capital formation in UK, France and EEC (in billions of dollars — 1963 prices)

Dates	UK		France		EEC	
	GNP	GFCF	GNP	GFCF	GNP	GFCF
1960	78.9	12.4	70.1	14.0	221.6	49.2
1961	81.7	13.6	73.9	15.7	234.4	54.5
1962	82.7	13.5	78.9	17.1	247.1	58.6
1963	86.1	13.8	83.4	18.6	258.5	61.5
1964	90.8	16.0	89.0	21.1	274.2	67.3
1965	93.1	16.7	93.1	22.6	287.4	69.4
1966	95.1	17.1	98.3	24.6	299.8	72.6
1967	97.1	18.3	103.2	26.1	309.9	73.3
1968	100.0	19.2	108.0	27.6	328.4	78.6
1969	102.0	19.0	116.3	30.6	352.3	86.3
1970	104.1	19.3	123.3	32.9	372.0	93.6
1960–1970 Yearly	%	%	%	%	%	%
average rate of increase	+2.9	+4.9	+5.7	+8.7	+5.2	+6.0

II Evolution of the growth rate (% of GNP — 1963 prices)

Dates	UK	France	EEC
1960	4.8	7.1	7.5
1961	3.5	5.4	5.8
1962	1.3	6.8	5.4
1963	4.1	5.8	4.6
1964	5.4	6.6	6.0
1965	2.6	4.7	4.8
1966	2.1	5.6	4.3
1967	2.1	5.0	3.4
1968	3.0	4.6	6.0
1969	2.0	7.7	7.3
1970	2.0	6.0	5.6

III Gross fixed capital formation (% of GNP)

Dates	UK	France	EEC
1960	15.7	20.0	22.2
1961	16.6	21.2	23.3
1962	16.3	21.7	23.7
1963	16.0	22.3	23.8
1964	17.6	23.7	24.5
1965	17.9	24.7	24.1
1966	18.0	25.0	24.2
1967	18.8	25.3	23.7
1968	19.2	25.6	23.9
1969	18.6	26.3	24.5
1970	18.5	26.7	25.2

Source: *Revue économique de la Banque Nationale de Paris*, October 1972.

was in the event too optimistic. As figure 11.1 on page 174 shows, the main aims of the plans were not met: expansion slowed instead of accelerating; productive investment scarcely increased as a percentage of GDP; and, far from Britain closing the gap between her and her neighbours, it continued to widen. Planning had not, therefore, remedied the structural problems of the British economy, which remained precisely what they had been before. Subsequently they were added to by the ravages of a world inflation which, as a result of her inherent weakness, Britain found even greater difficulty in combating successfully than other countries. There had been no lack of attempts over the previous decade to stop inflation. All had been in vain.

CHAPTER 13

An Assessment of the Prices and Incomes Policy

The PIB was just one cog in the machinery of prices and incomes policy, which was decided by the government (which was of course responsible to Parliament), and which was the direct responsibility initially of the minister of economic affairs and, later, the minister for employment and productivity. The PIB interpreted, informed, advised — but always within a policy laid down at this political level. Consequently we can assess neither the work of the PIB nor the prices and incomes policy itself without first considering how official policy developed.

The broad lines of prices and incomes policy were closely related to the Labour government's needs in its day-to-day management of the economy. Labour had gone firmly on record in 1964 that one of the basic principles of its policy was that it would be wholly voluntary; it was on this understanding that the employers and unions were prepared to endorse the Statement of Intent. But in July 1966 the government took powers to prohibit increases in prices and incomes without reference to the PIB. This obviously made for more effective government, but it also raised many doubts. Most particularly, it roused growing hostility among trade unionists — not just the minority who had always been opposed even to a voluntary prices and incomes policy, but also the majority who had been prepared to try and make one work. This was to have important political consequences for the whole Labour movement, since it was a major factor in strengthening the trade union Left at the TUC itself and, indirectly, within the Labour Party.

Thus there were two main phases in the development of Labour's prices and incomes policy, one voluntary, the other compulsory.

The Voluntary Phase

The different stages of the voluntary phase were as follows. (The early stages have been discussed earlier and so are simply listed here for the sake of completeness.)

December 1964: The Statement of Intent sealed the agreement of unions and employers to a voluntary policy for prices and incomes.

February 1965: Announcement of the setting up of the PIB.[1]

April 1965: The government, unions and employers promised to observe voluntarily a number of criteria in wage settlements and setting prices;[2] announcement of the composition of the PIB; introduction of a norm of between 3.0 and 3.5 per cent per annum on average for wage increases. (This was not an arbitrary figure but was in line with the growth of productivity; thus an average increase of this order should not have an adverse effect.) No norm for prices, but they were to be held as stable as possible.

November 1965: Introduction of a voluntary early warning system for both prices and incomes.[3] Proposed increases were to be submitted to the appropriate department for scrutiny before they came into force.[4]

This completed the machinery of the voluntary policy, which remained in operation until July 1966.

So far as prices were concerned, manufacturers or suppliers could not be asked to notify every price change. Consequently only a limited range of items was affected (the list varying from year to year). If any increase was envisaged for one of these items it was notified to the appropriate department. If the ministry had said nothing after twenty-eight days it was deemed to have agreed; if it did not agree, it referred the matter to the PIB.

The system for incomes was that all proposed increases in wages, salaries, dividends or professional fees were submitted to the DEA, which decided whether or not they were in keeping with official policy. If not, the matter was referred to the PIB. Those affected could decide to defer implementation of their agreement until the PIB had given its ruling. In November 1965 the TUC introduced its own pay vetting system which examined pay claims by its affiliated unions before they were formally lodged. This was meant as a tangible proof of the TUC's sincerity in attempting to obtain a measure of order in the field of wages. It also marked the high-water mark in the TUC's willingness to co-operate with the government. However, the employers would not agree to adopt a similar system for prices, as the CBI considered it unworkable; the TUC was later to attack it bitterly for this.

The Statutory Phase

The first cycle of the incomes policy was intended to produce results in the long term, but the short-term outcome was rather disappointing for the government. Between April 1965 and July 1966 the index of earnings rose twice as rapidly as the index of retail prices (see table 13.2) — which had also risen fairly steeply. This was mainly due to a severe shortage of labour in a number of regions. But the short-term economic problems were such that this was quite an inadequate result. One outcome of the July 1966 crisis was therefore stricter control of prices and incomes.

The July 1966 White Paper announced a six months' standstill during which there were to be no increases in incomes or dividends and price increases would be severely limited.[5] The freeze would be followed by a further six months of 'severe restraint' during which wage increases were to be restricted to the lower paid or to instances where they arose directly from increased output. Price increases were to be held to an absolute minimum (e.g. where there had been large increases in the cost of imported raw materials), and the freeze on dividends was maintained.

The Prices and Incomes Act of August 1966 empowered the government to prohibit any increase in either wages or prices for the life of the Act (which was to expire in July 1967) without any need to refer the matter to the PIB.

The restraint the government was seeking was accepted to a remarkable degree, and the government was obliged to use its powers on only fifteen occasions (fourteen times over wages, affecting 36,000 workers out of some 23 million, and once on prices). The outcome was what the government had hoped to achieve: incomes rose less rapidly than prices (see p. 206) and, even more important, export prices remained stable. Nevertheless, these sacrifices did not prevent devaluation; furthermore, they could not be sustained for too long and there was a danger that once they ended there would be furious competition to 'catch up'.

The next stage, running from July 1967 to March 1968, was marked by rather more flexibility and a partial return to the system that had operated before July 1966,[6] but with two important differences which class this with the compulsory phase. The zero norm remained for incomes; increases would only be allowed in exceptional cases, either where there was a direct contribution to higher productivity, or where workers were receiving particularly low pay, or where there was a need to attract or retain manpower or correct gross anomalies. The government also retained the power to defer implementation of wage and price increases on condition that the matter was referred to the PIB. (In the previous year it had complete discretion.) This could mean a delay of as long as seven months — one month to decide on a reference to the PIB, three for the PIB's investigation and three more if the PIB's report was adverse.

Despite this considerable measure of control incomes began to 'take off' during the second quarter of 1967. Earnings rose 6 per cent over the year while retail prices rose only 2.5 per cent; the increase in incomes was not matched by a comparable improvement in productivity, and it seemed clear that the unions were engaged in a determined attempt to make good the losses of the previous year; certainly their mood was markedly more militant after the 1967 Congress and devaluation of the pound.

During the third stage the emphasis was even more on productivity. It began on 20 March 1968 with the introduction of a budget that was designed to extract the greatest possible advantage from devaluation, and it continued to the end of 1969.[7] The new Act provided that nobody had an *automatic* entitlement to a wage increase, but authorised increases of up to 3.5 per cent in dividends, wages and salaries, provided the four criteria already mentioned were adequately met. Additionally, however, higher increases were authorised for productivity bargains that met the criteria laid down by the PIB (see p. 203) and to allow major reorganisations of the wage structure with the aim of greater efficiency and productivity. Prices could be increased only if productivity had not risen sufficiently for it to be possible to raise wages in line with the norm; where costs of raw materials, fuel, services and distribution had increased to the point where they could not be absorbed; where there had been unavoidable increases in capital costs per unit of output, and where there was the need for a company to finance investment to meet increased demand. There was also a ceiling of 3.5 per cent on increases in dividends.

The Act also gave the government several additional powers, allowing it to defer implementation of any proposal for up to twelve months (instead of seven), provided it was referred to the PIB; it could invoke Section II of the 1966 Act to peg wages by order (it should perhaps be noted that while there was a fresh Prices and Incomes Act each year, none of these completely repealed its predecessor and they complemented each other); it could compel prices to be reduced on a recommendation by the PIB; it could moderate and phase increases in rents and it could enforce dividend restraint.

These measures were scheduled to expire at the end of 1969, and during the autumn the government considered retaining them for the following year, but with a more flexible application of Section II (which could be extended by Order in Council). Eventually it decided not to do so. For even with its existing powers, the government was finding it increasingly difficult to hold back the pressure for higher wages, which had been building up steadily during the previous few months. Even the most moderate unions were now tending to consider 3.5 per cent as the starting point for bargaining rather than as a ceiling. Soon the norm went completely by the board. In October the dustmen won an immediate rise of about three times the official ceiling after a long strike. While they were lower-paid workers, shortly afterwards the miners, electricians and teachers all won increases that were well over the norm. The average percentage rise agreed in wage settlements during the last quarter of 1969 was 7.8 per cent – more than twice the norm – and the rate was accelerating. By the beginning of 1970 prices and incomes policy survived only in name. Retail prices had also risen 5.4 per cent in the twelve months to October 1969, and it was clear they were unlikely to stabilise in the face of a wage surge on such a scale. As in 1964 it was very difficult to maintain any significant degree of control or restraint over prices and incomes in the period immediately before a general election.

In 1964 a prices and incomes policy had been seen as just one strand in the whole general strategy of economic planning. The planned distribution of prosperity should go hand in hand with the planned use of national resources. But, whereas national economic planning was in eclipse after the abandoning of the National Plan in 1966, the prices and incomes policy, far from fading away, continued to develop, becoming ever more closely linked to the government's short-term handling of the economy rather than to the remaining vestiges of medium-term planning. So the role of the PIB was both strengthened and modified after 1966; strengthened because its rulings had a greater influence on government decisions, modified because it had become an instrument of short-term management of the economy rather than a tool for long-term education, though to some extent it was able to maintain that role through its continuing advocacy of higher productivity.

An Assessment of the PIB's Work

With the Conservative victory of June 1970 the PIB was doomed. It was officially abolished on 31 March 1971. Since then there have been a number of attempts to evaluate either the prices and incomes policy as a whole, most notably in Mr Aubrey Jones's able defence, or to consider the working of the Board and its contribution to the Labour government's economic policy, including studies by Joan Mitchell[8] and Alan Fels. So while it may still be rather early to reach a final verdict on the PIB, sufficient time has elapsed for a considered assessment.

Every year there are over a million price changes, thousands of wage agreements and hundreds of wage negotiations. Had it been free to decide for itself which matters it would look at – and as we have seen it was not – the PIB might perhaps have done no better than what it actually achieved over a little more than four years. But it might have chosen better 'test cases', such as the car industry, which for much of its life it was hoping would be referred to it, but on which the government never sought its views – perhaps because it was too politically explosive.

During the six years of its existence the PIB issued 170 reports, about 80 of which dealt with wages and 70 with prices, though some dealt with both. Each report on incomes affected an average of over 250,000 workers. Allowing for the fact that some industries were the subject of more than one report, it is estimated that forty per cent of the working population had its wages or working conditions directly affected by the work of the PIB. This is substantial enough, but on top of this the PIB issued a series of guides, providing practical advice to everyone involved in wage negotiations. The best known were *Help Yourself: NBPI Productivity Guide*, of which 250,000 copies were distributed, *Payment by Results* (160,000 copies) and *Job Evaluation*. The Board's educational and informational effort was therefore also quite considerable.

Although towards the end of its existence the Board issued more reports on prices than in its early years, its influence in this field was less marked and never more than piecemeal. Its main responsibility was to keep prices down in accordance with the criteria the government laid down at each successive stage in the prices and incomes policy rather than actually to reduce prices, though at least one PIB report led to a reduction in prices.[9] In addition, in September 1967 the PIB was given the important further responsibility of reviewing prices in the nationalised industries, which permitted it to investigate their efficiency. This led it to consider, for instance London Transport fares[10] and the structure of parcel post rates.[11]

In the area of incomes other than wages and salaries, the Board investigated the fees of barristers, solicitors and architects, building society mortgage rates and council house rents. Its report on council housing brought to the public's attention the fact that the local authorities were not as vulnerable to criticism (particularly over their allocation systems) as had often been alleged. Indeed, the PIB's work was most highly prized in just those areas where previously there had been little or no solid information. Mr Clive Jenkins, whom few would suspect of sympathy for the prices and incomes policy, nevertheless acknowledged the PIB's contribution here. After noting that 'The basic arithmetic of wages, profits and costs is still a secret in Britain,'[12] he went on to give his view that the Board's reports had 'provided the first comprehensive material on pay in engineering, costs in banking, profits in detergents and fees in the practice of law'.[13] Again, most of the union leaders whose opposition to the government's policy grew steadily over the years spared the PIB despite its role in the formulation of that policy. No doubt, like Clive Jenkins, they realised how useful the PIB had been in unearthing information and clarifying issues – sometimes thereby providing them with useful ammunition. Some observers have suggested that the pressure among car industry workers for parity with other workers whose work and responsibility were very similar to their own – which embittered relations in the car industry for many years – would perhaps not have been so intense had not the PIB made comparison easier.[14]

From the beginning the PIB laid great stress on improving productivity; so in assessing its achievement we should also consider what influence it was able to exercise in this field. We have already noted the importance of its guidance to negotiators; such headway as the government made was probably due in no small measure to the determined campaign by the PIB, which constantly stressed the link between improvements in productivity and in real wages. In recent years a growing number of restrictive practices have been abandoned, but there is still a long way to go, and it has to be admitted that sometimes productivity bargaining was the only way employers could, at a price, persuade the unions (particularly the craft unions) to relinquish quite unjustifiable privileges. But 'productivity bargaining' was sometimes productivity bargaining in name only, and became a backstairs way of getting round the official norms. It was to the PIB's credit that it was able to draw on the experience of earlier agreements and produce a list of reasonably clear and firm criteria, to work out a coherent theory of productivity, and to make some progress in securing acceptance for it. It may be hoped that though the PIB itself has gone its work in this area will have had some lasting effect.

Table 13.1a.   The growth of output and productivity from 1963

	All industries and services		Production industries	
	Output*	Productivity†	Output*	Productivity†
1963	100	100	100	100
1964	105.9	104.5	108.3	106.5
1965	108.8	106.5	111.7	108.7
1966	110.7	108.1	113.2	110.4
1967	112.5	111.4	113.9	114.1
1968	117.0	116.7	119.8	121.7
1969	119.5	119.4	122.9	124.9
1970	121.8	122.5	124.2	128.2
1971	123.9	126.8	125.0	133.7

* Gross Domestic Product (GDP).
† GDP per head.
Source: Department of Employment *Gazette* (October 1972), Table 134.

Table 13.1b.   Output per head by broad industrial sectors

	1963	1966	1969	1970	1971
Whole economy	100	108.1	119.4	122.5	126.8
Production industries	100	110.4	124.9	128.2	133.7
Mining and quarrying	100	106.5	124.1	128.8	135.5
Metal manufacture	100	107.0	117.1	116.5	117.5
Mechanical, instrument and electrical engineering	100	112.7	128.1	130.7	137.1
Vehicles	100	114.1	124.4	120.4	122.1
Textiles	100	111.7	137.4	145.1	156.8
Gas, electricity and water	100	110.0	137.0	150.4	169.1

Source: Department of Employment *Gazette* (October 1972), Table 134.
Notes:
1. Tables 13.1a and b show that during the years we are considering productivity increased by an average of about 3 per cent per annum for the industrial and service sectors as a whole (and by 3.5 per cent in manufacturing industry alone). This was a clear improvement on the late fifties and early sixties, as will be recalled from the debate between NEDO and the Treasury over the underlying trend in productivity (see chapter 4). But what is most striking is that the increase in productivity only really begins to accelerate in 1968, while — apart from 1968 itself — the rate of expansion was beginning to slow down. Thus increases in productivity were due less to improvements in the terms of trade than to other factors, such as the influence of the Selective Employment Tax in the service sector, and probably also to productivity agreements in industry. But another factor was probably crucial: the change in the nature of investments, with new plant and machinery being designed less to increase output than to economise on manpower, as a reaction to higher labour costs.
2. Table 13.1b clearly shows the varying rates of growth of productivity in different sectors of industry. While the textile industry shows up particularly well, probably reflecting the high efficiency of the artificial fibres side, two industries had a particularly unimpressive record, namely vehicles (in marked comparison with what was happening in continental Europe) and metal manufacture, which lagged well behind the German and even the French industries (probably as a result of the continuing uncertainties affecting the steel industry).
3. While the improvement in productivity towards the close of the period (18 per cent for the four years 1970—3) appears impressive, it should not be overlooked that this represented growth from a very modest base. In 1969, in the time taken by an English worker to produce 74.4 tons of cement, his French counterpart produced 100 tons; in steel again, British output per head was only 59.4 per cent of French levels. Also in 1969 the French railways, SNCF, carried 229.8 tons of freight per employee, compared with only 88.2 for British Rail.

Prices and Incomes Policy to 1970

The outcome of each of the main stages in the development of government policy is shown in table 13.2. The only period when incomes rose less rapidly than prices was during the time of freeze and severe restraint between July 1966 and July 1967. The restraint that was asked for then was generally accepted owing to the support of the great majority of unions and employers, both nationally and locally. But such restraint could not last indefinitely. While in theory the burden was shared equally by all sections of the community, in practice it fell most heavily on those least able to bear it. In addition the appeal to the Dunkirk spirit was bound to arouse greater scepticism and opposition at each successive airing. Finally, the declared aim in 1966 had been to stave off devaluation, but since that could not be prevented, what was the point of continued sacrifices? This argument was frequently aired at union meetings and conferences in 1968 and 1969.

But although the prices and incomes policy created some discontent, this may have been one sign of success. The PIB's fourth report suggested that periods of wage restraint — whether austerity under Cripps, the Selwyn Lloyd pay pause or the incomes policy operated since 1965 — had resulted in a reduction in the rate of increase in wage rates by something like one per cent a year.[15] The PIB emphasised that this could only be a very rough estimate. But assuming it to be about right, was a reduction of this order of any economic significance? The PIB report thought it was. Firstly, *The Task Ahead* emphasised that in the ten to fifteen years before devaluation unit costs of labour had risen in Britain by about one per cent per year more than among her main competitors. If that was the case, then a reduction of one per cent in the growth of money incomes leading to a reduction in unit costs of about the same order, spread over ten or fifteen years, would have been enough to prevent the 1967 devaluation. The report added that: 'other things being equal, a sustained reduction of more than one per cent a year in the rate of growth in labour costs per unit of output — that is, a fuller realisation of the objectives of the policy — would have given the United Kingdom a handsome surplus in the balance of payments.'[16] It might be thought that such a speculation is now of interest only to economic historians, since after all devaluation did happen. Yet could not the lesson still be put to good account? At the time of the 1967 devaluation it was estimated that British exporters had a price advantage of 10 per cent over their main competitors — but it was officially calculated in 1969 that this had already dropped to 7 per cent.[17] Thus it was more necessary than ever to limit the increases in labour costs per unit of output in order to maintain this advantage. Between 1967 and 1968 the prices and incomes policy had a measure of success in containing this rise; it averaged 3.1 per cent between 1957 and 1966, 2.3 per cent in 1967 and 2.4 per cent in 1968.[18] This was of course encouraging only in comparison with the earlier record of the British economy; compared with other European economies much remained to be done.[19]

The 1969 report also touched on another important problem: the need for

Table 13.2.   **Prices and incomes policy 1965–70: some economic and social indicators (Percentages of increase at annual rates)**

Different phases	GDP (output-based)	Retail prices	Earnings (seasonally adjusted)*	Hourly wage rates†	Wages and salaries per unit of output	Unemployment (percentage of civilian labour force)	Unfilled vacancies
April 1965–June 1966	1.2	5.1	7.6	7.4	7.0	1.28	1.68
July 1966–June 1967	2.0	2.5	1.7	2.8	0.3	1.82	1.26
July 1967–March 1968	4.6	2.8	8.8	9.2	4.5	2.30	1.08
April 1968–Dec. 1968	3.4	5.5	7.6	4.5	0.7	2.35	1.17
Jan. 1969–Dec. 1969	1.5	5.1	8.3	5.6	7.6	2.32	1.24
Jan. 1970–June 1970	1.8	8.8	13.6	12.6	12.1	2.44	1.20
Whole period	2.1	4.7	7.3	6.5	5.0	1.99	1.31

* Earnings figures relate to all industries and services.
† Hourly wage rate figures relate to manual workers.
Source: Combined from two tables by A. Fels in *The British Prices and Incomes Board* (pp. 29–31).

taxation and monetary policy to be consistent with the prices and incomes policy: 'The complementary nature of the three policies — fiscal, monetary, prices and incomes — requires that their use should be combined in a coherent strategy and with proper regard to their sequence in time.'[20] It was really rather paradoxical that at a time when the government was so worried about price stability it should seek to cut back consumption by way of higher taxes, which of course raised prices on the home market and generated still more wage demands. One may also wonder whether the level of indirect taxation, and even of direct taxation (since at the higher rates of income very large rises in gross income were needed to secure a significant increase in income after tax), may not have been the main reason why so many excessively large wage demands were lodged after the end of 1969. Turner and Wilkinson have demonstrated in their study of this problem that, when allowance is made for tax changes and variations in national insurance contributions, the increase in real incomes during this period was in fact very small.[21] They calculated that for the median wage-earner with two children it was only of the order of one per cent per year between 1964 and 1968, as compared with 1.9 per cent for the years 1959—64, and that it rose to about 2.7 per cent in 1968—70, i.e. the period following the acceleration we have previously noted. This is certainly one possible explanation for the wage explosion, which was all the more remarkable because it came at a time when unemployment was rather high.

In 1968—9 the level of unemployment varied between 2.25 and 2.50 per cent, but the rate of increase in wages gathered momentum. Had the relationship between wages and unemployment remained the same in 1968—9 as it had been in 1952—60, the rise in wages should have been under 2 per cent; in fact it was 7.8 per cent.[22] The trend in wages differed because the overall situation differed. But surely the main difference between the fifties and the latter half of the sixties was the existence of a prices and incomes policy? Lipsey and Parkin made a rather disturbing analysis of this point.[23] In their view incomes policy had had an unexpected disruptive effect on the relationship between unemployment and wages. The level of incomes became insensitive to variations in levels of unemployment; wage inflation, far from being damped down, was actually exacerbated by the incomes policy when unemployment went over 1.8 per cent. The explanation of this disruption of the 'normal' pattern was in their view as follows. If there is a norm or ceiling this disturbs the normal working of the market. While usually the demand for labour would be too low to allow wage increases, negotiations rapidly take the norm as given and use it as a point of departure for further discussions. In other words, far from working against the interest of the workers, as many trade unionists believed, incomes policy worked in their favour in periods of high unemployment when their bargaining power would otherwise have been eroded.

If Lipsey and Parkin were right, then the Labour government was wrong — in view of its policy of resisting wage inflation — to persist with the incomes policy once unemployment went over 1.8 per cent, as it did in 1967. It could be argued that once unemployment exceeded this figure a return to free collective bargaining would have been preferable to running an incomes policy, from the government's point of view.[24] But it is far from clear which course would have carried the greater political dangers — the anxiety arising from unemployment or the discontent generated by control of incomes.

Incidentally, their 'discovery' did not really contradict the work of earlier theorists like Barbara Wootton, who had always made it clear that the incomes policy they were advocating was intended to fight inflation in a context of full employment — which had been the situation ever since 1945. However, if incomes policy had in fact been abandoned at the end of 1967 this might very well have been seen as a deliberate challenge to Britain's foreign creditors and a capitulation to the trade union Left. The controversy is now of purely historic interest, since in 1970 wages took off at a quite unprecedented rate, even though unemployment was once more over 1.8 per cent and there was no incomes policy to 'disrupt the market'.

However, towards the end of 1969 many economic observers and politicians, who had noted Lipsey and Parkin's analysis and were aware of the growing antagonism of the unions, set aside their fear of runaway inflation and felt the time had perhaps come to discontinue the incomes policy, at least in its existing form, since its economic benefits were at best uncertain and certainly did not outweigh the political problems it was creating for the government. Mr Jeremy Bray, who had resigned as parliamentary secretary to the Ministry of Technology in 1969, asserted that 'if Lipsey and Parkin's conclusions are right, then while unemployment remains at 2.5% we should quietly drop incomes policy, thus reducing the rate of wage inflation'.[25] Less daringly a *Times* editorial asked whether, without completely abandoning incomes policy, the time had not come to reconsider its aims, and recalled the co-operative spirit that prevailed at the time of the Statement of Intent in 1964. Unfortunately, 'the reality has been a policy that degenerated quickly and strayed too far from its worthy objective under the dictates of short-term economic considerations'.[26] This of course was where the shoe pinched. There had to be a choice between a sustained, determined effort which would produce results in the long term, and the more striking measures which would produce purely short-term results. At the end of 1969 the choice was reduced to two possibilities: the government would have either to abandon incomes policy or to relax it so much that to all intents and purposes it would no longer exist. It preferred the second course. It announced that it was continuing along the same lines as before, that the PIB would be merged with the Monopolies Commission to form a new body which would deal with monopolies and competition as well as prices and incomes.[27] (This raised some alarm among employers.) But though Mr Wilson and Mr Jenkins gave warnings in rather general terms, and Mrs Castle fought a brave but fruitless rearguard action, the Labour government had lost the will to resist the complete collapse of its policies. It seemed that, for the time being at least, the experiment was at an end. This at least was the sad conclusion of *The Times*, which also suggested what was needed in the future: 'For the time being this chapter is closed. But in any industrial society there will, in the longer run, have to be some more rational incomes policy than one under which the race goes solely to those who are more strongly organised. The task of the next five years will be to educate public and political opinion to this fact in a less emotional atmosphere.'[28] But, five years further on, after yet another brave and unsuccessful attempt by the Conservatives, not only did the problem remain unresolved, but it was hard to see much progress with the thankless task *The Times* had mapped out.

CHAPTER 14

The State and the Modernisation of Industry

Planning as such made only a modest impact on the sluggish development of the economy. Over the long term the various attempts to modernise the economy and make it more competitive were to prove more fruitful. These took three main forms: the promotion of greater technical efficiency through the Little Neddies; encouragement to create larger, more financially efficient units through the Industrial Reorganisation Corporation, and direct encouragement of innovation through the Ministry of Technology. In addition, to protect consumers and workers from any adverse effect of these policies the government strengthened legislation against restrictive trade practices and monopolies, and tried to increase labour mobility and to prepare workers for modernisation by improving facilities for technical training and redeployment. This policy was not entirely consistent. For instance, one function of the Little Neddies was to encourage the development of new products or processes that would result in import saving; how was this tendency towards autarky to be reconciled with a policy of encouraging greater competition? More generally, the encouragement of mergers surely ran counter to the attack on monopolies? Even at the end of Labour's term of office the answer was still not clear.

The Quest for Greater Efficiency

The Work of the Little Neddies

Unlike the modernisation committees of the French Plan, the development committees were permanent bodies with a dual role. Like their French counterparts they gave the views of their industry on draft plans. This was scarcely a major task; when the NEDC plan was being prepared in 1962 the committees had not yet been set up; they had a very minor role in the drafting of the National Plan in 1965 and were really fully operational only during the preparation of the 'definitive estimate' for 1972.[1] But they also had a continuing role of suggesting ways in which their industry could be reorganised and rationalised so as to achieve greater efficiency. The failure of the National Plan and the long period of uncertainty that ensued naturally tended to throw this side of the councils' work more into the limelight. Yet whenever he defended Neddy, in the press or on other occasions, Fred Catherwood, while invariably putting the emphasis on the microeconomic work of NEDO and the development committees, insisted that it must be accompanied by appropriate action by the government. 'The NEDC view has always been that national economic policy and structural change in industry must march hand in hand and that each is, in fact, dependent on the other and unlikely to succeed alone. . . . So attempts at structural change must rely to some extent on the prospect of some degree of economic growth and that, in Britain's finely balanced economy, requires government policies to maintain demand and, so far as Government can, to keep exports profitable.'[2] Not only were the unions more willing to agree to improve productivity if the higher output was accompanied by stable employment, but it was also easier to persuade companies to invest to improve efficiency if they were confident of a buoyant demand for their products.

Not surprisingly, the failure of the government's macroeconomic policy and the resulting near-stagnation did not make the Little Neddies' job any easier. Yet most were very active, and published a number of reports either on the industry generally or on specific aspects, such as forecasts and production targets, manpower requirements, training and comparative efficiency.[3] The committees could not, of course, take action directly on these reports since they were purely advisory, and consequently their impact depended on the committee's influence within its industry. Not all the committees were equally energetic and their reports did not all carry the same weight. Among the most influential was the September 1968 report of the Little Neddy for agriculture which attempted to forecast agricultural expansion over the five years ahead and to quantify the possibilities for import saving.[4] The government, which was always on the alert for ways of keeping down the import bill, was quick to give the report's main recommendations its blessing.

Similarly, the Little Neddy for the chemical industry sent a mission to North America and subsequently published a report on manpower problems that was a major event in the industry.[5] It resulted in the Association of Chemical Industries deciding to establish a productivity service and to set up a joint working party to lay down the basic criteria to be used in negotiating productivity agreements.

The Hotel and Catering Committee investigated labour problems too, but also reported on the shortage of hotel rooms, especially in London, in the light of the fact that the number of foreign visitors, who were such a valuable source of foreign exchange, was growing far more rapidly than the government had expected.[6] The committee's recommendations for tackling the problem were very largely accepted and proved their worth.

These three committees were perhaps the most active. Most others published reports on the competitiveness of their industry, usually comparing it with its main competitors; among these were civil engineering and machine tools. But few were able to bring about any major reorganisation of their industry, which was of course a far more difficult matter. However, the Electrical Engineering Committee did have a hand in the reduction of the number of companies making transformers from twenty-eight to twelve.

At the time the committees were established some observers thought that only those where the industry was already well organised with well-established trade associations and a strong trade union structure would succeed in working out a coherent policy. This proved true in the chemical industry, where large companies predominate, but it also became clear that Little Neddies could be successful in industries that were not so highly organised. For instance the Hotel and Catering Committee proved valuable even though there had been little organisation in the industry on either the employers' or the unions' side. Indeed, it not only provided a way for unions and employers to discuss efficiency, but also brought together people who until then had had little or no contact.

Nevertheless this may seem a fairly modest record. Indeed one would be hard put to find one really major change that can be credited to the committees. But in fairness it should be said that what they were trying to do needed time to produce results. Their work is by no means easy to assess because obviously they cannot be judged on the number and thickness of their reports, but on the more underlying changes they were instrumental in bringing about. There would be fairly general agreement that they have been useful. The press has often pointedly contrasted the failure of national planning and the success of microeconomic planning by the development committees, and on the whole would agree with Frances Cairncross that 'Thanks to the Little Neddies, planning is once again respectable.'[7] To a broad section of British opinion 'respectable' was associated with what was achieved through *concertation* and persuasion. So there was a measure of affection for the Little Neddies, in contrast with the widespread suspicion of the IRC, whose effectiveness no one doubted, but which was widely feared and resented.

The Role of the IRC

Four months after the publication of the National Plan, the DEA issued a White Paper proposing the establishment of the Industrial Reorganisation Corporation. The IRC was therefore Mr Brown's baby. However, owing to the 1966 election and a protracted passage through Parliament, with the Conservatives — particularly Mr Macleod — fighting it every inch of the way, the Bill to set up the IRC did not finally receive the royal assent until the end of December. However, right from the publication of the White Paper it had been known that Sir Frank Kearton would be the chairman, though he was already a member of NEDC and the Atomic Energy Authority, as well as being chairman of Courtaulds.

The IRC was set up as a public body with 'non-public' management, to put money into companies to assist and promote modernisation. Its board of eleven were almost all businessmen.[8] It contained no government representative. The full-time staff numbered under thirty. It was the sort of interventionist body the Labour manifesto had adumbrated, but, as mindful as ever of industry's susceptibilities, Mr Wilson acted cautiously. For the IRC had a large measure of independence of the government, which laid down its powers and responsibilities and then left it to the Corporation to decide for itself its priorities and mode of operation. It was made clear that the IRC was not part of the normal machinery of state (though of course it co-operated with sponsoring departments and the Little Neddies). As the Act put it, 'It is hereby declared that the Corporation is not to be regarded as the servant or agent of the Crown, or as enjoying any status, immunity or privilege of the Crown.'[9]

The Act also set out the IRC's aims and objects as follows:

The Corporation may, for the purpose of promoting industrial efficiency and profitability and assisting the economy of the United Kingdom or any part of the United Kingdom —

(a) promote or assist the reorganisation or development of any industry; or
(b) if requested to do so by the Secretary of State, establish or develop, or promote or assist the establishment or development of, any industrial enterprise.[10]

An initial sum of £150 million was made available to the IRC for these purposes — a sizeable enough amount to make a significant impact.[11]

The IRC found itself with two questions to resolve: it had to work out its priorities for intervention, and to win over management, which viewed it with a mixture of suspicion and apprehension, if their initial reactions were any guide. While the Corporation did its best to heal this breach, it nevertheless took a very active role, doing its best to see, as the prime minister put it, that companies were 'dragged, kicking and screaming if necessary, into the twentieth century'.

Accordingly it went out looking for ways of bringing about sweeping changes in industrial organisation, both through 'mergers between companies or hiving off of subsidiaries, to eliminate wasteful duplication and permit economies of scale in production, marketing and research'.[12] But it was not just a matter of creating companies that could take their place in the 'international league'; the IRC also wanted to promote mergers that 'by increasing efficiency, will have a significant impact on the industry concerned and hence on the economy as a whole'.[13] Also, since the Conservatives were alleging that the IRC was just another way of providing handouts for 'lame ducks', the IRC insisted that it gave support only to 'schemes of rationalisation offering good prospects of early returns in terms of increased exports or reduced imports'.[14]

The IRC soon made its mark. The most important takeover in which it was concerned involved GEC and AEI in 1967 and then GEC and English Electric in the following year, which resulted in the formation of one of the world's major industrial corporations; but it was also significant because, while IRC gave advice and moral support, it did not take a direct financial stake. The merger would have taken place even if the IRC had not existed, but it would not have come as soon, and it would have shown results more slowly.

Another major undertaking was the merger of British Motor Holdings (BMH) and Leyland Motors to form BLMC, with the object of both strengthening BMH's management and of ensuring the survival of a major British-owned car producer, rather than leaving the industry entirely in the hands of American corporations — Ford, Vauxhall (General Motors) and Chrysler-Rootes.[15] This operation would probably not have succeeded without a loan of £25 million from IRC.

The third major IRC operation was the reorganisation of the nuclear industry, along lines advocated by Kearton. Design and construction of nuclear power stations were to be shared between two new consortia (this was in preference to the proposal of the Commons Select Committee on Science and Technology that there should be a single company). In January 1969 the British Nuclear Design and Construction Company and the Nuclear Power Group were created, with both the AEA and IRC contributing. The IRC's activities in the electronics industry led to the creation of International Computers Ltd, the largest computer manufacturer outside American control. On top of this the IRC was involved in forty-three mergers up to the end of 1969 and was, at the same date, engaged in talks with about a further sixty companies in a wide range of industries. And yet IRC was one of the most widely criticised of all the Wilson government's innovations. Its very success was probably a contributory factor.

From birth the Corporation came under fire for two quite contradictory reasons, from the Right and from the Left. These criticisms were aired during the Commons debates preceding the setting up of IRC, and thus owed much more to doctrinaire attitudes than to actual experience. For the Right, IRC was simply a tool of state intervention which raised dangers of backdoor national-isation, and which was far too ready to step in and rescue firms that were irretrievably inefficient. The Left, on the contrary, considered IRC had too much independence, and argued that the government should intervene directly to modernise the economy and stimulate growth, resorting to compulsion if need be. With rather more justification Mr Clive Jenkins argued that 'The IRC has assisted in the creation of monopolistic and oligopolistic undertakings by providing the finance and, more importantly, the arguments for them.'[16] In his view, rationalisation had led to the abolition of many jobs in industries where reorganisation had not been accompanied by increased demand. (He mentioned heavy electrical engineering as a particular case in point.) He did not blame IRC for this, since it was not equipped to take social consequences into account. Nor did he suggest that the pace of mergers should be slowed down. But he argued that the unions should insist on a 'code of conduct' to help 'those displaced as a direct result of the work of the IRC', and he suggested that the IRC should be responsible for enforcing this code. The IRC itself was acutely aware of this problem, and in June 1969 obliquely answered Jenkins:

IRC is acutely conscious that many of the schemes for industrial reorganisation . . . have far-reaching implications for trade union members and their
leaders . . . . IRC therefore took the initiative in approaching the Economic
Committee of the Trades Union Congress . . . to discuss with them their
suggestion that there should be a code of practice in merger situations and
ways in which IRC could help to secure such practice.[17]

This intention was put into practice when, at the time of the merger of
Hoffmann Manufacturing and Brown Bayley Steels, in which IRC was involved,
there was close consultation with the unions over redundancies that might result.
Had a merchant bank, rather than the IRC, been involved, it could not have
behaved in the same way — nor is it likely it would have wished to.

The IRC was undeniably effective. It is probably true that larger companies
with a tendency towards monopoly or oligopoly benefited most.[18] Smaller
companies, where the spirit of free enterprise and competition often burned
brighter, were suspicious of the Corporation and rarely sought its help. It was
chiefly their pressure that led the Conservatives to abolish IRC. Yet these were
the very firms that most needed to merge or reorganise.

Sometimes the IRC seemed to behave rather high-handedly, most notably in
the takeover battle involving Kent-Cambridge Instruments and the Rank
Organisation. It was severely criticised for this in the Commons, particularly by
Conservatives such as Sir Keith Joseph (then opposition spokesman on industry).
But the IRC could usually count on the unwavering support of *The Times*,
which was scarcely suspect of pro-Labour bias but which was still writing as late
as June 1970 that 'its general objectives are very much in line with what British
industry needs. Like many other British institutions the most useful attacks are
those which concern the behaviour of the institutions rather than the doctrinal
attacks on whether it has a right to exist at all'.[19] For the moment, however, the
doctrinaires on the Conservative side were to prevail — not just over IRC but
over the whole issue of governmental intervention.

Other Measures

No theme was closer to Mr Wilson's heart during the 1964 election than the need
for British industry to exploit the technological and scientific revolution. This
led to the establishment of the Ministry of Technology in October 1964. The
new ministry took under its wing a wide range of committees, institutes and
foundations which, under a variety of names and in a variety of ways, were
responsible for encouraging and assisting technical innovation and scientific
research.

The aim of the Industrial Expansion Act of 1968, which was vigorously
opposed by the Conservatives, was to give greater powers to Mintech to promote
innovation. The Act authorised it to help companies that either wanted to
introduce new techniques that might not be profitable in the short term, or to

market new products for which there was no assured commercial future. Aid could take one of several forms: direct loans and financial guarantees by the State, or even the State taking a stake in the company. This latter provision roused the particular ire of the CBI and the Conservatives. In their view state holdings in companies were an even bigger threat than the operations of the IRC, particularly since the fact that some £150 million had been set aside for the purpose indicated that action would be on a large scale. In the event, however, the result was neither as substantial nor as effective as expected. Its main impact was felt by established companies like Rolls Royce, and it would be hard to establish whether it really succeeded in promoting any significant degree of innovation, or whether it simply amounted to indirect subsidy on exports. At all events Mr Benn, Labour's last minister of technology, won little applause.

Safeguards

The Struggle Against Monopolies and Restraints of Trade

It was Mr Wilson, as president of the Board of Trade in 1948, who introduced the first Monopolies Act.[20] It was only a very tentative first step in the development of regulation of monopolies and restrictive practices. Over the years the Monopolies Commission, which was set up by the 1948 Act, was more concerned with educating and informing than with acting very decisively against monopolies. Consequently in 1956 the Conservatives decided to give the system more teeth. The Restrictive Trade Practices Act of 1956 set down a list of practices that would be held to be in restraint of trade and created the Restrictive Practices Court to deal with them.

Companies were required to register all such agreements and cartels with the Court. Over two thousand agreements were notified in this way, but the Court was not called on to examine them all; over half were either abandoned or amended in the light of the first rulings by the Court, which rapidly built up a body of case law by judicious choice of test cases and a strict interpretation of the Act. This partly compensated for the fact that the Court moved so slowly. Its rulings were of considerable significance because an agreement that it held to be illegal immediately lost all validity without any need for further action by the Board of Trade.

But the Monopolies and Restrictive Practices Act of 1948, despite its title, and the Restrictive Trade Practices Act of 1956, which retained the Monopolies Commission, though leaving it a smaller staff and reduced workload, were really concerned only with restrictive trade practices, and they did almost nothing about mergers. With the rising number of takeovers during the sixties this situation could not be allowed to continue. So on returning to power Labour brought in the Monopolies and Mergers Act of 1965 which took a tougher line on monopolies and extended both the scope and powers of the Monopolies Commission. The degree of continuity in the legislation in this field is quite striking. Far from its becoming a battleground between the parties, at each successive stage the two main parties have tried to bring legislation into line with the developing needs of the situation. The most one can say is that the Conservatives were rather tougher on restrictive trade practices, while Labour concentrated more on attacking monopolies. This may have reflected a greater Conservative concern with promoting competition, where Labour was more interested in controlling the power of big monopolistic companies.

This concern was to the fore in 1965 when the Monopolies and Mergers Act restored the Monopoly Commission's size and powers to what they had been from 1953 to 1956, while retaining the Restrictive Practices Court. The Monopolies Commission was an independent body, with its own headquarters and staff. The chairman was the only full-time member.[21] He had a part-time deputy and there were up to twenty-five part-time members[22] serving for three years — businessmen, professional economists (mostly from the universities) and trade unionists. The Commission recruited its own staff, most of them seconded civil servants; it occasionally 'borrowed' civil servants for short periods from the Board of Trade to help it carry out particular investigations.

The Commission's role was to examine actual or potential monopoly situations, and the likely effects of mergers that had either been announced or were contemplated, to consider whether or not these operated in the public interest, and to report accordingly. The Act defined a 'monopoly situation' as one where a company held at least one-third of the market for a particular product or service, or where a group of companies acted together in a way that restricted competition over the entire country or some substantial part of it. The Commission both investigated whether such a monopoly situation existed, and determined whether or not its operation was contrary to the public interest. The Commission had wide powers to investigate, summon witnesses and call for the production of documents. But it had no power of decision. It could not initiate an investigation; this was a matter for the Board of Trade. And the Commission's rulings were not binding; it was again the task of the Board of Trade to decide what action, if any, should be taken in the light of the report.

The Commission's procedures were very similar to those of the PIB. The initial investigation took a considerable time — anything up to two years.[23] Hearings might be held at the headquarters of the Commission, and were conducted along quasi-judicial lines. Following the investigation a team of civil servants drafted a report for approval by the Commission. Rulings of the Commission required the support of two-thirds of the members dealing with the case (the Commission never sat in plenary session). There could be minority reports and notes of dissent.

The Commission was therefore limited to advising the Board of Trade,[24] which had wide powers under the 1965 Act. The decision on which matters should be considered by the Commission lay with the Board. Companies were not required to notify proposed takeovers or mergers – unlike agreements in restraint of trade. Consequently it was up to the Board to keep an eye open for mergers that required its intervention. Apparently it was dependent for its information on the financial press.[25] It might either tacitly approve a merger by doing nothing or refer it to the Commission, which had to give a ruling within six months. Once the Commission reported, the Board was responsible for publishing the report and deciding what subsequent action to take. It could bar any proposed merger or nullify one that had already taken place.

The Board's powers in relation to monopolies (rather than the possibility of monopoly arising from a merger) were considerable. It could declare any monopoly unlawful, terminate agreements that might tend to restrict the supply of any product or service or to discriminate between customers through prices or other means, break up a monopoly, or intervene to regulate prices.

Governments have preferred to tackle monopolies or potential monopolies by administrative action while restrictive trade practices are dealt with by a special court. Perhaps there is a difference between Conservatives and the Labour Party here – with the latter more prepared to trust administrators to interpret the public interest!

The slow pace at which the Monopolies Commission worked meant that it did not have the same public impact as the PIB or the IRC. Between August 1965 and November 1968 it issued five reports dealing with colour films, detergents, cinematograph films, plate glass and artificial fibres. Over roughly the same period the Board of Trade considered 318 mergers but referred only 12 to the Commission.

In every case of monopoly it investigated except one (Pilkingtons and plate glass) the Commission found matters that were not in the public interest. However, it held eight of the twelve mergers that were referred to it to be in order. The other four involved Ross Group and Associated Fisheries, United Drapery Stores and Burtons, Rank Organisation and de la Rue, and Barclays with Lloyds Bank and Martins Bank, and were held not to be in the public interest. In these four cases the Board was not called on to use its powers under the 1965 Act, because immediately the Commission's report appeared the companies concerned announced that they no longer intended to continue with the proposals.

In its pamphlet *Mergers* the Board of Trade attempted to reconcile the work of the IRC and the Monopolies Commission on mergers: 'It is in no way contradictory to have on the one hand the IRC, which was set up to encourage and assist structural reorganisation, including mergers where appropriate; and on the other hand the 1965 Act and the Monopolies Commission offering a procedure for scrutinising specific mergers to see whether or not they are contrary to the public interest and, if they are, to prevent them taking place.'[26] The pamphlet also emphasised that a 'working relationship' had developed which should avoid 'any conflict between decisions by the Board to refer particular mergers to the Commission, and the IRC's decision to give its backing to any particular merger'.[27] In fact the Board of Trade appeared to have carefully avoided interfering with mergers supported by the IRC. However, there was at least potentially a difficulty, and in the autumn of 1968 Mr Crosland, who was then president of the Board of Trade, considered strengthening the Commission and defining its role rather more clearly so as to avoid any possibility of a clash with the IRC. However, he ran into opposition from such interventionists as Mr Shore (DEA), Mrs Castle (DEP) and Mr Benn (Mintech). As a result Mr Wilson proposed a rather different approach at the time of the ministerial reshuffle of October 1969: the PIB and the Monopolies Commission would be merged to form a 'superboard' under Aubrey Jones, which would deal with monopolies, prices and incomes and productivity. However the defeat of Labour in the 1970 election threw the matter back into the melting pot again.

Redeployment of Manpower

In the Statement of Intent the government pledged not only to create conditions favouring rapid growth and to get rid of restrictive practices and abuses of monopoly power, but also to see that greater productivity and increased industrial efficiency were not achieved at the expense of the workers, which meant that everything possible must be done to deal with redundancy, particularly by facilitating mobility of labour and better facilities for retraining workers. The unions promised not to oppose this.

Before Labour returned to power only workers in the public sector (including the nationalised industries) could be sure of any compensation, apart from unemployment pay, if they were made redundant. The Redundancy Act of 1965 extended these benefits to all workers with over two years service and introduced a system of redundancy benefits related to pay and length of employment. This compensation would be paid from a special Redundancy Fund (expenditure from which was estimated at around £25,000,000 a year) financed 40 per cent by the employers and 60 per cent by the State. In 1966 this was supplemented by a special rate of unemployment benefit for a period of six months. The declared aim was to help workers through a particularly difficult period — that is, the emphasis was on the social welfare aspect rather than the specifically economic aspect. More positive economic action was needed to make it easier to redeploy labour. Financial provision had to be made to encourage workers to move elsewhere either permanently or temporarily; this might involve assisting them to move to an appropriate job elsewhere or persuading key workers to move as part of the policy of regionalisation. This involved a range of removal grants, travel grants, subsistence allowances and training grants.

The most important thing was to absorb back into employment workers who had either become redundant or were scheduled for redundancy, many of whom were in declining industry. In other words there was a need to secure a better balance between supply and demand for skilled labour.

The idea of a national scheme for retraining redundant workers was of course by no means new. The main legislation during the period we are considering was in fact the Industrial Training Act of 1964, which the Conservatives carried shortly before leaving office.[28] Here again we see the Conservatives identifying a problem during the early sixties, and introducing appropriate measures some time later, which were then implemented by the Labour government. The 1964 Act provided for a national system of occupational training financed by the employers. It had three main objects: to bring the supply of skilled labour roughly into line with demand; to improve occupational training; and to see the financial burden was shared fairly between companies. Since Labour took office very shortly after the Act was passed the system that was subsequently set up was primarily their work. Its central feature was the creation of an Industrial Training Board for each industry; by 1969 there were twenty-six, with thirty more scheduled.[29] The various boards were co-ordinated by a Central Training Council, serving as an intermediary between the boards and the DEP. Each board administered its own training schemes, fixing and collecting levies from companies, laying down standards for training and gathering information on manpower requirements. The resulting system involved over fifteen million workers and more than a million firms.

The occupational training centres have about 25,000 instructors, whose training is undertaken by some thirty-one colleges and two universities. While by 1970 only 16,650 people were receiving full-time training in the official training centres, some half a million more were undergoing full-time or part-time training or retraining in their place of work or elsewhere. Numerically at least this seemed a satisfactory result.[30] The problem was whether this form of training and redeployment was in keeping with the developing needs of the economy as a whole. At the end of 1964 there were about 250,000 unfilled vacancies and about 300,000 unemployed. Five years later there were about 200,000 unfilled vacancies for some 540,000 unemployed.[31] Progress had scarcely been spectacular, and yet the main object of the entire exercise was to achieve a better balance between supply and demand in the labour market. However, the conclusion one draws from this must be highly qualified; for manpower planning is particularly difficult, especially if one is wholly dependent on financial and intellectual incentives for success. It is not enough to ensure that the number of workers trained matches projections for employment – the projections themselves have to be right. But this is a field where accurate forecasting is notoriously difficult. Moreover, although training schemes are in principle a way of balancing supply and demand, obviously it is much easier to achieve this in practice if there is a generally high level of economic activity, including employment. It is extremely difficult to break out of the vicious circle created by insufficient expansion.

It should also be added that some unions, mostly older craft unions, gave no help in improving mobility; they resisted as long as they could any increase in numbers being trained in their skill, even where there was a chronic shortage, as a means of keeping their pay up. Sometimes they tried to prevent men who had been trained at the training centres from being given jobs. So, in their various ways, government, unions and employers all failed to honour fully the commitments they had made in the statement of intent: the government failed to provide sustained expansion; the TUC was unable to prevent some of its constituent unions from clinging to the old restrictive practices – and many employers were quite prepared to turn a blind eye.

Conclusion

In an attempt to cope with the problems of industrial modernisation, the State produced a wide range of new legislation and new institutions. Its financial contribution was in keeping with the size of the problem. Shortly before the 1970 election *The Economist* estimated that the government would spend £2,000 million on aid to industry in 1970 and commented: 'It has taken an inordinately heavy priming of the pump in the four years since the last general election to produce a modest growth of 10% in Britain's industrial production: equivalent to an annual 2½%, well below the other industrial economies of the west . . . .'[32] The financial effort seemed quite disproportionate to the results. The paper went on, 'The inescapable conclusion is that much of the aid has been ill-directed.'[33]

The Economist's view was that Whitehall was ill-suited to the new roles it was being called on to perform, and it called for an overhaul of the machinery of government, planning techniques and aid to industry, and recommended merging the two departments most closely concerned with industry, the Board of Trade and Mintech, to form a single department. (And this was of course done by the next government.)

But the problem could not simply be explained in terms of inadequate machinery; it was vain to imagine that any revamping of institutions would make the crucial difference. The gulf between the enormous intellectual and financial effort expended on modernisation and the very modest results was due, rather, to the fundamental contradiction in the government's conduct of the economy over the preceding five years: while industry was constantly being exhorted and induced to change and modernise, the main brake on these changes was in fact the failure of the government to maintain a favourable economic climate. Almost throughout those five years the atmosphere nurtured an economic malaise which was a major factor in crippling the attempt to transform industry. Government aid enabled many firms to survive but few to be revitalised in the way ministers hoped. Admittedly the balance of payments improved appreciably after August 1969, but this was achieved only at the cost of near stagnation in output, and came very belatedly after years of sacrifices and devaluation. Also, although unemployment had risen sharply, the fear of inflation immediately came to dominate the thinking of those who were responsible for the economy much as the balance of payments had in the past.

So the degradation in the economic climate provoked a growing malaise, which blighted industrial relations and was particularly damaging to relations between the government and the unions. The deterioration became evident after the devaluation of the pound in November 1967, reached its peak in 1968 with the argument over growth and the incomes policy and culminated in 1969 in the abandoning of the most controversial provisions of the government's proposals on industrial relations reform.[34] The way that these differences turned into a virulent political battle was all the more surprising because Labour is so much an emanation of the unions. It was hardly to be expected that the party would come into conflict with a majority of its supporters. On the other hand, nobody would have been in the least surprised if there had been bitter disagreement between Labour and the *employers*, for a mixture of ideological reasons, strengthened by memories of the postwar Labour government and the fact that Labour's new programme heralded an extension both of compulsion in planning and of state intervention to speed up economic modernisation. Yet in the event there was something close to peaceful coexistence, and private industry managed to come to terms with a Labour government remarkably successfully. One explanation that was widely favoured on the Left was that the government repeatedly sided with the employers and that its policies were anti-union. But one has only to recall how many of the government's measures were opposed by the CBI — the creation of the DEA, the establishment of the IRC and the Industrial Expansion Act to name only three examples — to feel that the employers by no means always got their way. On the other hand a good many firms did manage to reconcile themselves with remarkable alacrity to accepting the funds that 'socialist intervention' made available to them — and which they had reason to fear they would lose if the Conservatives returned (though in the event the Conservatives were to temper the wind to almost as many shorn lame ducks as Labour).

But to return to the unions; examination of incomes policy shows that it did not work against the workers' interest as was sometimes claimed, since with the exception of a single year incomes always rose more than prices. On top of this the government tried to ease the inevitable problems associated with modernisation by improving the range of grants and benefits and facilities for occupational training. Nevertheless, rightly or wrongly, many trade unionists felt that they were being asked to shoulder more than their fair share of the sacrifices. Also, by tackling the problem of industrial relations, particularly the unofficial strikes which a broad section of the public looked on as an abuse of union power, the government gave the impression it was more prepared to listen to socialism's detractors than to its own supporters. And yet *In Place of Strife* contained many provisions that were favourable to the unions, and the chairman of the new Commission for Industrial Relations was George Woodcock (who had recently retired from the general secretaryship of the TUC). The CIR was to be an instrument for both improving relations between employers and workers through persuasion and negotiation and diminishing inter-union disputes. The DEP retained its traditional role as mediator in industrial disputes, with the CIR having only an advisory role. Unfortunately the CIR took a long while to get under way, and its first three reports only appeared at the end of 1969. All three dealt with union recognition; in two cases the employers refused to accept the CIR's ruling, and in the third the outcome was not completely negative, but the CIR's recommendations were not fully implemented. A bad start.

At all events, the deterioration in the climate of industrial relations, the most obvious sign of which was the proliferation of unofficial strikes, was having a depressing influence on British industry during 1969 and 1970, particularly since the government capitulated over its industrial relations reform in May 1969 and followed this by a strategic withdrawal over prices and incomes in October. These two episodes were widely seen as political defeats. Both must have had their impact on the outcome of the 1970 election, for they lost Mr Wilson the support of the marginal voters without regaining the approval of the left-wing militants.

PART IV

The Heath Government – Between 'Freedom' and Intervention

CHAPTER 15

Reforming the Machine

For much of 1969 Whitehall was buzzing with speculation and rumours about the fate of the DEA. It was known that the head of the civil service, Sir William Armstrong,[1] was considering a reallocation of responsibilities between departments, and it was generally expected that this would reflect the fact that the DEA had failed and that the system established in 1964 had been too cumbersome and inefficient.

As we have seen, the setting up of the DEA (like that of NEDC) was based on the hope that the existence of two poles of economic policy-making would develop a creative tension which would promote economic expansion. It was only too evident in 1969 that this had not happened, and it was widely held that:

> The right machine of high command in economic policy ... is to place supreme authority on one senior economic minister clearly responsible for the balance of payments, the Budget, planning, prices and incomes, investments, the currency reserves and the inter-relations of these .... In the absence of one clearly responsible coordinating minister, you will necessarily get blurred responsibility, indecision, delay and finally, in the economic circumstances of postwar Britain, sooner or later ... crisis. ... The cardinal mistake of setting up the DEA in 1964 was to ignore this principle.[2]

In Douglas Jay's view the British economy had never been so well run as under Sir Stafford Cripps. While Cripps's own personal qualities certainly had a lot to do with this, the more important factor was that he had sole responsibility for policy-making. Mr Jay argued that the best solution would be to give back to the chancellor all the powers he had held in Cripps's day – which implied not only disbanding the DEA but also radically recasting the relationship between the Treasury and the other economic departments.

It was also clear in 1969 that the government had suffered a bad attack of 'institutionitis', as Michael Shanks described the tendency to react automatically to every new problem by setting up a new body to deal with it. On the economic side alone, since 1964 Labour had established three new ministries (DEA, Mintech and the DEP),[3] the regional economic councils and boards, the PIB, the CIR, the IRC, the Central Council for Industrial Training with its twenty-six ITBs, as well as creating or reorganising a substantial number of specialised public or semi-public bodies or companies[4] of varying importance but all in their various ways representing an extension of the bureaucracy. Moreover, the party programme approved at the 1969 Labour conference, far from showing any awareness of the danger of bureaucratisation, displayed all the symptoms of an even more acute attack of 'institutionitis':[5]

> [The] solution to every problem in *Labour's Economic Strategy* appears to be the setting up of a new board, committee, corporation or government department. Not all of these are otiose or misconceived individually, but the cumulative effect is. For every close observer of the Whitehall scene knows that today we already have too many overlapping committees, boards and government departments, and that this proliferation is a source of time-wasting and inefficiency.[6]

An overgrown bureaucracy was not the only danger. 'Institutionitis' could also lead to paralysis and disguise an absence of policy:

> It is much easier for a hard-pressed minister to set up an institution than to hammer out a policy. Too often in the past few years, in my view, energies in government have been diverted from the hard task of choosing policies to the more congenial option of setting up an institution, choosing and briefing its bosses and determining its terms of reference.[7]

Michael Shanks was also understandably apprehensive about the consequences of a Conservative victory at the forthcoming general election, fearing they might go too far in the opposite direction. 'There is thus the growing danger that there will be an overreaction after the next election, and that an incoming Tory administration will throw out the baby with the bathwater, the useful committees and institutions (of which there are many) along with the superfluous (of which there are some).'[8]

These were by no means empty warnings, as we shall see in the next chapter. Meanwhile, however, Mr Wilson's 1969 reorganisation prepared the ground for a degree of simplification. Indeed, the changes Mr Heath was to introduce the following year should be seen as complementing and completing Mr Wilson's work rather than as a fresh change of course.

The Labour Reorganisation of October 1969

Basically the Labour reorganisation entailed the abolition of the DEA and the distribution of its responsibilities to other departments, but it also affected the Ministry of Fuel and Power and the Board of Trade. The new allocation of responsibility for economic matters was as follows.

The Treasury. Apart from retaining all its existing responsibilities the Treasury took over the DEA's medium- and long-term forecasting division — which to all practical intents and purposes restored the old National Economy group in the Treasury, which had been disbanded when the DEA was formed. This amounted to at least a tacit admission that it would probably have been better if the various functions had never been separated in the first place. Thus there were once more three groups in the Treasury (Public Sector, Finance and

National Economy). The last of these had four divisions (economic forecasting, national economy, industrial and incomes policy, and monetary policy) corresponding to the four main areas of forecasting, economic strategy, communications and the other aspects of economic policy for which the Treasury has a shared responsibility, such as monetary questions, prices and incomes and industry. Also, the Economic Section was no longer to be assigned specific responsibilities but was to serve as a pool of economic expertise on which all the other groups could call according to their needs. Mr Heath's later reorganisation (see figure 15.1) was to leave this system intact, though of course from 1970 to the end of 1972 incomes policy was in a state of suspended animation.

The Ministry of Technology and Energy became in fact if not in name the Ministry of Industry. In addition to its existing responsibilities it was now made responsible for almost the entire range of public and private industry and for structural policy and productivity, which were transferred to it from the DEA. This involved oversight of the IRC and the Little Neddies (which of course depended directly on NEDC). The department also took over responsibility for regional development from the DEA, and industrial location and investment subsidies from the Board of Trade. To complete the list, it took over energy and mineral prospecting from the Ministry of Fuel and Power, which was abolished.

The Ministry of Local Government and Regional Planning took over direct responsibility for regional policy from the DEA (though regional development went to Mintech); with this went supervision of the regional planning councils and boards. It was also made responsible for co-ordination of housing and local government and transport, whose ministers were no longer in the cabinet.

The Board of Trade retained responsibility for overseas trade and internal communications, such as merchant shipping, civil aviation and the tourist and hotel industries, and for regulating such matters as patents, copyright, insurance and companies, but it lost most of its responsibility for industry to the enlarged Mintech.

The Department of Employment and Productivity, while retaining the functions assigned to it when it was established in March 1968, also took over from the Board of Trade the supervision of several bodies concerned with productivity and industrial efficiency such as the British Productivity Council, the British Institute of Management, and the Centre for Inter-Firm Comparisons. Also, the Commission for Industrial Relations and the proposed new 'Super-board',[9] which was to replace both the Monopolies Commission and the PIB, were to be attached to the DEP – though in the event the 1970 election intervened before Mrs Castle had time to set up the new board.

The five ministers responsible for these departments (at the time, respectively, Mr Jenkins, Mr Benn, Mr Crosland, Mr Mason and Mrs Castle), together with the paymaster-general, Mr Lever, who had special responsibility with Mintech for energy questions, all had seats in the cabinet.

The position of NEDC was unchanged, and the prime minister retained his chairmanship. Apart from the proposed merger of the Monopolies Commission and the PIB, the other government agencies dealing with planning matters also kept their existing powers and responsibilities.

The 1969 reorganisation was generally well received. The disappearance of the DEA caused little surprise and few regrets. Nevertheless it was important as giving expression in terms of administrative organisation to the failure — and abandonment — of a certain idea of planning. But there was some apprehension that the Treasury would emerge again as the Whitehall 'superpower'.[10] For this reason *The Economist* and Sam Brittan both advocated the creation of a Council of Economic Advisers on the American model, attached directly to the cabinet, and providing independent advice on the major economic policy issues.

There was also some satisfaction that industry had been brought under a single department, though Mr Crosland's new super-ministry also aroused a measure of scepticism and apprehension. While it was logical for the ministry concerned with local government to deal with regional planning too, it was more surprising that it was not also responsible for regional economic development (particularly such matters as the location of industry), for, as *The Times* argued, 'Industrial development is the dynamic of regional planning, yet the minister responsible for the latter has no executive powers in relation to the former.'[11] This was illogical, to say the least.

Moreover, the new organisation of planning at the national level also seemed rather confused. For although NEDC was officially attached to the cabinet office, for such macroeconomic functions as the preparation of the plan, consultation and co-ordination between the economic departments and industry and reports on matters of general interest it had to work in close conjunction with the National Economy group at the Treasury, while its microeconomic functions in relation to the Little Neddies came under Mintech for industry and the Board of Trade for services.

However, the Labour government had little time to put this new structure to the test. Indeed, one criticism that could be made of Mr Wilson was that he left the reorganisation until the election was almost upon him. For at the time it seemed highly probable that if the Conservatives won the election they would make more changes, thus prolonging administrative upheaval and uncertainty, and this was likely to have an adverse effect on policy-making. In the event, though, the Wilson and Heath reforms complemented more than they contradicted each other. This is perhaps not as surprising as it might seem at first glance. For not only had the Conservatives been laying their plans while in opposition, but a number of senior civil servants were also considering possible reforms — though they were thinking more in terms of improving the existing machinery than of radically reorganising it, and their views were to carry considerable weight. However, the motives underlying the Labour and Conservative reforms were very different. For while Labour was concerned with strengthening and rationalising government control of the economy, the Conservatives' aim was to rid the state machine of a burden of intervention which, in Mr Heath's view, did not really belong to it.

The Conservative Reorganisation of October 1970[1][2]

The guiding principle of the new organisation was set out unequivocally in the opening words of the accompanying White Paper: 'This Administration believes that government has been attempting too much. This has placed an excessive burden on industry, and on the people of the country as a whole, and has also overloaded the government machine itself . . . . The weakness has shown itself in the apparatus of policy formulation and in the quality of many government decisions over the last 25 years.'[1][3]

The basic argument was quite clear: the size and complexity of the machinery of government had become an obstacle to good decision-making and efficiency. In attempting to remedy this the reform had a three-fold aim:

(i) To improve the quality of policy formulation and decision-taking in government by presenting ministers, collectively in Cabinet and individually within their departments, with well-defined options, costed where possible, and relating the choice between options to the contribution they can make to meeting national needs . . . .

(ii) To improve the framework within which public policy is formulated by matching the field of responsibility of government departments to coherent fields of policy and administration.

(iii) To ensure that the government machine responds and adapts itself to new policies and programmes as these emerge, within the broad framework of the main departmental fields of responsibility.[1][4]

With these general aims, the reorganisation attempted to apply a functional approach to the allocation of responsibilities. In the economic field the White Paper identified three principal functions: national economic policy, industrial policy and land-use planning. It did not discuss the first of these but it was clear that this was to be the responsibility of the Treasury. The other two were to be entrusted to two new super-ministries, one dealing with trade and industry and the other with the environment.

The Department of Trade and Industry (DTI). This new department was something other than a straight merger of the Board of Trade and Mintech. While it took over all the functions of the old Board of Trade and most of Mintech's, it lost aerospace research and aviation supply, which were assigned temporarily to the Ministry of Aviation Supply and later to the Ministry of Defence. However, it also assumed responsibility for monopolies, mergers and restraints of trade, which had come under the DEP during the Wilson government. The first secretary of state for trade and industry was Mr John Davies (he was succeeded in November 1972 by Mr Peter Walker). Below him were ministers for trade and for industry, who were not in the cabinet, who were joined soon afterwards by a minister for aerospace, and in April 1972 by a minister for industrial development. In November 1972 the minister for trade − at the time Sir Geoffrey Howe − became the minister for trade and consumer affairs and was given a seat in the cabinet.

The Department of the Environment (DOE). Here the Conservatives were following the Labour reform through to its logical conclusion. For Mr Crosland's

Figure 15.1. Central economic organisation under the Conservatives 1970–74.

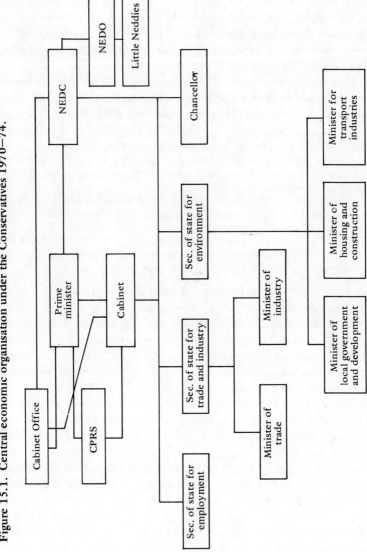

old department had taken over the responsibilities of the old Ministries of Housing and Local Government and Transport. The new DOE also absorbed the Ministry for Public Buildings and Works. In England (for in Scotland and Wales most of these responsibilities stayed with the Scottish and Welsh Offices) the DOE, in the words of the White Paper, 'will cover the planning of land — where people live, work, move and enjoy themselves'.[15] It also embraced housing policy and finance, relations with the building industry, the road construction programme, co-ordination of urban and transport planning, the investment programmes of the nationalised industries, ports policy, the control of all forms of pollution, the preservation of amenity and the protection of the countryside, and (in co-operation with the DTI) regional development. Finally, it was responsible for the reform of local government, which the Conservatives were to carry through soon afterwards.

Heading this vast conglomerate was a secretary of state, Mr Peter Walker (until he moved to the DTI in November 1972 and was succeeded by Mr Geoffrey Rippon in November 1972), and three ministers with specific responsibility for local government and development, transport industries, and housing and construction.

Such were the broad outlines of the October 1970 reorganisation of the machinery of government as it related to the economy. It should be noted that the DEP, having lost responsibility for both productivity and prices and incomes, became simply the Department of Employment — essentially the old Ministry of Labour under a different name.

However, Mr Heath's reforms had a less enthusiastic welcome than Mr Wilson's (partly at least because the earlier changes had still not been fully digested). There was particular scepticism about the two new monster-ministries, and especially the vast range of the DTI's responsibilities. The criticisms of the DTI were not wholly immune from political overtones, since the White Paper made no secret of the fact that one reason for the merger was to improve co-ordination in the negotiations on EEC, and thereafter to prepare more effectively for Britain's entry.[16] At all events the DTI frequently found itself having to counter charges that it was too big and too unwieldy. Eight months after the DTI was formed the permanent secretary, Sir Anthony Part, argued in the *Financial Times* that it was quite wrong to see the DTI as a Whitehall monster.[17] Indeed, its staff of 26,000 came fifth in size to the Ministry of Defence (with 112,000 non-industrial civil servants), the Ministry of Health and Social Security (92,000), the DOE (39,000) and the Department of Employment (31,000). Moreover over 10,000 of those working for the department were in sections which were 'in essence separately manageable operations' like air traffic control and safety services (7,000), the Export Credit Guarantees Department (1,600), Export Promotion Services (1,200), the Patent Office (1,600) and the Business Statistics Office (800), which clearly did not need continuous co-ordination. But Sir Anthony also noted that 'The main challenge lies not in the large numbers of staff, but in the range of policy issues', and he admitted that, while the problem of co-ordination had largely been overcome, there was still room for improvement in communication between the different branches of the department.

Be that as it may, in November 1972 Mr Heath felt that the DTI needed strengthening politically and he replaced Mr Davies — whose tenure had at best been undistinguished — with Mr Peter Walker, who was generally thought to have done a good job at the DOE, and brought in an additional cabinet minister (Sir Geoffrey Howe) as minister for trade and consumer affairs — for by now 'consumer protection' was the fashionable issue in succession to 'the environment'. It is worth noting that when Mr Wilson returned to power in 1974 he split the DTI into four separate departments, each under a secretary of state with a seat in the cabinet: Industry (Mr Benn), Trade (Mr Shore), Energy (Mr Varley) and Consumer Affairs (Mrs Williams). But here again there was a striking measure of continuity, for the lead in breaking up the DTI had already been taken by Mr Heath when he created a new Ministry for Energy under Lord Carrington only a few weeks before the election, in order to tackle both the internal and external aspects of the energy problem. Mrs Williams, while keeping all Sir Geoffrey Howe's responsibilities, also took over price control from the Treasury. It is hard to be sure whether Mr Wilson was simply responding to the criticisms that had been levelled at the DTI, whether he wanted to find suitably important posts for some of the most able and ambitious members of the Labour front bench, or whether there was an element of 'divide and conquer' about the operation. At all events this has been the only major change in the economic machinery of government since 1970.

The Improvement of Forecasting and the Control of Public Expenditure

The attempt to improve the control of public expenditure of course began well before October 1970. Indeed, this has been one of the traditional functions of the Treasury, though the 1962 reform, following the report of the Plowden Committee,[18] was one of the most significant landmarks. Most reforms of the Treasury — those at least that come to fruition — spring chiefly from dissatisfaction within the Treasury over some aspect of its work. The 1962 reform was no exception, since its prime cause was the dissatisfaction of the Treasury knights with their inability to hold the growth of public expenditure in check during the fifties. Moreover, during periods of deflation it had proved extremely difficult to make sizeable genuine reductions in public expenditure. When cuts were announced they rarely had any significant impact on either the current year or the ensuing one. Consequently they were attracted by the possibility of being able to consider public expenditure as a whole five years in advance. This of course was what the Plowden Committee recommended, and since its recommendations had the advantage of being in harmony with the preoccupations of the chancellor of the day, Selwyn Lloyd (who wanted to introduce a system of indicative planning, and so was receptive to the idea of a five-year programme for public expenditure), the introduction of the Public Expenditure Survey (PES), and the Public Expenditure Survey Committee (PESC) was rapidly agreed. The PESC is an interdepartmental committee under the chairmanship of an under-secretary from the Treasury's Public Sector group, with members drawn from the Treasury and the finance officers of the spending departments. The first PESC exercise, which appeared in 1963, dealt with expenditure for 1963–4 and attempted projections for up to 1967–8.[19] It was followed by a regular series of reports, which appeared annually after 1968.[20] The PESC system was strengthened several times between 1966 and 1970.[21] However, from 1966 onwards the system was concerned more with controlling and reducing the general level of expenditure than with planning it, the Public Sector group having rather unhappy memories of indicative planning, because the optimistic forecasts of the growth of national income in the plans had led the spending departments to raise their sights in proportion. In later years they had to lower them again, and bring expenditure into line with the resources that were actually available rather than those it had been hoped would be available (despite the fact that the ratio of public expenditure to GDP rose from about 43 per cent in 1962 to 52 per cent in 1968!).

As described by Heclo and Wildavsky,[22] the annual PES cycle begins around November or December when the Treasury circulates a memorandum to the spending departments setting out the economic basis on which they should prepare their forecasts of expenditure. These projections are sent to the Treasury at the end of February and indicate the levels of expenditure that will arise simply from continuing existing policies over five years. The Treasury sends these figures to the relevant divisions which examine and discuss them with the departments between March and May. In May the PESC meets and prepares a report that provides a detailed projection of current expenditure commitments and a list of points that are still to be resolved. In June this report goes to the chancellor, who sends a copy to each ministry. In conjunction with his senior officials the chancellor then decides the total expenditure that is permissible in current economic circumstances. Usually this means that there must be further reductions. In June, too, the last disagreements are settled by the cabinet, and with three months for any final discussions and drafting the annual White Paper finally appears in the autumn, when the cycle begins again. The PESC report is not published; the White Paper reflects the final compromises and decisions of the cabinet. In theory PESC's job is simply to work out how much it will cost to maintain current policies and it is not concerned with the desirability of these or alternative policies; that is a matter for direct discussion between the Treasury and the department concerned, with the level at which negotiations take place depending on the size of the problem. In practice it is obvious that even this limited conception of the PESC has considerable implications for policy. So PESC should be seen as a modernised form of the Treasury's traditional function of guardian of the public purse. For although it was originally introduced as a forecasting mechanism, it has become essentially a control mechanism. In that case how useful are the five-year projections, given the fact that medium-term economic planning has been abandoned? For the Treasury, the five-year projections are less a target than a ceiling. They offer a way of extracting a public commitment by ministers not to try and obtain more than they have been allocated, while allowing them to press forward with commitments that have been agreed with greater confidence. This method also facilitates parliamentary scrutiny.

There were important changes in the area of parliamentary control in January 1971. Publication of the annual White Paper is now followed by a major debate in the Commons, lasting two full days and sometimes longer. This debate, which is intended to give MPs an opportunity to express their views on the broad outlines of the White Paper, then shifts to the new Select Committee on Expenditure, which with the aid of six sub-committees, each corresponding to a major area of expenditure, submits the projections to detailed scrutiny. When it was first introduced this new procedure was hailed by *The Times* as 'historic' and the *Financial Times* as 'highly democratic'. This procedure has the merit of letting the House make its views known before decisions are taken — it had always been extremely difficult for members to make any significant impact on expenditure during discussion of the Finance Bill, because by then most expenditure was irrevocably committed by earlier decisions. It then was argued that now members had the five-year projections in front of them, they would be better placed to make real choices and vary priorities to a significant extent. The Treasury put the greatest emphasis on the third or 'focal' year. This is far enough ahead for Parliament to be able to indicate its wishes without hampering short-term management by the departments, yet close enough for the projections to be reasonably accurate. These efforts by the Treasury to see that Parliament has a real chance to make its views effective is, in Heclo and Wildavsky's view, in keeping with the long-standing complicity between it and the House of Commons arising from a common concern to hold public expenditure in check,[23] a concern that has perhaps been honoured in the breach rather than the observance in recent years. In fact Heclo and Wildavsky note that, while there is a common interest, the aims are by no means identical, and that members are concerned with the control of the level of expenditure largely so that they can contain the level of revenue. Here again, the judgement must be qualified, and it would be incorrect to suggest that members are not concerned with the way public money is spent, particularly locally. Be that as it may, until December 1972 the executive would not let Parliament have the overall assessment of the economy on which its choice of a particular ceiling for public expenditure was based. It was also far from clear that most MPs had any great interest in this new role. Certainly the ensuing debates have been so far rather disappointing and the Expenditure Committee has failed to make the 'revolutionary' impact some had expected.

Programme Analysis and Review

In addition to the reorganisation of Whitehall, the October 1970 White Paper announced two more changes in the working of central government: Programme Analysis and Review (PAR) and the Central Policy Review Staff (CPRS). While the CPRS was intended to provide a source of continuous scrutiny and challenge to government policy, PAR was more concerned with controlling public expenditure. But where PESC was intended to keep the level of expenditure down, the function of PAR was to monitor the effectiveness of expenditure by detailed analysis of specific departmental proposals and examination of the various policy options that were open. While in opposition Mr Heath had formed a small team from the City and industry which he hoped might imbue his future ministers (and civil servants) with the basic principles of programme budgeting and systems analysis, which had been all the rage on the other side of the Atlantic for some years past, and which was essentially a way of applying the principles of corporate planning to running the State. But what in fact happened was much more limited. On taking office Mr Heath assigned his team of businessmen to the Civil Service Department to prepare the introduction of PAR. However, it was soon clear that the Treasury had been beginning to move along similar lines, and, realising that there was little point in trying to work outside the Treasury and in opposition to it, the team recommended that PAR be handled by the Treasury, which soon afterwards set up a PAR Committee of Under-Secretaries from the Treasury and departmental representatives, under the chairmanship of the chairman of PESC. Heclo and Wildavsky comment:

> From its outset, therefore, PAR has departed from many of the original hopes behind its creation. Location in the Treasury means that PAR is likely to exclude analyses of subjects lacking significant and immediate expenditure content. Invariably PAR is also run by the same old faces, people who are familiar with each other's problems and assumptions through the normal expenditure process. PAR has not fallen to a detached independent group of thinkers.[24]

But this may well have been the only way of ensuring a certain level of effectiveness. Although it is still too early to say whether the PAR system has met the minimum expectations of its progenitors, it seems to have been less readily accepted by the departments than PES, since they have tended to see it as a threat to their expenditure programmes. The two declared aims of PAR — to improve the quality of governmental policy formulation and to enable regular reviews of the government's long-term aims and strategy — carry the threat of increased Treasury interference in areas that the other departments have always looked on as their private preserves, particularly the laying down of priorities in the use of the funds allocated to them.

The CPRS

Unlike PES and PAR, the CPRS (more usually known mildly derisively as 'the think tank') was unequivocally intended to concern itself with general policy issues. Indeed it was set up to help in the working out of government strategy, for, in the words of the October 1970 White Paper, 'under the pressures of the day to day problems immediately before them, governments are always at some risk of losing sight of the need to consider the totality of their current policies in relation to their longer-term objectives; and they may pay too little attention to the difficult, but critical task of evaluating as objectively as possible the alternative policy options and priorities open to them'.[25] Heclo and Wildavsky note that the words 'strategy' or 'strategic' appear four times in three paragraphs and observe drily, 'to anyone unacquainted with the preceding six years of Labour Government, it could seem a little obsessive'.[26]

Though the CPRS was officially heralded in the White Paper it was some months before it actually began operations.[27] However, unlike the uncertainty over the introduction of PAR, there was never any argument about its place in the governmental machine. It was immediately attached to the cabinet office where, incidentally, like the cabinet office as a whole, it is available to all departments and is not the personal possession of the prime minister. However, unlike the cabinet office, it is not concerned with co-ordinating the work of the government or with mediating between departments. On the contrary it was very much envisaged as the grit in the oyster, 'rocking the boat' whenever necessary. For it was mainly intended as a source of advice, chiefly for the prime minister, completely independent of the Treasury and the other departments. This is why, although many of the matters it deals with are technical, its basic task is political. (The prime minister's private office, which is quite small, has a partisan nature, and apart from its role as a secretariat is mainly concerned with the prime minister's responsibilities as a party leader.)[28] Moreover, unlike the cabinet office the CPRS has extensive contacts with the world outside Whitehall, and particularly with the most important social and economic groups. Its nearest 'ancestor' in terms of British administrative history, is Churchill's wartime Statistical Section, which helped the prime minister and played a vital role in controlling the arms programme. The only difference — which is more theoretical than real — is that the Statistical Section was at the disposal of the prime minister alone. But the function of the two bodies was basically the same: to detect basic errors or omissions in government strategy in good time and to suggest ways in which they may be overcome. Given the government's record in social and economic policy, and the benefit of hindsight, it is obviously tempting to write the CPRS off as a failure. This would almost certainly be an unwarranted oversimplification, however, particularly since as yet little is known officially about the issues on which the CPRS has been consulted and the extent to which its advice has been followed. But it is noteworthy that, although Mr Wilson strongly criticised the CPRS on occasion while he was in opposition, on returning to power in 1974 he decided to retain it.[29] It seems that this has at least the merit in his eyes of strengthening the power of the prime minister.

In the event it seems that the CPRS's advice was a major factor in leading the Heath government to execute at least some of the 'U-turns' that were a notable feature of its period in office. In particular, it is said that the CPRS was influential in the change in industrial and regional policy embodied in the Industry Act of 1972, and in science policy relations with the research councils, prices and incomes policy (notably the November 1972 'freeze'), and even the Northern Ireland policy, with the introduction of direct rule from Westminster in March 1972. If this is correct then the influence of the CPRS has been far from negligible — though at the same time it would suggest that, in economic and social affairs, its achievement in effect amounted to bringing Mr Heath back to the 'middle way' of the Macmillan period and steering him further and further away from the 1970 Tory programme — possibly because the programme was politically impracticable. Whether all this was in the national interest is of course a matter of opinion; what is not is that it did much to tarnish the leader's image within his party. It also led to an appreciable increase in governmental intervention. Coming to office with a neo-liberal programme not only in economic affairs but more generally (for at first the prime minister constantly stressed 'the need for less government'), the Heath government ended up as the most interventionist Conservative administration Britain has ever seen.

CHAPTER 16

Years of Confrontation 1970–1972

What we all have to recognise is that, with the present system of wage bargaining, no union leader, nor any individual management can afford to put the community interest first.[1]

Between 1964 and 1970 the Conservative Party did not attack planning in principle as it had between 1945 and 1951. There were several reasons for this. Firstly, through Mr Selwyn Lloyd, the Conservatives had themselves taken the initiative in reviving planning in 1962. Again, planning had changed from a system of centralised governmental control to being merely indicative. Finally, the Party itself had changed.

The Conservatives and Planning Between 1964 and 1970

The first attempt to set out a coherent Conservative view on planning came from one of the Party's most liberal and open-minded leaders, Sir Edward Boyle.[2] He wrote at the time when the National Plan had just been published, and had received a sceptical if not hostile reception. It was an opportune moment for a clear assertion of the Conservatives' position. A firm believer in the 'middle way', Boyle saw the Conservatives as standing midway between Labour interventionism and the complete rejection of all forms of planning advocated by the Institute of Economic Affairs[3] and Professor Jewkes.[4] He directly rejected the Jewkes line with the assertion that it was rejected by industry. Boyle was a strong believer in the State taking the lead in stimulating growth. He wrote, 'One clear condition of sustained growth must be that we have a long-term strategy to which short-term policies ought to conform.'[5] As we have seen, that condition had almost never been met in British planning. From this angle the value of planning lies less in preparing a thick document full of striking but barely credible proposals than in forecasting and co-ordinating industrial investment to avoid bottlenecks or undue strains on the balance of payments.

> It seems to me that the main value of indicative planning lies not so much in overall targets.... I suggest that as part of one economic strategy ... for breaking out of the stop–go cycle ... we should encourage key sectors of

British industry to plan together and to plan for success. The advantage of this approach to planning is that it is wholly consistent with the emphasis which conservatives would wish to lay on individual enterprise and on consent.[6]

Boyle concluded with an assertion of his belief in a voluntary incomes policy, not as a panacea but as a practical way of checking the wage–price spiral. In this he was very much in line with the policy followed between 1962 and 1964 by Selwyn Lloyd and Reginald Maudling, but it is much less certain that his views reflected the feelings of the party generally, firstly because it was no secret that Lloyd's and Maudling's policies had been unpopular with grass roots Conservative opinion, and also because Boyle himself was scarcely in the mainstream of Conservative thought – his withdrawal from active political life in 1969 was generally seen as a reflection of his unhappiness over the line being taken by Mr Heath and his senior colleagues. Yet the line taken by the party's 1970 *Campaign Guide* came very close to Boyle's except on prices and incomes policy, though the Conservative manifesto supported free collective bargaining and freedom to set prices. As to planning, the *Guide* assigned it three roles: to inform industry 'what is likely to happen in the rest of the economy',[7] 'to help everyone to make their own decisions more sensible and realistic by improving some of the relevant background information to which they must be related'[8] (these were both reasons that had been employed to justify the setting up of NEDC), and to 'strengthen the effectiveness of democratic political choice by exposing to public discussion the likely increase in the country's wealth and the various uses to which it might be put'.[9] But the *Guide* insisted that planning must not go beyond this, and it must be 'flexible, tentative and relatively informal so that decisions can be modified if they turn out to have been mistaken or when unforeseen events occur'.[10] Herein lay the value of a semi-independent body like Neddy which did not commit the government, and of independent forecasting bodies like the National Institute of Economic and Social Research whose forecasts and analyses were so often at variance with the official advice of the Treasury.

Despite this apparently moderate approach, the Selsdon Park conference, called by Mr Heath in February 1970 to finalise Conservative policy for the forthcoming election, had clearly indicated that a future Tory administration would not be as conciliatory and committed to compromise as the governments of the 1951–64 period. For the emphasis in economic policy was on reducing the role of government and cutting the level of public expenditure, on greater freedom for industry and wider resort to the market mechanism and free competition (implying that 'lame ducks' should be left to their fate) even in the public sector, and the ending of the 'privileged position' of the trade unions. Obviously such proposals would not meet universal approval. Indeed, they implied that sooner or later there would be serious friction with a sizeable part of the work force. It is by no means sure the Conservative leaders fully realised this, though it should at least have been clear that this line would be incompatible with the development of a close working relationship between the government and the two sides of industry in tackling the major issues of economic policy.[11]

The Heath Government's First Measures

Addressing the Conservatives' Youth Advisory Committee on 7 March 1970, the party's shadow minister for industry and technology, Sir Keith Joseph, gave a detailed outline of the fate the party had in store for the 'interventionist' bodies set up by the Labour government. He envisaged abolition of the Little Neddies, replacement of the PIB and revamping of the Monopolies Commission. While the fate of the IRC was left uncertain, at the very least it would be 'stripped of power to impose its will on the market'.[12]

The following October, soon after taking office, the Heath government resolutely embarked on the implementation of this programme, though its 'doctrinaire' side was partially concealed by the way the changes were presented as part of a general pruning of public expenditure. And so abolition of the IRC was one of a list of economies announced in Mr Barber's October 1970 'mini-budget'. According to the chancellor this would bring an economy of between £20 million and £30 million in 1971—2 and around £40 million in the following year. And when Mr Davies, then secretary of state for trade and industry, made a further statement a few days later this concentrated on the arrangements for transferring the IRC's responsibilities to his department during the period when its activities were being phased out rather than on the policy underlying the decision. This led Mr Lever, for the Opposition, to accuse the government of wanting 'the minimum amount of public witness and attention to what is an act of wanton and ritual slaughter'.[13] At NEDC's November meeting several members sharply criticised the way the government had abolished the IRC — which had been done in such a rush that the board of IRC had not even been consulted. It seemed clear that the IRC had been sacrificed to the hostility of small business and to pressure from the party's rank and file for a reduction in state intervention.

On the neighbouring but less controversial terrain of the Little Neddies, the government acted with equal speed. In July 1970 it set up a special co-ordinating committee under Sir Douglas Allen (then permanent secretary at the Treasury) to consider reduction in the number of Little Neddies. The intention was to lessen the administrative and technical load on NEDO by weeding out those committees that had failed to prove their value. In December 1970 NEDC discussed the Allen committee's proposals (which were relatively mild — it recommended abolishing three committees, retaining ten, and deferring action on nine more). It decided — probably on the insistence of the government members — to abolish five: paper and board, Post Office, rubber, hosiery and knitwear and food. But it gave the remaining sixteen a vote of confidence and in the event they all survived.

There had been no serious threat to NEDC itself, and when the government announced in March 1971 that Sir Frank Figgures, formerly director of trade and finance at OEEC (1948—51) and secretary-general of EFTA between 1960 and 1965, would succeed Sir Frederick Catherwood on 1 May, it was clear that the government did not intend to do away with NEDC, and was considering the post an important one. The government was obviously influenced by the fact that both the TUC and the CBI favoured keeping Neddy, and it may well also have been swayed by *The Economist's* argument that 'So much power, in terms of the country's economic management, is now vested in the Treasury, short though it is in talent and expertise, that it would be wrong to remove Ned without putting something better in its place. Mr Heath could eventually decide to have a special economic council in which the interests of members are less vested than those of the NEDC. But in the meantime it is right to give the Ned organisation at least another year of life.'[14] So Neddy was reprieved, and today it is fully accepted by all the major parties and groups. But to what end? Sir Fred Catherwood had worked tirelessly to promote expansion, in keeping with Neddy's original brief. He even suggested in 1970 that NEDC should initiate a new 'planning exercise' for the period up to 1976, but while this was well received by the other members, it did not find favour with the government. Sir Frank Figgures played a less prominent role. During 1971 and 1972 he was mainly concerned to prevent the tension between the unions and the government causing an open breach within the Council itself. Thanks to his efforts, even when relations between the TUC and ministers were most strained, NEDC still served as a meeting point — if sometimes also as a battleground — between the two sides. The fact that it survived the storms of this period proved its strength if not its effectiveness. But these are problems to which we shall return later.

A harsher fate was in store for the PIB. Given the Heath government's rejection of the prices and incomes policies of its predecessor, the PIB no longer had much point, and there was no surprise when its demise, to take effect after the necessary legislation on 31 March 1971, was announced in November 1970. It was replaced by three review bodies which were responsible for advising the government on the salaries of seven specific groups: chairmen and members of the boards of nationalised industries, judges, senior civil servants, senior officers of the armed forces and 'such other groups as might be appropriately considered with them' (for the first review body); the pay of the armed forces as a whole, for the second, and doctors' and dentists' pay for the third. These bodies were intended to co-operate with each other, and their membership to some degree overlapped, and all were serviced by the Office of Manpower Economics, an independent non-statutory body with a staff of around fifty, mostly drawn from the old PIB — thus enabling the government to continue drawing on the PIB's accumulated experience and expertise. In April 1971 the government announced that the chairman of the first review body would be Lord Boyle, and that it would also be asked to handle the payment of ministers and members of parliament. Reviews were to be conducted at least every two years (except for ministers and MPs, whose salaries were to be reviewed once in the lifetime of each full-length parliament — i.e. roughly every four years). Also, until the Pay Board was established, the OME serviced a number of *ad hoc* inquiries and arbitration bodies such as the inquiries into consulting engineers' fees and the pay of probation officers and allied occupations, and most notably the Burnham Committee on teachers' salaries and the Wilberforce inquiry into miners' pay of February 1972.

The death of the PIB stopped any possibility of progress towards an overall policy for incomes, and meant there was no machinery at all to deal with prices. The Labour opposition was quick to attack the imbalance between the total freedom the government was allowing prices (apart from taking a rather tougher line on monopolies and restrictive practices), and the partial scrutiny and control it continued to exercise over salaries in a number of areas. This imbalance was aggravated by the determination of the prime minister to oppose any 'unreasonable' wage increases, at least in the public sector. In its final annual report the PIB put this same criticism rather more indirectly. It argued that neither the Monopolies Commission nor the Office of Manpower Economics was capable of dealing with these problems adequately, particularly since, unlike the PIB, neither was in a position to take an overall view: 'While we feel each will do valuable work, the advantage which we have of considering individual problems in the light of a consideration of productivity, prices and incomes as a whole will be denied them.'[15] At the press conference at which he presented the report Lord Peddie, who had succeeded Mr Aubrey Jones as chairman of the PIB in October 1970, declared, 'The ghost of the PIB will haunt the corridors of Whitehall and industry for many years to come. We go out knowing it was a job well done. The significance to government and industry will not be lost.'[16] And he prophesied, 'A body of this type must inevitably come into existence in the future.'[17] Probably even he would not have guessed just how soon the future would arrive. A page had been turned in the long battle against inflation, at the very moment when the rate of cost inflation was accelerating and there was a growing campaign for the reintroduction of a wage and price freeze, which was reinforced by an OECD report that appeared at the end of 1970. Part of the Labour movement still favoured control of prices and incomes along lines proposed by Lord Balogh in September 1970.[18] He had argued yet again that full employment was incompatible with a moderate rate of inflation if at the same time wages were left to completely free collective bargaining. He was also highly sceptical about the possibilities of voluntary restraint under the auspices of the TUC, suggesting that there would be more chance of success if the government set up an arbitration and conciliation body which, unlike the PIB, had effective powers of decision and compulsion. But the political climate was clearly not propitious; the unions ranged from suspicious to openly hostile, while the Conservatives had no faith in the Balogh approach. Having divested himself of the PIB and all other means of compulsion, the only way open to Mr Heath to resist 'inflationary settlements' was to rally public opinion behind him in standing up to strikes and in attempting to secure a progressive lowering of the level of wage settlements. But this blunt, crude weapon soon showed itself quite inadequate.

The Deterioration of Government-Union Relations and the Industrial Relations Act

It is doubtful whether the election of a Conservative government has ever led to trade unionists dancing in the streets in celebration. But when that government declares that one of its first priorities will be to regulate the conduct of industrial relations in ways that the unions consider gravely prejudicial to their interests, their suspicion rapidly turns to unqualified hostility. This is what happened after the publication in October 1970 of the Conservatives' Green Paper on the reform of industrial relations. Mr Vic Feather, the general secretary of the TUC, immediately made clear that it was utterly opposed to the proposals and declared that the Bill would cause 'complete confusion in industry and bring the law into disrepute'.[19] It was attempting to 'turn the clock back 100 years – that is literally back to 1871 – in curtailing the basic rights of workpeople and their unions'.[20] A month later the TUC spelled out its objections to the government's proposals in detail,[21] branding them a direct attack on 'the very root of a union's bargaining strength – its power to bring pressure to bear on the employer – and the very root of a union's democratic strength – its responsiveness to the wishes of the rank and file members'.[22] Not altogether surprisingly the TUC made no attempt to persuade the government to amend its proposals, which were scarcely changed when its Bill was published in early December, insisting simply that they should be withdrawn, lock, stock and barrel. Given the Conservatives' insistence on industrial relations reform in the 1970 election campaign, this was of course not on the cards for a moment. Despite the vigorous opposition of the Labour Party (in what Mrs Castle, who had apparently forgotten her own attempt to introduce a not wholly dissimilar reform of industrial relations only a year earlier, called a tooth and nail fight) and a national campaign by the TUC that was backed (against its wishes) by three unoffocial strikes only two of which commanded really significant support, the Bill was carried by the Commons in March 1971 and became law the following August, though it did not actually come into force until the end of the year. Meanwhile, at a special congress in March the TUC voted by a small majority not to call a national strike against the Act, but instructed member unions not to co-operate with any body that might be set up under the Act, not to register under the Act, not to allow any agreements to become legally binding and to insist on maintaining existing custom and practice in negotiations with employers.

What led the great majority of unions to challenge the very existence of the Act in this way? Without entering into a detailed analysis, it may be useful to recall the main controversial points. These included the banning of the pre-entry closed shop and the authorising of the agency shop — which gave the individual worker potentially greater autonomy in relation to his union branch; the decision that all 'labour-collective agreements' would in future be legally binding on the signatories unless it was expressly resolved to the contrary when the agreement was signed; the introduction of a special Registrar for trade unions and employers' associations (in place of the existing system by which they were registered, mainly for statistical purposes, with the chief registrar of Friendly Societies — who remained responsible for associations other than the unions);[23] the strengthening of the CIR, which ceased to be an independent consultative body and became part of the machinery for enforcing the Act, and which consequently could have matters referred to it by the National Industrial Relations Court (NIRC) as well as by the secretary for employment.

The NIRC, which was to have a standing comparable to the High Court, and was to include judges from the High Court, the Court of Appeal and the Court of Session selected for their special experience in the area of industrial relations, was unquestionably the most original feature of the new Act. The Court, which had Sir John Donaldson as president throughout its life, had the power to impose fines of up to £100,000, and had original jurisdiction over the more important cases involving unfair labour practices, breach of contract, unfair dismissals, etc., and appelate jurisdiction over secondary matters that had been dealt with by the industrial tribunals (which were already in existence but were given wider powers under the Act). In addition the NIRC could intervene directly in industrial disputes if the secretary for employment asked it to do so in a national emergency. It could impose a sixty-day cooling off period to allow negotiations to continue, or require a ballot to be held of the membership where there was some doubt about whether or not the workers involved really wanted to strike. This amounted to a fairly stringent codification of industrial relations, even at plant level. Moreover this oversight was to be in the hands of the courts. In the event, while legal processes might have the merit of clarity and impartiality (which many would contest), they were to prove dangerously rigid, particularly since the majority of unions were to refuse to have anything to do with the working of the Act. And yet many of its provisions were unquestionably favourable to the unions — full recognition in law rather than in custom and practice, the right to join a union, better protection against unfair dismissal, the requirement that companies reveal certain information to the unions, and a recognition of the unions' virtual monopoly in bargaining over wages and conditions. This was far from negligible, but from the beginning the TUC insisted that it was too high a price to pay for what it considered nothing more than its normal basic rights; as Vic Feather put it, there was never any question of 'trading one crumb for a whole loaf and we can do without the crumb'.

Apart from the decision of most of the big unions to refuse to register under the Act, and to invite and later compel other unions to fall into line,[24] the TUC's attitude had three immediate consequences: the implementation of the Act (the Registry was established in October 1971, the new CIR in November, and the NIRC in December) took place gradually but steadily without any discussion between the unions and the government; moreover most of the trade union members of the old CIR resigned (Mr Allen and Mr Paynter at the beginning of 1971 and George Woodcock, the chairman, in July). Mr Woodcock was succeeded at the end of the year by Mr Len Neal of British Rail, but the government had great difficulty in replacing the other members, because not only could it not recruit members from the unions but a number of people it approached in the universities declined because they were unwilling to be involved in working an Act of which most of them disapproved.[25] The third outcome was that, given the hostility of the unions, most employers left negotiating procedures as they were and did not insist on agreements being legally binding so as not to cause more friction. So the new Act got off to a very bad start, particularly since the government and the unions were at cross-purposes not only over industrial relations but over how to stop inflation. In the government's view the main cause of inflation was excessive wage increases, while the unions insisted their wage demands were simply the consequence of higher prices, and in January 1971 they launched the idea of protecting workers' purchasing power by means of threshold agreements.

Nevertheless, the government seemed to be making some headway in the battle against inflation. In January 1972 Mr Barber, then chancellor of the Exchequer, noted with some satisfaction that the index of retail prices which had risen at an annual rate of 11 per cent during the first half of 1971, had gone up at an annual rate of only 5¾ per cent in the second half of the year. So it seemed that the rate of inflation was slowing. This was accompanied by a fall in the average level of wage settlements from 11—15 per cent to 7—8 per cent, despite a number of major industrial disputes such as the dockers' strike of July 1970, the power workers' action of December 1970 and the resulting Wilberforce settlement of March 1971, and the seven-week strike of postal workers, quite apart from the political strikes against the introduction of the Industrial Relations Act.

But there was another side to the medal. In November 1971 unemployment had reached a national average of 3.7 per cent; in the North and Scotland (where it reached 6.4 per cent) it was almost three times the level in the South East (2.2 per cent). This recession was due partly to the gloomy prospects that seemed likely in light of the financial measures adopted by the United States in August 1971, and it persisted despite three reflationary packages from Mr Barber in October 1970 and March and July 1971, which among other things pumped £1,400 million into the economy over a full year. But this was also the result of the Jenkins deflation of March 1968. (Mr Jenkins had refused to reflate in the April 1970 budget, which at the approach of a general election earned him full marks for political integrity but was nevertheless an economic mistake. While many economic mistakes arose from the desire of successive governments to make themselves popular, Mr Jenkins' error arose from a determination not to leave himself open to a charge of buying votes — a rare enough occurrence to be emphasised.) The stop–go cycle had not been beaten, and as in the past chancellors had if anything made it worse, whether by deflating too late and too harshly or by reflating too little at first and then too strongly later because they were in too much of a hurry to secure results.

Nevertheless, early in 1972 it seemed the government was beginning to get the situation in hand again, and it had been strengthened by the decisive vote in the Commons on membership of EEC — which at the time was considered as a historic turning point. But this had not been achieved without a measure of ruthlessness and the opposition made great play of the fact that the policies it had promoted the most energetically, such as the reform of industrial relations, reduction of taxation and membership of the Common Market, were all profoundly divisive. In other words, the consensus that governments of both parties had observed since 1945 seemed increasingly to be called into question.

As we have seen, since 1945 the major parties had been in general agreement on the three pillars of the welfare state, to which they had pledged themselves at the close of the war: full employment, a comprehensive system of social welfare, and greater educational opportunity. This consensus implied the politics of 'the middle ground' and close co-operation and consultation between the government and the two sides of industry. In the forties it was typified by Cripps, in the fifties by Butskellism, and in the sixties by attempts to introduce indicative planning and the Statement of Intent. But there seemed to be no counterpart at the beginning of the seventies. On the contrary, it seemed that the new government had espoused the neo-liberal view that the mainspring of progress is competition, and therefore conflict rather than conciliation. If the references to a 'free society', which were so often on Mr Heath's lips during the 1970 campaign, meant the neo-liberals' 'conflictual society', then he was well on the way to achieving his wishes. For unquestionably there had been conflict. This is not to say he was wrong in trying to regulate industrial relations or oppose excessive wage increases, but above and beyond that he seemed completely uninterested in encouraging moderation, in reducing tension or in discussing and compromising on details. Indeed, at times (particularly during the postmen's strike) there seemed a barely concealed desire to make even the most moderate union leaders lose face. This was a grave tactical error for which later he was to pay dearly. Finally he seemed to relish flying in the face of opinion, whether over reductions in income tax, which favoured the middle or wealthier classes, or over squalid little economies on school meals and milk or museum charges.

Since Labour reacted furiously against the government's 'class policies' there was a consequent hardening of ideological conflict between the two major parties. This was not necessarily bad, for the 'return of ideology' meant that politics became rather more meaningful. But it was important that such clashes should not distract attention from the basic, underlying problems, for experience had shown that the remedies that were needed must not unduly divide the country. But, for the moment at least, the understandings and the processes of consultation that had been built up over the previous quarter-century suddenly seemed to be called into question.[26]

The Miners' Strike and the Unhappy History of the Industrial Relations Act

On 9 January 1972 the coal miners came out on a national official strike for the first time since 1926. The government had reason to feel that it was well placed to win: the decision to strike had been supported by only 59 per cent of those voting in a national strike ballot; coal stocks at the power stations represented about eight weeks' supply at the normal rate of winter consumption, despite the fact that the miners had been operating an overtime ban since November. Also, rightly or wrongly, the government thought that the rejection of the Coal Board's offer of an average overall increase of 8 per cent (which was roughly in line with other recent settlements in the public sector, though the miners were asking for 20 per cent) owed more to rivalry between the newly elected president of the NUM, Mr Joe Gormley, a moderate, and the union's left-wing general secretary, Mr Laurence Daly, than to genuine grass roots pressure. But it completely failed to foresee how, despite their earlier divisions, the miners would close ranks once the strike began, or how they would paralyse the power stations by the skilful deployment of mass pickets, some of which were not beyond resorting to violence. Far from the rivalry between the two leaders working in the government's favour, it meant that neither was willing to be the first to accept a compromise settlement, and each was vying with the other. During the first month of the strike the government seemed unconcerned, but as a growing number of generating stations began to run out of coal, and negotiations between the NCB and the NUM again broke down on 11 February, it announced drastic restrictions on the use of power by both industrial and domestic consumers and appointed a court of inquiry under Lord Wilberforce to investigate miners' pay. Its recommendations were published a week later, on 18 February. In general the miners' contention that their wages had fallen behind since the abolition of piecework was accepted, but it was only after the prime minister had personally intervened and a number of further concessions had been extracted that the NUM executive was prepared to recommend a return to work on 28 February. This was a complete defeat for both the government and its policy of containing wage inflation, particularly since the Chrysler workers at Linwood had just won an increase of £6 per week – even more than the miners! Though this settlement had attracted relatively little attention during the wider national coal and power crisis, it did not escape the attention of other workers in the car industry, which throughout this period was plagued by almost continuous disputes.

On top of this the Industrial Relations Act, and its 'secular arm' the NIRC, were being put to their first major tests. The challenge came on two fronts: in the dispute between Heatons Transport and the TGWU and in the rail dispute. In the former the Court was called on for the first, but by no means the last, time to deal with the blacking by a number of local groups of dock workers of vehicles belonging to container transport companies that refused to employ dock labour in their warehouses. The blacking was intended to force them to employ registered dockers to pack and unpack the containers rather than the independently recruited workers who were then doing the job. It took the form of refusing to load the companies' vehicles or to let goods enter or leave their warehouses — paralysing them completely. This unofficial action did not have the backing of their union, the TGWU, because it was harming drivers employed by the firms concerned, who were also members of the TGWU. Considering a complaint from one of the companies affected, Heatons Transport, the NIRC ordered the TGWU to end the blacking, but it continued. The TGWU refused even to appear before the Court and was thereupon fined £5,000 for contempt in March, followed by a further £50,000 in April. It paid this sum 'voluntarily' at the beginning of May, to avoid seizure of its entire assets, and promptly called on the TUC to reimburse it. The General Council then agreed reluctantly that member unions might defend themselves before NIRC, with only the AUEW maintaining right to the very end its complete refusal to appear before the Court or to co-operate with it in any way. It even refused to pay the heavy fines resulting from this attitude and these were consequently recovered by partial seizure of its assets.[27] However, the Heatons Transport dispute was never really satisfactorily settled because the fines were first quashed by the Court of Appeal and then restored by the Lords (the differing decisions turning on whether or not the union could be held responsible for the illegal acts of its shop stewards), and because new blackings at the Port of London in the Chobham Farm and Midland Cold Storage disputes led NIRC to imprison five rank and file leaders for contempt, and the resulting outcry was prevented from swelling into a dispute of national proportions only by the Lords' decision to maintain the fines on the TGWU. This allowed Sir John Donaldson, the president of NIRC, to rule that the Lords' judgement implied that responsibility lay with the union rather than with the shop stewards, and consequently to release the five dockers without seeming to capitulate to external pressure. So in its attempt to apply legal procedures to industrial relations the government found itself forced to conduct an apparently unending battle from which it seemed increasingly doubtful it would extract any significant advantage.

It fared no better in its attempt to use NIRC in the rail dispute. In April 1972 NIRC intervened in the railwaymen's go-slow to order a fourteen-day cooling off period, at the request of the minister for employment, Mr Maurice Macmillan. After some hesitation the unions obeyed the order, and the government could claim a minor victory. But the cooling off period expired without any settlement being reached and industrial action resumed. The government now went to the

Court to obtain a mandatory secret ballot of the union's membership on whether the strike should continue. The outcome of the postal vote at the end of May was an overwhelming majority in favour of continuing the strike.[28] Once more the government had lost; it had been wrong about both the mood of the rank and file and the use of the cooling off period. It could do little else but try and reach a settlement with the railwaymen as quickly as possible. The agreement reached on 12 June granted increases averaging 13.5 per cent, compared with the British Rail Board's initial offer of about 10 per cent. The disappointing outcome of both these affairs, which did considerable economic damage to the economy and seriously undermined the government's credibility, led the government to alter its policy and make a serious attempt to explore with both sides of industry ways of fighting inflation. But the climate of opinion was scarcely auspicious for negotiation.

Table 16.1 shows just how serious a problem strikes became in 1972, with more days being lost through industrial disputes than in any year since 1926 (when 162 million working days were lost).

Table 16.1.   Days lost through stoppages 1970–72

	Days lost (million)	Stoppages	Workers involved (million)	Increase in basic wage-rate (%)
1970	11.0	3,906	1.8	13.5
1971	13.6	2,228	1.2* (including 281,000 laid off)	12.4
1972	23.9	2,490	1.7* (including 312,000 laid off)	13.8

* Not included are the so-called 'political' stoppages:
– in 1971: in March, nearly 1.5m. workers were involved in the twenty-four-hour strike protesting at the third reading of the Industrial Relations Act. Very few workers were involved in the previous protest stoppages.
– in 1972: in July, involving about 170,000 workers protesting at the fining of the AUEW by the NIRC.
Comment: – There is a clear trend towards longer, if fewer, strikes.
– The number and importance of stoppages does not alter much the average progression of basic rates.
Source: Department of Employment (January 1973).

The Quest for Co-operation

Although, as we have seen, the period after the Conservatives returned to power in June 1970 produced a whole series of conflicts between the government and the unions, this is not to imply that it was entirely dominated by disagreements and that there were no attempts to bring the two sides together. Throughout, the CBI and the TUC met three ministers, the chancellor, the minister for employment and the minister for trade and industry, every month at meetings of Neddy. Even when relations with the government were at their worst the TUC never contemplated boycotting Neddy, and this could be taken as a more general indication of their wish to avoid a total breach. Nevertheless for at least a year meetings were rather tense and not very productive. The TUC was at odds with the government over the Industrial Relations Act, and later it clashed with the CBI over the memorandum on inflation drawn up by the TUC's Economic Committee, which argued that wage increases of 14 per cent were fully justified and suggested the introduction of threshold agreements to protect workers' purchasing power against erosion by inflation. Nevertheless, the climate changed slightly before the July 1971 meeting, and this improvement was sustained in August. The chancellor had, meanwhile, announced on 19 July a number of measures aimed at stimulating the economy and the CBI had put forward the idea that its members might pledge themselves to restrict price increases to 5 per cent over a period of twelve months. (That autumn this commitment was accepted by 176 major companies of the 201 approached. It was extended for six months in July 1972. On the whole it was kept remarkably well.) The August 1971 meeting also set up a committee of 'four wise men' (Mr Campbell Adamson, Mr Feather, Sir Frank Figgures and Sir Douglas Allen) to report on the theory and practice of threshold agreements. The report, which was discussed in November, had no immediate outcome; then there followed the miners' strike, the outcome of which was that the unions partly avenged their defeat over the Industrial Relations Act. So there was considerable interest when it was announced that Mr Feather would lead a delegation of the TUC to meet Mr Heath on 9 March — apparently the first official meeting between the prime minister and the TUC since the Conservatives had returned to power almost two years earlier. As yet there had been only the slightest change in the government's position, but Mr Heath must by now have grasped that a hard line and refusal to compromise did not pay (particularly when they were not — or appeared not to be — linked with fairness), and that the influence of unofficial rank and file leaders was increasing at the expense of official leadership, particularly of the TUC. The time was ripe to encourage the TUC to participate once more in discussions of major economic problems. Moreover, a number of important decisions would shortly have to be taken about the economy, and it seemed desirable to sound out the two sides of industry. Finally, since the October 1971 party conference, Mr Wilson had been conducting discrete negotiations with the unions, and notably with Mr Jones and Mr Scanlon, in an attempt to heal the breach between the political and industrial wings of the Labour movement, after the strains their relationship had suffered in the last years of the Labour government. (After many difficulties these negotiations were eventually to produce the 'social contract' between Labour and the TUC.) The problem of the TUC (as with the CBI, though the CBI had shown through its programme of voluntary price restraint that it could commit its members up to a point) was that it was virtually impossible to make any binding agreement with them, not of course because of any duplicity on their part, but because they themselves were never quite sure what they could persuade their members to accept.

Such was the case in the summer and autumn of 1972. The initial contacts between the two sides were extremely circumspect – not surprisingly, considering that they had been at daggers drawn only a few weeks earlier. So negotiations began only after a meeting between the three sides, which was held under the auspices of Neddy but at 10 Downing Street. (This was a compromise, since the TUC and CBI would have preferred the meeting to have taken place on the neutral ground of Millbank Tower, while the prime minister wanted them to come to him in recognition of the primacy of government.) In a television interview on the eve of the meeting Mr Heath proclaimed he was ready to negotiate right through the summer if need be. But to what end? After three preliminary meetings the three sides agreed to set up three working parties under Sir Frank Figgures, to study ways and means of containing inflation, and to report back to a full meeting of all three sides at Chequers on 14 September. As the official programme for the negotiations shows (table 16.2), by agreeing to discuss low pay, threshold agreements, the implementation of equal pay legislation, aid to industry and industrial investment, the government was running the risk of being trapped into concessions that in one way or another were bound to lead to greater inflation. Consequently a number of commentators such as Sam Brittan[29] were tempted to hope the negotiations would fail,

Table 16.2.   The government–TUC–CBI work programme (official text)

1.   An assessment of the practicability of action by the participants in collective bargaining to improve the relative position of the lower paid consistently with slowing down the rate of inflation. This will include:

a. A consideration of the definition of the lower paid.
b. Ways and means of implementing a programme for the improvement of their relative status.
c. A consideration of the relevance of threshold agreements in pay negotiations.
d. An assessment of the expected relationship between the future movement of pay and conditions (compatible with such a programme) and the movement of unit costs during the relevant period.
e. The implications for employment in the sectors mainly affected by the programme.
f. The requirements for the implementation of the Equal Pay legislation.
g. The implication of such developments for social security and similar arrangements including pensions.

2.   An assessment of the practicability of action which could be taken by the parties to reduce the rate of increase in prices during the next 12 months, having regard to:

a. The viability of any industries affected.
b. The need for increased investment and the means of providing for it.
c. The possible consequences for employment.
d. The desirability of reducing speculation in land and building.
e. The consequences for government expenditure/taxation.

Source: Financial Times (31 August 1972).

since in their view any possible agreement would prove more economically damaging than no agreement. Moreover, an increasing number of influential voices were being raised in favour of a prices and incomes policy, if need be a statutory one. Among them was Mr Reginald Maudling (who had recently returned to the back benches as a consequence of the Poulson affair). An article he wrote in *The Times*[30] favouring incomes policy had brought an accusation of fascist tendencies from Mr Enoch Powell, who made it clear that the introduction of a statutory policy would lead to the final break between him and the government. (Mr Powell had already shown his hostility to the government for a mixture of personal and political reasons, such as membership of the Common Market and his preference for neo-liberal economic policies, but the danger that he might now take a small section of the Conservative Right with him into opposition was naturally of some concern to the government.)

Nevertheless, the prime minister continued his attempt to reach agreement with the TUC and the CBI. On 26 September he proposed a four-point package deal: annual wage increases should be kept down to £2 per week; price rises should not exceed 5 per cent (with threshold agreements above that); a promise by the government to aim for 5 per cent growth over a two-year period, and the setting up of a new body to inquire into the problems of low pay.

Although these proposals were not rejected out of hand by the union negotiators, the following day the TUC announced its intention of submitting counter-proposals, which was a polite way of rejecting the government's proposition. At the time an increase of £2 per week in wage rates (with wage drift of up to 60 pence) represented about 8 per cent on the average wage, or an increase of around 3 per cent in real terms, which was far from negligible considering the rate of increase of GNP and productivity. Moreover, it was particularly favourable to the lower paid, many of whom were earning under £20 per week. But the main defect of the government's proposals in the unions' eyes may well have been precisely its emphasis on a flat rate increase. For although it pays periodic lip-service to the idea of a guaranteed minimum wage, the TUC has always given more weight to the higher-paid sections of the working class, either because they are better organised, or because they have greater economic bargaining power. Not surprisingly it was unimpressed by the offer of £2 per week, particularly since a fairly hefty slice of it would be taken by tax. However, negotiations continued for a further six weeks during which it became increasingly obvious that the TUC was unwilling to enter into any commitments, probably because it would be unable to see they were kept. This was evident in the way in which in mid-October it began to call for statutory controls on a wide range of retail prices without any comparable readiness to see a similar system applied to wages. The TUC was of course well aware that the CBI, which had been operating its system of voluntary restraint for fifteen months, would not be prepared to go on doing so without any return. Despite a last minute proposal from the Retail Consortium, representing some ninety per cent of British retail food sales, which suggested that ceilings might be set for the prices of a number of basic foodstuffs, negotiations broke down on the evening of 2 November despite all the efforts of Mr Campbell Adamson and of Mr Feather, who was being watched closely by his left-wing colleagues. It also seems that at the last moment the prime minister suddenly took a tougher line and insisted the union leaders must accept or reject proposals that were little different from those he had originally put forward on 26 September. This gave them the impression that the negotiations (which, significantly, Mr Heath referred to throughout as 'discussions') had been pointless. It is hard to avoid feeling that this final misunderstanding would not have occurred if the general climate of industrial relations had not been so deplorably bad over the previous two years. This seems to have been the real reason why the negotiations broke down. While they were still in progress Mr Frank Chapple, the electricians' leader, had won an increase of rather more than £3 per week for his men — and in so doing just escaped the freeze on prices and incomes that was announced on the following Monday, 6 November. The prime minister and the chancellor, Mr Barber, were not to take direct responsibility for the new measures.

CHAPTER 17

Prices and Incomes Policy and Other Forms of State Intervention

The idea of a statutory prices and incomes policy was no closer to rallying unanimous agreement in November 1972 than during the sixties. Even as Mr Heath was locked in his negotiations with the TUC and the CBI, the 'Economic Radicals', a group of monetarist economists headed by Richard Body, a Tory back-bencher, were publishing a short pamphlet in the form of an open letter to the prime minister challenging the view that a prices and incomes policy had any part to play in the fight against inflation.[1] They argued that inflation had nothing to do with higher wages because, for all the militancy and monopoly power of a number of unions, statistics showed that, while they were able to vary the differentials between one job and another, they had made no significant impact on the proportion of national income going into wages, net of tax and national insurance contributions. They urged the case for a number of monetary and fiscal remedies, including a cut of between 6 and 8 per cent in the money supply; reduction of the budget deficit, whether by higher taxes or lower public expenditure (to reduce public borrowing); a lower rate of economic growth, and major changes in the way the level of unemployment was calculated. (They argued that when the existing system reported one million unemployed, there were in fact only about 300,000 'genuinely' unemployed.) Clearly some of their arguments were music to the unions' ears (notably their views on the relationship between wage increases and inflation), because they were in line with the traditional union view that higher wages reflected rather than caused inflation, and that workers should not only be compensated for increases in the cost of living but should also receive a fair share of the sums accruing from improvements in productivity in the companies they were working for. At least one leading figure in the international trade union movement, Charles Levinson, has argued forcefully[2] that cost inflation is due mainly to the burden of capital investment, whether as a consequence of high interest rates or because when firms try to finance their capital programme from their own cash-flow this forces them to keep their profit margins at very high levels. This situation is aggravated by the relative indifference of multi-national corporations to the monetary policies of individual countries, since they plan their investments over a fairly long period on the basis of their own assessments of likely demand for their products and carry them through regardless of the credit restrictions which may happen to be operating in the country concerned.

Prices and Incomes Policy

Nevertheless, the announcement of the freeze came as something of a relief, both because negotiations had dragged on for so long that the public now felt the time had come for decisive action, and because the man in the street is in any case probably rather more favourable to this form of regulation than political and union leaders have often professed,[3] particularly since in this instance about a million workers had managed to squeeze home with new wage settlements just before the freeze was imposed. This considerably eased the pressure on the government, though of course it brought the danger that there would be ill-feeling between those who had beaten the freeze and those who had not, either because their leaders had not moved rapidly enough or because they had no negotiations under way at the time. The reactions of the politicians were almost entirely predictable; the opposition was unable to resist the temptation to exploit the government's embarrassment and made great play of the fact that it was making yet another 'U-turn' in policy (though in fact the 1972 freeze was very much like Labour's 1966 standstill). Government back-benchers were rather more divided than the majority of twenty-nine on the third reading suggested, when the defection of thirty or so Conservatives was more than outweighed by Labour absences or abstentions (the government's nominal majority over other parties at the time being twenty). The debate was notable for a violent attack by Mr Powell on the prime minister ('Have you taken leave of your senses?').[4] Although most Conservatives were rather relieved that the tripartite talks had not produced agreement, because they had been afraid that Mr Heath would end up by giving too much away, the *laissez-faire* Cobdenite wing of the party, represented among others by Mr Powell and the supporters of Sir Keith Joseph, took the freeze very badly — they felt it more deeply than the resort to indicative planning in 1961, which they had always viewed as a futile exercise which, while doing no good, would at least do little actual harm. Now they were deeply worried about the distortions incomes policy would inflict on the market economy.

Phase I — The Freeze[5]

The government's Bill, which was rushed through all its stages in the Commons and became law on 27 November, froze prices, rents, rates, and all forms of income, including dividends at their level of 6 November for a period of three months after it became law; the freeze could subsequently be extended for further periods of up to two months at a time (Phase I was in fact to end for wages on 31 March 1972), until such time as more detailed legislation had been drafted and become law. So this was a strictly temporary measure which had the virtue of simplicity. Even so there were a number of problems. So far as prices were concerned, the government realised that the freeze might create difficulties for firms that had already been conscientiously observing the voluntary CBI restraint for the previous fifteen months. So firms that could not hold their prices because of exceptionally large increases in costs could apply through their sponsoring department to be treated as special cases. But it was expected that such exceptions would be rare. In addition wholesalers and retailers were forbidden to increase their cash margins. The only areas where there was greater flexibility were vegetables, fruit, meat and fish, where some fluctuation was unavoidable. The freeze on incomes covered not only money payments but all other improvements in the terms and conditions of employment. While existing settlements were not affected, the Act laid down that, where increases had been agreed but not as yet implemented, then they could not be paid until the freeze ended. Wage negotiations and arbitration could continue as usual during the freeze, but awards could take effect only when it was over. The Act also prescribed fines for breaches of the freeze.

Contrary to what might perhaps have been expected Phase I was implemented with little difficulty, though a few ASTMS branches, urged on by their general secretary, Mr Clive Jenkins,[6] did their best to exploit loopholes — but to their great annoyance the secretary for employment, Mr Maurice Macmillan, for the most part succeeded in thwarting them. The only real difficulty arose when the prime minister tried to halt negotiations on a number of wage claims, among them those of the gas workers and the hospital ancillary staffs. While the Act did not bar such negotiations, he was worried that they might lead to settlements above the eventual Phase II limit. In February the dispute took a more serious turn when the gas workers decided on industrial action, but by then the government had won a good three months' respite and the main details of Phase II were known.

Phase II — The End of the Freeze and the One-Plus-Four Ceiling[7]

Every country which has operated a wage or price freeze has found that, while the freeze itself is relatively easy to run and is generally well accepted by the public because it treats everyone alike, the real problems come with the thaw, when there is a danger that, once pent-up demands are released, there will be such a scramble to make up for lost ground that anything the freeze has gained will rapidly be lost. So the transitional stage must be handled particularly carefully, especially when, as was the case in Britain at the beginning of 1973, there remain very strong inflationary pressures — which the freeze may conceal for a time but cannot remove.

Phase II, which was to cover this difficult transition, was outlined in a White Paper that was published in January, and subsequently embodied in a Bill that became law five weeks later and came into force on 31 March, when the complete freeze on wages ended. (The price freeze was extended to 28 April to cover the period when VAT was being introduced.) A second White Paper, *The Operation of Phase II*, appeared just before the new Act came into force. While offering a first survey of the results of Phase I, and offering some indication of the likely later lines of development of the prices and incomes policy, it was mainly devoted to setting out the code for Phase II.

For incomes the main principles were that increases in salaries and wages should be held down somewhere nearer to the rate of increase in the national income, that there should be an effort to improve the relative position of the lower paid, and that negotiations on increases within the Phase II norm could continue as usual. At least twelve months should elapse between major settlements. In hard cash this meant a limit of one pound per week plus four per cent of the average wage bill of the workers concerned over the previous twelve months. This limit was to cover all forms of income – basic wages, piecework bonuses, payments in kind and fringe benefits, allowances and lump sum payments and overtime rates. There was also an absolute limit of £250 to what any individual might receive – though this did not include overtime payments and 'certain personal increments' such as the annual increments paid to civil servants. The code was to be policed by the Pay Board, which came into existence on 2 April with Sir Frank Figgures as chairman and two deputy chairmen, Mr Derek Robinson, formerly of the PIB, who was to advise the government on the working out of Phase III and deal with pay anomalies and relativities, and Mr Ken Johnson, the former industrial relations director at the CBI, who was to administer the Phase II code. The Board itself had between five and twelve members. To service it there was a research and investigation staff under Mr Ian Hudson, secretary to the Board, comprising between 150 and 250 lawyers, statisticians, economists, industrial relations specialists and administrators, many of whom had moved over from the Office of Manpower Economics (which was otherwise unaffected). If we add that the Pay Board was housed in the same building as the Price Commission, which was established at the same time to act as watchdog over prices, and that the two bodies were expected to work very closely together, the result looked remarkably like a thinly concealed resurrection of the PIB. In fact both bodies had rather greater powers than the PIB because unlike the PIB they could take their own decisions and enforce them directly.

The Pay Board worked as follows. Wage agreements involving over a thousand workers had to be notified to the Board and could only be implemented with its approval; agreements involving from one hundred to a thousand workers had to be notified within a week of coming into force but could be implemented without the Board's prior agreement. Firms employing between ten and one hundred workers were simply required to keep records of wage increases which could be inspected if need be. An agreement covering more than a thousand workers was deemed to have been approved if the Board did not veto it within twenty-eight days or indicate that it wanted a further twenty-eight days in which to make its decision. If the agreement was approved it could be implemented retrospectively to the date it was signed; if the Board did not approve, then it would issue an order giving reasons and specifying the maximum amount that could be paid under the code. So the Board had a large measure of discretion and its powers of decision were considerable, and they could be used without reference to a minister, unlike the old PIB, which could deal only with matters that were referred to it, initially by the DEA and later by the DEP. However, the secretary of state for employment could reverse a decision of the Board where he decided that there were 'exceptional circumstances' and this provided a kind of appeal mechanism which the unions were to do their best to exploit.

The system of price control was by no means as clear-cut, and in the unions' eyes it was quite inadequate. It had to be designed to cope with much greater diversity and to provide for a wide range of possible exceptions, though its basic principles were in fact simple:

(I)   to limit the extent to which prices may be increased on account of increased costs, and to secure reductions as a result of reduced costs;
(II)   to reinforce the control of prices by a control on profit margins while safeguarding investment;
(III)   to reinforce the effects of competition and to secure its full benefits in the general level of prices.[8]

These rules did not apply to exports, or to imports on their first introduction to the United Kingdom market. They did not apply where controls would be a breach of the government's international undertakings, or to goods normally sold by auction, or to the London commodity markets, or to second-hand goods (except cars), international transport rates, medical supplies covered by agreements between the secretary of state for social services and manufacturers, or defence contracts (which had a separate system of controls), or insurance premiums (which were controlled by the DTI) or to charitable bodies. Prices of fresh fruit and vegetables, eggs, meat and fish were not controlled, but distributors' margins were.

Controlled prices could be increased only if there had been an increase in total costs per unit of output, in which case the increase in price must in no event exceed the increase in costs, the base point being the level of unit costs on 30 September 1972.

The Price Commission, which came into being at the end of the period of total freeze in April, had Sir Arthur Cockfield as chairman, assisted by a number of part-time members.[9] (Unlike the Pay Board it was to be retained by Labour when it returned to power in 1974.) As table 17.1 shows, its procedures varied with the type of economic activity a company was engaged in and the size of its annual turnover. Firms in Category I had to submit proposals to alter prices to the Commission, and required its direct or tacit approval along much the same lines as with the Pay Board. Those in both Categories I and II had to accompany their applications with full supporting evidence.

Dividends remained under Treasury control, and increases were limited to 5 per cent over the previous year, unless the Treasury gave special permission. (Investment trusts and close companies were exempt.) The freeze on business rents continued, but the government maintained the 'fair rents' provisions of the 1972 Housing Finance Act — which in most cases meant higher rents, though there was a comprehensive system of rebates and allowances. The government made no firm commitment on rates, though it did raise its central grant to local authorities as a way of encouraging them to keep increases down. Land prices

Table 17.1.   Price Commission procedures

	Category I Pre-notification and reporting	Category II Reporting	Category III Record-keeping
	(£m. annual turnover)	(£m. annual turnover)	(£m. annual turnover)
Manufacturing, mining, public utilities, transport, postal services and telecommunications	over 50	5–50	1–5
Wholesalers, retailers, and other distributive trades	–	over 10	0.25–10
Services	over 20	5–20	0.25–5
Construction	–	over 10	1–10
Professional services	National scales or rates	over 0.5	0.1–0.5

were outside the Act, though the government did announce its intention of introducing a tax on speculative gains. This underlines one of the major weaknesses of an incomes policy in a market economy — its inability to deal satisfactorily with incomes arising from capital.

When Phase II was announced most observers were struck by the extent to which the government had gone back on its earlier policies. For during Phase I it had been concerned mainly to freeze prices and incomes as a way of winning time to persuade the public to break with its bad inflationary habits. While this was striking psychologically, politically the decisive step came only with Phase II. For while it was scheduled to last only until the autumn, the machinery to operate it was given a life of three years — which took the government until after the next election. Some ministers, or at least Mr Heath himself, had made a two-fold switch. The first, which has perhaps not been given as much attention as it deserved, was psychological. The old eagerness to take on the unions had given way to a desire to seem fair and reasonable, to persuade rather than to defeat. There should be no misunderstanding: the formula of '£1 + 4%' did not result from a strictly economic calculation. Had it done so the figure would have been much lower. It also favoured the lower paid at the expense of the higher paid workers, salary-earners and the professions. In addition the government announced an inquiry into relativities and anomalies, problems that had been embittering industrial relations for years. Politically there was an obvious desire to look beyond the immediate situation and work out longer-term solutions, which were bound to require major changes in the management of the economy. Indeed, this was just what Mr Powell and those who thought like him found it most difficult to forgive in Mr Heath. They were really the only people within the Conservative Party who fully grasped just what was entailed ideologically and electorally: Mr Heath was sacrificing the party's non-interventionist principles in a way that was bound in some degree to harm the interests of the middle class. It is hardly surprising that even now Mr Heath is so unloved by so many rank and file Conservatives.

For all that, Phase II had a hostile reception from the unions. The General Council even refused to take part in talks on the working out of the draft prices and pay code, and in February 1973 the atmosphere deteriorated still further with the first strike of civil servants and a fresh outbreak of trouble at Ford, where the unions were demanding rises of £10 per week (as against the £2.70 they might hope to receive under Phase II). The greatest dissatisfaction was expressed by those who had already been the victims of Phase I, such as the gas workers and the hospital ancillary staffs. But though some hospitals were forced to close and others had the greatest difficulty in carrying on, while reductions in gas pressure created the danger of explosions and forced a number of factories to shut down, and there were also demonstrations by the civil servants and the gas workers, there was never a head-on clash between the government and the trade union movement as a whole. On 23 March the gas workers accepted the Gas Board's offer on terms that differed very little from what they were originally offered. This was the signal for a general improvement in the situation. Early in April the miners agreed to a settlement within Phase II despite their executive's recommendation to reject. Next the Ford workers, while still rejecting the management's offer, refused to introduce a ban on overtime. Then the railwaymen and the hospital workers both settled, and though they managed to extract a few more minor concessions, this did not dent Phase II all that gravely. Indeed, by the time of the May Day 'national day of protest' against the government's incomes policy, the temperature had fallen considerably and it received only limited support.[10] Mr Hugh Scanlon, usually considered among the most intransigent of union leaders, admitted on 9 April that the government had, temporarily at least, won the upper hand — though he also warned that there was trouble ahead if prices were allowed to rise sharply while wages were being held down. The way was now clear for fresh negotiations in preparation for Phase III — although, as Mr Scanlon said, the government had won only a battle; it was far from winning the war on prices and so persuading the public of the merits of its policy.

The government's success was in large measure due to the fact that Britain was then enjoying one of her rare periods of rapid growth. Between December 1972 and June 1973 GDP was rising at an annual rate of 7 per cent. As always, the inadequate level of industrial investment in earlier years meant that there was not enough spare capacity to cope, and ways of curbing demand were soon being considered, particularly since the pound had been allowed to float, and this had led to a *de facto* devaluation of 11 per cent over the past year, and the balance of payments deficit was running at an annual rate of £700 million over the first quarter. (It was to reach an annual rate of £2,328 million by November, even before the effects of higher oil prices had been felt.) The pound would have fallen even lower had not high interest rates attracted money to London. So the chancellor had to choose between cutting interest rates, which would encourage investment but would cause a further depreciation of the pound, which would bring still higher prices in its train, and the *status quo*, which put a brake on capital expenditure and was an indirect cause of inflation. Despite the five-month·freeze retail prices were still rising. In November 1972 they were 7.6 per cent higher than a year earlier, in March 1973 8.2 per cent higher, in June 9.3 per cent and in November 10.3 per cent. So the rate of increase was also rising despite Phase I and Phase II. Nevertheless, controls had made a major contribution to controlling inflation, for between November 1972 and November 1973 a 43.9 per cent rise in industry's input prices led to a rise of only 9.5 per cent in output prices. No prices policy could have been totally effective in such a situation. At the time the guidelines for Phase II were drawn up the government was expecting world prices to be stable. It failed to take into account the precarious condition of the international monetary system, and it seems to have assumed that Britain would be the only country to expand and increase its purchases of raw materials; in the event 1973 proved to be a good year in most industrial countries and, urged on by speculation, raw material prices soared.[11] The *Financial Times* was later to show how 'inflation made an ass of Phase II'. This is also why the CBI was complaining increasingly loudly about price controls. The Price Commission, however, was unimpressed. It challenged the validity of the CBI's complaints and drew attention to a number of gaps in the prices code that needed plugging; in its judgement the CBI had not proved that profits had been seriously affected by Phase II. However, it estimated that in its first five months it had saved the public some £316 million.[12]

Results on the wages front were equally modest. Many wage agreements that had been caught by Phase I had come into force again on 1 April. So although increases under Phase II were limited to about 8 per cent, the DEP's statistics showed that the actual rise was considerably greater. In January 1973 weekly wage rates were 12.8 per cent above their level of a year earlier; in April they were 15.4 per cent higher, and in July they were again up 15.4 per cent. Earnings were up 15.0 per cent in January; 13.4 per cent in April and 15.4 per cent in July. Wage increases were still comfortably outstripping prices, but they were now beginning to level off while prices were starting to rise rather more rapidly. Be that as it may, these figures help to explain why there was so little industrial unrest at the time.[13] Only 7,173,000 days were lost through industrial disputes during 1973, compared with 23,909,000 in 1972 — a fall of 70 per cent — though against this the number of strikes was actually slightly up, at 2,854 compared with 2,497, and the picture was to change sharply at the end of the year.

Nevertheless, the fight against inflation was by no means won. In August NIESR warned against any loosening of controls on prices and wages,[14] and in a speech in September that offended many by its frankness, Lord Rothschild declared flatly that: 'Unless we give up the idea that we are one of the wealthiest, most influential and important countries in the world ... we are likely to find ourselves in increasingly serious trouble.'[15] Such was the uncertain atmosphere in which the preparations for Phase III got under way.

Phase III — Decline and Fall

Phase II was due to end at the close of October. Contacts between the government and the two sides of industry were resumed in May — Mr Heath had met union leaders privately somewhere around Easter. But they were still very far apart. While the government's attitude had changed considerably, and it was more relaxed and ready to listen, the unions were still very suspicious, partly because they thought that the government was capable of changing its mind yet again and going back to a hard line, and partly because they had come so badly out of Phases I and II. In a speech to the Institute of Personnel Management in May Mr Feather admitted the TUC 'had much to gain on behalf of the working people of this country and in terms of our involvement in running the economy — that includes taxation and pensions — if we engage in these sorts of commitments with the government'.[16] But in September the TUC was expecting negotiations to deal with 'a wide range of issues', including food and housing costs, pensions, taxation, investment and economic growth, when at the last moment it heard that most of these were not negotiable. This only deepened its suspicions. Also, at the end of June the AUEW executive refused to allow Mr Scanlon to join the TUC delegation. Around the same time too Sir Frank Figgures was talking about the difficulty of devising more flexible rules for pay, suggesting that he was being asked to square the circle in devising a form of words that would take account of the needs of productivity, the need of a number of essential services to hold labour during a period of economic expansion (he had in mind particularly the problems of London Transport, which was suffering chronic staff shortages because of the unsocial hours that had to be worked), the requirements of wage restructuring and the special problems of low pay. In the end, after the three sides had met a number of times during the summer and autumn, it was clear that nothing short of a return to completely free collective bargaining would satisfy the unions. So there was little likelihood of their approving the government's Phase III proposals, which were officially unveiled on 8 October,[17] despite the fact that its proposals for wages contained a considerable measure of flexibility.

The proposals set a limit of 7 per cent for increases in basic rates, which was then equivalent on average to £2.25 per week, with an absolute limit of £400 per year. But there was provision for negotiating further rises either nationally or locally in the form of efficiency schemes or additional payments for 'unsocial hours' up to a limit of 11 per cent. On top of this — and the government was running a serious risk, in view of the inflationary situation — agreements could provide for threshold payments by which, if retail prices increased more than 7 per cent over the year, there would be a flat rate wage increase of 40 pence per week for each additional 1 per cent rise in the cost of living. Finally, an additional 1 per cent was available for pay restructuring, correcting of anomalies noted by the Pay Board, increases in London weightings and progress towards the implementation of equal pay.

Few major changes were proposed in the system of price controls. The compression of price margins was limited to 10 per cent to avoid adverse effects on the level of investment. Although a few minor relaxations were made, few concessions were made to the protests from the CBI; indeed at the request of the Price Commission firms were no longer allowed to subdivide themselves artificially to escape limitations on their profits. Also, companies in Category II now had to notify increases when they occurred rather than once a quarter. Dividend increases continued to be limited to 5 per cent.

The government announced at the same time that it would compensate the nationalised industries for losses they had incurred by being required to keep their prices down (only gas and electricity had been allowed significant rises). The freeze on business rents was maintained; pensioners were to be given a £10 Christmas bonus; bank profits were reduced by £30 million thanks to a stricter formula to control their interest earnings (the fact that the banks earned more money because of higher interest rates, supposed to fight inflation, had been widely criticised); a scheme was introduced to help first-time house purchasers, and New Year's Day was declared a public holiday! Together with a number of lesser measures this made up the government's 'social package', which was intended to demonstrate its new concern to be 'fair'. This at least was how the prime minister presented the proposals in his Lancaster House speech.[18]

Ministers were once again gambling on the fall in world prices, which they had been predicting and hoping for for over a year, but which obstinately failed to materialise. (Later the steep rise in oil prices from November 1973 for some time concealed the fact that most other commodity prices were levelling out and some were actually falling.) Immediate reactions to the government's statement were not encouraging. The CBI was 'disappointed'. The new general secretary of the TUC, Mr Len Murray, saw little point in further negotiations with the government. The Labour Party issued a strongly worded attack on the prime minister for revealing his proposals outside Parliament while the House was in recess, and branded them as 'unfair and unworkable', laying special emphasis on the refusal to freeze rents or subsidise basic foodstuffs or increase pensions — all of which Labour did in fact decide on taking office the following March. But, more seriously for both the government and the fate of its policy, almost immediately after the announcement, the NUM executive rejected a settlement within Phase III, even though the pay code had practically been tailor-made for the miners and the Coal Board had exploited every possible provision within the code to produce an offer of 13 per cent. It may well have made a fundamental psychological error to do so because all union leaders like to be able to show their members that they have managed to screw a few additional concessions out of the management during negotiations. By making an offer that from the start went right to the very limit of Phase III, the Coal Board, and indirectly the government, made this impossible — and certainly made things no easier for the three leading officials of the NUM who were watching and vying with one another.[19]

The outcome scarcely requires recapitulating. The miners continued to insist on being treated as a special case and on 12 November began an overtime ban. On 17 November the retail price index showed that prices had gone up 2 per cent in October, largely because of higher food prices,[20] which are always felt the most. As table 17.2 shows, confidence in the government's policy was beginning to fall. It was probably no coincidence that, just as prices seemed to be catching up wages, more people were inclined to blame the government than the unions for the country's economic problems.

In December, although Mr Whitelaw was brought in as secretary of state for

Table 17.2.

Q. *In your opinion are the Government's new controls on prices and wages fair or unfair?*

	Stage I 20 Nov. 1972	Stage II 29 Jan. 1973	Stage III 13 Oct. 1973	Stage III 28 Oct. 1973
	(%)	(%)	(%)	(%)
Fair	55	44	40	37
Unfair	33	44	49	47
Don't know	11	12	11	16

Q. *Do you think the measures recently announced by the Government to control the level of prices and wages will work or not?*

	Stage I 20 Nov. 1972	Stage II 29 Jan. 1973	Stage III prices 28 Oct. 1973	Stage III wages 28 Oct. 1973
	(%)	(%)	(%)	(%)
Will work	40	33	(26)* 20	(29) 24
Will not work	41	50	(61) 54	(56) 52
Don't know	19	17	(13) 26	(15) 24

* Figures in brackets are 13 Oct. 1973.

Q. *Who do you think is most to blame for Britain's economic problems?*

	Stage I Nov. 1972	Stage II Jan. 1973	Stage III 28 Oct. 1973
	(%)	(%)	(%)
The government	25	31	41
The trade unions	50	45	40
Employers	10	11	14
None of these	3	6	7
Don't know	12	13	15

Source: NOP, *Financial Times* (16 November 1973).

employment, the government's optimism, which to this point had been unquenchable, began to falter. The most notable feature of Mr Barber's 17 December mini-budget was how little direct relationship it had with the immediate crisis. (It was mainly concerned with reducing the budget deficit by cutting programmes of public expenditure, though it did contain the promise of a tax on speculative capital gains.) A few days earlier the government had announced that, owing to the effect on coal stocks of the miners' overtime ban, from 1 January industry would be put on a three-day week. This was bound to be unpopular — but who would the public blame, the miners or the government? Mr Heath was clearly banking on its being the miners, and there were many who felt that he was staking his future on the outcome. Events were to suggest that this was not an overstated view of the situation.

So the auguries for 1974 were bleak, even bearing in mind Sam Brittan's reflection that:

> The pendulum of influential opinion swings from wishful thinking to sado-masochistic doom-mongering. During most of 1972—3 it was the wishful thinking end . . . . This year the danger is the opposite — an over-reaction to the oil shortage, and excessive fiscal restraint of the usual 'too much, too late' variety . . . .
> [He further commented] The coal situation with its threat of confrontation and class war is basically more worrying than the oil position. Nevertheless, within three months at the very most, the coal dispute is likely to have been settled one way or another; and one of the most predictable of economic surprises is how quickly output lost in a strike can afterwards be recovered.[21]

His remarks were apt, for the great surprise of the three-day week, which lasted two months, was that output did not fall by any means as much as had been feared, but held up at around eighty per cent of normal — which said something about the efficiency of British industry in normal times. However, production failed to pick up as rapidly as had been hoped in the spring.

The New Year began with the two sides eyeing each other warily. On 9 January Mr Heath set up a separate energy ministry with responsibility for both the home and overseas aspects of the energy crisis. On the same day the miners rejected a direct appeal from Mr Whitelaw to think again, and the government had a majority of twenty-four in the Commons at the end of a debate on the energy crisis. Meanwhile the train drivers were continuing their separate guerilla action in support of a demand that they too should be treated as a special case outside Phase III. On the tenth a TUC delegation suggested to the prime minister that, if he would agree to the miners being treated as a special case, then other unions would pledge themselves to settle within Phase III. While Mr Barber's instinctive reaction was to dismiss the idea out of hand, Mr Heath agreed to discuss it with the TUC, which submitted a thirty-six-page document drawn up by its Economic Committee. However talks on the fourteenth were inconclusive, and the rumours of an early election began to circulate more persistently. Initially the prime minister resisted pressure for a dissolution. The government and the unions met again on the twenty-first and again failed to reach agreement. Three days later the NUM executive called a strike ballot, and the Pay Board published a report on relativities which offered the government a face-saving way out — which it was to adopt too late. Mr Mick McGahey, the NUM vice-president, was now calling on Scottish miners to form a 'popular front' against the government, to the displeasure of Labour leaders because this gave credence to the increasing tendency of the Conservatives to accuse the miners of being politically motivated. On 4 February there was a further fruitless meeting between the prime minister and the TUC, and the result of the miners' ballot was announced: 81 per cent of those voting favoured strike action (compared with only 59 per cent in December 1971). The strike was set for 10 February. On the eighth the prime minister called a general election for the twenty-eighth. The miners decided to continue with their planned strike notwithstanding, but the train drivers suspended their industrial action until the election was over. During the ensuing campaign all parties vied with each other in depicting themselves as moderates. Meanwhile Mr Heath had asked the Pay Board to prepare a report on miners' pay relative to that of other occupations. So the government was striking two contradictory attitudes at the same time. On the one hand it was being firm and insisting that the country must give it a clear mandate to stand up to the miners, and on the other it was showing signs of weakness by referring the matter to the Pay Board — for all the precedents indicated that reference of a dispute of this kind to any kind of arbitration is one of the first moves towards capitulation. This apparent contradiction did not escape the voters, and may well have contributed to the government's defeat. It only remained for the new Labour government to settle with the miners — at a price: they received £100 million compared with the original Coal Board offer of £43 million. So the miners had won a two-fold victory: industrially they had won very large wage increases; politically they had brought down the government. It was hard not to feel that this episode would cast its shadow over the pattern of union—government relations for many years ahead.

But this was not quite the end of the road for Phase III. While the price of coal leaped 48 per cent, the new secretary for employment, Mr Michael Foot, reached a tacit agreement with the TUC, as part of Labour's much-heralded social contract, that Phase III and the Pay Board would remain in existence temporarily while the government gave first priority to the repeal of the Industrial Relations Act. Nevertheless, the days of statutory incomes policy were numbered. The Pay Board was abolished in July,[22] and under the Prices Act the prices and pay code became simply the price code. Thus completely free collective bargaining was restored while prices were still subject to fairly comprehensive control. The new government also inherited the poisoned chalice of threshold agreements, which had assumed much greater significance than its authors had ever imagined — a rise of 3.4 per cent in the cost of living index for March, largely as a consequence of increases imposed in Mr Healey's first budget, triggered three threshold payments, giving some seven million workers an additional £1.20 per week. Many now envied a provision that had seemed of little consequence only six months earlier.

Other Aspects of State Interventionism

Industrial and Regional Policy

The government changed its mind on industrial and regional policy far more quickly than it did over incomes policy. In 1970 Mr Heath's 'free society' had no place for 'lame ducks'; sad though it was, the government must leave them to their fate rather than keep them alive artificially. This was why the IRC was one of the first victims of the chancellor's economy drive in October 1970 — for it was accused of having bailed out too many ailing firms. Yet even before the IRC was finally laid to rest, the government became entangled in the problems of Rolls Royce. In November 1970 the secretary for trade and industry, Mr John Davies, announced that the government was making £42 million available to enable the company to develop the RB-211 engine. In January 1971 the government had to intervene again — this time to partially nationalise the company. Rolls Royce, it was clear, was not to receive the lame duck treatment — though if it was not a lame duck, what was? However, the government was apparently not prepared to see such a key company in the aircraft industry — already burdened by that ailing white elephant, Concorde — collapse, for a number of reasons, part international (Rolls Royce had contracts with Lockheed, which was itself in difficulties), part related to prestige (it was unthinkable that one of the most celebrated names in British industry should vanish) and part social.

Social considerations were certainly foremost in the second major crisis the government had to confront in this area, at Upper Clyde Shipbuilders (UCS). Shipyards had been the special objects of government largesse ever since the war. Many were unprofitable and inefficient, riddled with demarcation disputes and other forms of restrictive practices, and survived only with the help of government subsidies. No government had been prepared to grasp this particular nettle, partly because of tradition (they were linked with the days of Britain's maritime supremacy), partly for social reasons (most were located in depressed areas where closure would aggravate existing unemployment problems) and partly from political opportunism (their workers were notoriously inclined to militancy and were capable of reacting vigorously to defend not only their jobs but traditional custom and practice). This was what happened at UCS. When the company was found to be on the verge of collapse in June 1971 this was a shock for Mr Davies, who had tried to put the firm back on its feet in December 1970, aided by a management that mingled undue optimism with a very modest level of competence. (The government already held 48 per cent of the company's capital following a reorganisation and merger negotiated by Mr Benn in 1967.) But it was an even greater shock to the workers. Threatened by the closure of the yard and the loss of a large number of jobs, they organised a work-in to force the State to come to their aid. After months of argument and negotiations involving the unions and the Labour Party (which, both collectively and personally, through Mr Benn, must take a considerable share of responsibility for the situation), in the wake of the miners' strike in February 1972, the government finally agreed to provide £35 million to enable a private industrialist to take the company over. Once more the government had been forced to abandon one of the main pillars of its economic philosophy, mainly by events but also by a small group of determined men, and perhaps, too, by fears of completely alienating the Scots.[23]

There was clearly a need for the government to restate its policy on industry and the regions. In March 1972 it published a White Paper[24] which the luckless Mr Davies had to defend in the House of Commons. The ensuing Industry Act had two salient features: it revised the system of investment incentives and assisted areas and completely reorganised the way development aid was administered, both nationally and locally.

The new investment incentives, for which provision had already been made in the 1972–3 budget, took two forms: taxation allowances, which were available throughout the country, and regional development grants, which were confined to the assisted areas (see table 17.3). The boundaries of the assisted areas were slightly modified, though intermediate area status was extended to the whole of the North West and Yorkshire and Humberside regions.

On the administrative side the Act introduced a minister for industrial development (Christopher Chataway) attached to the DTI with general responsibility for the private sector and special responsibility for industrial development in the assisted areas. He was to co-operate closely with the

Table 17.3.   The new investment incentives and regional development grants

Taxation allowances countrywide		
	First-year allowance of 100%	
All plant and machinery (new and second hand — other than passenger cars), for use in both services and manufacturing	Initial allowance of 40% and annual writing down allowance of 4%	
New industrial buildings and structures		
Regional development grants in assisted areas	Plant, machinery and mining works	Buildings
	(%)	(%)
Special development areas	22	22
Development areas	20	20
Intermediate areas	–	20
Derelict land clearance areas (until March 1974)	–	20

Source: Survey of Current Affairs (April 1972).

secretary for the environment and the secretaries for Scotland and Wales. There was also to be an industrial development executive (IDE) at the national level, combining the DTI divisions dealing with regional development and small business (which had been set up on the recommendation of the Bolton Committee[25]), and the regional offices of the DTI. The IDE could recruit its staff from the City and industry as well as the civil service. The minister was also to be advised by an industrial development board, whose members included senior representatives of industry, business and banking. In the assisted areas regional industrial development boards (RIDBs) replaced the existing DTI regional offices (which were retained in the other regions). These were to work with the regional economic planning councils and boards. Each RIDB had a regional director from the civil service and an industrial director with a background in industry. This new machinery was to operate the new scheme for selective assistance introduced in October 1972.[26] The White Paper had made it quite clear that the aim was not just to create new jobs but even more to encourage companies to modernise. Naturally the government did not lose sight either of the need for industry in the regions to prepare for Britain's entry into EEC. The emphasis on selectivity was itself quite striking, since until then the Conservatives had always rejected the idea, arguing that discrimination between firms impaired free competition and the normal working of the market. The Industry Act also indicated that henceforth there would be more flexibility in the granting of industrial development certificates – though this carried the obvious risk of regions such as the South East where the unemployment rate was already very low becoming 'overdeveloped'. At all events, the sum of £250 million that was initially made available, together with two possible further instalments of up to £150 million, meant that the DTI would have considerable scope for intervention – and Mr Benn was to delight in taking full advantage of it on becoming minister for industry in 1974.

Hand in hand with a regional policy for industry went vocational training. As we have seen, the Conservatives had severely criticised Labour's use of the Industrial Training Act, so they were expected to make major changes on returning to power. But although Mr Carr, minister of employment between 1970 and 1972, announced that plans for reform were being considered, they were a long while in seeing the light of day, and the fate of the industrial training boards, for instance, was still in doubt up to the end of 1971. The government's 'Green Paper' that finally appeared in February 1972 proposed the introduction of a Training Opportunities Scheme, which would pull together the whole range of government schemes for training and retraining and increase the number of trainees from 18,000 to 60,000 by 1975 and eventually to 100,000.[27] After long discussions and some uncertainty the resulting Bill finally became law at the end of 1973. A new Manpower Services Unit was established under Sir Dennis Barnes. It was to operate through two agencies: the Employment Service Agency, which was to deal with everything relating to employment and unemployment, and the Training Services Agency, which was to cover the whole range of vocational and occupational training schemes. So the reform involved the decentralising of a number of functions that had previously been run directly by the Department of Employment, and brought together those who were most knowledgeable about employment needs and those who were best placed to see those needs were met. It seemed a useful reform, though it might prove short-lived because it seemed all too likely that Mr Michael Foot or his successors would decide to make still more changes before the new system could prove itself.

At the beginning of 1974 two big queries hung over regional development policy: how would it be affected by the new European regional policy, which was the object of seemingly endless discussions in Brussels, and what would be the impact of the proposals of the Kilbrandon Commission.[28] EEC might affect the issue in two ways. On the one hand it was possible that some features of the British system would prove to be incompatible with the EEC's own legislation, but on the other hand, if the European Regional Fund was as generously financed as Britain was hoping, then considerable additional funds might be available to the regions. However, when the Wilson government came to office it was more concerned with renegotiating existing commitments than with pressing forward with fresh ones. On the second point, the slowness and ambiguity of the government response to the Kilbrandon Commission's complicated and rather inconsistent proposals[29] meant that it was not immediately clear what the effect would be, though it seemed that in the short run Scotland would be given quite a substantial measure of devolution, Wales considerably less, and the English regions practically none. It is too early to see what the implications of this would be for regional policy.[30]

Consumer Protection and Fair Trading

On their return to power in 1970 the Conservatives announced their intention of strengthening the Monopolies Commission and the Restrictive Practices Court.[31] However, they also abruptly abolished the Consumer Council, which they themselves had set up in 1963, ostensibly to save £240,000 in public expenditure, but also because they considered that consumers were perfectly capable of defending themselves through voluntary bodies. Here again experience produced a change of heart. The growing number of mergers made it more necessary for the government to intervene to stimulate competition. According to the chairman of the City's unofficial panel on mergers and takeovers,[32] mergers were running at an average of eight a week — a sizeable figure, given that about 3,200 companies were quoted on the London Stock Exchange. Two years later the figure had doubled.

However, the government did not announce fresh plans until December 1972, shortly after Sir Geoffrey Howe's appointment as minister for consumer affairs, with the publication of the Fair Trading Bill. Sir Geoffrey was to be assisted by a director of fair trading, who was to have a staff of around 175 and an annual budget of £500,000. According to the *Financial Times* he was to be 'the consumer's watchdog over an area stretching from the shopper in the High Street to monopolies and mergers'.[33] In addition to these new responsibilities the director-general of fair trading took over a number of functions from the registrar of restrictive trading agreements, which entailed co-ordination of the work of the Restrictive Practices Court, the Monopolies Commission and a new agency, the Consumer Protection Advisory Committee. The nationalised industries were brought within this type of legislation for the first time, but otherwise there was much less change in the machinery for dealing with monopolies and restrictive practices than had been generally expected.

A notable feature of the Fair Trading Act was its avoidance of detailed regulation and the wide measure of discretion it gave to the new 'Consumers' Ombudsman'. The director-general could propose to the Consumer Protection Advisory Committee draft statutory instruments to deal with trading practices that were unfair to the consumer, and if approved then they would be sent to the minister for him to make the appropriate order. The first director-general was Mr John Methven, a part-time member of the Monopolies Commission. Sir Geoffrey had earlier announced the government's intention of setting up a national network of consumer advice centres in conjunction with the local authorities. At about this time the Monopolies Commission reported on parallel pricing,[34] coming down with some qualifications in favour of those who believed it was not in the public interest and recommending that the government keep an eye on firms practising it. Again, in September Sir Geoffrey published a White Paper on the reform of the law relating to loans and hire purchase agreements.[35] A once neglected area of policy seemed suddenly to have become a hive of activity.

In the field of monopolies and mergers, the Monopolies Commission was now known as the Monopolies and Mergers Commission but was otherwise unchanged. However, the director-general of fair trading was given powers to refer monopolies (except the nationalised industries, which could only be referred by the minister himself). But he could only refer mergers through the minister, and with the minister's approval. Outlining the government's policy on mergers in November 1973, Sir Geoffrey Howe recalled that the Fair Trading Act reduced the market share that was held to constitute a 'monopoly situation' from one-third to one-quarter and brought within its scope mergers involving the acquisition of assets worth £5 million or more. He noted that previously only 120 of the 800–1,000 mergers taking place in the course of a year (involving total assets of something like £3,500 million) fell within the terms of the Act. Over the previous twelve months the DTI had considered 137 proposed mergers and had referred six to the Commission. Since five of these had promptly been abandoned, in the end the Commission had reported only on one.[36] So there was a case for a rather finer net, rather than the contrary as a number of people in industry were suggesting. In fact the government had shown by referring the proposed merger of Boots and House of Fraser to the Monopolies and Mergers Commission to report within five months that it wanted to make greater use of the Commission and to speed up its work.

One conclusion emerges quite clearly: that the law on restrictive practices, monopolies and consumer protection is a striking instance of political bipartisanship. It was Harold Wilson who as president of the Board of Trade introduced the first legislation dealing with monopolies in 1947; the Tories strengthened it in 1956 by establishing the Restrictive Practices Court, and in 1963 they set up the Consumer Council; in 1965 the Labour government gave the Monopolies Commission its present form; and while in 1970 the Conservatives broke with convention by abolishing the Consumer Council, they themselves restored it under the Fair Trading Act of 1972; Mrs Williams, as Labour secretary for prices and consumer protection, was to declare her intention of giving full effect to the Fair Trading Act and strengthening the Restrictive Practices Court. Here was a field, then, where, far from the alternation of parties in office producing incoherence and discontinuity, there was a continuous adjustment to changing economic circumstances irrespective of which was in power. The Conservatives talked more about strengthening competition, while Labour seemed more interested in controlling monopolies, but at bottom both were trying to see that British capitalism had a less unacceptable face.

Planning or Non-Planning?

> *Planning has now acquired so many possible meanings that it tends more to confuse than to clarify.* — Ely Devons[37]

In the article from which this quotation is drawn Professor Sandford offers a useful classification of the various types of planning. We are in his debt because the literature (particularly the literature in English) has never been notable for precise definitions. To Professor Sandford, 'planning or more fully national economic planning, is taken to mean all attempts by the government to exercise conscious direction over the economy as a whole', which, he adds, 'distinguishes planning from individual policy measures, though of course policy measures may be used to implement a plan'.[38] On the basis of this general definition, he distinguishes between three kinds of planning:

> ... administrative or physical planning [which is] the attempt to manage the economy by an apparatus of controls — licences, rationing, price and profit controls backed by the force of law ... financial or overall financial planning [which] consists primarily of monetary and budgetary policy and is in essence an attempt to manage the economy by influencing demand and prices [and] indicative planning [which is] ... the compilation of detailed programmes for the public and private sectors of the economy ... which are intended as a consensus view of the likely growth of the various sectors of the economy over the next five years or so.

His first category covers the wartime government, the Labour government of 1945 and the various periods of statutory prices and incomes policy under

Labour and the Conservatives. The third covers the work of Neddy and the DEA, and the second covers practically all other forms of economic management that have been employed under the influence of Keynes since the war.

While Professor Sandford's clarity is admirable, his definitions are not wholly convincing. Indeed, he really takes us little further than Lewis's celebrated but ambiguous 'we are all planners now'. If we accept his three categories, then every country in Western Europe that has tried to steer its economy by controlling the overall level of demand by monetary or fiscal measures has been planning without realising it, and perhaps even without wanting to, as with Germany under Adenauer. For Dr Erhardt's 'social market economy' must presumably be considered a form of 'financial planning' even though the very word 'planning' was anathema to the father of the 'German miracle'. The view of planning that emerges from these pages is, of course, strongly influenced by the French view summarised in the phrase so often heard in French political circles that 'to govern is to foresee', and not just to administer. These were the grounds on which the French Left criticised M. Giscard d'Estaing when he was minister of finance — that he ran the economy purely on short-term considerations, endlessly tinkering with it but never taking into account the Plan or indeed any other longer-term aim. And this is the crux of the matter; what distinguishes planning from mere day-to-day management or even *dirigisme* is the existence of some 'longer-term aim'. However, it is by no means sure that there can be truly 'national' planning in countries that are so dependent on the largest national economy of all — that of the United States, which notoriously is the least likely to be planned.

It follows that planning can really be said to be taking place only when at least two of Professor Sandford's categories are simultaneously present — and this has clearly been the case most of the time since the war in Britain. Even during those periods of Conservative rule that were covered rather rapidly here, precisely because they were not thought to be planned, there was always a certain degree of 'administrative planning', such as the system of industrial development certificates. But its survival was more a matter of administrative convenience than the outcome of any clearly formulated political intention, which is why there seemed no need to give it more than a passing mention.

The later period of Conservative rule, though begun with the best of neo-liberal intentions, clearly falls into at least two of Professor Sandford's categories — administrative planning from November 1972 onwards and, of course, financial planning, since after all this is the normal business of chancellors; there were more full-scale and mini-budgets than usual, while one marked feature of economic management, particularly towards the close of the period, was the emergence of a large budget deficit intended to stimulate demand and get the economy growing again, and the policy of dear (but not particularly scarce) money to combat price increases. This was rather inconsistent and, as we have seen, it was on the whole unsuccessful.

It seems more useful to ask whether, after the collapse of planning under

Labour, a number of features did not nevertheless carry over into the later period, for the absence of any official plan is not in itself wholly conclusive. There were two factors of note, though in themselves they are not wholly conclusive either. In discussing PESC we noted that until December 1972 the government refused to publish the 'economic assessment' on which its five-year projection of public expenditure was based. In December 1972 it did this in the form of a long-term projection for the whole economy, provoking Sam Brittan to comment that 'growthmanship rides again'.[39] As table 17.4 shows, alternative hypotheses of growth were presented — but in the light of the past performance of the British economy both looked optimistic, and as Sam Brittan also pointed out, there was nothing in the White Paper, apart from prices and incomes policy, to ensure that the targets were achieved. However, as he said, the drama was 'unlikely to be played out to the end because of our old friend the balance of payments'.[40]

NEDC of course continued to explore the future in its unpretentious yet important reports. One of Sir Frank Figgures' most valuable achievements as director-general of NEDO was to maintain the dialogue between the government and the two sides of industry, particularly the TUC — even if it was a dialogue of the deaf at times. He also played an important part in the various attempts at closer consultation in 1971 and 1972, and though they were eventually unsuccessful, he emerged with a considerable reputation as a mediator. It was not surprising that the government turned to him when it set up the Pay Board, where his talents would now be displayed in a more controversial role. His place at NEDC was filled temporarily by Mr Tom Fraser, who had been Neddy's industrial director for eight years, and then by Mr Ronald McIntosh, who headed the Prices and Incomes Policy section of the Treasury, and who had been closely involved in the talks with the CBI and TUC during the summer and autumn of 1972. This was of course no coincidence. He was already well known to the TUC and CBI, and a colleague described him as an 'untypical civil servant and a bit of an entrepreneur'[41] — qualities that would certainly be called on at NEDO. For all his skill the December 1973 and January 1974 meetings of Neddy were marked by heated exchanges between union representatives and members of the government — notably Mr Barber.

At least one of Neddy's reports around this time could fairly be considered a 'planning exercise',[42] since it worked through the two hypotheses, previously mentioned, of 3½ or 5 per cent growth, and examined the likely response of eleven key sectors of the economy: electrical engineering, electronics, machine tools, mechanical engineering, motor manufacturing, chemicals, iron and steel castings, paper and board, agriculture, manufactured food, textiles and clothing. This report, which was largely based on inquiries undertaken by the Little Neddies concerned, reached relatively optimistic conclusions. The authors cautiously argued that efforts over the previous decade to improve the efficiency of British industry were at last beginning to bear fruit, but still more needed to be done by way of structural reforms, better use of manpower, improved training and higher profitability — for the rate of return on capital was still

Table 17.4. Resources and claims: average annual change, 1971–7 (1972 factor cost prices)

| | 3.5% growth rate | | | | 5.0% growth rate | | | |
| | Low investment | | High investment | | Low investment | | High investment | |
	(£m)	(%)	(£m)	(%)	(£m)	(%)	(£m)	(%)
A. Gross Domestic Product	1,970	3.5	1,970	3.5	2,900	5.0	2,900	5.0
B. Claims on Gross Domestic Product								
1. Private investment	320	6.2	410	7.8	540	9.8	650	11.2
2. Balance of trade	−50	–	−50	–	170	–	170	–
3. Public expenditure								
(a) Public consumption	370	3.2	370	3.2	370	3.2	370	3.2
(b) Public investment	130	2.8	130	2.8	130	2.8	130	2.8
(c) Total direct public expenditure ((a) + (b))	500	3.1	500	3.1	500	3.1	500	3.1
(d) Indirect public expenditure	190	3.1	190	3.1	190	3.1	190	3.1
(e) Total public expenditure ((c) + (d))	690	3.1	690	3.1	690	3.1	690	3.1
4. Resources available for privately financed consumption	1,010	3.5	920	3.3	1,500	5.0	1,390	4.8

Source: Public Expenditure to 1976–1977 and Financial Times (4 January 1973).

falling. But this had been said so often in the past! Furthermore, while in many ways progress depended on the individual firms, performance of some of the largest companies was very dependent on the general economic policy of the government, which has to take account of such external constraints as the balance of payments, the tendency of financial institutions to export capital, the possibility that the energy crisis might invalidate the more optimistic forecasts. At all events, NEDO continued examining such basic problems as the structural obstacles to growth, though it was also concerned with finding ways of coping with short-run fluctuations in the economy.[43]

It would not be in the least surprising if the return of Labour to power brought fresh attempts to introduce indicative planning. Perhaps the party might even be rather bolder than in the past. But it seemed even more likely that there would be an extension of administrative planning in at least two directions. The first of these obviously is the continuation of price controls; the introduction of subsidies on a number of basic foodstuffs did not involve any extension of controls but did give them a more 'administrative' character. If the system were to continue for some time, 'administrative' prices would bear less and less relationship to market prices, and the need to keep public expenditure getting out of control would make rationing seem increasingly attractive. While perhaps not as intolerable as it might appear at first glance, what a contrast it would imply with the affluence of the Macmillan era! The second way in which administrative planning seemed likely to expand arose from the new industrial policy operated by Mr Benn, particularly the proposed planning agreements between the State and the private sector oulined in his White Paper.[44] Although in principle these involved nothing more than 'a new and improved framework for cooperation between the government and leading industrial companies'[45] and a 'series of consultations . . . leading to an agreement about plans for the following three years', given the views and personality of Mr Benn, the anxiety of employers was in some measure justified. Under the new Industry Act a National Enterprise Board will have between £700 million and £1,000 million at its disposal, and it will be under the tight control of the minister for industry, who will enjoy a considerable margin of discretion. Yet, as the Bill was fiercely contested by the opposition and challenged by the CBI, the government had to water down its plans and it seemed that the old dream of the Labour Left, 'planning with teeth in it', will not be quite realised. But what with 'reconstruction', 'liberation', 'reorganisation', 'redeployment', 'hiving off' and 'regeneration', one might well wonder what will remain of British industry.

And there was one other obvious question: how long would Labour be able to maintain its control of prices without any control on incomes? For the social contract was only a frail device which was almost bound to be temporary. Admittedly the relative failure of earlier attempts to control incomes has tended to accredit a new orthodoxy, and not only in Labour circles, that an incomes policy entails such a degradation of relations with the unions that any slender benefits that might accrue were won at much too high a price.[46] The debate continues — and there is certainly no sign of its ending.

Conclusion

Western planning is in crisis. Since 1965 – i.e. the beginning of the Fifth Plan – French planning, which had so often been taken as a model by other countries, is no longer the object of universal admiration, and has first been challenged (as with the Fifth Plan), and then treated with indifference (as with the Sixth). Recent attempts to rescue it from the near oblivion into which it had fallen have been, to say the least, ambiguous. First there was the 'jonquil plan', which was drawn up early in 1974 for President Pompidou by the former commissaire-général au plan, M. Montjoie. This considered how the French economy could meet the energy crisis during the period up to 1976. It died with President Pompidou. Next came M. Claude Gruson's 'report on waste' which so far at least has had little practical outcome. And finally, in September 1974, there was the creation by President Giscard d'Estaing of a 'planning council', which was surprising in view of his reputation for economic liberalism. This meets monthly under his chairmanship, its other members being the Prime Minister, the Ministers of Finance and Labour, the new Commissaire-Général, M. Ripert, and two of the President's economic advisers. It is hard to see what the outcome of this will be. Many politicians and political observers, not only on the Left, but including some hard-line Gaullists, fear that under cover of claiming to revitalise planning its nature may be transformed.[1]

One can scarcely speak of a crisis in British planning, if only because it has never been more than a succession of isolated efforts which have led to nothing and which have been temporary expedients rather than thoroughgoing reforms. As a former member of the DEA remarked, 'It was not integrated with policies and in particular the urgent triumphed as always over the important.'[2] Nevertheless, while its economic impact may have been no more than marginal, one cannot say the same of its influence on British political life and institutions.

Firstly, it is worth noting that, in Britain as in France, if we set aside the *dirigisme* of the wartime and postwar period, the introduction of indicative planning into a capitalist system owed more to non-socialists of the Right and Centre rather than to those on the Left who are more ideologically inclined in that direction. However, whereas in France the political success of planning was ensured by the fact that a number of key posts – not only in the civil service but in public and private industry – were held by men who were deeply committed to planning (men Professor Duroselle has described as 'neo-realists'[3], by which he means that they are pragmatic and more interested in methods than in political dogmas), developments in Britain were both slower and less decisive. They were slower because planning emerged only in the early 1960s, and less decisive because the 'cabal' responsible for the establishment of NEDC in 1961–2 lacked the cohesion of a permanent pressure group, and was deficient in political realism. Indeed, in this field of planning the celebrated realism of the

British has been conspicuous largely by its absence. This is perhaps because it was an imported 'foreign' device, and because the civil service was unable to call on an equivalent of the French *polyvalents* to work the new system. For not only was the civil service at first not capable of supplying the necessary experts, but it was ill-adapted to operate the new institutions and procedures. And the lack of realism was more generally characteristic of the management of the economy; the attitude of Labour leaders to the problem of devaluation between 1964 and 1966 is particularly revealing in this respect.

All in all, in Britain planning has been rather more like a religion than a technique of running the economy, and as a result it has not been treated seriously by the tough-minded leaders of the higher civil service, industry and the City. Like a primitive religion it had an initial tendency towards magic formulae and a belief in the efficacy of simple incantations. Like the Church of England its doctrines have always remained imprecise. Becoming a state religion after the (partial) conversion of the ruling élites, it has nevertheless always attracted more iconoclasts than idolators and, what is worse, more sceptics. While, unlike the Church of England, it has never become permanently 'established', it too has been struggling against the rise of fresh orthodoxies and the declining numbers of the faithful, and its future seems problematical. In a country where traditions are simply accumulated rather than being directly overthrown, the iconoclasts may in the end be defeated by sheer force of inertia. But true believers will not be deceived into mistaking the sporadic celebration of the old rituals as a sign of the genuine survival of the faith.

The decline in planning has obviously owed much to the mediocre performance of the British economy, but it has also been due to the political disappointments suffered by its initiators. The advocates of planning have always tended to feel that it should also be a means of extending and deepening democracy, both because it offers traditional political institutions clear choices about the development of the economy, and because it offers the producer and the consumer – and thus the citizen – a chance to have his say in an area of direct personal concern to him. In Britain the Conservatives have tended to give the greater emphasis to these potential features of planning, beginning as far back as Harold Macmillan in 1938 and continuing right down to the present; for instance the 1970 *Campaign Guide* wrote that planning 'can reinforce the efficacy of democratic political choice by exposing to public debate the probable increase in the country's wealth and the various uses to which this can be put'.[4]

Every country that has introduced planning has found the role of Parliament a major problem. In a democracy there is something deeply disturbing about the idea that a programme of measures that may affect the life of the entire nation for four or five years may not be thoroughly considered by the elected representatives of the people. For Parliament is the only channel through which minority views can be heard. Moreover, indicative planning is basically the product of negotiations between the government and the producers, both workers and employers. But the government's role is rather ambiguous because it is at one and the same time the defender of the general public – and thus of the consumer – and the spokesman for the public sector – and thus for part of the producers. So it seems highly desirable, even essential, that the voice of the public in the widest sense should not only be heard, but where possible heeded.

In France, after a number of false starts, Parliament has been given a role in the preparatory phases of the Plan.[5] Two parliamentary debates are held. The first, to discuss the main policy options on which the Plan should be based, is held a year before it is due to come into force, while the second takes place on the Bill to approve the Plan. In this later debate the House must decide whether to accept or reject the Plan as a whole – they cannot amend it. However, high hopes were placed in the earlier discussion of the main policy options because it was to be held while it was still possible to include any changes Parliament might want, and also because the planners could put a number of variants before the House and ask it to choose between them. This seemed the best way of making the choice more democratic. However, in the event, practical difficulties like the amount of technical work required and the complexities of decision-making by committee have been such that planners cannot – or will not – present more than one completely worked-through proposal. So when the Fifth Plan was being prepared, Parliament had to discuss a single model, and had to take it or leave it. In 1970 Parliament spent four days discussing the Sixth Plan, but here again it was discussing a package of interlocking priorities rather than a series of discrete choices.

All this, while far from satisfactory, and doing no more than pay lip-service to democratic choice, has at least the merit of existing, whereas Britain has so far failed to devise anything comparable. The first plan was simply a semi-official report prepared by NEDC and it was never debated by Parliament, though members did obtain some information about its preparation and general tenor through questions, and its general outlines were discussed during the debate on the 1963 Finance Bill. The second National Plan was published as a White Paper, and consequently Mr Brown made a Commons statement which was followed by a debate.[6] However since members had had no time for detailed consideration of the White Paper, the discussion and subsequent endorsement by the House could be only in the most general terms.[7] *The Task Ahead* was published as a Green Paper and, interestingly, offered three possible models – though these were prepared for discussion by the Little Neddies and NEDC working parties rather than with Parliament in mind. The final version, which appeared in May 1970, still included two models, though these were to be put to the leaders of industry rather than to members of parliament. Clearly, parliamentary control of planning in Britain has been completely inadequate.

On the other hand, Parliament is now in a better position to control the programme of public expenditure since the 1971 reforms – though as we have seen the practical impact of these changes is questionable. Certainly this is not enough to prevent our concluding that the development of planning has concentrated still greater power in the hands of the executive, even though this power has been partially qualified by the 'participation' of a wide range of economic and social groups.

Since the revival of planning in 1962 one notable feature has been the relationship between the government and the two sides of industry within NEDC and the Little Neddies. On NEDC itself there is strict parity between the two sides: six employers and six trade unionists. This is not the case in the Little Neddies, where employers have about forty-five per cent of the places and trade unionists about twenty per cent. In the regional development councils spokesmen for trade and industry make up about one-third of the membership, about as many as the local authorities, while trade unionists have only a sixth. The unions were also closely involved in the PIB where they played an active key role, and the unions had a small but significant role in the IRC – which was something of a departure for them. Despite being so outnumbered, this machinery has provided a way of involving trade unionists in consideration of most of the major national economic problems, such as the balance of payments and the conditions for growth, and in matters relating to the competitiveness of particular industries and the profitability of companies – and these were matters on which they had rarely been consulted in the past. The TUC has welcomed this and has usually attached considerable importance to achieving representation at every level. Even the leaders of left-wing unions have been prepared to accept the challenge. In addition, as its contribution to the wider economic debate, the TUC began in 1967 to publish an annual economic review, setting out its views on the main problems confronting the economy.

There has obviously been considerable participation by public and private industry, since they supply basic information to the economic departments, the planners, NEDO, the development councils and a wide range of other bodies. Indeed, it was partly in order not to be totally beholden to the trade associations for information, with the accompanying danger that they might exploit their monopoly, that Labour established a number of public and semi-public bodies, so sparing British planning from an undue degree of corporatism, which had seemed a danger in 1962–4. But it is only too easy to go too far the other way, and it cannot be said that the right balance between bureaucracy and corporatism has yet been found.

But participation along these lines is inadequate in many ways. The most glaring weakness is that by no means all the main interests are included. The representation of industry, for instance, is monopolised by the CBI and its member-companies, the nationalised industries, the TUC and its member-unions. Although agriculture and the service industries are represented on the Little Neddies they are not on NEDC itself. Manufacturing industry has, generally speaking, been given the lion's share, though admittedly its role in the national economy is very important – more important than in, say, France. (This situation will be formally recognised when, as it has been announced, Neddy becomes 'Niddy' – the National Industrial Development Council. This apparent narrowing of its scope will have no real effect on its activities.) Moreover, agriculture has its own special machinery for consultation, negotiation and planning which has altered little since the war.

It should also be said that all this network of participation makes very little sense unless it makes some genuine impact on economic development; we have indicated earlier just how circumscribed the influence of the various plans was on the very limited development of the economy that did occur. Employing a distinction suggested by François Perroux, the British economy is less a 'concerted economy' than an 'informed economy' and a 'discussed economy'. But however intensive and far-ranging discussion may be it cannot achieve the greater integration of society that is usually credited to it unless it has some real impact on the way the economy actually works. At the time of the 'events' of May 1968 in France some British anti-planners lost no time in portraying them as a rebuff for planning. For instance Mr Russell Lewis wrote:

> The main virtue of French planning was supposed to be not its economic but its political effects. It claimed to be planning by consent. The process by which officials of the planning commission drew up a plan and then submitted it to criticism by the organised interests of the nation were said to be an extension of democracy . . . . Many French theorists even found in this frenzied dialogue a dynamic modern expression of Rousseau's general will. Now, whatever else the recent riots did or did not show, they certainly made any French claim to have found a new dimension of democracy in the economic field look like a lot of baloney.[8]

There can be no questioning the fact that May–June 1968 was a serious setback for planning in France. Yet it can fairly be argued that this setback was not the outcome of a surfeit of dialogue and negotiation but on the contrary reflected the fact that the process was not democratic enough. The 'events' might have taken a very different course if the Fifth Plan had given more weight to the unions' arguments in favour of a shorter working week and a reduction in unemployment.[9] Certainly one of the greatest obstacles to planning in France now is the attitude of the left-wing unions which no longer pay lip service to *concertation*.

Britain's own social unrest arises to a large extent from the fact that *concertation* has produced very limited results indeed, particularly in relation to prices and incomes, but it is also partly due to the wish of workers to have more say in the decisions their companies take, particularly when these affect them directly. This is one reason why Labour decided that greater provision must be made for the involvement of workers in management, whether by introducing worker-directors on the boards of companies or by creating (or reviving) joint machinery where necessary. Certainly the unions' own 'philosophy' on these questions has changed considerably since the forties, and with their greater strength they seem less afraid of accepting responsibility for decisions. One of the avowed aims of the new director-general of NEDC, Mr Ronald McIntosh, has been to recruit more junior officials from the unions into the Office to accustom them to operating these new forms of *concertation*.

M. Pierre Massé has said of the French Plan that 'it does not limit itself to heralding what is probable; it also proclaims what is desirable. It is not only a reducer of uncertainty; it is also a statement of intent'.[10] This was probably more true of the Fourth Plan, with its attempt to spare France the less attractive features of the 'affluent society', than of the Fifth Plan which, as Professor Hayward has argued, was less a 'bearer of the future' than a 'bearer of conservatism' because of the way it so confidently extrapolated the past into the future.

This seems to have been even more true of planning in Britain, where there was such an obsession with growth that progress was seen basically as the current economy writ larger, instead of as an opportunity to eliminate deficiencies and injustices. It took some considerable time before incomes policy began to get to grips with the problem of redistribution; engrained traditions and the bargaining power of some of the stronger unions do not make for any speedy progress towards a better deal for the lower paid; also the benefit of increases in productivity almost always goes to those who are already relatively privileged because employers have always been more prepared to reach settlements with the unions in industries where productivity is rising most rapidly. But this is only one of the drawbacks of the mania for growth. The gravest has been the failure to give adequate attention to the adverse consequences of economic expansion such as pollution and a whole range of other forms of damage to the environment, such as the destruction of natural beauty. This is not a matter of yearning for the days when only a privileged few reaped the benefits of technical and economic progress, but of reckoning the cost in such a way that the people can decide whether or not to embark on growth in full knowledge of the likely consequences. This was one of the themes discussed by E. J. Mishan in *The Costs of Economic Growth*, which seemed unorthodox when it first appeared in 1967, but which subsequently gained far wider currency. Lumping planners and neo-liberals together he rejected the idea that growth was *per se* desirable, and emphasised the importance of improving the quality of life:

> [The] essay urges a reconsideration of the place of growth in the economic policy of a technologically advanced society. The notion of economic expansion as a process on balance beneficial to society goes back at least a couple of centuries, about which time, however, the case in favour was much stronger than it is today when we are not only incomparably wealthier but also suffering from many disagreeable byproducts of rapid technological change. Yet so entrenched are the interests involved, commercial, institutional and scientific, and so pervasive the influence of modern communications, that economic growth has embedded itself in the ethos of our civilisation. Despite the manifest disamenities caused by the post-war economic expansion, no one today seeking to advance his position in the hierarchy of government or business fails to pay homage to this sovereign concept.
>
> The general conclusion of this volume is that the continued pursuit of economic growth by Western societies is more likely on balance to reduce rather than to increase social welfare.[11]

In reply to Mishan it could be argued, and some optimists have done so, that Britain's slow growth offered the prospect that she would preserve her environment more successfully than other developed countries. Although the point is certainly not devoid of substance to someone acquainted with both Britain and the continent, this seems a somewhat mixed blessing – and insufficient to reassure the environmentalists. It remains true that such arguments about the quality of life receive a better hearing now than in the sixties. In 1970, showing he was responsive to something which, though perhaps seemingly only a fleeting fashion, was in fact a basic objection to industrial society, Mr Heath set up the super-Department of the Environment and made it responsible for co-ordinating the entire range of matters that could avoid or counterbalance the 'costs of growth'.

Even so, in even the richest of contemporary societies – among which of course the British people is not (as it knows only too well, having been repeatedly told so for fifteen years, by its own gurus and other wiseacres such as the OECD, General de Gaulle, the gnomes of Zurich and more recently the Hudson Institute (Europe) and the Brussels Commission) – there remain many needs, principally social needs, that are only too real. And it will always be politically easier to meet such needs when the resources available are increasing rather than declining or stagnating. In addition, the economic growth of the developed world was largely based on the availability of abundant supplies of cheap energy and raw materials. The need to find substitutes, particularly for oil, now that those days appear to be over may well lead to pollution problems being overlooked once more, and to the improvement of the environment being treated as an expensive luxury. The root problem, however, is one of adapting the economy to dearer energy. While Britain is obviously in a better position than many other western countries because she can look forward to oil from the North and Celtic seas, the measure of control she will have over her own energy supplies in a few years will give rise to new economic and social problems which a combination of devolution and a new approach to planning the distribution of resources could enable her to overcome successfully.

Paris, December 1974

APPENDIX A

Membership of the National Economic Development Council at Various Dates

1. *Initial membership, March 1962 (20 members)*

   Government (3): S. Lloyd (Chancellor), chairman; F. Errol (President, Board of Trade); J. Hare (Minister of Labour).

   Employers (6): J. A. Cockfield (Chairman, Boots); R. M. Geddes (Chairman, Dunlop); Sir Cyril Harrison (Deputy Chairman, English Sewing Cotton); E. J. Hunter (Deputy Chairman, Swan Hunter); J. M. Laing (J. Laing & Sons); J. N. Toothill (member of the board of Ferranti).

   Unions (6): Sir William Carron (President, AEU); Frank Cousins (General Secretary, TGWU); H. Douglass (General Secretary, ISTC); S. J. Greene (General Secretary, NUR); R. Smith (General Secretary, UPW); G. Woodcock (General Secretary, TUC).

   Nationalised industries (2): R. Beeching (Chairman, BTC); Lord Robens (Chairman, NCB).

   Independent members (3): Sir Oliver Franks (Provost of Worcester College, Oxford); Prof. E. H. Phelps Brown (LSE); Sir Robert Shone (Director-General, NEDO).

2. *After Labour came to power in October 1964 (22 members)*

   Government (5): George Brown (Chairman); Frank Cousins (Minister of Technology); Ray Gunter (Labour); Douglas Jay (Board of Trade); F. Catherwood (Chief Industrial Adviser).

   Employers (6): J. Davies (Deputy Chairman, Shell Mex and BP); R. M. Geddes; K. A. Keith (Chairman, Philips, Higginson, Erlangers); J. M. Laing; Sir Dennis Pearson (Deputy Chairman, Rolls Royce); Sir Peter Runge (Chairman, FBI).

   Unions (6): Sir William Carron; J. Cooper (General Secretary, NUGMW); H. Douglass; S. J. Greene; R. Smith; G. Woodcock.

   Nationalised industries (2): Sir Ronald Edwards (Chairman, Electricity Council); Lord Robens.

   Independent members (3): W. Coutts Donald (Chairman, Association of Management Consultants); Professor Phelps Brown; Sir Robert Shone.

3. *With the Prime Minister as chairman, summer 1968 (24 members)*

Government (6): H. Wilson (Chairman); A. W. Benn (Technology); B. Castle (Employment and Productivity); A. Crosland (Board of Trade); R. Jenkins (Chancellor); P. Shore (Economic Affairs).

Employers (6): Sir Stephen Brown (Chairman, Stone-Platt Industries); J. Davies (Director General, CBI); Sir Frank Kearton (Courtaulds and IRC); K. A. Keith (Deputy Chairman, Hill Samuel); A. G. Norman (Chairman, de la Rue; President, CBI); J. Partridge (Chairman, Imperial Tobacco).

Unions (6): A. W. Allen (General Secretary, USDAW); Lord Carron; Lord Cooper; Frank Cousins (General Secretary, TGWU); S. J. Greene; George Woodcock.

Nationalised industries (2): Sir Ronald Edwards and Lord Robens.

Independent members (4): F. Catherwood (Director-General, NEDO); A. Jones (Chairman, NBPI); Sir Stewart Mitchell (Chairman of the ITB for the Shipbuilding Industry); Professor D. J. Robertson (Glasgow).

4. *Composition in November 1971 (19 members)*

Government (3): A. Barber (Chancellor), Chairman; R. Carr (Employment); J. Davies (Trade and Industry).

Employers (6): W. Campbell Adamson (Director-General, CBI); J. S. Clapham (Deputy Chairman, ICI and the CBI); Lord Netherthorpe (Chairman, Fisons); Sir Arthur Norman (Chairman, de la Rue); Sir J. Partridge (Chairman, Imperial Tobacco; President CBI); G. Richardson (Chairman, Schroders).

Unions (6): A. W. Allen; Lord Cooper; V. Feather (General Secretary, TUC); Sir Sidney Greene; J. Jones (General Secretary, TGWU); H. Scanlon (General Secretary, AUEW).

Nationalised industries (2): Lord Melchett (Chairman, BSC); R. Marsh (Chairman, British Railways Board).

Independent members (2): Sir Eric Roll (Deputy Chairman, S. G. Warburg); Sir Frank Figgures (Director-General, NEDO).

Sir Douglas Allen attended as an observer.

5. *Composition in late 1974 (23 members)*

Government (7): D. Healey (Chancellor); M. Foot (Employment); S. Williams (Prices and Consumer Protection); A. W. Benn (Industry); P. Shore (Trade); H. Lever (Chancellor of the Duchy of Lancaster).

Employers (6): W. Campbell Adamson; R. M. Bateman (Chairman, Turner & Newall; President, CBI); Sir John Clapham; R. E. B. Lloyd (Chief Executive, Williams & Glyns Bank); Lord Netherthorpe; Sir John Partridge.

Unions (6): A. W. Allen; D. Basnett (General Secretary, NUGMW); Sir Sidney Greene; J. Jones; L. Murray (General Secretary, TUC); H. Scanlon.

Nationalised industries (2): H. M. Finniston (Chairman, BSC); R. Marsh.

Independent members (2): Sir Eric Roll; R. R. D. McIntosh (Director-General, NEDO).

APPENDIX B

Membership of the National Board for Prices and Incomes

Name	Dates of membership	Office or position	Appointments held*
Rt Hon. Aubrey Jones	26.4.65–31.10.70	Chairman	Former Chairman, Staveley Industries, and former Minister Fuel and Power and Supply
Lord Peddie	26.4.65–31.3.71	Full-time member (1965–8); Jt Dep. Chairman (1968–70); Chairman (1970–1)	Former Director, CWS and CIS
Rt Hon. H. A. Marquand	3.5.65–2.5.68	Jt Dep. Chairman	Former Minister of Pensions and of Health
D. A. C. Dewdney	8.6.65–31.12.69	Jt Dep. Chairman (1965–6); part-time member (1966–9)	Managing Director, Esso; later Chairman, Anglesey Aluminium
R. Turvey	1.9.67–31.3.71	Full-time member (1967–8); Jt Dep. Chairman (1968–70); Dep. Chairman (1970–1)	Former Chief Economist, Electricity Council
J. E. Mitchell	26.4.65–25.10.68	Part-time member	Reader in Economics, University of Nottingham
R. G. Middleton	26.4.65–11.10.68	Part-time member	Solicitor
J. F. Knight	26.4.65–25.4.67	Part-time member	Financial Director, Unilever
P. E. Trench	26.4.65–10.5.68	Part-time member	Director, National Federation of Building Trade Employers
R. Willis	26.4.65–31.7.67	Part-time member	Former General Secretary National Graphical Association
Prof. H. A. Clegg	1.3.66–31.8.67	Full-time member	Fellow of Nuffield College

Prof. B. R. Williams	12.12.66–31.8.67	Part-time member	Professor of Political Economy, Manchester
Prof. W. B. Reddaway	1.9.67–31.3.71	Part-time member	Professor of Applied Economics, Cambridge
R. C. Mathias	1.9.67–15.4.68	Full-time member	South Wales Regional Secretary, TGWU
Prof. H. A. Turner	1.10.67–31.3.71	Part-time member	Professor of Industrial Relations, Cambridge
E. Brough	1.10.67–31.3.70	Part-time member	Head, Marketing Division, Unilever
Prof. J. Woodward	1.2.68–31.8.70	Part-time member	Professor of Industrial Sociology, Imperial College
W. L. Heywood	1.3.68–30.6.70	Full-time member	General Secretary, National Union of Dyers, Bleachers, Textiles; Member, Restrictive Practices Court
M. B. Forman	1.4.68–31.3.70	Part-time member	Personnel Director, Tube Investments
Lord Wright	1.7.68–31.3.71	Part-time member	General Secretary, Amalgamated Weavers Assoc.; ex-Chairman, TUC
J. E. Mortimer	5.8.68–31.1.71	Full-time member	National Officer, Draughtsmen & Allied Technicians' Association; Board Member for Industrial Relations, London Transport
	1.2.71–31.3.71	Part-time member	
G. F. Young	19.9.68–31.3.71	Part-time member	Chairman, Tempered Group Ltd
Admiral Sir Desmond Dreyer	28.10.68–31.3.71	Part-time member	Former Chief of Naval Personnel and Second Sea Lord
H. G. Reid	1.4.69–31.3.70	Part-time member	General Manager (Commercial Services), ICI

Secretaries to the Board

A. A. Jarratt	1.6.65–31.3.68
K. H. Clucas	1.4.68–31.3.71

* Appointments shown are those held either before or at time of appointment.
Source: A. Fels, *The British Prices and Incomes Board*.

Notes

Introduction

1. Abnormal Imports Act (November 1931); Horticultural Products Act (December 1931); Import Duties Act (February 1932).
2. The May Committee was the Committee on National Expenditure and the Macmillan Committee, the Committee on Finance and Industry. Their reports formed a basis for many of the measures taken in 1931 and the following few years.
3. For further details on this period see: Sir Oswald Mosley, *My Life* (London, 1968); R. Skidelsky, *Politicians and the Slump* (London, 1967).
4. S. and B. Webb, *Soviet Communism: A New Civilisation?* (London, 1935). The quotations that follow are taken from the third edition (London, 1944) – by which time the question mark had disappeared from the title.
5. ibid., p. 495.
6. ibid., p. 499.
7. ibid., p. 500.
8. ibid., p. 517.
9. H. Macmillan, *The Middle Way* (London, 1938), p. 12.
10. ibid., p. 15.
11. J. A. Hobson (1858–1940) marked himself off from other economists as early as 1898 with his theory of underconsumption, first formulated in his *Physiology of Industry* and later developed in *Wealth and Life: A Study in Values* (London, 1930) and *Rationalisation and Unemployment* (London, 1930).
12. G. D. H. Cole, *A Plan for Democratic Britain* (London, 1939), p. 25.
13. Macmillan, op. cit., p. 11.
14. B. Wootton, *Plan or No Plan* (London, 1934), p. 310.
15. ibid., p. 312.
16. G. D. H. Cole, *The Next Ten Years in British Social and Economic Policy* (London, 1929), p. 51.
17. ibid., p. 52.
18. G. D. H. Cole, *Practical Economics or Studies in Economic Planning* (London, 1937), p. 248.
19. ibid., p. 252.
20. Macmillan, op. cit., p. 102.
21. ibid., p. 102.
22. ibid., p. 185.

Chapter 1

1. *Employment Policy*, Cmd. 6527 (London, 1944). At the time this was considered a revolutionary document.
2. *The Beveridge Report in Brief* (London, 1943), p. 59. The Report was primarily concerned with a programme of social reform, and was not an economic plan, though a plan might incorporate such reforms, relating their financing to the availability of resources.
3. Association of British Chambers of Commerce, *Report on Post-War Industrial Reconstruction* (May 1942).
4. FBI, *Report on Reconstruction* (April 1942).
5. Conservative Party, *Work: The Future of British Industry* (January 1944).
6. Labour Party, *The Old World and the New Society* (1943).

7. TUC, *Statement on the Post-War Transitional Period* (1943).
8. ibid.
9. The term was used well before the war in Macmillan's *Reconstruction* (London, 1933) and *The Middle Way* (London, 1938).
10. Quoted by H. Pelling, *The Challenge of Socialism* (London, 1954), pp. 328–9.
11. In his memoirs Macmillan suggests that it may well have been the reading of Hayek's *Road to Serfdom*, which appeared in 1944, that led Churchill to pursue such a violently anti-socialist line in the 1945 general election – when his extreme language alienated a number of voters.
12. Influenced by both Benthamite utilitarianism and Marxian egalitarianism, Laski feared that the struggle between capitalism and socialism would prove fatal to the political liberalism to which he was so deeply attached. In 1936 Cripps had called for sweeping constitutional reforms, all of them aimed at crushing the resistance of the Establishment to socialist policies – but which by the same token would have reduced the influence of the opposition.
13. Michael Young, *Labour's Plan for Plenty* (London, 1947), p. 11.
14. J. Schumpeter, *Capitalism, Socialism and Democracy* (London, 1941). Quoted here from Unwin University Books edition (1955), pp. 229–30.
15. F. A. Hayek, *The Road to Serfdom* (London, 1944), p. 64.
16. ibid., p. 85.
17. See Raymond Aron, *Essai sur les libertés* (Paris, 1965), pp. 123–46.
18. Hayek, op. cit., p. 36.
19. Hayek, *Collectivist Economic Planning*, Routledge & Kegan Paul (London, 1935).
20. Hayek, op. cit., pp. 49–50.
21. Aron, op. cit., p. 131.
22. Hayek, op. cit., p. 42.
23. Ibid., pp. 55–6.
24. This is still a matter of debate. Should there be discriminatory treatment of firms, encouraging or discouraging them according to the requirements of the plan? The issue has still not been clearly settled.
25. From 1941 to the end of the war Professor Jewkes was director of the economic section of the cabinet secretariat. Later he was professor of economics at Manchester (1946–8) and professor of economic organisation at Oxford (1948–69).
26. J. Jewkes, *Ordeal by Planning* (London, 1948), subsequently republished as *The New Ordeal by Planning: The Experience of the 40s and the 60s* (London, 1968).
27. ibid., p. 108.
28. He mentions, for example, integration, stability, orderly progress, orderly marketing, concerted progress, price management. These no longer seem particularly shocking.
29. Jewkes, op. cit., p. 117.
30. ibid., p. 126.
31. Evan Durbin, *Problems of Economic Planning* (London, 1949).
32. ibid., p. 92.
33. ibid., p. 95.
34. ibid.
35. ibid.
36. ibid., p. 97.
37. ibid., pp. 97–8. His emphasis.
38. ibid., p. 98.
39. ibid., p. 105.
40. Barbara Wootton, *Plan or No Plan* (London, 1934).
41. Barbara Wootton, *Freedom under Planning* (London, 1945), p. 12.
42. ibid., p. 13.
43. A. Salter, *The Framework of an Ordered Society* (London, 1933).
44. ibid., p. 16.
45. Wootton, *Freedom under Planning*, p. 63.
46. ibid., p. 95.
47. Sir Arthur Lewis, prominent Fabian, was professor of economics at Manchester (1948–58), then held posts in a number of Commonwealth universities, and moved to Princeton in 1963.

48. Arthur Lewis, *The Principles of Economic Planning* (London, 1949), pp. 8—9.
49. ibid., p. 14.
50. ibid.
51. ibid., p. 109.
52. ibid., p. 110.
53. Lionel Robbins, *The Economic Problem in War and Peace* (London, 1947), p. 68.
54. ibid., p. 69.
55. This was the subtitle of Meade's *Planning and the Price Mechanism* (London, 1948).
56. ibid., p.v.
57. J. M. Keynes, *How to Pay for the War* (London, 1940).
58. *H. C. Debates, 5s 378*, col. 38 (24 February 1942).
59. In a slightly different category were the economists and statisticians of the prime minister's Statistical Section, a working group of some twenty people, including six economists, six statisticians, a scientific adviser, an administrator and about four experts in matters of statistical and graphic presentation. Their task was to be a source of independent advice for the prime minister on all matters for which he had sole responsibility. The bulk of the work of this group, which was under Lord Cherwell, was in relation to the armed forces. The existence of such a working group specially attached to the prime minister was particularly justified because his personal staff was extremely small, and if he was to be able to settle disagreements between the Treasury and the spending departments he required a relatively independent source of information.
60. D. N. Chester, 'The Central Machinery for Economic Policy', *Lessons of the British War Economy* (London, 1972), p. 10.
61. ibid., pp. 14—16.

Chapter 2

1. Cmd. 6550 and 6551.
2. ibid.
3. Cmd. 6502.
4. Cmd. 6527.
5. W. H. Beveridge, *Full Employment in a Free Society* (London, 1944).
6. In a speech in the autumn of 1946, quoted in R. A. Brady, *Crisis in Britain* (Cambridge, 1950), p. 523. This work is useful less for its conclusions, which are rather superficial, than for the wealth of detailed information it contains.
7. ibid.
8. ibid.
9. ibid.
10. On the abolition of the Ministry of Production in August 1945 most of its functions were transferred to the Board of Trade, with the exception of those that were no longer needed, such as the Anglo-American Joint Committees and the Joint Services Staff for War Production. The Raw Materials Directorate of the Ministry of Supply was also transferred to the Board of Trade on the adoption of the Ministers of the Crown (Transfer of Functions) Act in March 1946, which also attached to it the former Ministry of External Trade, which became the Directorate for Export Promotion.
11. *H. C. Debates*, 419, col. 1965 (26 February 1946).
12. ibid., col. 2129 (27 February 1946).
13. ibid., col. 2130 (27 February 1946).
14. See P. Huet and J. de Sailly, *La Politique économique de la Grande Bretagne depuis 1945* (Paris, 1969), p. 458. While the cheap money policy has become inextricably linked with the name of Hugh Dalton, it should be noted that bank rate had in fact been held stable at around 2 per cent ever since 1932. Successive chancellors were well aware of one enormous advantage of this policy — its contribution to reduction of the National Debt, which reached catastrophic levels during the economic crisis. The most

that can be said about Dalton is that he pursued cheap money more systematically than his predecessors. It should be noted that in 1945—6 he benefited from a particularly favourable set of circumstances: on the one hand personal incomes were buoyant as a consequence of a combination of compulsory savings, rationing and the fact that prices had risen less than incomes, while on the other hand there was less competition because the money market had not returned to normal peacetime operations. Consequently short-term Treasury loans enjoyed a near monopoly. This favourable situation rapidly disappeared, never to return.

15. Ernest Davies, quoted in Brady, op. cit., p. 48.
16. Hugh Dalton, *Memoirs, Vol. III; 1945—1966* (London, 1962).
17. To take one example, there was the reaction to Labour's nationalisation programme. The first measures, taking over the mines, road transport, airlines, gas and electricity, were conceded without much of a struggle, partly because they could be justified on grounds of efficiency but mainly because public opinion was in favour of them. Once public opinion had altered and nationalisation proposals were justified only in terms of 'socialist dogma', then Conservative opposition became increasingly vigorous, and the party's leaders were prepared to employ all the resources of press and publicity open to them and carry the debate beyond the confines of Westminster. This was particularly true during the battle over iron and steel nationalisation.
18. Law of 3 December 1945, amended by the Law of 17 May 1946.
19. Dalton, op. cit., p. 96.
20. The Committee had received instructions along similar lines in a Memorandum of Guidance issued in May 1945, before Labour came to power. This laid down that the Committee should give priority to issues in the following areas: exports, establishment of new industries in the depressed areas, building and construction, and products replacing imported goods.
21. Dalton, op. cit., p. 97.
22. However, the chancellor rejected a proposal for a National Investment Board, which would have taken decisions independently or semi-independently of the government. Dalton argued that responsibility for decisions of this kind must lie with ministers, and that decisions of major importance in the field of economic or financial planning must rest with the cabinet, in the light of parliamentary opinion. We see here a continuing feature of Labour's attitude, at least during the early phases of the Attlee government: what ministers can decide, they should decide, and there should be no delegation of authority to civil servants beyond what was strictly necessary. Morrison acted in the same way when he rejected the proposal to establish an Economic Planning Board, preferring to continue with the existing machinery of interdepartmental co-ordination.
23. Dalton, op. cit., p. 3.
24. E.g. during the Commons debate on economic policy of 6 August 1947.
25. Roy Harrod, *Are These Hardships Necessary?* (London, 1947).
26. *Economic Survey for 1947*, Cmd. 7046.
27. The second section moved from theory to attempted application with a draft programme for between nine and twelve months.
28. This was supplemented by the publication of a short popular version of the Survey in April 1947, which sold some 200,000 copies under the title *Battle for Production*.
29. *Economic Survey*, (op. cit.,) p. 4, para. 1.
30. The 1947 *Economic Survey* was prepared by the Lord President's secretariat in co-operation with the Economic Section, the Central Statistical Office and the cabinet secretariat, under the auspices of the Lord President and his committee.
31. *Economic Survey*, (op. cit.,) p. 5, para. 81.
32. ibid., pp. 5—6, para. 12.
33. ibid., p. 6, para. 14.
34. ibid., p. 7, para. 22.
35. ibid., p. 8, para. 27.
36. *H. C. Debates*, 434, col. 968—969 (10 March 1947).
37. ibid., col. 1412 (27 March 1947).
38. ibid., col. 1413.
39. ibid.
40. Brady, op. cit., pp. 514—15.

41. The members were Sir William Coats, Sir Graham Cunningham and W. R. Verdon-Smith (FBI/BEC); V. Tewson, A. Naesmith, J. Tanner (TUC); A. S. Le Maitre, H. T. Weeks, F. W. Smith and R. L. Hall (CEPS), and Sir John Woods, Sir Godfred Ince, and Sir Archibald Rowlands (permanent secretaries to, respectively, the Board of Trade, the Ministry of Labour and National Service and the Ministry of Supply). It also included Sir Robert Hall, then director of the Economic Section.
42. *H. C. Debates*, 439, col. 1804 (7 July 1949).
43. Its membership in 1951 was seven employers, seven trade unionists and two representatives of the nationalised industries. After the abolition of the Ministry of Production it was chaired first by the lord president and later by the chancellor.
44. This at least is what Dalton implies in a letter to Attlee reprinted in his *Memoirs* (op. cit., p. 195):

    1. We four ministers were appointed to make the Economic Survey for 1947 (Chancellor, Lord President of the Council, President of the Board of Trade, Minister of Labour). And we were served by as good an official committee – an 'Economic General Staff' it has been called – as could be collected, with Sir Edward Bridges in the chair. After long labour both by ministers and the officials, we presented our report. I consider that this has been treated by the Cabinet with much less attention than we were entitled to expect. Much of it was brushed aside last week in an emotional impatience and intellectual levity.
    2. We were told in Cabinet that the manpower gap of 630,000 was a mere trifle – only 2 per cent of the total working population, you yourself said – and that it could be closed by a 'small increase in productivity'.... But this, I am afraid, is mere escapist arithmetic....
    3. Our two principal economic anxieties over the next few years must be the balance of external payments and our production for the home market.

    This was by no means the last instance of 'escapist arithmetic'.
45. *Statement on Personal Incomes, Costs and Prices*, Cmd. 7321 (February 1948).
46. *European Cooperation: Memoranda Submitted to the OEEC Relating to Economic Affairs in the Period 1949 to 1953*, Cmd. 7572. At this time terminology was still somewhat fluid; it was only later that 'medium term' was generally accepted as meaning any period over eighteen months but under five years, while 'long term' meant five years or over.
47. Cmd. 7572, Introduction.
48. *Economic Survey for 1949*, Cmd. 7647.
49. J. Mitchell, *Groundwork to Economic Planning* (London, 1966), p. 107.
50. The *Economic Survey* appeared at the end of the first quarter and included forecasts up to December; the period covered was therefore only nine months.
51. *Economic Survey for 1948*, Cmd. 7344.
52. *Economic Survey for 1949*, op. cit., p. 43, para. 125.
53. *Economic Survey for 1950*, Cmd. 7915.
54. *Economic Survey for 1951*, Cmd. 8195.
55. *The Economist* (1 April 1950), p. 689.
56. In G. D. D. Worswick and P. H. Ady, *The British Economy, 1945–50* (London, 1952), p. 360.
57. The programme of further nationalisation proposed in 1950 would only have increased the public sector by a further two or three per cent of the country's productive capacity. Nevertheless, this played a significant part in Labour's defeat in 1951.
58. *The Economist* (1 March 1941), p. 264, quoted by A. Rogow and P. Shore, *The Labour Government and British Industry, 1945–1951* (Oxford, 1955). Most of the examples below are drawn from their study.
59. *H. C. Debates*, 440, col. 570 (17 July 1947).
60. Rogow and Shore, op. cit., p. 68.
61. *Report of the Committee on Intermediaries*, Cmd. 7904 (March 1950).
62. *Administrative Staff College Handbook* (1951), p. 7.
63. For this reason it seems excessive to speak, as Brady does, of a 'Burnhamite' revolution in the British ruling elites.

64. See, for example, Cole's *Self-Government in Industry* (London, 1920).
65. Obviously this refers to participation in managerial decision-making rather than to participation in advisory bodies, such as joint committees, tripartite commissions, ministerial consultative committees, etc. As has already been noted, the TUC took part in Whitehall committees from 1940, and was quite happy to do so because not only did this leave its hands completely unfettered in negotiations but gave it a position comparable to that enjoyed by the employers' associations — which was far from the case before the war. We will see later that after 1961 the TUC was to adopt a more flexible position and favour a fuller commitment to participation.
66. *Report of the Labour Party Conference, 1948*, p. 170.
67. The industries concerned were cotton and wool textiles, hosiery, lace, jute, carpets, heavy clothing, light clothing, shoes, rubber-proof clothing, pottery, glassware, furniture, jewellery and silverware, linoleum, cutlery and porcelain.
68. Board of Trade, *Terms of Reference for Working Parties*.
69. *H. C. Debates*, 433, col. 547 (13 February 1947).
70. ibid., col. 552.
71. Established by the Monopolies and Restrictive Practices Act, 1948.
72. In *Rex v.* Tronoh Malayan Tin Group of Companies, and Tate and Lyle *v.* Inland Revenue, the court in the first case accepted that such expenditure was within the law, and in the second held that expenditure on opposing nationalisation was a legitimate tax-deductible business expense.
73. P. Foot, *The Politics of Harold Wilson* (London, 1968), p. 91.
74. ibid., p. 83.
75. See, e.g., Shaw's *The Apple Cart* (London, 1929), which has worn badly in literary terms but remains an interesting example of left-wing anti-parliamentary attitudes.
76. C. R. Attlee, *As it Happened* (London, 1954), pp. 163—6.
77. Brady, op. cit., p. 661.
78. Rogow and Shore, op. cit., p. 171.
79. P. Huet and J. de Sailly, *La politique économique de la Grande Bretagne depuis 1945* (Paris, 1969).
80. *The Economist* (13 June 1970).
81. ibid.
82. The year 1937 is taken as base because 1938 was a poor year in most countries and thus unrepresentative of the average levels reached.
83. A. Shonfield, *British Economic Policy Since the War* (London, 1958), p. 174.
84. ibid., p. 176.
85. Even here judgement must be qualified. For raw material allocations were usually based on prewar consumptions, and thus favoured established firms, whether efficient or not, at the expense of more dynamic but recently-established firms.
86. Shonfield, op. cit., p. 163.
87. Rogow and Shore, op. cit., pp. 178—9.
88. However, they did not completely restore the 1939 *status quo*, since they retained specific controls on these industries.

Chapter 3

1. Samuel Brittan defines 'Butskellism' as follows: 'It was an interesting mixture of planning and freedom, based on the economic teachings of Lord Keynes. Planning during this period was concerned with one global total . . . the "level of demand" in economists' language'. (*The Treasury under the Tories* (London, 1964), p. 162.) This is another case where 'planning' really meant '*dirigisme*'.
2. On this see the interesting account of the reception of the April 1952 budget in N. Macrae, *Sunshades in October* (London, 1963), pp. 36—7.

3. According to Macrae the Conservative decline began with Butler's last budget in the autumn of 1955. Brittan thinks the turning point came rather later, at the time of the sterling crisis of 1957. Macrae was deputy editor of *The Economist* and Brittan economic editor of the *Financial Times*.

4. The various volumes in the Penguin 'What's Wrong With . . .?' collection are a good example of this tendency to challenge existing attitudes and institutions. One can also quote a series of articles in *Encounter* which caused a considerable stir and were published shortly afterwards, edited by Arthur Koestler, under the title *Suicide of a Nation* (London, 1963). See also, Michael Shanks, *The Stagnant Society* (London, 1961), which went through two editions within a year of publication.

5. In 1957 the Conservative government had realised the urgency of setting down a rather more long-term policy, and had set up a committee of 'three wise men', the Council on Prices, Productivity and Incomes, to report on these three elements in growth (see ch. 4).

6. Brittan, op. cit., p. 288.

7. 'Economic Planning in France', *Planning*, 454 (14 August 1961).

8. Brittan, op. cit., p. 216.

9. Before the merger of 1965 that gave birth to the CBI there were three employers' organisations, the FBI, the BEC and the National Association of British Manufacturers; the FBI was the most influential of these.

10. Brittan, op. cit., p. 216.

11. ibid.

12. Later Viscount Amory.

13. Federation of British Industry, *The Next Five Years, Report of the Brighton Conference*, November 1960.

14. ibid.

15. 'Economic Planning in France', *Planning*, op. cit.

16. ibid.

17. ibid., pp. 218–19.

18. ibid., pp. 219–20.

19. ibid., p. 235.

20. *Control of Public Expenditure*, Cmnd. 1432 (July 1961).

21. *Public Expenditure in 1963–1964*, Cmnd. 2235 (December 1963).

22. An attempt was made to revitalise it in the weeks following the FBI conference, but this was overtaken by the proposal to establish Neddy.

23. In a memorandum published by fourteen MPs in 1935, advocating planning as a means of tackling unemployment.

24. Harold Macmillan, *Reconstruction* (London, 1933) and *The Middle Way* (London, 1938). See introduction to this book.

25. For example, A. Shonfield in *Modern Capitalism* (London, 1966).

26. 'Neddy' arose from the initial letters of National Economic Development Council and National Economic Development Office. Here and later it may be used to refer to either or both.

27. *H. C. Debates*, 645, col. 220 (25 July 1961).

28. ibid., col. 439 (26 July 1961).

29. ibid.

30. ibid., col. 484 (26 July 1961).

31. Labour Party, *Challenge to Britain* (1953).

32. Labour Party, *Industry and Society* (1957), p. 57.

33. Labour Party, *Plan for Progress* (1958).

34. ibid., p. 9.

35. ibid.

36. ibid., p. 10.

37. It revealed this temptation in a statement published in 1963 (*Economic Development and Planning*). This statement also shows how far the TUC had moved from its 'anti-participationist' attitudes of the forties.

38. *H. C. Debates*, 651, col. 980 (18 December 1961).

39. ibid., col. 1062.

40. This decision was endorsed by a very large majority at the TUC in September 1962.

Chapter 4

1. Council on Prices, Productivity and Incomes, *First and Second Reports* (London, 1958); *Third Report* (London, 1959); *Fourth Report* (London, 1961).
2. By now the membership of the Council had changed. Its chairman was Lord Heyworth, formerly chairman of Unilever, and the other members were Professor Phelps Brown of London School of Economics and Sir Harold Emmerson, a former permanent secretary at the Ministry of Labour.
3. For NEDC's initial membership see Appendix A.
4. However, the appointment of development committees (see below) was to lead to a diversification of *concertation*. In addition, as we have seen in the Introduction, agriculture already had a system of *concertation* that had worked satisfactorily for many years.
5. Joan Mitchell, 'The Function of the NEDC', *Political Quarterly*, 34(4) (1963), pp. 354–65.
6. *The National Economic Development Council in Britain*, COI R.5438/64.
7. In 1953 the Economic Section ceased to be attached to the cabinet secretariat and became part of the Treasury.
8. A similar working group had prepared the earlier *Economic Surveys*; this was accordingly by no means a new responsibility. The *Surveys* had been replaced by 'economic reports', which merely reviewed the previous year without attempting any forecasts.
9. E. E. Bridges, *The Treasury* (London, 1964).
10. One of the few who understood Mr Lloyd's position was Sir Frank Lee, joint permanent secretary on the Finance and Economic side, who, though opposed to planning, realised just how little room for manoeuvre the chancellor had.
11. To demonstrate its autonomy, at one of its early meetings the Council refused to discuss a Treasury paper on obstacles to growth, thus showing it was determined to be briefed by the Office rather than by the Treasury.
12. See Michael Shanks, *The Stagnant Society* (London, 1961).
13. Michael Shanks, 'What Future for Neddy?', *Political Quarterly*, 33(4) (1962).
14. Samuel Brittan, *The Treasury under the Tories* (London, 1964), pp. 329–30.
15. In his *Modern Capitalism* (London, 1965), p. 152, Andrew Shonfield writes unambiguously, 'The planning officials had no right of access to official documents or to the Government's discussions about its own plans.' Shonfield is right on the second point, but on the first further investigation suggests a rather complex state of affairs. The Treasury was supposed to provide Neddy with official information and did so, but it seems clear that on occasion it was less than wholly candid. In particular, it seems that NEDO had some difficulty in securing details of the five-year programme for public expenditure in advance of publication.
16. NEDO, *NEDC, History and Functions* (July 1962), p. 7.
17. The Treasury view was that achievement of over 4 per cent growth was highly problematical because industrial productivity was increasing so slowly. Analysis of figures for earlier years indicated that productivity had grown on average 2¼ per cent, while Neddy was postulating an increase of 3½ per cent. The Treasury concluded that the margin was too great to be bridged in the immediate run. The economists at NEDC replied that their inquiries showed that the improvement in productivity had been accelerating in recent years, that the amount of productive investment in 1960–1 had been substantial and that most industrialists were of the view that they could increase output considerably with only a little additional labour. They concluded that production per head was bound to improve of its own accord over the next few years, and with the right policies would increase even more.
18. NEDC, *Growth of the United Kingdom Economy to 1966* (HMSO, 1963).
19. *H. C. Debates*, 675, col. 455 (3 April 1963).
20. Joan Mitchell, op. cit., p. 143.
21. *H. C. Debates*, 695, col. 1283 (4 June 1964).
22. NEDC, op. cit., p. 1.
23. ibid.

24. ibid., p. 2.
25. A similar method was employed for the second plan. Criticisms which can be made of it will be discussed later.
26. Joan Mitchell, op. cit., p. 139.
27. NEDO, *Activity Report* (HMSO, 1964).
28. In order of their establishment in the spring and summer of 1964, these were the committees for machine tools, chemicals, electronics, heavy engineering, wool textiles, heavy electrical engineering, distribution, paper and board.
29. The role of the development committees is considered more fully in the next chapter.

Chapter 5

1. NEDC, *Growth of the United Kingdom Economy to 1966* (HMSO, 1963).
2. ibid., p. 60. It should be noted that the report somewhat ambiguously calculates growth of 'national output'. In the ensuing discussion it is assumed, following Polanyi, that this relates to Gross Domestic Product at market prices.
3. This was the term constantly employed by a wide range of commentators at the time.
4. NEDC, *Conditions Favourable to Faster Growth* (HMSO, 1963).
5. It was even said that the report bore a strong resemblance to the paper the Treasury submitted for the first meeting of NEDC — which the Council refused to discuss because it had not been produced by its own office!
6. NEDC, op. cit., p. 52.
7. NEDC, *The Growth of the Economy* (HMSO, 1964).
8. The first two reports were followed in June 1963 by one on the problems of exporters (*Export Trends*). Realising that its target for exports would be difficult to achieve, the Council wished by means of this paper to present a detailed analysis of the pattern of British exports in earlier years and the reasons for the decline in Britain's share of world trade, and to discuss possibilities for the future. At bottom its prime concern here was not very different from what it had been in the previous reports: to increase the growth rate of the British economy.
9. 'Loud Cheers for Ned', *The Economist* (12 May 1962).
10. *The Observer* (11 February 1962).
11. A. Day, 'The Myth of Four per cent', *Westminster Bank Review* (November 1964).
12. OEEC, *The Problem of Rising Prices* (HMSO, 1961).
13. According to Brittan (*The Treasury under the Tories* (London, 1964) p. 237), the conversion of the government to the idea of an incomes policy must have been facilitated by the arrival of new men at the Ministry of Labour. In July 1961 Sir Laurence Helsby, a one-time economics don, became permanent secretary. Helsby thought that the Ministry should no longer step in as conciliator in labour disputes irrespective of the damage this might cause to the economy generally, which had been the line taken by Conservative ministers of labour since 1951. By a fortunate accident the then minister of labour, Mr John Hare, was a personal friend of Selwyn Lloyd, and willing to listen to the Treasury point of view.
14. *Incomes Policy: the Next Step*, Cmnd. 1626 (1962).
15. Prime ministers very rarely 'short-circuit' their ministers in this way; in all probability Macmillan's action was due to the serious malaise within the cabinet as a result of disagreements between ministers, particularly over economic policy. The April 1962 budget had a frigid reception from the cabinet, which thought it too 'neutral' after the restrictions of July 1961. Moreover it was widely expected that unemployment would rise to over 500,000 in the winter, and there had been a run of particularly disastrous by-election results. This malaise was to lead to the 'Macmillan purge' of July 1962, the most drastic cabinet reshuffle since the war, in which seven members of the cabinet lost their places, including Selwyn Lloyd.
16. Its chairman was Sir Geoffrey Lawrence (a lawyer); the deputy chairman was H. S. Kirkaldy (formerly professor of industrial relations at Cambridge), and the other members were Sir Harold Banwell (former secretary of the Association of Municipal

Corporations); L. C. Hawkins (chartered accountant) and R. C. Tress (professor of political economy at Bristol).
17. *Conditions Favourable to Faster Growth,* op. cit., p. 51.
18. However it should be added that the employers' representatives had proposed the setting up of a watchdog body for prices that would have had a similar standing and role to NIC.
19. *Financial Times* (7 February 1964).
20. These different measures were listed in an OEEC document published in 1964, *Policy for Prices, Profits and Non-Wages Incomes.*
21. *Resale Price Maintenance Act* (16 July 1964).
22. With the title 'secretary of state for industry, trade and regional development'.
23. The government, NEDC and NIESR advanced different figures for the norm. See the *First Report of the National Incomes Commission* (April 1963), pp. 8–9.
24. Most of the figures and graphs quoted here are drawn from Polanyi, *Planning in Britain: the Experience of the 1960s* (London, 1967).
25. Shonfield, *Modern Capitalism.*
26. Brittan, op. cit., p. 333.
27. Shonfield, op. cit., p. 164.
28. The Conservatives had set an example during their last year in office by dividing responsibility for economic matters between the chancellor, Mr Maudling, and Mr Heath, at the head of a strengthened and expanded Board of Trade, along the following lines: the former took the macroeconomic and financial side, and the latter took trade and industry, but there remained grey areas between and it took all the diplomatic skills of their respective permanent secretaries to avoid trouble.

Part III Introduction

1. *Signposts for the Sixties.* This policy statement was approved by the 1961 Labour Party Conference.
2. 'Some Implications of Planning', *Moorgate and Wall Street Review* (Autumn 1963).
3. *Daily Mail* (5 March 1964).
4. T. Balogh, 'Planning and Persuasion in a Mixed Economy', *Political Quarterly* (April–June 1964).
5. M. Stewart, *Planning for Progress,* Fabian Tract 346 (July 1963).
6. ibid., p. 149.
7. Throughout this section the past tense is employed to describe the organisation and procedures of a number of bodies even though these may have continued unmodified up to the present. This is because the section is concerned with the situation in 1964–70. The ways in which the various bodies discussed here were affected by changes during the period of Conservative government to February 1974 are dealt with in the concluding section.

Chapter 6

1. It has often been suggested, a trifle maliciously, and probably inaccurately, that the creation of the DEA was decided on the spur of the moment in the back seat of a taxi, as a means for finding a post for George Brown. For Brown's version see his autobiography, *In My Way* (London, 1971), p. 97. Chapters 5 and 6 provide a particularly lively account of the DEA's main battles. But a different version of the genesis of the DEA is given by Harold Wilson in his account of the 1964 Labour government: *The Labour Government, 1964–70* (London, 1971).
2. In October 1965 the DEA's staff numbered 544 in all, compared with 1,580 at the Treasury, which in turn looked modest compared with the 9,500 at the Board of Trade.
3. Sir Eric Roll, 'The Machinery of Economic Planning, I; The Department of Economic Affairs', *Public Administration* (Spring 1966).

4. *H. C. Debates*, 703, col. 1829 (10 December 1964).
5. The industrial advisers survived Mr Wilson's departure from office in June 1970, but they were by then attached to the Ministry of Technology.
6. R. W. B. Clarke, 'The Formulation of Economic Policy', *Public Administration* (Spring 1963).
7. Roll, op. cit.
8. A sentiment that was often expressed during the row over the visit of South African cricketers in the summer of 1970.
9. Sir Douglas Allen, 'The Department of Economic Affairs', *Political Quarterly*, 38(4) (October–December 1967).
10. The minister of labour in October 1964 was Mr Ray Gunter.
11. The president of the Board of Trade in October 1964 was Mr Douglas Jay.
12. In October 1970 the Board of Trade and the Ministry of Technology were combined to form the Ministry of Trade and Industry, which was in turn split in 1974 into separate ministries for trade and industry when a new Labour government came to power.
13. The minister of technology in October 1964 was Mr Frank Cousins.

Chapter 7

1. Brittan, 'Inquest on Planning in Britain', *Planning*, 499 (January 1967), p. 6.
2. His reasons are discussed in greater detail on pp. 183ff.
3. Mr (later Sir) Fred Catherwood remained director-general until 30 April 1971; his place was taken by Sir Frank Figgures, who in turn was succeeded on 1 April 1973 by Mr R. McIntosh, a civil servant who earlier had been in charge of the Prices and Incomes Section of the Treasury. Since it was established in 1962 NEDO has therefore had only four directors-general.
4. Mr Fraser, who for fifteen years previously had held senior posts in the wool industry, held his position at NEDO for eight years. After leaving in the summer of 1970 he became chairman of the Little Neddy for the woollen industry.
5. 'The Machinery of Economic Planning, II, The National Economic Development Council', *Public Administration* (Spring 1966).
6. CBI, 'The National Economic Development Council and Office: History and Functions', duplicated (late 1966), p. 3.
7. ibid.
8. Mr John Davies left the CBI in September 1969; in June 1970 he entered Parliament as a Conservative; in July of the same year he was made minister of technology, and in October secretary of state for trade and industry. This meteoric political advancement did not rouse universal enthusiasm, for the new minister had often been accused of taking too conciliatory a line in the face of 'socialist interventionism'. Mr Davies was later minister for European affairs until the defeat of the Conservatives in February 1974.
9. CBI, op. cit., p. 4.

Chapter 8

1. See above, pp. 109–10.
2. These responsibilities were transferred to the Ministry of Technology in 1969, then to the new Ministry of Trade and Industry when it was set up in October 1970, and subsequently to the Ministry of Industry when the 'monster' was broken up on the return of Labour in 1974.
3. On the other hand, several working parties that tended to have a rather more restricted brief than the committees were set up between 1966 and 1968. These were for process plants, paper and board packaging, large industrial construction sites, management education, and training and development.

4. This was the title of an article by T. Fraser in the *Journal of Management Studies* (May 1967). (The question mark is mine.)
5. CBI, 'The National Economic Development Council and Office', duplicated (late 1966), p. 4.
6. ibid., p. 5.

Chapter 9

1. NEDC, *Conditions Favourable to Faster Growth* (HMSO, 1963).
2. *Municipalisation by Provinces* (Fabian Society, 1905).
3. See, for example, G. Lansbury, *My England* (London, 1934).
4. See p. 122, Fig. 5.16.
5. *The North East: A Programme for Regional Development and Growth*, Cmnd. 2206, (1963); *Central Scotland, A Programme for Development and Growth*, Cmnd. 2188 (1963); *Development and Growth in Scotland, 1963—4*, Cmnd. 2440; Ministry of Housing and Local Government, *The South East Study, 1961—1981* (1964); *South-East England*, Cmnd. 2308, (1964); DEA, *The North West: A Regional Study* and *The West Midlands: A Regional Study* (1965).
6. Regional headquarters were opened in Newcastle, Leeds, Nottingham, Norwich, London, Bristol, Birmingham, Manchester, Edinburgh and Cardiff, which thus became 'regional capitals'.
7. See below, pp. 188—9.
8. Originally, in 1965, there had been an effort to recruit a more varied range of chairmen; in particular the number from the universities was greater.
9. Northern Ireland is not included, since for so many obvious reasons it is a very special case.
10. *The Scottish Economy, A Plan for Expansion*, Cmnd. 2864 (1966).
11. A. W. Peterson, 'Regional Economic Planning Councils and Boards', *Public Administration* (Spring 1966).
12. Hence the importance of the establishment of the Royal Commission on Local Government under Lord Redcliffe-Maud in 1966, and the ensuing debate on local government reform discussed further below, pp. 191—2.

Chapter 10

1. 'Joint Statement of Intent on Productivity, Prices and Incomes', *The Times* (17 December 1964).
2. ibid., para. 1.
3. ibid., para. 6.
4. ibid., para. 7.
5. ibid.
6. ibid., para. 8.
7. ibid.
8. ibid., para. 9.
9. ibid., para. 10.
10. He did not resign until July 1966, by which time it was clear that he would be unable to stop the government from following what he considered to be a right-wing policy.
11. The accurate abbreviation would of course be NBPI, but we will employ PIB, which was the abbreviation in fact used almost universally.
12. *Machinery of Prices & Incomes Policy*, Cmnd. 2577 (14 February 1965).
13. *Prices and Incomes Policy*, Cmnd. 2639 (April 1965).

14. PIB, *Meet the PIB* (September 1969).
15. See Appendix B.
16. *Prices and Incomes Policy*, p. 10.
17. Aubrey Jones, 'The National Board for Prices and Incomes', *Political Quarterly*, 39(2) (1968).
18. *Road Haulage Rates*, Cmnd. 2695, quoted in Jones, op. cit.
19. ibid.
20. ibid.
21. The criteria changed over the years with the government's prices and incomes policy as a whole. The first criteria were laid down in the White Paper of April 1965 (Cmnd. 2639).
22. It is true that most writers considered the incomes policy to be among the short-term measures open to the government, but it had not been presented to the unions in this light.

Chapter 11

1. *The National Plan*, Cmnd. 2764 (1965) (hereafter *Plan*).
2. Quoted in part by *The Times* (17 September 1965).
3. *Plan*, p. v. This lack of enthusiasm is confirmed by George Brown (*In My Way* (London, 1971), pp. 104–105), when he tells how he wrung the assent of the employers out of them.
4. *Plan*, p. 24.
5. *The Banker* (October 1965), p. 645.
6. *Plan*, p. 2.
7. ibid., p. iii.
8. ibid.
9. ibid.
10. ibid., pp. 17–21.
11. ibid., pp. 1–2.
12. ibid., p. 9.
13. *The Banker* (October 1965), p. 647.
14. *Plan*, p. 1.
15. ibid., p. 79.
16. ibid., p. 4.
17. Spartacus, *Growth Through Competition*, Hobart Paper No. 35, IEA (London, 1966). 'Spartacus' is the pseudonym of an economist employed by the government who remained anonymous because of his opposition to official economic policy.
18. J. Brunner, *The National Plan*, Eaton Papers No. 4, IEA (London, 1965), p. 7.
19. Quoted by Ian Gilmour, *The Body Politic* (London, 1969), p. 12.
20. *The Times* (17 September 1965).
21. ibid.
22. *The Economist* (18 September 1965).
23. *The Observer* (19 September 1965).
24. 'The National Plan: Its Contribution to Growth', *Planning*, 493 (November 1965), p. 338.
25. *The Banker* (October 1965); the article was headed 'Brown Study'.
26. Also, before publication the very notion of planning was the subject of a lively controversy between Mr Albu and the economist John Brunner. See J. Brunner, *The National Plan*, 2nd edn. (July 1965).
27. 'The National Plan', *Planning*, op. cit., p. 336.
28. ibid., p. 351.
29. ibid., p. 353.
30. *The Economist* (18 September 1965).
31. Labour Party, *Time for Decision* (1966).
32. Party political broadcast (29 March 1966).

33. Sam Brittan, 'Inquest on Planning in Britain', *Planning*, 499 (January 1967).
34. There was at least one precedent. In France, M. Félix Gaillard's measures of 10 August 1957 ('Operation 20%') were of limited application initially but were made general by a full devaluation in October 1957.
35. *H. C. Debates*, 718, col. 1075 (3 November 1965). Macleod was shadow chancellor at the time.
36. According to Sam Brittan, in his revised and updated version of *The Treasury under the Tories*, covering the first years of Labour rule and published under the new title of *Steering the Economy* (London, 1969), Mr Wilson even went so far as to forbid the word 'devaluation' to be mentioned in cabinet. Hence the title of Harold-the-Parity bestowed on him by one of the government's economic advisers.
37. J. and A.-M. Hackett, *L'Economie britannique: Problèmes et Perspectives* (Paris, Armand Colin, 1966) p. 136.
38. *H. C. Debates*, 732, col. 1849 (27 July 1966).
39. This view was originally advanced in the original edition, written in 1971, but it has received subsequent confirmation in the extracts from Richard Crossman's diaries published by *The Sunday Times* (particularly the issue of 16 March 1975). There was in fact a cabinet cabal led by Crossman himself (with the backing of George Brown, Roy Jenkins, Anthony Crosland, Barbara Castle and Anthony Wedgwood Benn – and not, therefore, a 'left-wing' conspiracy), which favoured floating the pound, and thus by implication eventual devaluation, but this group had no agreed alternative strategy, and had to settle for a promise from Harold Wilson to give consideration to a strategy for meeting the next crisis!
40. P. Foot, *The Politics of Harold Wilson* (London, 1968).
41. See for example the article by Angus Maddison, 'How Fast Can Britain Grow?', *Lloyds Bank Review* (January 1966). According to Maddison, even without the constraints imposed by the balance of payments, Britain's growth rate would have been below that of other Western countries.
42. This gave rise to the idea of the complete or partial underwriting or 'consolidation' of the sterling balances, which would guarantee a given rate of exchange against the dollar, thus stopping their tendency to fluctuate with the pound. The outcome was the Basle Agreement of September 1968, which 'consolidated' ninety per cent of the 'official' balances – i.e. balances held on behalf of other national governments. The holders of sterling balances accordingly had nothing to fear from any possible devaluation of the pound. The agreement also provided for the gradual conversion into dollars of the 'unofficial' holdings. To this end the Bank of International Settlements opened a three-year credit line of $2,000 million to the Bank of England, the sum to be repaid between the sixth and tenth years, starting in 1968. This agreement was renewed in 1971.
43. Mr Callaghan resigned shortly after devaluation. His name had been linked too closely to the struggle to hold the old parity for it to be possible for him to stay on as chancellor. According to Richard Crossman, Callaghan invariably followed the advice of his Treasury officials, whose influence by way of the senior officials of other departments was such that the cabinet was left with no other possibility than to follow the Treasury line. Only Mr Wilson could have imposed any other decision on the civil service, and Crossman reports him as saying, in a private conversation on 19 July 1966, 'I'm not adamant against devaluation, but we shall have to get the pound stabilised first so that we can float from strength not from weakness.' In effect this meant nothing could be done, because between then and November 1967 there was never to be a time when it was possible to 'float from strength'.

Chapter 12

1. Not, of course, to be confused with Professor John Jewkes, the well-known opponent of planning.
2. DEA, *The Task Ahead, An Economic Assessment to 1972* (HMSO, 1969).

3. S. Brittan, 'Inquest on Planning in Britain', *Planning*, 499 (January 1967), p. 23.
4. 'Interview with the Minister of Economic Affairs', *The Banker* (October 1966).
5. CBI, *Britain's Economic Problems and Policies: the Next Five Years* (London, 1965).
6. ibid., p. 20.
7. CBI, 'The National Economic Development Council and Office', duplicated (late 1966), p. 3.
8. Notably by setting up the International Reorganisation Corporation.
9. In July 1966 there were 305,000 people unemployed, after correcting for seasonal factors. Twelve months later this had risen to 543,000 and it was thought that it would remain at this level throughout the winter.
10. 'Report of the Conference of Union Executives Held at Croydon on 28 February 1968', *TUC Economic Review* (1968), p. 6. The TUC decided in 1967 to publish an annual economic review giving its view of the general state of the economy in a fuller and more precise form than was possible at the annual Congress. It is to be hoped that the minimal influence this has had to date will not lead the TUC to abandon its efforts.
11. ibid., pp. 88–9.
12. The figures quoted are taken from NEDO, *Productivity, Prices and Incomes: A General Review 1969* (September 1970).
13. See on this the articles by M. André Bettencourt, 'La Politique régionale à l'échelle de l'Europe', *Le Monde* (21 and 22 April 1970).
14. *The Intermediate Areas* (HMSO, 1969).
15. See below, part IV.
16. DEA, *The North West* (HMSO, 1965), and *The West Midlands* (HMSO, 1965).
17. In 1966, *The East Midlands Study, Review of Yorkshire and Humberside*, and *Challenge of the Changing North*; in 1967, *A Region with a Future: A Draft Strategy for the South West* and *A Strategy for the South East*.
18. *East Anglia, A Study* (HMSO, 1968).
19. *A Region with a Future*, op. cit., p. 8.
20. Scottish Office, *The Scottish Economy, 1965–1970: A Plan for Expansion*, Cmnd. 2864.
21. Welsh Office, *Wales, The Way Ahead*, Cmnd. 3334.
22. G. McCrone, *Regional Policy in Britain* (London, 1969), p. 232.
23. ibid., p. 233.
24. ibid., p. 234.
25. 'Epitaph for a Planner', *The Observer* (16 March 1969).
26. ibid.
27. *DEA Progress Report*, 56 (September 1969), reprinting an article previously published by the *Manchester Evening News* (3 July 1969).
28. ibid.
29. *Royal Commission on Local Government in England, 1966–1969* (3 vols) Cmnd. 4040 (1969).
30. *Local Government in England: Government Proposals for Reorganisation*, Cmnd. 4584 (1971); *Reform of Local Government in Scotland*, Cmnd. 4583 (1971); *Reform of Local Government in Wales: Consultative Document* (HMSO, 1971).
31. *Revision of the Boundaries of the Economic Planning Regions in England*, DOE Circular 69/74 (HMSO, 11 April 1974).
32. *Royal Commission on the Constitution, 1969–1973*, Cmnd. 5460 (1973).
33. Cmnd. 5460–1 (1973).
34. See *Devolution Within the United Kingdom, Some Alternatives for Discussion*, (HMSO, 1974).
35. i.e. as a 'consultative document' for comment and discussion rather than as a formal statement of government policy.
36. *The Task Ahead*, p. 1.
37. ibid.
38. *The Observer* (2 March 1969).
39. T. S. Barker and J. R. C. Lecomber, 'Economic Planning for 1972', *Planning*, 515 (November 1969).
40. ibid., p. 786.
41. *The Task Ahead*, p. 29.

42. Barker and Lecomber, op. cit., p. 783.
43. G. and P. Polanyi, 'National Plan Mark III: An Analysis of *The Task Ahead*', *Economic Age*, 194 (May–June 1969). See also G. Polanyi's *Planning in Britain: The Experience of the 1960s* (London, 1967), which is a closely reasoned criticism of British planning.
44. Polanyi and Polanyi, op. cit.
45. ibid.
46. HM Treasury, *Economic Prospects to 1972: A Revised Assessment* (HMSO, May 1970).

Chapter 13

1. *Machinery of Prices and Incomes Policy*, Cmnd. 2577.
2. *Prices and Incomes Policy*, Cmnd. 2639.
3. *Prices and Incomes Policy, An Early-Warning System*, Cmnd. 2808.
4. The DEA dealt with incomes and the appropriate sponsoring department with proposed price increases.
5. *Prices and Incomes Standstill*, Cmnd. 3073.
6. See *Prices and Incomes Policy After 30th July 1967*, Cmnd. 3235 (March 1967), the provisions of which were codified in the Prices and Incomes Act, 1967.
7. See *Productivity, Prices and Incomes Policy in 1968 and 1969*, Cmnd. 3590 (April 1968), the provisions of which were embodied in the Prices and Incomes Act, 1968.
8. J. Mitchell, 'The National Board for Prices and Incomes', *Public Administration* (Spring 1970).
9. See *Increase in Prices of Mercury Hearing Aid Batteries Manufactured by Mallory Batteries, Ltd.*, PIB Report No. 64 (May 1968). This related to an instance where the price of the article was particularly high and there had been public protests. But a cut in the price of hearing aid batteries was going to have little impact on the cost of living. See also PIB general reports Numbers 19 (August 1966), 40 (August 1967), 77 (July 1968), 122 (July 1969), 170 (April 1971).
10. Report No. 112, Cmnd. 4036 (15 May 1969).
11. Report No. 121, Cmnd. 4115 (15 September 1969).
12. Quoted in an internal document, 'Speakers' Notes on NBPI', p. 14.
13. ibid.
14. This was of course not of the PIB's own seeking. It was simply rendered inevitable by the publicity given to its major reports in the press, and the perfectly legitimate exploitation of these by the unions.
15. PIB, *Fourth General Report, July 1968 to July 1969*, Cmnd. 4130.
16. ibid., p. 3.
17. Statement by the president of the Board of Trade in April 1969.
18. *Fourth General Report*, p. 8.
19. ibid., Table 2. But costs began increasing more rapidly in 1969.
20. ibid., p. 9.
21. H. A. Turner and F. Wilkinson, 'Real Incomes and the Wage Explosion', *New Society* (25 February 1971).
22. According to calculations by Mr Malcolm Crawford in a *Sunday Times* article (23 November 1969), 'Wages, Exploding the Incomes Policy Myth', based on the Phillips curve. See A. W. Phillips, 'The Relation Between Unemployment and the Rates of Change of Money Wage-Rates in the United Kingdom, 1861–1957', *Economica* (November 1958).
23. R. G. Lipsey and J. M. Parkin, 'Incomes Policy – A Reappraisal', *Economica* (May 1970).
24. According to Professor Paish (see below) prices would become stable when unemployment reached 2.25 per cent. However, events disproved these various hypotheses; after 1970 though unemployment was high and there was no incomes policy the increase in wages was higher than ever.
25. 'What Next on the Pay Policy?', *The Times* (16 December 1969).

26. 'Incomes: A Fresh Start is Needed', *The Times* (8 December 1969).
27. *Productivity, Prices and Incomes Policy After 1969*, Cmnd. 4237.
28. 'Requiem for a Prices and Incomes Policy', *The Times* (20 March 1970).

Chapter 14

1. See Chapter 12.
2. 'Neddy: Advocate or Judge', *The Times* (12 July 1967).
3. See *Neddy in Print, A Catalogue of Neddy Publications.*
4. NEDO, *Agriculture's Import-Saving Role* (HMSO, 1968).
5. NEDO, *Manpower in the Chemical Industry* (HMSO, 1967).
6. e.g. NEDO, *Visitors to Britain* (HMSO, 1967); *More Hotels?* (HMSO, 1967); *Investment in Hotels and Catering* (HMSO, 1968).
7. 'What will the Neddies do Now?', *The Observer* (1 March 1970).
8. There was one trade unionist, Mr Les Cannon.
9. *Industrial Reorganisation Corporation Act 1966*, Section 1(6).
10. ibid., Section 2(1).
11. It is worth noting that when the French government subsequently established the Institut de Développement Industriel, which was to some extent inspired by IRC, the sum initially put at its disposal was between £25 million and £35 million.
12. IRC, *Report and Accounts, 1967–8*, p. 7.
13. ibid.
14. ibid.
15. This should not be taken to mean that the IRC was opposed to foreign investment; it had in fact earlier supported Chrysler's takeover of Rootes.
16. 'The Jobs Dilemma', *The Times* (21 October 1968).
17. IRC, *Report and Accounts 1968–9*, pp. 15–16.
18. See *Le Monde* (4 November 1969).
19. *The Times* (9 June 1970).
20. Monopolies and Restrictive Practices Act, 1948.
21. The first chairman was Sir Ashton Roskill (now Lord Roskill).
22. In July 1969 there were sixteen.
23. In the case of a merger the total delay must not exceed six months.
24. The arrangements discussed here have been somewhat modified by the Fair Trading Act, 1973. See below, pp. 272–4.
25. Board of Trade, *Mergers* (HMSO, 1969), p. 20.
26. ibid., p. 1.
27. ibid., p. 23.
28. It was based on a White Paper, *Industrial Training: Government Proposals*, Cmnd. 1892 (1962).
29. In fact, only one more was actually created. In February 1972 when the Conservative government announced its intention of modifying the system (*Training for the Future, A Plan for Discussion*, Department of Employment, (1972)), there were twenty-seven ITBs covering fifteen million workers, collecting about £200 million a year in levies, of which ninety per cent was returned in the form of grants, the boards spending about £15 million a year on their advisory and direct training services and administration. In 1974 the Central Training Council was abolished, and its functions transferred to the new Manpower Services Agency, which also operates the Government Training Opportunities Scheme.
30. See Local Government Act 1972 and Local Authority (Scotland) Act 1974.
31. NEDO, *Productivity, Prices and Incomes: A General Review 1969* (1969), p. 5.
32. 'Aims for Industry', *The Economist* (23 May 1970).
33. ibid.
34. *In Place of Strife: A Policy for Industrial Relations*, Cmnd. 3888.

Chapter 15

1. The Civil Service Department was formed from the old Pay and Management side of the Treasury and the Civil Service Commission. This lessened the burdens of the Treasury, though in its role of guardian of the public purse it continued to be consulted about the level of civil service pay.
2. Douglas Jay, 'Government Control of the Economy: Defects in the Machinery', *Political Quarterly* (April–June 1968), pp. 134–44.
3. However, the DEP was for the most part a reincarnation of the old Ministry of Labour.
4. The National Freight Corporation, Overseas Marketing Corporation, British Steel Corporation, Post Office Corporation, Freight National Council, Apple and Pear Council, Shipbuilding Industry Board, British Hydrocarbons Company, British Airports Authority, Land Commission.
5. Labour Party, *Labour's Economic Strategy* (1969).
6. Michael Shanks, 'Institutionitis: the Danger for Labour', *The Times* (4 September 1969).
7. ibid.
8. ibid.
9. The proposed title was the Commission for Industry and Manpower. Mr Aubrey Jones, chairman of the PIB, had agreed to become chairman of the new body.
10. See 'The Ministry of Super Power', *The Economist* (11 April 1970).
11. 'A Better Shape', *The Times* (6 October 1969).
12. See figure 15.1.
13. *The Reorganisation of Central Government*, Cmnd. 4506 (October 1970), p. 3.
14. ibid.
15. ibid., p. 10.
16. ibid., p. 8.
17. Sir Anthony Part, 'The Running of the DTI', *Financial Times* (25 June 1971).
18. *The Control of Public Expenditure*, Cmnd. 1432 (1961).
19. *Public Expenditure in 1963–4 and 1967–8*, Cmnd. 2235 (1963).
20. *Public Expenditure in 1968–9 and 1969–70*, Cmnd. 3515 (1968); *Public Expenditure 1968–9 to 1970–71*, Cmnd. 3936 (1969); *Public Expenditure 1968–9 to 1973–4*, Cmnd. 4234 (1969); *Public Expenditure 1969–70 to 1974–5*, Cmnd. 4578 (1971); *Public Expenditure to 1975–6*, Cmnd. 4829 (1971); *Public Expenditure to 1976–7*, Cmnd. 5178 (1972). Note the change in the titles from 'and' to 'to' which is not without significance. For initially the five year projection was given without describing the intervening years; from 1969 the projection was given for each individual year.
21. *Public Expenditure: Planning and Control*, Cmnd. 2915 (1966); *Public Expenditure: A New Presentation*, Cmnd. 4017 (1969); *New Policies for Public Expenditure*, Cmnd. 4515 (1970).
22. H. Heclo and A. B. Wildavsky, *The Private Government of Public Money* (London, 1974), which provides a very illuminating description of procedures and practices within British government, and particularly of the working of the Treasury.
23. ibid., pp. 247–50.
24. ibid., p. 280.
25. *The Reorganisation of Central Government*, Cmnd. 4506, p. 13.
26. Heclo and Wildavsky, op. cit., p. 308.
27. Lord Rothschild, a prominent scientist and Labour peer, was appointed as head of the CPRS in November 1970. It was received in much the same vein as Mr Aubrey Jone's appointment to the PIB in 1965, i.e. a recognition of the element of political fair play involved, but anxiety at the introduction of a foreign body into the Whitehall machine. In 1972 the CPRS had a staff of sixteen, including seven permanent civil servants – two from the Ministry of Defence, two from the Treasury, two from the DTI and one from the Foreign and Colonial Office. Lord Rothschild's principal assistants were Mr Peter Carey, a permanent civil servant, and Professor C. R. Ross, an Oxford economist who had represented the Treasury at OECD between 1961 and 1968. In November 1971 Mr Brian Reading, the prime minister's personal economic adviser, was attached to the CPRS.

28. It seems that in 1972 serious consideration was given in Whitehall to the possibility of merging the CSD, CPRS and the cabinet office to form a sizeable Prime Minister's Department. However this raised great opposition, not least from those who feared it would lead to a concentration of 'personal' or 'presidential' power in the hands of the prime minister. However, the existence of a rather large staff at the Hotel Matignon had little effect on the power of French prime ministers under the Third and Fourth Republics!

29. However, he also established his own, personal think-tank at Number 10 Downing Street under Mr Bernard Donoghue of LSE. This small group, all active supporters of the Labour Party, is mainly intended to see that the permanent civil service does not hold back Labour's reform programme. This still left room for the CPRS, which appears accordingly to be becoming a permanent element in the machinery of government. In the autumn of 1974 Lord Rothschild was succeeded as head of the CPRS by Sir Kenneth Berrill, a former civil servant and head of the University Grants Committee. *The Economist* argued (23 November 1974) that his earlier Whitehall background might lead to a strengthening of the cabinet secretariat, where Sir John Hunt had succeeded Sir Burke Trend in 1973. In addition, Sir Douglas Allen left the Treasury to become head of the Home Civil Service in succession to Sir William Armstrong, who had retired to take up a post in the private sector — a rare example of *pantouflage* in Britain!

Chapter 16

1. Lord Beeching, *The Financial Times* (24 March 1971).
2. Conservative Party, *Conservatives and Economic Planning* (1966). This reprints a speech he made at the party's October 1965 conference at Brighton.
3. The Institute of Economic Affairs, a research body that is financed by private donations and the sale of publications, was created in 1951 mainly to carry out microeconomic analysis of the problems of the market economy. Although it insists it is independent of any political party, it has tended to serve as an intellectual powerhouse of neo-liberal thought, supplying theoretical backing for neo-liberal politicians like Mr Enoch Powell, who has often contributed prefaces or conclusions to IEA publications, or to other Conservatives who have perhaps been closer to the mainstream of the party's thought in recent years than Mr Powell, such as Sir Keith Joseph. When *Encounter* published its famous 'Suicide of a Nation' special issue in July 1963 (see chapter 3), shortly afterwards the IEA brought out a symposium with the significant title, *Rebirth of a Nation: A Symposium of Challenging Essays*. Most of the contributors took the opposite tack from the *Encounter* collection, and also advanced neo-liberal solutions to a wide range of problems. The contributors included, in addition to the familiar names of John Jewkes, Enoch Powell and Colin Clark, Ralph Harris and Arthur Sheldon, who were respectively director-general and director of publications of the IEA, and also John Brunner, the author of a number of attacks on planning which have already been quoted, and Jocelyn Hennessy who, jointly with Professor Paish, proposed a neo-liberal solution to excessively rapid increases in wages — *Policy for Incomes?*, 3rd ed (London, 1967).
4. He returned to the attack against planning in his *New Ordeal by Planning: The Experience of the 40s and the 60s* (London, 1968). This was a revised and expanded edition of his earlier study which was published in 1948.
5. Conservatives and Economic Planning (1966), p. 10.
6. ibid., pp. 24—5.
7. Conservative Party, *Campaign Guide* (1970), p. 59.
8. ibid.
9. ibid.
10. ibid.
11. M. Corina, 'Setting Industry Free', *The Times* (9 March 1970).
12. ibid.
13. *H. C. Debates*, 836, col. 566 (30 October 1970).

14. 'Ned Spared the Axe', *The Economist* (5 December 1970).
15. PIB, *Fifth and Final General Report, July 1969 to March 1971*, Cmnd. 4649, and *Supplement*, Cmnd. 4649T.
16. *Financial Times* (30 April 1971).
17. ibid.
18. Lord Balogh, *Labour and Inflation*, Fabian Tract 403.
19. *Financial Times* (10 October 1970).
20. ibid. He was referring to the Trade Disputes Act, 1871, which gave the unions a measure of protection at law.
21. TUC, *Reason: The Case Against the Government's Proposals on Industrial Relations* (1971).
22. ibid.
23. In his *Final Report on Trade Unions* the chief registrar of Friendly Societies reported that there were 398 trade unions (compared with 491 in 1960). (The term 'trade union' here covers both 'employees' unions' and 'employers' associations'. It was the Industrial Relations Act that officially introduced the distinction between the two.)
24. The 1972 TUC Congress decided to suspend for one year thirty-two unions, with about 500,000 members, representing about five per cent of its affiliated membership, because they had registered under the Act. The following year twenty unions, with 370,000 members (four per cent of the membership of Congress) were expelled because they had not obeyed the TUC's order to deregister.
25. Despite the unions' boycott, the CIR continued with its work of attempting to resolve recognition and demarcation disputes, and criticising employers' resistance to the spread of white collar unionism. The CIR was abolished when the Industrial Relations Act was repealed, and replaced by the Conciliation and Arbitration Service, which has a considerably wider brief. For a description of the work of the CIR, see CIR, *Trade Union Recognition, CIR Experience* (HMSO, 1974).
26. See *Rebirth of a Nation*, ch. XVI, 'A Plan for Competition', pp. 223–41.
27. However, the final sum of £47,000 in damages and costs that was owed to CON-MECH, a small company which had been seriously affected by a dispute over trade union recognition in 1973, was paid by an anonymous donor (in all probability a number of industrialists) in order to prevent the strike which the AUEW had called for 8 May 1974 in protest against seizure of its assets. However, the intransigeance of Mr Scanlon's union came at a moment which was much more politically favourable to the unions, since they had just won their last battle against the Conservatives and the NIRC had only a few weeks left to live.
28. The voting was 129,441 for continuing industrial action and 23,181 against. The postal ballot was organised by the CIR.
29. *Financial Times* (31 August 1972).
30. *The Times* (12 September 1972).

Chapter 17

1. In addition to Mr Richard Body, MP, a member of the Monday Club, the group included Professor Harry Johnson (LSE and Chicago), Professor A. Walters (London), Professor D. R. Myddleton (Cranfield School of Management), Professor E. V. Morgan (Manchester), Dr Malcolm Fisher (Downing College, Cambridge), Mr B. Griffiths (LSE), Professor S. H. Frankel (Oxford) and Professor D. Laidler (Manchester). The pamphlet was entitled 'Memorial to the Prime Minister'.
2. Most notably in *Capital, Inflation and the Multinationals* (London, 1971).
3. See, for example, survey results reported in *New Society* (7 February 1974), which suggest that under the Labour government the working class was on the whole favourable to incomes policy and the middle class sceptical, but when the Conservatives introduced an incomes policy the balance of support was reversed.
4. *H. C. Debates* (6 November 1972).

5. *A Programme for Controlling Inflation: The First Stage*, Cmnd. 5125 and *A Programme for Controlling Inflation: The First Stage, A Draft Bill*, Cmnd. 5200.
6. See *The Observer* (18 February 1973).
7. *The Programme for Controlling Inflation. The Second Stage*, Cmnd. 5205, *The Programme for Controlling Inflation. The Second Stage, A Draft Bill*, Cmnd. 5206.
8. *The Counter-Inflation Programme. The Operation of Stage II*, Cmnd. 5267, (HMSO, March 1973), p. 5.
9. On 2 April 1973 the secretary of state for the environment and the minister of agriculture jointly appointed Miss Sheila Black (women's editor of the *Financial Times*), Professor Douglas Hague (Manchester Business School, and former NEDC consultant and former member of the EDC for paper and board), Miss M. E. Head (chairman of the Board of Management of the National Chamber of Trade and member of the Retail Consortium), Mr A. W. Howitt (president of the Institute of Cost and Management Accountants), Mr F. B. Kitchen (chairman of Van der Bergh and Jurgens). Sir Arthur Cockfield is a former commissioner of Inland Revenue.
10. There were about 1,600,000 strikers – or as the government put it, 85 per cent of workers ignored the TUC's instructions.
11. High prices for raw materials were not the only factor in inflation. During 1973 the money supply (M3) increased by 28.3 per cent.
12. *Price Commission Report for the Period June 1–August 31 1973*, House of Commons Sessional Paper 403.
13. In addition on 13 September the Pay Board had published its report *Anomalies Arising Out of the Pay Standard of November 1972*. The report proposed allocation of £145 million to correcting these anomalies. While this was concerned with seeing that justice was done, nevertheless the resulting increases were to increase still further the costs of the public services – in which most of those who were affected were employed.
14. *Economic Review* (August 1973).
15. *Financial Times* (24 September 1973).
16. *Financial Times* (1 June 1973).
17. *The Price and Pay Code for Stage 3. A Consultative Document*, Cmnd. 5444.
18. *The Counter-Inflation Policy Stage 3. A Statement by the Prime Minister*, Cmnd. 5446.
19. i.e. Mr Joe Gormley, the president, generally considered a moderate, but a redoutable negotiator for all that; Mr Laurence Daly, the general secretary, a man of strong left-wing sympathies, and Mr Michael McGahey, vice-president and president of the Scottish miners, a member of the Communist Party.
20. On 22 November 1973 Mr Godber, the minister for agriculture, had to admit to the Commons that between June 1970 and October 1973 the cost of food had risen 44.8 per cent.
21. *Financial Times* (3 January 1974).
22. In its *Fifth Quarterly Report* (July 1974), the Pay Board noted that, between 7 November 1973 and 31 May 1974, 5,071 agreements covering 14,500,000 employees had been notified, and of these 3,760, covering 12,100,000 workers, had been screened by the Board. Settlements in excess of the norm had been agreed for 6,100,000 workers covered by threshold agreements, 876,000 receiving allowances for anomalies, 252,000 increases in London allowances, and 1,600,000 women affected by progress towards equal pay. The average increase for all settlements considered by the Board was 9.1 per cent.
23. Had this been the case, the attempt failed, as the result of the two 1974 general elections showed.
24. *Industrial and Regional Development*, Cmnd. 4942.
25. *Small Firms. Report of the Committee of Enquiry on Small Firms*, Cmnd. 4811.
26. The Conservatives later proposed to discontinue the Regional Employment Premium of £1.50 introduced by Labour in 1967, but on returning to office, far from implementing this decision, which would have been effective in September 1974, the new Labour government doubled the premium.
27. Department of Employment, *Training for the Future. A Plan for Discussion.*
28. *Royal Commission on the Constitution 1969–73*, 2 vols. Cmnd. 5460 and 5460–1 (1973).
29. The Labour government's response came in the pale 'Green Paper', *Devolution Within*

the United Kingdom — Some Alternatives for Discussion, (HMSO, June 1974), and in the slightly more compromising White Paper, *Democracy and Devolution: Proposals for Scotland and Wales*, Cmnd. 5732 (September 1974). From the White Paper it appeared that Scotland was to be treated substantially more favourably than Wales (perhaps because the SNP had proved a more dangerous electoral challenge than Plaid Cymru), at least in relation to general devolution. Yet in both regions the new constitutional arrangements would be expected to have considerable repercussions on regional economic development policies.

30. For a fuller discussion of these problems see T. Wilson, 'British Regional Policy in the European Context', *The Banker* (February 1973); D. Donnison, 'The Economics and Politics of the Regions', *Political Quarterly* (April—June 1974); N. Johnson, 'The Royal Commission on the Constitution', *Public Administration*, 54 (Spring 1974).
31. See *Financial Times* (10 September 1971).
32. See *Trade and Industry* (1 November 1973).
33. *Financial Times* (2 December 1972).
34. *Parallel Pricing. A Report on the General Effect on the Public Interest of the Practice of Parallel Pricing*, Cmnd. 5330 (July 1973).
35. *Reform of the Law on Consumer Credit*, Cmnd. 5427.
36. *Trade and Industry* (1 November 1973).
37. Quoted by Professor C. T. Sandford, 'Is Planning Back in Fashion?', *The Banker* (January 1974).
38. ibid.
39. *Financial Times* (4 January 1973).
40. ibid.
41. *Financial Times* (15 June 1973).
42. NEDO, *Industrial Review to 1977* (October 1973).
43. See NEDO *Proposals for a Counter-Cyclical Policy* (August 1974), a report of the Machine Tools EDC, or *The Increased Cost of Energy: Implications for UK Industry* (July 1974).
44. *The Regeneration of British Industry*, Cmnd. 5710 (August 1974).
45. ibid., p. 3.
46. See Pay Board *Fifth Quarterly Report* (May 1974), and *Report on Public Expenditure — Inflation and the Balance of Payments*, a report by the Sub-Committee on Public Expenditure of the House of Commons Committee on Expenditure. While the Pay Board does its best to defend the policy it is responsible for implementing the sub-committee, though under the chairmanship of a Labour MP, Mr Michael English, appears to have embraced the monetarist arguments put to it by Professor Walters, an adviser to the sub-committee, and Professor Laidler, who appeared before the sub-committee during its hearings, which the director of NIESR, Mr David Worswick, described as 'the best free show in town'. See, too, the comments by William Keegan in *Financial Times* (25 July 1974), and Lord Kahn and Michael Pozner, *Financial Times* (22 August 1974), and the NIESR report in *Economic Review* (29 August 1974).

Conclusion

1. See the articles by M. Michel Jobert, *Le Monde* (21 and 22 November 1974).
2. Roger Opie, 'Planning in the United Kingdom', in M. Faber and D. Seers *The Crisis of Planning* Vol. 2, pp. 208—216.
3. In F. Goguel (ed.), *France: Change and Tradition* (London, 1963).
4. Conservative Party, *Campaign Guide* (1970), p. 59.
5. Only since the preparation of the Fifth Plan.
6. *H. C. Debates*, 718, cols. 993—1163 (3 November 1965).
7. While many Conservatives criticised the Plan there was no division.

8. 'Planning, Collapse of a Myth', *Daily Telegraph* (21 June 1968).
9. See the interesting contribution by Professor J. E. S. Hayward to the International Political Science Association Round Table at Salzburg, 16–20 September 1968, 'Political Problems of Planning: Projection, Political Choice and the Preparation of the Fifth Plan', and his 'The reduction of working hours and France's Fifth Plan', *British Journal of Industrial Relations*, 7(1) (March, 1969), pp. 110–12.
10. P. Massé, *Le plan ou l'anti-hasard* (Paris, 1965), p. 50.
11. E. J. Mishan, *The Costs of Economic Growth* (London, 1967), p. 171.

Select Bibliography

I. General Works

A. British Economic Policy

D. H. Aldcroft and P. Fearson *Economic Growth in Twentieth Century Britain* London, Macmillan (1969).
W. Beckerman *et al. The British Economy in 1975* Cambridge, University Press (1965).
S. Brittan *Steering the Economy* London, Secker & Warburg (1969).
R. F. Caves & Associates, *Britain's Economic Prospects* London, The Brookings Institution/ Allen & Unwin (1971).
J. C. R. Dow *The Management of the British Economy 1945—1960* Cambridge, University Press (1964).
P. Huet and J. de Sailly *La politique économique de la Grande Bretagne depuis 1945* Paris, Armand Colin (1969).
M. Lipton *Assessing Economic Performance. Some Features of British Economic Development 1960—1965 in the Light of Economic Theory and the Principles of Economic Planning* London, Staples Press (1968).
A. R. Prest and D. J. Coppock (eds) *The U.K. Economy: A Manual of Applied Economics* 4th edn London, Weidenfeld & Nicolson (1972).

B. The Politics of Planning and Growth

J. Hayward and M. Watson (eds) *Planning, Politics and Public Policy: The British, French and Italian Experiences* London, Cambridge University Press (1975).
W. A. Lewis *Principles of Economic Planning* London, Fabian Society (1949) and Allen & Unwin (1969).
P. Massé *Le plan ou l'anti-hasard* Paris, Gallimard (1965).
J. Meynaud *Planification et Politique* Lausanne, privately published (1963).
E. J. Mishan *The Costs of Economic Growth* London, Staples Press (1967).
A. Shonfield *Modern Capitalism* London, Oxford University Press (1965).

II. The Emergence of the Idea of Planning

G. D. H. Cole *The Next Ten Years in British Social and Economic Policy* London, Macmillan (1929).
G. D. H. Cole *Principles of Economic Planning* London, Macmillan (1935).
G. D. H. Cole *Practical Economics or Studies in Economic Planning* London, Penguin (1937).
G. D. H. Cole *The Machinery of Socialist Planning* London (1938).
G. D. H. Cole *A Plan for Democratic Britain* London, Labour Book Service (1939).
J. A. Hobson *Rationalisation and Unemployment, An Economic Dilemma* London, Allen & Unwin (1930).
H. Macmillan *The Middle Way, A Study of the Problem of Economic and Social Progress in a Free and Democratic Society* London, Macmillan (1938).
A. C. Pigou *Socialism Versus Capitalism* London, Macmillan (1937).
A. Salter *The Framework of an Ordered Society* Cambridge, University Press (1933).
R. Skidelsky *Politicians and the Slump. The Labour Government of 1929—1931* London, Macmillan (1967).
S. and B. Webb *A Constitution for the Socialist Commonwealth of Great Britain* London, Longman, Green (1920).
S. and B. Webb *Soviet Communism: A New Civilisation?* London, Longman (1935).
B. Wootton *Plan or No Plan* London, Gollancz (1934).

313

III. Planning in Wartime and Under the
Postwar Labour Government

S. H. Beer *Modern British Politics* London, Faber (1965).
W. H. Beveridge *The Beveridge Report in Brief* London, HMSO (1943).
R. A. Brady *Crisis in Britain* Cambridge, University Press (1950).
D. N. Chester *The Organisation of British Central Government 1941–1956*, London, Allen & Unwin (1957).
D. N. Chester (ed) *Lessons of the British War Economy* London, Greenwood Press (1972).
E. M. F. Durbin *Problems of Economic Planning* London, Routledge & Kegan Paul (1949).
J. W. Grove *Government and Industry in Britain* London, Longman, Green (1962).
F. A. Hayek *The Road to Serfdom* London, Routledge (1944).
J. Jewkes *Ordeal by Planning* London, Macmillan (1948).
W. A. Lewis *The Principles of Economic Planning*, London, Fabian Society/Allen & Unwin (1950).
J. E. Meade *Planning and the Price Mechanism, The Liberal–Socialist Solution* London, Allen & Unwin (1948).
F. W. Paish *Studies in an Inflationary Economy, U.K. 1948–1961* London, Macmillan (1962).
A. A. Rogow and P. Shore *The Labour Government and British Industry (1945–1951)* Oxford, Blackwell (1955).
B. Wootton *Freedom under Planning* London, Allen & Unwin (1946).
B. Wootton *The Social Foundations of Wage Policy* London, Allen & Unwin (1955).
G. D. N. Worswick and P. H. Ady (eds) *British Economy 1945–1960* Oxford, Clarendon (1952).

Official Documents

Economic Survey annually from 1947, particularly 1947.
Employment Policy, Cmd. 6527, London, HMSO (1944).
The Long-Term Programme, Cmd. 7572, London, HMSO (1947).
Statement of Personal Incomes, Costs and Prices, Cmd. 7321, London, HMSO (1948).

IV. Planning Under the Conservatives

V. Bogdanor and R. Skidelsky (eds) *The Age of Affluence 1951–1964*, London, Macmillan (1970).
E. E. Bridges *The Treasury* London, Allen & Unwin (1964).
S. Brittan *The Treasury Under the Tories* London and Harmondsworth, Secker & Warburg (1964).
Lord Butler *The Art of the Possible* London, Hamish Hamilton (1971).
J. B. Christoph *Cases in Comparative Politics* Boston, Little, Brown (1965).
Federation of British Industry *The Next Five Years* London, FBI (1960).
J. Mitchell *Groundwork to Economic Planning* London, Allen & Unwin (1966).
Political and Economic Planning *Growth in the British Economy* London, Allen & Unwin (1960).
M. Shanks *The Stagnant Society*, Harmondsworth, Penguin (1961).
R. Shone *Planning in a Dynamic Economy* York, University Press (1964).
A. Shonfield *The British Economy Since the War* Harmondsworth, Penguin (1958).

Articles

– 'The Suicide of a Nation' *Encounter* (special issue, July 1963).
R. Bailey 'Neddy and the Planning Process' *Westminster Bank Review* (November 1965).
C. F. Carter, 'The Uses of Nick and Neddy' *District Bank Review* (September 1962).
A. Day 'The Myth of Four Per Cent' *Westminster Bank Review* (November 1964).
J. C. R. Dow 'Problems of Economic Planning' *Westminster Bank Review* (November 1961).
S. Lloyd 'Neddy and Parliament' *Crossbow* (October–December 1963).

M. MacLennan 'Economic Planning In France' *Planning*, 454 (1961); 'French Planning, Some Lessons for Britain' *Planning*, 475 (1963).
A. Shonfield 'Economic Planning in Great Britain, Pretence and Reality' *Modern Age* (Spring 1963).

Official Documents

Conditions Favourable to Faster Growth London, NEDO (1963).
Control of Public Expenditure, Plowden Report on the Machinery of Government Cmnd. 1432, London, HMSO (1961).
Council on Prices, Productivity and Incomes *Annual Reports* London, HMSO (1958–61).
The Growth of the Economy London, NEDO (1964).
Growth of the United Kingdom Economy to 1966 London, NEDO (1963).
Public Expenditure in 1963–4 and 1967–8 Cmnd. 2235, London, HMSO (December 1963).

V. Planning Under Labour

A. Theory

T. Balogh *Planning for Progress* London, Fabian Tract 346 (1963).
A. K. Cairncross *The Short Term and the Long in Economic Planning* Washington, Economic Development Institute (1966).
M. Stewart 'Planning and Persuasion in a Mixed Economy' *Political Quarterly* (April–June 1964).

B. The Machinery of Planning and the Plans

J. Brunner *The National Plan, A Preliminary Assessment* London, IEA (1965).
G. Denton, M. Forsyth and M. MacLennan *Economic Planning and Policies in Britain, Germany and France* London, Allen & Unwin (1968).
A. J. Harrison *The Framework of Economic Activity* London, Macmillan (1967).
G. Polanyi *Planning in Britain: The Experience of the 1960s* London, IEA (1967).
E. A. G. Robinson *Economic Planning in the United Kingdom, Some Lessons*, Cambridge, University Press (1967).

Articles

– 'Brown Study' *The Banker* (October 1965).
– 'Indicative Planning' *Political Quarterly* (April–June 1965).
– 'The New Planning System' *The Banker* (December 1964).
– 'Some Implications of Planning' *Moorgate and Wall Street Review* (Autumn 1963).
A. Albu, R. Prentice and J. Bray 'Lessons of the Labour Government' *Political Quarterly* (April–June 1970); also *Public Administration* (special number, Spring 1966).
Sir Douglas Allen 'The Department of Economic Affairs' *Political Quarterly* (October–December 1967).
A. Barber 'The Department of Economic Affairs' *Moorgate and Wall Street Review* (Spring 1966).
T. S. Barker and J. R. Lecomber 'Economic Planning for 1972: An Appraisal of *The Task Ahead*' *Planning*, 513 (November 1969).
W. Beckerman 'The National Plan' *J. Royal Statistical Society*, 129(1) (1966).
S. Brittan 'Inquest on Planning in Britain' *Planning*, 499 (January 1967).
A. Cairncross 'Economists in Government' *Lloyds Bank Review* (January 1970).
G. Denton 'Reflections on Economic Planning' *Banker's Magazine* (November–December 1968).
G. Denton, M. Forsyth, M. MacLennan 'The National Plan. Its Contribution to Growth' *Planning*, 493 (November 1965).
W. A. Eltis 'Is Stop–Go Inevitable?' *National Westminster Bank Quarterly* (November 1969).

T. C. Fraser 'Economic Development Committees: A New Dimension in Government Industry Relations' *J. of Management Studies* (May 1967).
A. Maddison 'How Fast Can Britain Grow?' *Lloyds Bank Review* (January 1966).
G. Owen 'The Department of Economic Affairs' *Political Quarterly* (October–December 1965).
G. and P. Polanyi 'National Plan Mark III, An Analysis of the Task Ahead' *Economic Age* (May–June 1969).
G. Radice and R. Elsworth 'Life Among the Little Neddies' *Management Today* (March 1969).
R. Shone 'Before the 1970 Plan' *Moorgate and Wall Street Review* (Spring 1965).

Official Documents

Board of Trade *Mergers, A Guide to Board of Trade Practice* London, HMSO (1969).
The National Plan Cmnd. 2764, London, HMSO (1965).
DEA *The Task Ahead. Economic Assessment to 1972* London, HMSO (1969).
Treasury *Economic Prospects to 1972. A Revised Assessment* London, HMSO (1970).

C. Regional Planning

G. McCrone *Regional Policy in Britain* London, Allen & Unwin (1969).
M. Sant (ed.) *Regional Policy and Planning for Europe* Farnborough, Hants, Saxon House (1974).

Articles

A. F. Leemans 'Organising the Region' *Public Administration* (Autumn 1969).
N. Johnson 'The Royal Commission on the Constitution' *Public Administration* (Spring 1974).
A. V. Wiseman 'Regional Government in the United Kingdom' *Parliamentary Affairs* (Winter 1965–6).

Official Publications

Royal Commission on the Constitution 1969–73, Report and *Memorandum of Dissent* Cmnd. 5460 and 5460–1, London, HMSO (1973).

D. Prices and Incomes Policy

H. A. Clegg *How to Run an Incomes Policy and Why we Made Such a Mess of the Last One* London, Heinemann (1971).
J. Corina, A. J. Meyrick *The Performance of Incomes and Prices Policy in the United Kingdom, 1956–68* Geneva, International Institute of Labour Studies (1969).
A. Fels *The British Prices and Incomes Board* Cambridge, University Press (1972).
J. Mitchell *The National Board for Prices and Incomes* London, Secker & Warburg (1972).

VI. Planning Under the Tories: The Debate Continues

E. Boyle *Conservatives and Economic Planning* London, Conservative Party (1966).
H. Heclo and A. B. Wildavsky *The Private Government of Public Money, Community and Policy Inside British Politics* London, Macmillan (1974).
A. Jones *The New Inflation: The Politics of Prices and Incomes* London, Deutsch (1973).
J. E. Meade *The Theory of Indicative Planning* Manchester, University Press (1970).
J. E. Meade *Wages and Prices in a Mixed Economy* London, IEA (1971).

Articles

S. Brittan 'Politics and Markets' *The Banker* (October 1973).
F. Catherwood 'Economic Planning and the Market Economy' *Economic Age* (January–February 1970).
P. Fosh and D. Jackson 'Pay Policy: What Britain Thinks' *New Society* (7 February 1974).
F. Hirsch 'Empty Shelves on the Market Counter' *The Banker* (June 1973).
M. Peston 'Conservative Economic Policy and Philosophy' *Political Quarterly* (October–December 1973).
W. A. Robson 'The Reorganisation of Central Government' *Political Quarterly* (January–March 1971).
W. A. Robson 'The Constraints on British Government' *Political Quarterly* (April–June 1973).
C. T. Sandford 'Is Planning Back in Fashion?' *The Banker* (January 1974).
M. Scott 'A New Way to Attack Inflation' *The Banker* (April 1974).

Official Publications

The Counter-Inflation Policy Stage 3. A Statement by the Prime Minister, Cmnd. 5446, London, HMSO (1973).
The Counter-Inflation Programme. The Operation of Stage II, Cmnd. 5267, London, HMSO (1973).
The Price and Pay Code for Stage 3. A Consultative Document, Cmnd. 5444, London, HMSO (1973).
A Programme for Controlling Inflation: The First Stage, Cmnd. 5125, London, HMSO (1972).
A Programme for Controlling Inflation: The First Stage, A Draft Bill, Cmnd. 5200, London, HMSO (1972).
The Programme for Controlling Inflation. The Second Stage, Cmnd. 5205, London, HMSO (1972).
The Programme for Controlling Inflation. The Second Stage, A Draft Bill, Cmnd. 5206, London, HMSO (1972).
The Reorganisation of Central Government, Cmnd. 4506, London, HMSO (1970).

Index

Wales Tourist Board, 162
Walker, P., 231, 233—4
Webb, S. and B., 3—6, 10, 29, 53, 66, 72, 76
Weeks, S., 85—6
Welsh Arts Council, 162
Welsh Office, 162, 233, 271
West Midlands (Region), 155, 158—60
West Riding, 11
Whitelaw, W., 266—7
Wilberforce inquiry, 244, 247, 249
Wildavsky, A. B., 235—7
Wilkinson, F., 207
Williams, S., 234
Wilson, H., 52, 58—9, 61, 93, 112, 129, 133,

137, 141—3, 147, 177—83, 186—7, 208, 214—6, 219, 223, 228, 233—4, 238, 274
Wissel, 4
Woodcock, G., 115, 117, 222, 247
Wootton, B., 9, 10—11, 21, 25, 27—8, 31, 56, 208
Works, Ministry of, 53

Yorkshire and Humberside (Region), 155, 158—60, 188, 270
Young, M., 21
Youth Advisory Committee, 242

Zurich, 285